RECOGNITION OF GOVERNMENTS

STUDIES IN DIPLOMACY

General Editor: G. R. Berridge, Centre for the Study of Diplomacy, University of Leicester

Andrew Cooper (*editor*)
NICHE DIPLOMACY AFTER THE COLD WAR

David H. Dunn (*editor*)
DIPLOMACY AT THE HIGHEST LEVEL: The Evolution of International Summitry

M. J. Peterson
RECOGNITION OF GOVERNMENTS: Legal Doctrine and State Practice, 1815–1995

Gary D. Rawnsley
RADIO DIPLOMACY AND PROPAGANDA: The BBC and VOA in International Politics, 1956–64

Recognition of Governments

Legal Doctrine and State Practice, 1815–1995

M. J. Peterson
Associate Professor of Political Science
University of Massachusetts, Amherst

First published in Great Britain 1997 by
MACMILLAN PRESS LTD
Houndmills, Basingstoke, Hampshire RG21 6XS and London
Companies and representatives throughout the world

A catalogue record for this book is available from the British Library.

ISBN 0-333-65763-2

First published in the United States of America 1997 by
ST. MARTIN'S PRESS, INC.,
Scholarly and Reference Division,
175 Fifth Avenue, New York, N.Y. 10010

ISBN 0-312-17519-1

Library of Congress Cataloging-in-Publication Data
Peterson, M. J., 1949–
Recognition of governments : legal doctrine and state practice,
1815–1995 / M. J. Peterson.
p. cm. — (Studies in diplomacy)
Includes bibliographical references and index.
ISBN 0-312-17519-1 (cloth)
1. Recognition (International law) I. Title. II. Series.
JX4044.P48 1997
341.26—dc21 97-16329
CIP

10 9 8 7 6 5 4 3 2 1
06 05 04 03 02 01 00 99 98 97

Printed in Great Britain by
The Ipswich Book Company Ltd
Ipswich, Suffolk

Contents

Preface

This study began as a doctoral dissertation defended at Columbia University in December 1975. Efforts to revise it for submission to publishers were abandoned in 1979 when President Carter completed the process of 'normalizing relations' with the People's Republic of China by formal recognition of the Beijing government. I thought that a study of recognition of governments would attract little attention, particularly for the political scientists among whom I was trying to make a career, a belief based on the state of international relations scholarship in the USA at the time. Though vaguely aware of a distinctive 'British school' of international relations with greater interest in institutions, I knew that the proposition that institutions are epiphenomenal was one of the few points on which members of the contending realist, behaviouralist, and Marxian schools of international relations theory in the USA could agree. I drew two article-length studies from my research notes in 1980–81 then moved on to other projects.

The suggestion that increased interest in international institutions on both sides of the Atlantic would extend to a study of recognition of governments came from Professor Alan James in late 1994. He wrote from Keele that Professor Margaret Doxey at Trent in Canada had told him about the dissertation, and that the organizers of this series wanted to consider it for publication. Fears that I had discarded the manuscript and notes proved unfounded, but rereading confirmed my initial reaction that an unmodified 1979 manuscript was now useless. Encouraged by Professor James and Professor G. R. Berridge of Leicester University I have brought the research up to date and written a new manuscript.

Research and writing of the original dissertation was supported financially by the Institute for the Study of World Politics, then known as the Inter-University Consortium for World Order Studies. The late Professor Oliver J. Lissitzyn, chair of my dissertation committee, and Professor Louis Henkin, second reader on the committee, displayed great patience with the ways political scientists use legal materials and prodded me to deeper analysis. The other members of the committee – Professors Robert W. Cox, Henry Graaf, and the late John N. Hazard – provided additional guidance based on their vast knowledge of international practice and diplomatic history. My graduate-school buddies, particularly Michael G. Schechter, Linda S. (Marasco) Mullenix, and Peter M. Leo, put up with the usual round of frustration-venting and odd-fact recounting that are part of any lengthy research project. My parents and younger siblings also tolerated moodiness and all-hours typing during much of the writing and the post-defence revisions. The editors and anonymous reviewers at *World Politics* and *The American Journal of International Law* provided the mix of sharp comments and encouragement that helps young scholars find their feet as the shorter studies were turned from wobbly first submissions into publishable works.

Professors Berridge and John W. Young read and commented on the entire new manuscript. Chapter 9 is far better thanks to comments and materials provided by Professor Colin Warbrick at Durham. The University of Massachusetts has no law school, though it and its Five Colleges partners together possess a good collection of basic research resources. I had access to the fuller range of materials needed for updating such a specialized study thanks to a grant of reading privileges by the Librarians at the Harvard Law School. At Macmillan, Sunder Katwala had overall charge of the book; John M. Smith saw the typescript and disks through to production and Jocelyn Stockley provided sharp-eyed copy-editing and matching of notes to bibliographic references.

M.J. PETERSON
Amherst, Massachusetts

Abbreviations Used in the Notes

AJIL	*American Journal of International Law*
Ann. française	*Annuaire française de droit international*
Annual Digest	*Annual Digest* and *Reports of International Law Cases*
FRUS	*Foreign Relations of the United States*
GAOR	*General Assembly Official Records*
ICLQ	*International and Comparative Law Quarterly*
ILR	*International Law Reports*
Japanese Annual	*Japanese Annual of International Law*
RGDIP	*Revue générale de droit international public*
UNRIAA	*United Nations Reports of International Arbitral Awards*
YBIL	*Yearbook of International Law*
ZaoRV	*Zeitschrift für ausländisches öffentliches Recht und Völkerrecht*

1 The Institution of Recognition of Governments

In international law, the term 'recognition' means acknowledgement of the existence of an entity or situation indicating that the full legal consequences of that existence will be respected. In public international law, states, governments, and belligerent or insurgent groups within states are the entities to which it is commonly applied; war, foreign military occupation, neutrality, and territorial or jurisdictional claims the most prominent of the situations. While the recognition of any entity or situation has significance, the recognition of new states and new governments in existing states has attracted the most attention and inspired the most effort to state and refine international rules.

This is unsurprising given the key place of states and governments in the international order. The growing prominence of intergovernmental organizations in the twentieth century has not affected the basic Westphalian approach to defining membership in the international community. States remain the primary members of the community – not merely the entities with the greatest range of capabilities, but also the entities with the widest range of rights, duties, and legal capacity under the rules of international law. However, these states are abstract collective entities unable to accomplish anything except through designated human agents. Those who rule domestically also serve as the state's agents in international affairs – exercising its rights, ensuring fulfilment of its obligations, and committing its resources and reputation in relations with other states and other types of actor on the world scene.

No legal system can function properly without identifying its various types of legal person and the agents (if any) entitled to act on their behalf. In national legal systems the law defines the criteria of eligibility for status as a legal person or agent and some government organ – sometimes an administrative agency and sometimes a court – certifies or determines what entities and persons fit into each category. In the international system, there is no central government that can fulfil these functions. Instead, the agents of the primary legal persons, the governments of the various independent states, have assumed this function. Guided by the rules of international law, each government determines for itself what entities qualify as states and who qualifies as their governments.

This pattern of decentralized acknowledgement is the basis of the institution of recognition well-entrenched in diplomatic practice by the start of the nineteenth century. In these key questions of status, nineteenth-century practice rested on highly formalized dichotomies between recognized states and other political communities (such as protectorates and colonies), and between established governments and other claimants (such as dynastic pretenders, exiles, opposition parties, and rebels). The formalism was so strong that many legal scholars and diplomats alike believed that recognition by others gave a political community the status of a state and a particular set of individuals the status of its international agents.

A few legal scholars have treated recognition of states and recognition of governments as a single legal process.[1] However, it is more accurate to regard them as two closely related, but distinct forms of the broader institution of recognition. All forms of recognition involve appreciation of a status or situation and willingness to give that appreciation full legal effect; yet the criteria for appreciation and the legal consequences of giving the status or situation legal effect vary according to the particular sort of status or situation being considered.[2]

Though the collapses of the Soviet Union and Yugoslavia have made recognition of states the more prominent issue in recent years, concern about recognition of governments has not disappeared. It is more likely to increase again as some states, newly-independent or long-established, undergo periods of political turmoil. Leaders and citizens in many states are now trying to develop democratic political systems where the question of who shall rule will be decided in periodic competitive elections, but the possibility of resort to other modes of selection cannot be excluded. So long as that is true, the question of recognizing new governments will remain on the international agenda.

Recognition of governments can be studied from a number of perspectives. One perspective focuses on the works of legal scholars and the statements and actions of government leaders and diplomats to analyse how the institution is understood and used in a particular era. Most legal scholarship does just that: it seeks to describe the current state of the institution and the rules defining action within it, and to offer some commentary on how the institution could be improved. Policy debates also focus on the rules of the moment and what they suggest about accepting or refusing to accept some new regime as the government of another state. Participants in policy debates are less interested than legal scholars in the rules themselves and much more interested in whether some plausible interpretation of the rules can be used to promote their preferred policy or frustrate competing proposals. This does not mean, though, that they treat the rules as irrelevant. Just as hypocrisy is the tribute vice pays to virtue, tortured interpretation is the compliment policy expediency pays to the broad sense that a good member of the international community respects the common rules.

Policy debates suggest a second perspective: studying the use of recognition of governments as a political tool for reaching foreign policy goals. As long as new regimes need recognition, and other governments' recognition decisions are not so predetermined by application of legal rules that they become matters of routine, governments can exploit a new regime's need of recognition for policy ends by withholding recognition unless or until the new regime does certain things. These policy ends might involve collective protection of particular shared values, but more frequently have involved the seeking of individual advantages. Such political uses of recognition of governments have been studied extensively, most frequently by those who condemn the activity. Yet most such studies focus on a particular government's activity. While this work has produced considerable knowledge of some individual governments' tendencies to seek or avoid opportunities to use recognition for their own advantage, there has been little comparison or analysis of trends in political use of recognition.

A third perspective uses knowledge of how legal scholars have interpreted and policy-makers have used recognition of governments to learn more about the place of legal institutions in world politics and the foreign policy calculations of governments. This perspective requires an explicitly long-term and comparative analysis of how legal scholars and policy-makers have understood and acted on the rules over time. Some legal scholarship takes this longer view, addressing how rules have changed, assessing the impact of the changes on governments' and other actors' behaviour, and judging whether the changes promote or hinder development of the sort of world order the particular scholar prefers. Yet students of international relations are also interested in the broader questions of how legal institutions affect the behaviour of governments and other actors and of how the development and functioning of legal institutions is affected by the character of the international system. Addressing the first question requires a close inquiry into the decision-making processes of governments and other actors to determine how various considerations – including the shape of the legal institutions – affected their choices and actions.[3] A study of this type is well beyond the resources of a single scholar, so will not be attempted here. Rather, attention will focus on the second question of how the character of the international system affects the legal institution.

This study proceeds in two stages. The first consists of tracing the evolution of the legal doctrines expounded by scholars and the actions of governments as they reacted to extra-legal changes of government in other states from 1815 to the present. The year 1815 has been selected as the starting point for two reasons. First, it marks the beginning of a distinct phase in the development of the European, and later global, states system. Second, it is late enough that the major features of what is now regarded as 'classical' international law were well established and legal scholars were both numerous enough and sufficiently aware of each other to form a transnational intellectual network imparting a degree of uniformity to the conceptions of the legal institutions that guided policy-makers and diplomats.[4] The ensuing years have been divided into four periods for purposes of comparison: (1) the nineteenth century, extending from 1815 through to the outbreak of World War I in August 1914; (2) the interwar period extending from the start of World War I through to the immediate aftermath of World War II; (3) the Cold War era extending from roughly 1947 through to the collapse of the Soviet Union in December 1991; and (4) the short post-Cold War era.

The ninty-nine years of the diplomatic historians' 'nineteenth century' appear today as the period when the Westphalian states system was most fully developed. Though the spread of socialist ideas inspired considerable domestic concern in Europe and the spread of European rule and influence created major changes in many non-European areas, the nineteenth century looks like a period of stability, particularly in international institutions, compared with subsequent eras. In particular, discontented rising powers were revisionist rather than revolutionary and the relevance of European conceptions of organizing international relations was not questioned.

Contrary to conventional usage, the 'interwar period' is extended here to include both World Wars. Rather than being the short war almost everyone in Europe expected, the long combat of 1914–18 had broken up the nineteenth-century system before it ended. One need recall only the Russian Revolution to concede the point; those who regard World War I as the pivotal event in shaping the twentieth century would insist on the strong continuities of the entire 1915–45 period. Similarly, the shape of the post-World War II order was not clear in 1945; few perceived the bipolar order until 1947 or 1948.

Dating the end of the Cold War at December 1991 involves taking a cautious view of events. Many feel that the dissolution of the Soviet bloc in 1989 was far more important. Yet a united Soviet Union would have meant the persistence of bipolarity, and the policy preferences of those responsible for the August 1991 coup attempt suggest that anti-reform elements in the Communist Party of the Soviet Union might have pulled the country back closer to its old Leninist ways. Though leaving less material for assessing post-Cold War developments, a cautious dating seems prudent.

Material for this longterm comparative survey of legal doctrine and government practice has been assembled by reading four types of works: book-length scholars' treatises on recognition of governments, article-length scholars' or practitioners' discussions of recognition of governments or particular questions that arose in its application to particular events, introductory textbooks of international law, and official and unofficial reports of government practice. Limits of linguistic ability confine the readings to works appearing originally in or translated into English, French and German. This means writings and reports from Latin America, the Middle East, and parts of East Asia are not as well represented as they should be in a truly global comparison.

This survey includes almost all of the book-length treatments on the subject of recognition of governments in those three languages. The survey of article-length works on recognition generally or on particular situations is equally extensive. However, the vast law review literature on the effects of nonrecognition in proceedings before domestic courts has been read more selectively with a view to developing an overview of comparative jurisprudence. The reading of general international law textbooks is also selective, choosing from among the many available in all parts of the world. They include works by scholars enjoying global renown in their time, but also include others chosen partly for their region and partly (it must be confessed) because of their availability in the north-eastern USA.

The survey of state practice depends heavily on a number of privately-compiled sources to supplement the available government reports. These vary in their legal sophistication, and have been treated accordingly. In the years since 1945 governments have more actively assembled and published reports on their own practice, either through government printing offices or through associations of international law scholars. News media have also become a source of greater information. Thus the discussions of state practice get more detailed for later periods not only because there were more situations calling for recognition decisions but also because there is more information available.

The second phase of the study focuses on identifying how the institution of recognition of governments was affected by the character of the international system. There have been few efforts to gauge the impact of the international system on the institution of recognition of governments.[5] Legal scholars have not felt competent to undertake such inquiries, and the political scientists interested in international institutions have focused their attention on more prominent ones.

Three aspects of the international system have the greatest impact on the institution of recognition of governments: the competition among the great powers, the level of inter-state ideological conflict, and the extent of transnational interconnections among societies. Competition among the great powers has obvious relevance; the great powers have always asserted a particularly prominent role in the process of accepting new states as members of the international community and new regimes as their agents. Though diluted in the twentieth century by the claims of other states to help make decisions through multilateral processes, the great power management role remains and great power acceptance or nonacceptance is a significant factor in a new regime's international fortunes.

Similarly, the level of inter-state ideological conflict has obvious relevance. Most extra-legal changes of government reflect domestic discontents (though foreign policy misfortunes can trigger or reinforce them) and all new regimes must project some vision of domestic political order to win and retain support. The principle of territorial sovereignty means, however, that the working out of these visions is left to the government and citizenry of each state unless the modes of working them out threaten other states' rights or adversely affect citizens of other states. There are periods, however, when differences of domestic vision themselves become an international issue and foreign governments pay more attention to the domestic programmes of new regimes.

The level of interconnection among societies is also important. It determines the extent to which social groups, business firms, households, and individuals will be inconvenienced by the interruption of diplomatic relations and the reluctance to give effect to a new regime's internal acts that accompanies refusal to recognize a new regime as the government of its state. That, in turn, influences the extent to which social groups, legislators and opposition leaders pay attention to recognition decisions and try to influence government policy in general or in particular instances.

International relations scholars do not agree on how best to analyse the nature of great-power competition. Neorealists following Kenneth Waltz's lead[6] focus on the number of great powers and attribute the main differences to whether there is one predominant power (a 'hegemon'), two, three, or several. The classical realists[7] also paid attention to the objects and intensity of great-power conflict while more recent realists have paid attention to the shape of technology and the level of interaction.[8] Historical materialists[9] and world systems theorists[10] focus more on the shape of global and domestic production processes, in particular the dynamics of capitalism as it has evolved in the industrial era.

The nature of great-power competition can be characterized by four reasonably perceivable elements: (1) the number of great-power units – whether single states, stable alliances of individual great powers, or blocs of a great power and its weaker associates – active in the international system; (2) the degree of disparity in material capability between great powers and other states; (3) the degree of disparity of will between great powers and other states – the extent to which great powers expect and other states concede deference to great-power wishes; and (4) the fluidity of alignment – the ease with which great powers can shift alliances and other states can manoeuvre among rival great powers.

Using change in any two of the elements as indicating significant difference in great-power competition permits dividing the years since 1815 into eight distinct periods.

1. 1815–30, when the Concert of the Powers was constantly tested by disagreements between Great Britain and the Quadruple Alliance, great disparity of both capability and will between great powers and other states, and relatively low flexibility of alignment;

2. 1830–94, when there was multipolar competition among individual great powers, continued great disparity of capability and will between great powers and other states, and considerable flexibility of alignment;
3. 1894–1917, when there were two fairly stable great-power alliance systems (though Great Britain generally remained aloof), continued great disparity of capability and will between great powers and other states, and decreased fluidity of alignment;
4. 1919–38, when there was contention among three separable sets of status quo, revisionist, and revolutionary great powers but no firm alliances, continued high disparity of capability but decreased disparity of will between great powers and other states, and fluidity of alignment;
5. 1939–45, when two rival alliances formed in the course of World War II, there remained great disparity of capability and will between great powers and other states, and very little flexibility of alignment;
6. 1947–60, when two great power blocs contended, there was continued high disparity of capability but reduced disparity of will between great powers and weak states (particularly those outside the blocs), and little flexibility of alignment in Europe or East Asia though more elsewhere;
7. 1961–91, when the same two great power blocs persisted but each was subject to some degree of internal fracturing, there was reduced disparity of capability between great powers and certain regional powers but high disparity with the smallest or least industrialized states, and growing fluidity of alignment – again particularly for those outside the blocs;
8. 1992–, when there was one 'superpower' still leading an identifiable bloc but well short of being a hegemon, a similar situation as regards disparity of capability and will between great powers and other states, and considerable fluidity of alignment.

Ideology is a matter of belief, and needs to be distinguished from other sorts of beliefs that can affect foreign policy. Academic analysts of ideology have argued that everyone has an ideology, in the sense of a more or less coherent set of beliefs about the proper goals, norms, organization, and operation of society. The more coherent ideologies approach Leninism in the elaborateness of their propositions and the strength of claims about their truth. The less coherent may be little more than a preference for continuing to follow, or a vague discontent with, established social patterns. Both coherent and loose ideologies provide adherents with a vision of the 'best' (or 'best attainable') society, and the political programme needed to secure it. Nationalism has elements of ideology in that it stresses the importance of common identity, but must usually be fleshed out with other elements in order to provide a positive political programme. Another significant difference for foreign policy is that nationalists focus on the unique character of each separate people and tend to endorse the continued division of the world into autonomous states; they simply want to be sure they either have their own state or live in one that allows their community a wide degree of local autonomy. Ideologues, in contrast, tend to focus on similarities and universalizing principles. While they may accept division of the world into states, they are attracted to proposals for centralization under a world government or for an international community of like-minded states all organized along the same ideological lines.

The cycles of inter-state ideological conflict are somewhat different from those of distributions of capability, but also easy to identify from outward behaviour. Periods of low inter-state ideological conflict are marked by awareness of differences in domestic political programme but little or no interest in making them foreign policy issues by seeking to spread or contain an ideology through involvement in the politics of other countries. During periods of high inter-state ideological conflict, in contrast, efforts to spread or contain rival political visions become central elements in states' foreign policies. Using this rough binary categorization, the years since 1815 divide into 6 rather than 8 periods:

1. 1815–30, when there was competition – though mild by twentieth-century standards – between absolutism and constitutionalism, with the latter involving both constitutional monarchy and republicanism;
2. 1830–1914, when ideological differences were irrelevant in foreign policy though nationalism acquired increasing importance;
3. 1917–22, when the main line of competition was between liberal democracy (with the difference between constitutional monarchy and republicanism less relevant than the extent of sympathy with social democratic aspirations) and Leninism;
4. 1922–45, when a three-way ideological competition among liberal democracy, fascism, and Leninism prevailed – though adherents of

the first and third eventually lined up to eliminate the fascist powers;
5. 1947–91, when there was renewed competition between liberal democracy and Leninism;
6. 1992–, when the collapse of Leninist ideology[11] left liberal democracy facing less serious challenges from various nationalisms and non-European cultural reassertions.

Because nonrecognition of a new regime can cause significant inconvenience for groups, firms, and individuals dealing with counterparts in another state, the level of interconnection between societies affects the length of time over which governments are able to pursue nonrecognition. If interconnection is low, the inconveniences will be minor and recognition can be treated simply as a foreign policy matter where the well-known tendency of other branches of government and members of the public to defer to executive branch decisions will apply in full.[12] If interconnection is higher, the public is apt to get more involved for two reasons. First, greater interconnection means a greater material stake in having uninterrupted transactions. Where economic and other interest in continuing transactions is high, there will be pressure to end nonrecognition more quickly. Second, an important element of greater interconnection is the spread of information about events in other parts of the world. Possession of more information allows citizens and other government agencies to second-guess executive decisions more effectively.

Despite the importance of interconnection, and the extent to which notions of 'globalization' have become popular in recent years, there is no consensus on how to assess the degree and significance of interconnection at any moment. However, there does appear to be broad agreement that shifts in levels of interconnection since 1815 can be charted as follows:

1. Rising interconnection building on the new industrial, information, and transportation technologies developed in the nineteenth century;
2. Serious disruption of existing interconnections in 1914–18;
3. Some success at reviving interconnections, but not to pre-1914 levels except within colonial empires in 1919–29;
4. Renewed dismantling of interconnections as governments attempted to cope with the Great Depression;
5. Building of different sets of interconnections for fighting World War II;

6. A steady increase in interconnection among Western industrial powers and Third World areas incorporated into their economic network in the 1950s and 1960s;
7. Continued increase in interconnection, particularly in the field of travel and information, eventually encompassing the entire 'socialist bloc' since 1970.

Tracing the evolution of the institution of recognition of governments will occupy eleven chapters. Chapter 2 focuses on the legal doctrines that establish the broad confines of recognition of governments by defining the occasions when recognition decisions need to be made and the relations between states and governments that determine the outer limits of differential treatment accorded to unrecognized governments. Chapter 3 addresses the extent to which recognition decisions are guided by obligatory rules. Chapters 4 and 5 survey the optional criteria for recognition that have been advocated or used over the years. Chapter 6 deals with matters of form, both the way in which recognition decisions are communicated and the question of whether there are one or two types of recognition that can be extended to new governments. Chapters 7, 8 and 9 deal with the effects of recognition and nonrecognition in bilateral relations, multilateral relations, and internal law and administration respectively. Chapter 10 deals with one of the consequences of discretion in recognition decisions, attempts to use the institution for individual political advantage. Chapter 11 focuses on the two proposals to alter the institution in a fundamental way that have received the most attention in the twentieth century. The final chapter takes up the second phase of the inquiry and investigates how this evolution of the institution has been affected by changes in the international system within which it functions.

2 Limits to Recognition of Governments

Four broad prescriptions of general international law, two defining occasions and two defining effects, bound the implications of recognition decisions by identifying when recognition or nonrecognition of a new government in another state needs to be decided, and setting some outside limits on the legal consequences attached to recognition decisions. In tandem, the four define the area of choice within which governments set their recognition policies.

The rules limiting occasions confine recognition decisions to situations when a new government has come to power by methods that are not stipulated in the affected state's constitution, basic law, or other fundamental political customs and impart a one-way character to the act by treating recognition as irrevocable until the government recognized loses power. The doctrines defining effects limit how far others can discriminate against an unrecognized government. The doctrine of state continuity protects the state's rights and preserves its obligations under international law. The doctrine's precise impact on how others treat unrecognized governments depends on a fourth consideration, whether recognition is regarded as constitutive or declaratory of a government's status as international agent of its state. Regarding recognition as constitutive encourages making strong distinctions in the day-to-day treatment of recognized and unrecognized governments; regarding it as declaratory encourages reducing those distinctions.

The rules that recognition is irrevocable and that the state's legal personality is undisturbed by changes of government have held steadily since 1815. The definition of occasions requiring recognition has been manipulated a little, in the direction of somewhat reducing the number of occasions. This has made little difference in the overall impact of the rule, which is to confine recognition decisions to a minority of the changes of government occurring in the world. The fourth, stipulating whether recognition constitutes or declares status, has shifted over time toward the declaratory view, helping erode the strong differentiations of treatment accorded to recognized and unrecognized governments in the nineteenth century.

WHEN RECOGNITION IS NEEDED

No government or legal scholar has ever asserted that every change of government raises the need for recognition. Though a custom that new rulers or governments formally notify others of their accession to power was well-established by 1815, it was not linked to recognition. Everyone accepted that changes of government occurring according to the procedures specified in a state's constitution, basic law, or fundamental political customs maintained the domestic legal continuity of rule and raised no doubts about the new ruler's or government's claim to act as international agent of its state. Even the minority of legal scholars treating notification as a formal request for recognition[1] admitted that the possibility of withholding the requested recognition only arose with extra-legal changes of government.

Nineteenth-century legal doctrine rested on an assumption that the distinction between 'legal' and 'extra-legal' largely corresponded to that between peaceful and violent methods of ousting the preceding government. The possible uses of violence and other preliminary moves to engineer an ostensibly legal change were seldom discussed; though Holtzendorff did suggest an opening for ignoring them by noting that no question of recognition arises if the head of state resigns in favour of someone else.[2] In the nineteenth century, governments took the opposite view, paying more attention to the violent preliminaries than to the 'voluntary' resignation. Thus the British regarded recognition as necessary following a forced change of Portuguese regents in 1820 and most governments did so after the forced abdication of the Persian Shah in 1909.[3]

Both scholars and governments became more attuned to the possibilities of forcing resignations during the interwar period. Some of the scholars sought to clarify matters (or, on another view, to shore up the traditional dichotomy) by dividing all of the possible combinations into 'legal' and 'extra-legal' for purposes of recognition.[4] Governments preferred handling the problem on an ad hoc basis, but did increase the number of changes regarded as 'legal' by dispensing with recognition if the head of state remained in place or violence appeared as an ancillary element in an otherwise constitutional transition. This meant that two of the most significant changes of government in the period – Mussolini's accession in Italy and Hitler's in Germany – did not raise questions of recognition. The US government at least regarded two changes of premiers in Thailand during a hotly contested shift from absolute to constitutional monarchy as raising no recognition questions because the king remained in place.[5] Yet governments could focus on the preliminaries if other considerations came into play. The British and US governments explicitly denied recognition to a new Liberian president in 1931 even though he had also been careful to use a two-step transition to power. They were supporting League of Nations efforts to hasten the end of slavery and forced labour in Liberia and concerned that the new president's anti-reform supporters would end that process.[6]

Latin American and Iberian factions developed a routine for engineering 'legal' changes of government in countries where the president was both head of state and head of government. An insurgent faction would first secure replacement of the vice president (or first vice president in countries with more than one) with their own preferred candidate, and then prevail on the president to resign in his favour. Such manoeuvrings meant that recognition questions were not raised after two changes of president in Portugal in 1926, Urena's 1931 coup in the Dominican Republic, Montero's 1931 coup in Chile, and the 'Acción comunal' group's 1931 coup in Panama.[7]

In reaction against US nonrecognition policy, the Mexican government proposed narrowing the range of occasions when recognition is necessary. In a 1921 letter President Obregón argued that any government based on the same broad political tendency as its predecessor should be recognized no matter how it comes to power:

> Finally, I permit myself to draw your attention to a distinction which should be made in order to understand better the actual situation of the relations between the United States and Mexico. The moral entities 'American Government' and 'Mexican Government' should be separated from the physical persons who preside over them, or who comprise them, since, in the present case, the change of physical persons who form the Government of Mexico imports no break in the legal continuity of the entity 'Government of Mexico' constituted after the triumph of the revolution of 1913.... It is thus not admissible, unless in this case the principle of retroactivity should be applicable, that the present Government of the United States should disavow its former acts in denying recognition to the moral entity 'Government of Mexico,' before recognized and still in existence.[8]

However, neither the US nor other governments acted on Obregón's suggestion until a rash of Latin American coups in 1930–31. Most foreign governments chose to regard the Ocampo junta in Peru as another segment of the 'August 1930' movement that had been in power.[9] Yet there was no consensus on using this method of definition. The French government formally recognized that junta.[10]

Cold War and post-Cold War scholars knew that the line between 'legal' and 'extra-legal' changes of government was not always clear, and some proposed new ways of drawing the distinction. Two argued for treating a government's or head of state's efforts to remain in power longer than their alotted term or to increase their powers as being among the extra-legal changes.[11] A few narrowed the definition of 'extra-legal' by including only changes involving particularly gross violations of law or resulting in adoption of a very different form of rule or political ideology.[12]

Governments were willing to ignore irregularities on occasion. The traditional theory that there is no change if the head of state remains in place was used to avoid recognition issues after the 1948 coup in Czechoslovakia forcing appointment of an all-communist cabinet,[13] the 1957 coup in Thailand,[14] U Nu's forced resignation as premier of Burma in 1958,[15] and the 1967 coup in Greece.[16] The Australian government also used it to deflect opposition proposals for breaking off diplomatic relations with Poland after imposition of martial law in 1981.[17] This tradition also illuminates the Canadian position that recognition is seldom a problem within the Commonwealth:[18] member states have either the British monarch or a ceremonial president as head of state.[19]

There are limits to governments' acceptance of such expedients. The Greek colonels undertook a particularly convoluted form of transition. Their first two steps, ousting the prime minister and cabinet but leaving the king in place in April 1967 and naming a regent after the king fled that December, were not regarded as requiring recognition by the British, Canadian, French, or US governments. The April events even elicited a declaration of British policy that 'the question of a formal act of recognition does not normally arise unless there has been a change in the Head of State or two opposing regimes are each claiming to be the government of a State'.[20] Yet all four thought recognition was necessary when the colonels abolished the monarchy in 1973, and extended it fairly quickly because they all had such extensive relations with the colonels by then that they felt obliged to recognize.[21] Particularly sloppy engineering will also fail to cover an extra-legal change. The British and Canadian governments regarded recognition as necessary after the new military leaders of Nigeria deposed the president, killed the prime minister and other members of the cabinet, and intimidated the rest into endorsing the takeover.[22]

More generally, governments have been inconsistent in their reactions to changes that left the head of state in place. The 1951 Thai coup, which led to replacement of the prime minister without disturbing the king's position, was followed by some formal recognitions of the new government.[23] Soviet efforts to claim that continuity of the head of state, the Presidium of the National Assembly, meant that the Kadar government brought to power by their 1956 intervention in Hungary did not need recognition did not influence those Western governments explicitly denying it recognition.[24] The People's Republic of China (PRC) government regarded recognition of the new Burmese government in 1962 as necessary despite retention of the same president because of the shift away from its predecessor's neutralism.[25]

The idea that new governments sharing the same political orientation as their predecessor do not need recognition regardless of how they come to power was applied by Australia to the Ironsi government of Nigeria.[26] Many governments reacted similarly after the 1965 coup in Algeria,[27] the 1965 coup in South Vietnam,[28] the 1970 coup in Argentina,[29] and the 1971 coup in Bolivia.[30] However, they split along ideological lines in reacting to the 1970 proclamation of the Khmer Republic. Western governments focused on the National Assembly's endorsement to treat it as a 'legal' change while Leninist ones treated it as 'extra-legal'.[31] Nor were Leninist governments consistent in their doctrine that major ideological changes necessitated recognition. The PRC made no issue after the Iraqi government expelled its radical Ba'athist faction in 1963[32] and the Soviets avoided recognition questions after Amin overthrew Obote's socialist government of Uganda in 1971.[33]

The rule confining the need for recognition to extra-legal changes of government means that the occasions when recognition decisions need to be made have been irregular. They have usually been unanticipated as well because those who are planning coups seldom advertise their intentions very far in advance and rebellion is an uncertain enterprise. At most, policy-makers could identify states more or less likely to experience extra-legal changes of government. Some governments even followed different routines depending on how frequently a particular state experienced extra-legal changes of government.[34]

WHEN RECOGNITION ENDS

The need to recognize some new governments implies that recognition does have an end. Scholarly and governmental discussion of that end point has sometimes failed to make sufficient distinction between wilful retraction and automatic lapse. If allowed, wilful retraction – variously called 'revocation' or 'withdrawal' – would create additional problems for or exert additional pressure on governments by allowing any one to threaten another with taking back recognition at any time. Lapse – generally called 'termination' – occurs only when a government has lost power. In the vast majority of cases this means it has been supplanted by another, though occasionally there is no one faction clearly in control. The main question with lapse is identifying when the old government is no longer in power.

Few nineteenth-century specialists commented on the possibility of revoking recognition. Of the four who did, three rejected the idea while one permitted revocation if the new government proved unwilling or unable to maintain normal intergovernmental relations.[35] The only cases of apparent revocation in nineteenth-century state practice involved reversing a diplomat's error or exceeding of instructions, a step all governments accepted as legitimate. This problem seems to have been confined to the US government, which had to revoke recognitions of new governments in Sicily (1837), Nicaragua (1854), Mexico (1858), Venezuela (1862) and Mexico again (1913).[36]

Interwar scholars favoured viewing recognition as irrevocable. Most of those commenting on the issue regarded all recognitions as irrevocable,[37] though some believed that a *de facto* recognition was revocable[38] and others said that a recognition conditioned on meeting certain conditions could be revoked if those conditions went unfulfilled.[39] Governments generally restricted revocation to occasions of diplomatic error, though a few ambiguous cases did occur. In October 1944 the President of Nicaragua was ready to revoke his government's recognition of the new Salvadorian junta if other Western Hemisphere governments wished, and blamed the act on mistaken instructions issued by the foreign minister.[40] Two commentators said the French government had revoked recognition of the Finnish government in early 1918 while it appeared likely that a Hohenzollern prince would be invited to become king.[41] The Austro-Hungarian, German, and Ottoman imperial governments recognized the Soviet government by the Treaty of Brest-Litovsk, but for unexplained reasons – perhaps the later annulment of that treaty? – their republican successors all decided that they had to recognize it anew. Soviet recognition of communist-organized Polish and Finnish governments in 1918 and 1919 respectively implied revoking recognition of established governments in both states. This inspired little comment because the Soviets were at war with both states at the time of supposed revocation and abandoned their communist allies when it became clear that the established government could hold its own in the military contest.[42] Soviet revocations of recognition of Polish governments in 1939 and 1945 were more widely noticed. In September 1939 the Soviets informed the Polish government that the course of battle following the German invasion had proved the internal collapse of the Polish state and government, and required a quick Soviet response (military occupation of the eastern part of the country) to prevent anarchy. Though the initial Soviet note claimed this was termination, revocation is a better description in light of the later resumption of relations with the Polish government-in-exile in July 1941.[43] In January 1945 they implicitly revoked recognition again by recognizing a rival communist-organized government. The ensuing diplomatic crisis among the Allies was settled in September 1945 with the establishment of a new coalition government, including the communists, for Poland.[44]

The US government declined several proposals to revoke recognition. Its diplomats on the scene, who supported Sun Yat-sen's rival government in Canton, proposed revoking recognitions of successive Peking-based regimes claiming to rule all of China in 1923 and 1926.[45] They also proposed doing the same to the Cuban government in 1932.[46] The State Department also dissuaded formal debate on a proposed Congressional resolution that 'diplomatic recognition by the Government of the United States of the Union of Soviet Socialist Republics should be withdrawn' by objecting that recognition was irrevocable.[47]

Most Cold War era specialists believed that only a diplomat's error could justify revocation. A few believed that 'temporary'[48] or '*de facto*'[49] recognitions were revocable, but most rejected making any such distinction. Isolated commentators permitted revocation for political reasons,[50] or as an international sanction when mandated by a multilateral organization.[51] The division of opinion has remained much the same after the Cold War. A minority of scholars, all from the Commonwealth, were ready to accept '*de facto* recognition' as revocable[52] and one permitted revocation if the facts justified it.[53]

Governments generally maintained the view that recognition of another government is irrevocable except in cases of diplomatic error, making no distinction between *de jure* and *de facto* or 'permanent' and 'temporary' recognition. Western Hemisphere governments registered their rejection of revocability in responses to a 1953 query by the Inter-American Council of Jurists.[54] The British government overrode a diplomat's hasty recognition of the new Algerian government in mid-1965,[55] but explained its general objections to revocation in answers to parliamentary questions later the same year. Members criticizing the South Vietnamese government's 'fascist policies' were told that withdrawing recognition 'would create possibly a number of precedents and awkward examples. We did not withdraw recognition from the Soviet government after the Nazi–Soviet Pact was signed.'[56] A number of African governments pursued confusing policies *vis-à-vis* the rival Chinese governments in the 1960s, alternately establishing diplomatic relations with each at a time when both claimed to be the sole legitimate government of China.[57] Observers were not sure whether this involved revoking recognition, or an effort to recognize both while having diplomatic relations with only one at a time.[58] US courts confused revocation and termination on occasion, but were quickly corrected by appeals courts or commentators.[59]

The Cambodian situation inspired some loose rhetoric that could mislead the unwary into thinking that some governments do believe revocation is possible. In statements explaining their position, both the Australian and British governments spoke of having 'withdrawn' recognition from, or of having 'derecognized', the already-deposed Pol Pot regime.[60] They used these phrases to indicate that, unlike some other governments, they would have no relations with his faction. Though their mode of expression was unclear, the sequence of events is not: Pol Pot's regime had lost control of the country and had little hope of recovering it against Vietnamese troops by the time the Australians and British spoke; recognition had lapsed. Angolan, PRC, Haitian, Kenyan, Singapore, and Soviet delegates also used phrases suggesting they no longer recognized the South African government when voting against seating the South African delegation at the 1981 session of the UN General Assembly.[61]

Recognition terminates immediately when a recognized government loses power, without need for any statement or act by other governments. Nineteenth-century practice did allow governments to maintain contacts with the diplomatic and consular representatives appointed by the old government unless and until the new one sent its own appointees. By itself, this practice created no problems. Difficulties arose later, when governments began to continue these contacts while refusing to recognize a successor government that was clearly in control of the state. The only question directly connected to termination is determining when the former government fell. Since this is not always easy to determine, governments sometimes specify that they recognize a particular new government as from a certain day or hour.

CONTINUITY OF THE STATE

The idea that a state's existence is undisturbed by any change of government has a long history. Even in the sixteenth century there was consensus that all rulers, new or long-established, were bound by general international law. The notion that each reign was a separate sovereignty unfettered by earlier treaty commitments was replaced over the course of the seventeenth century. The new rule posited that a monarch's public treaties[62] bound any successor – whether an heir, a usurper, or revolutionaries establishing a non-monarchical government.[63] Well before 1815, then, there was consensus that the state's own international legal personality, and with it the rights and duties it holds under both general international law and the specific treaties to which it is a party, remain undisturbed by any change of government.

The principle that states are the possessors of complete legal personality under international law, and governments have only those rights and obligations necessary for carrying out their tasks as the human agents of states, was also well established by 1815. Though states are no longer the sole entities possessing international legal personality, governments remain agents of states rather than international legal persons in their own right. Yet this status as agent allows a broad range of government action. States are abstract entities unable to act on their own; governments retain their legal monopoly on speaking and acting for their state.

In nineteenth-century writings this doctrine of state continuity was sometimes expressed as a principle of 'solidarity of governments', a phrase stressing the elements of continuity between successive governments no matter how power was transferred between them. A separate principle of solidarity of government is logically superfluous because continuity of state personality determines the matter; politically, it served as a reminder of the legal continuities involved when one government supplants another on the whole territory of a state.

In the interwar period there was some dissent in favour of ideas that a great enough transformation in the form of rule amounts to creation of a new state. The Austrian Kelsen and the German Livonius argued that any extra-legal change of government produces a new state, but limited the practical implications of their view by positing that this new state immediately succeeds to all the general and specific rights and obligations of the old.[64] Early Soviet writers took such ideas much further. Building on Marxist theory that a government is formed by and for whatever class dominates in the relations of production which structure society, they argued that a change of government brought about by class revolution meant the creation of a new state.[65] This was only a partial attack on the doctrine of state continuity since most changes of government do not result from class revolution. Yet Soviet legal scholars soon realized they could not take even this partial attack too far because it interfered with efforts to claim succession to Tsarist Russian territories and other assets. They soon shifted to more traditional doctrines defining when states may seek release from obligations, to support their arguments that the Soviet Union should not be obliged to pay Tsarist debts.

There was less dissent after 1945, even among Leninists. The Chinese communists affirmed continuity of the Chinese state, and invoked class revolution simply as one of a few circumstances justifying exceptions to the general rule of succeeding to specific obligations.[66] The Khmer Rouge government of Cambodia followed a similar course. It repudiated certain acts of the Western-supported Lon Nol republic, but none of the earlier neutralist monarchy.[67]

The doctrine of state continuity has three main consequences for a new government. First, it is both bound and protected by international law as a consequence of the state's continued existence. Second, it must maintain the specific rights and obligations acquired from previous governments unless it renounces a right or can invoke acceptable reasons for nonperformance of an obligation. Third, even an unrecognized government that actually rules all or most of the territory of its state has certain competences that must be accepted even by those drawing strong distinctions in their relations between recognized and unrecognized governments.

Even in the nineteenth century, the capacity of an unrecognized government to act under the domestic law of its state was not challenged. This permitted holding them responsible for violations of international law arising from domestic actions, and even presenting claims for damage to the nonrecognizing government's own state or its nationals. Continuity of state rights and obligations was also interpreted to permit allowing an unrecognized government to represent its state to the extent needed to deal with specific concerns and to make temporary or provisional agreements on pressing matters.

Recognition made a difference in a few special situations. In 1815 the great powers permitted the Elector of Hesse to annul sales of previously-acquired state property undertaken by Jérôme Bonaparte on the grounds that an interim government (one replaced by the same government it had earlier overthrown) lacked the capacity to dispose of state assets acquired before its accession.[68] While this decision was made easier by the fact Jérôme's government could be regarded as either a military occupation or a puppet of Napoleon, the precedent could be used to limit the authority of other barely-established new governments. Similarly, recognition could bolster the authority of short-lived governments. Most of the governments whose nationals' interests would have been affected argued that recognition of the Pierola and Iglesias governments of Peru was the basis for affirming the continued validity of contracts against a successor's efforts to cancel them.[69] Only the US government argued that the fact of being a general government was itself sufficient for their continuing validity.[70]

The significance of recognition narrowed in the interwar and Cold War periods. The ability of a 'general *de facto* government', one ruling the whole state, to take actions engaging state responsibility was clearly upheld.[71] An unrecognized general government was also permitted to represent its state at multilateral forums, and to conclude a wider set of bilateral agreements.[72] In the Cold War period, effective rule rather than recognition became the basis of much international legal competence and foreign acceptance of domestic competence.[73] Though stemming from increased instances of prolonged nonrecognition of a clearly effective government, this new emphasis became the basis for narrowing the differences between the external competences of recognized and unrecognized governments.

RECOGNITION AND LEGAL EXISTENCE

Legal specialists have long debated whether recognition of states is constitutive or declaratory of their international legal personality. Those viewing it as constitutive argued that a new state had no international legal personality in the eyes of another state until recognition, while those viewing it as declaratory argued that the legal personality existed as soon as the state existed and recognition was merely the recognizing state's confirmation and pledge of respect for that personality. Advocates of the constitutive view sometimes compared the international system to a closed club in which approval from all current members was required for admission. Advocates of the declaratory view did not share a common image of the international system, but objected to the closed club one as unduly favouring established states over new ones.

A few legal scholars observed that constitutive and declaratory theories of recognition did not apply to governments since governments are agents, not legal personalities in their own right.[74] Most, however, drew governments into the controversy, sometimes by discussing the matter without clearly specifying what entity was being recognized, but most frequently by explicit inclusion. Most of the early inclusions of governments came from advocates of the declaratory view, who may have acted to bolster their case in the face of widespread support for the opposite view.[75] However, the greater difficulty of applying the constitutive theory to governments, which could be said to derive title to rule from acceptance by their own populations rather than by their foreign peers, did not stop advocates of the constitutive approach from continuing the expanded debate.[76]

Scholarly debate resumed after 1919, with inclusion or noninclusion of governments making little difference; the views of those who did not mention governments divided in roughly the same proportion as the views of those who did. Among those including recognition of governments in the discussion, about one-quarter – mainly writers of general texts – supported constitutive views,[77] about half supported declaratory views,[78] and the rest expressed intermediate positions.[79] A few decided that the issue was so confused that the very terms constitutive and declaratory should be abandoned.[80]

Abandoning the controversy was a more popular position after 1945,[81] but it continued anyway. Intermediate conceptions became more common as specialists tried to describe what governments actually believed. In one such description, recognition was partly constitutive and partly declaratory.[82] In another, recognition was declaratory of international legal capacity but constitutive of ability to undertake relations with the recognizing government.[83] Relatively few scholars continued to advocate purely constitutive conceptions.[84] Among those specifically including governments in the discussion, as among the others, declaratory views attracted more support as time passed. By 1975, the vast majority of specialists accepted the declaratory theory.[85]

The balance shifted towards mixed views after the Cold War. Many scholars avoided the debate, none defined recognition of governments as constitutive, and only one stated it to be purely declaratory.[86] Decades of discussion have inclined most legal scholars towards a mixed view that recognition declares awareness of existence and opens the way for the full range of bilateral relations.[87]

Governments made few comments on this controversy. Most statements came from new governments whose need for or recent acquisition of recognition inclined them towards the declaratory theory. The most elaborate was an 1848 circular sent by the new foreign minister to French envoys abroad:

> The French revolution is thus entering into its final period. France is a republic: the French Republic does not need to be recognized to exist. She is the product of national law. She is the will of a great people which seeks its title only from itself. Nonetheless, the French Republic desires to enter into the family of established governments as a regular power and not as a phenomenon disruptive of the European order. It is proper that you make known promptly to the government to whom you are accredited the principles and tendencies that will henceforth guide the policies of the French government.[88]

The one clear governmental comment on the other side was made during a domestic argument about whether to take up certain relations with an unrecognized government. In 1921 French premier Briand told the Senate that 'I cannot conceive of how one can make a juridically valid treaty with a de facto but juridically nonexistent entity. I do not see how, when one says to a government: "I do not recognize you, you are in my eyes nonexistent," one can make with that same government accords likely to create tangible realities.'[89]

The actions of governments show that they lean towards declaratory views. Even in the nineteenth century it was generally admitted that unrecognized governments could act for their states on international matters. No one challenged the new Italian government's right to expel consuls of nonrecognizing Bavaria in 1861 or its power to bind Italy to multilateral agreements.[90] Acceptance of an at least temporary competence to deal with pressing international matters underlay the whole justification of maintaining informal relations (*relations officieuses*) with unrecognized governments. Nor did governments challenge agreements between a government they did not recognize and a third government that did.[91]

Governments never pressed the consequences of nonrecognition as far as legal scholars. This became clearer as the twentieth century progressed and the extent of relations with unrecognized governments broadened. Governments realized, as Briand had concluded in 1921, that they could not combine constitutive notions of recognition and the range of contacts needed during prolonged nonrecognition of a well-established new government. Since they wanted, for various reasons, to engage in prolonged nonrecognition, they gave up constitutive notions. The lack of formal statements on the matter allowed them to do so discreetly. However, the shift was stated clearly in the Americas; Article 9 of the OAS Charter begins with the stipulation that 'The political independence of the State is independent of recognition by other States.'[92]

International and national tribunals also ruled on the issue, usually in relation to recognition of new states. Early in the interwar period, the Tinoco Claims Arbitration adopted a declaratory approach to recognition of governments, treating recognition only as additional evidence supporting a government's claim to be the effective ruler of a state.[93] Though the Permanent Court of International Justice's decision in *Certain German Interests in Polish Upper Silesia* seems to lean in a constitutive direction,[94] declaratory conceptions were adopted by some national courts.[95] There were instances of national courts refusing to give effect to acts of unrecognized governments, but doing so only because of nonrecognition, rather than on grounds that the particular act violated international law, became less prominent as time passed.[96]

Though phrased as a debate about the intrinsic character of recognition, the constitutive–declaratory debate is better viewed as an argument about its effects. Recognition, like other legal institutions, changes over time in response to the changing beliefs and needs of members of the social system in which it functions. To posit that a legal institution has some intrinsic character encourages thoughts that it has an unchanging essence. Too strong an insistence on that point can easily condemn legal institutions to ossification.

The competing conceptions can be related to a deeper philosophical debate. Methodological individualists, who believe that individuals or some other basic units are the primary elements, and social systems the product of interaction among the basic units, are more likely to feel at home with declaratory views. These base a government's legal existence on its own ability to win obedience from the population of the affected state, thus asserting the primacy of the national community. Methodological holists, who regard the social system as primary and the individuals or basic social units within as derivative, are more likely to feel at home with constitutive views. These base a government's legal existence on the collective judgement of its peers, asserting the primacy of the international community. However, few legal scholars explicitly raised these deeper issues, and governments did not consider them when deciding in favour of declaratory views. Relatively new governments, it is clear, saw declaratory views as more conducive to their efforts to acquire international status than the 'closed club' notions encouraged by constitutive views. Yet even well-established governments accepted declaratory views; constitutive ones appear to have been the province of legal theorists.

SUMMARY

The four legal doctrines examined in this chapter have provided the broad confines within which recognition decisions, and the political struggles they sometimes inspired, were pursued. Two operated to limit the number of occasions when recognition became an issue. The other two operated to limit, more strongly in the twentieth century than in the nineteenth, the impact of those decisions on the bilateral relations of states.

Acceptance of the legal doctrines that questions of recognition only arose with extra-legal changes of government and that recognition was irrevocable bounded the recognition policies of states by limiting the number of occasions when they had to make a conscious decision. Limiting recognition to extra-legal changes of government meant that recognition was an occasional, generally unforeseen, necessity. Decisions thus followed rather than anticipated events and were often improvised. Treating recognition as irrevocable meant that once recognition was given, the issue was settled until there was another extra-legal change of government in the same state. This was significant politically for two reasons. First, it limited the opportunities for demanding favours in return for recognition; each other government only had one chance to exploit a new government's greatest vulnerability. Second, irrevocability affected the terms of domestic policy debates about relations with new regimes. Debate could be avoided or reduced if recognition was granted early. If it was delayed, opponents of recognition explicitly or implicitly used the one-way nature of the step as another reason for proceeding cautiously. Those seeking to change a nonrecognition policy had to overcome such arguments or await developments that persuaded enough others that it was time to recognize.

The doctrine of state continuity provided even unrecognized governments with a floor of legal protection by limiting the amount of permissible discrimination between them and recognized governments. The exact implications of this doctrine depended on how recognition was characterized. Holders of constitutive views encouraged drawing great distinctions between the recognized and the unrecognized. In the nineteenth century this worked to produce a greater stress on the continuing obligations than on the continuing rights of the affected state. In the interwar and Cold War periods, the shift towards declaratory views paralleled and supported the concurrent shift towards expanding the range of relations with unrecognized governments. By 1975 the spread of declaratory views created a climate of opinion more encouraging to arguments that recognition of governments is an unnecessary formality.[97]

3 Legal Rules Guiding Recognition Decisions

Particular decisions about whether to recognize a new regime as the government of another state are neither completely governed by rules of international law nor left entirely to policy-makers' discretion. Even those legal scholars and policy-makers most inclined to regard recognition as a 'political act' have acknowledged that two sets of legal rules do limit discretion by defining the occasions on which recognition decisions are needed and by establishing the acceptable reasons to recognize or withhold recognition. Understanding the mix of rule-bound and discretionary choice involved requires tracing opinions on two related issues: why international law is structured to permit an area of discretion, and identification of the binding rules that have been accepted in various periods.

WHY DISCRETION PERSISTS

International law is a 'horizontal' legal system in which the rules are made by states as a group rather than by a central rule-maker. States (more accurately, their governments) retain considerable discretion in recognition decisions because they remain convinced that this best advances their longterm interests. The unwillingness to surrender all choice is apparent in discussions of two related issues: (1) whether recognition is a 'legal' act to be accomplished strictly according to rules, or a 'political' act involving considerable discretion, and (2) whether there is a duty to recognize as a government any new regime that meets certain criteria. The two questions are related in that there are clear logical connections between regarding recognition as a legal act and assuming that there is a duty to recognize in certain circumstances, or alternatively regarding recognition as a political act and rejecting any duty to recognize.

The question of whether recognition is a 'legal' or a 'political' act involves deciding whether governments may apply only those criteria for recognition specified in general international law or may also take other considerations into account. This is distinct from the question of whether there is a duty to recognize. Proponents of a duty generally argue that only one criterion – effective control over all or most of the state – is relevant, while some proponents of viewing recognition as a legal act have supported general application of additional criteria as well. Conversely, a belief that international law specifies all the criteria for decision does not necessarily mean the decision will be recognition; legal rules might as easily specify that certain characteristics or policies make a new regime ineligible for recognition.

Few nineteenth-century writers discussed whether recognition is a legal or a political act, but those who posited a duty to recognize did support their conclusion with arguments suggesting that recognition is a legal act. Lorimer wrote that allowing discretion in recognition decisions entailed denying that international law is law, while Bluntschli argued that recognition, like other international acts of governments, must proceed according to international law because that law binds all states in the international community regardless of their will.[1]

Interwar legal scholars hoped to reduce government abuse of recognition, but were aware that governments would not give up all discretion about entering into relations with new regimes. In 1931 the French diplomat Grenard argued that there is a duty to recognize once a new regime has demonstrated effective control of its state but that establishment of full diplomatic relations remains a matter of choice.[2] Kelsen adopted similar ideas in 1941 by distinguishing between acknowledgement of existence as the 'legal' aspect of recognition and establishment of diplomatic relations as the 'political' aspect.[3] Borchard, in noting the difficulties of separating recognition into legal and political aspects, argued that there was a duty to recognize but discretion in carrying out that duty – which amounted to saying there was no enforceable duty.[4] The Dane Møller, the Englishman Baty, and the German Arendt were probably closest to policy-makers' views of the matter when they argued that recognition is a discretionary act producing binding effects. In their conception, the act of recognition was political, but its consequences legal.[5]

Policy-makers' refusal to accept any duty to recognize led some Cold War era legal scholars to emphasize the legal character of decisions to recognize as a way of limiting government discretion. Lauterpacht, whose earlier insistence on a duty to recognize had been criticized as not reflecting the actual state of international law, wrote in 1950 that recognition should be based on unvarying principles.[6] Scelle argued that discretion is limited because the power to recognize is a consequence not of sovereignty but rather of the *dédoublement fonctionnel* of national authorities stemming from lack of a central world governing body. In the recognition of new governments, he argued, national policy-makers are actually undertaking tasks of international governance and are bound to follow international rules exactly.[7]

Other scholars revived interwar efforts to distinguish 'legal' – or acknowledgement of basic rights – and 'political' – or initiation of optional relations – aspects of recognition.[8] Frowein took off in a slightly different direction in separating a nondiscretionary 'recognition as a *de facto* regime', accepting a new government's ability to act for its state, and a discretionary 'recognition as a government', establishing wider relations.[9] O'Connell attempted to make a three-part division into 'cognition' – taking notice of an effective government's existence; 'cognizance' – acts by subordinate agencies indicating their cognition and respect for its legal consequences; and 'recognition' – cognizance when undertaken by the political leaders.[10]

Several thought that efforts to persuade governments to accept a duty to accord a certain level of respect to any effective government by calling that respect something other than 'recognition' were doomed to failure. Even though they also hoped to limit discretion, they believed that the legal and political aspects of recognition were too intertwined to permit clear separation.[11] Others took the impossibility of separating these aspects and the evidence from state practice as confirming that recognition is a discretionary act. Patel limited discretion only by arguing for a duty to avoid recognizing before effective control existed,[12] while the American Law Institute's Second Restatement expressed a widespread view in stating that recognition is a discretionary act with binding effects.[13]

Post-Cold War writers sought to increase the predictability of recognition decisions in a number of ways. Some agreed that recognition of governments was becoming obsolete and that a duty to treat any effective regime ruling the whole state was emerging.[14] One adopted the more indirect argument that failure to recognize a regime effectively ruling its state amounts to a violation of its rights.[15]

Governmental discussion of the matter since 1815 has been scanty but generally involved asserting discretion. A 1971 Canadian statement expressed the prevailing governmental view: 'While the act of recognition is essentially legal in nature, the relevance of political factors is recognized in modern international practice; each situation is therefore considered on its own merit.'[16] At most, governments have accepted that recognition has legal consequences; they have continued to insist that they enjoy discretion not only in whether to recognize but also in the choice of criteria and interpretations of criteria to apply in making recognition decisions.

Most governments and many writers confined their attention to the related question of whether there is a legal duty to recognize. During the nineteenth century as a whole, as many writers proposed that there should be a duty to recognize any government effectively controlling its state as denied the possibility or desirability of such a duty. Future trends were foreshadowed between 1900 and 1914 when twice as many denied as affirmed the usefulness of positing such a duty.

The arguments in favour of establishing a duty varied. Most advocates relied on arguments that the principle of sovereign equality of states or the principle of state continuity required others to accept and deal with any 'general government' – that is, any new regime that controls the whole state.[17] A few reached the same result from the premise that international law is superior to state law and specifies control as the only criterion for recognition as a government.[18] Two accepted a limited duty to recognize. Le Normand, a French specialist on civil wars, expressed a more widely-held reservation in not extending the duty to cover new governments endangering 'the fundamental laws of international society'.[19] The German Holtzendorff argued there was a duty to recognize any government in whose favour the predecessor had resigned.[20]

Failure to posit a duty did not mean accepting that 'anything goes'. Some scholars noted that governments could be held responsible for any damage done by a failure to recognize a new regime once it demonstrated effective control of its state.[21] Another group argued that international law provides all the relevant criteria but permits government discretion in their application to particular cases.[22] Others gave no clear reason for their conclusion.[23]

State practice in the nineteenth century decisively supported contentions that no duty to recognize exists. Governments might argue that regimes in control of their whole state normally should be recognized, but left themselves room for choice in the qualification 'normally'. 'Normally' did mean 'in the vast majority of cases'; prolonged nonrecognition of an effective regime was rare.[24] But nineteenth-century governments followed the same proclivities for reserving discretion in recognition that they followed in other areas of international interaction.

Few writers attempted to argue for a duty to recognize in the interwar period.[25] Many did try, however, to limit the extent of discretion in recognition decisions with other arguments. A few were confident that increasing levels of interaction among states would limit nonrecognition of an effective government to relatively short periods of time.[26] Others believed that long delays in recognition would be curbed by exercise of the counterpressures permitted under international law by effective but unrecognized governments.[27] Specialists splitting recognition into 'legal' and 'political' aspects attached a duty to the former and permitted discretion in the latter.[28]

Governments generally held to their earlier opinions, except in Latin America where proposals that the regional law of the Americas should include a duty to recognize were popular as responses to US policies tying recognition to various conditions. The US government obviously opposed the proposals, but so did a number of Latin American governments. Regional dissensus was so great that the Pan American Union was unable to adopt a regional treaty on recognition. The Union's Institute of International Law proposed a provision that:

> The new government has a right to be recognized if it meets the aforementioned conditions [ability to maintain internal order and 'disposition to fulfill international obligations']. Refusal of recognition by one of the Republics may be considered an unfriendly act.[29]

The terms were not materially altered during additional discussions before it was presented to the Sixth Interamerican Conference at Havana in 1928. Even so, the whole draft was rejected. Latin American governments secured some satisfaction of their demands that the US government curb its abuses of discretion when the 1933 Montevideo Declaration on the Rights and Duties of States condemned intervention in other states' internal affairs. By the end of the decade, Western Hemisphere discussions of recognition policy had shifted to an entirely different concern: the possibility of curbing fascist influence through nonrecognition of new governments coming to power through a coup d'état.

The Soviet government, which was still unrecognized by the US and several other governments, was also interested in making recognition of any government in effective control of its state a duty in the late 1920s. In 1928, it argued that the undertaking to resolve all disputes by peaceful means contained in Article 2 of the Kellogg–Briand Pact prohibited refusals to establish or resume diplomatic relations.[30] This was a roundabout way to condemn nonrecognition as well since an absence of diplomatic relations was one consequence of a refusal to recognize a new government.[31] By the time the Soviet Union joined the League of Nations in 1934 the Soviet government had been recognized by all the great powers, and no longer pursued these efforts.

Cold War era specialists advocating a duty to recognize divided more clearly into those arguing that the duty does exist and those arguing that it does not yet but should exist. Many of those claiming that a duty does exist derived it from what they regarded as fundamental principles of international law. The English scholar Lauterpacht based the duty on the argument that the right of a state to change its own government is one of the minimum rights of independence.[32] The Brazilian Azevedo argued from the duty of non-intervention and a need to avoid creating obstacles to international cooperation.[33] The Soviet scholars Kozhevnikov and Feldman argued that the right of self-determination, to which Feldman added a right to participation in international affairs derived from the principles of peaceful coexistence, creates a right to be recognized.[34] The English scholar Higgins believed a duty to recognize governments arising from indigenous rebellions was implied in the General Assembly's 1960 Declaration on the Granting of Independence to Colonial Countries and Peoples.[35] The French Marxist Charvin showed more ingenuity, citing the UN Charter, the General Assembly's 1970 Declaration on Principles of Friendly Relations and Cooperation among States, the rules of peaceful coexistence, and other unspecified general principles of international law in support of a duty to recognize new governments.[36] The French Sibert, the American Wright, and the Swiss Bindschedler used the simpler argument that because effective control is the sole test of a new government's claim to rule there is little or no room for discretion in its application to particular cases.[37]

The persuasiveness of these arguments was weakened by the controversies about the existence and identity of 'fundamental principles of international law'. Though the idea that there were or ought to be 'fundamental principles' was widely accepted by 1968,[38] there was far less agreement on which principles were fundamental. There was also considerable dissent from the proposition that effective control of its state is the only criterion on which recognition decisions can be based. The extent of such opinions did not entirely discourage advocates of a duty to recognize; they merely shifted from saying it does exist to saying it should exist. One, O'Connell, even argued that the idea of a duty to recognize must have some hold over governments because they offer at least quasi-legal explanations for decisions to refuse recognition.[39]

Again there was a substantial middle group accepting nonexistence of a duty to recognize but affirming the existence of real limits to government discretion in recognition decisions. The Tanzanian Kato argued that international law specified all the criteria governments could use in recognition decisions.[40] The Chinese K'ung argued that discretion does not permit the use of nonrecognition for seeking illegal advantages or promoting aggression.[41] The English editors of Oppenheim, the American Law Institute, and the Belgian Verhoeven all argued that there was a framework of legal rules imposing real limits on discretion.[42] The distinction between 'legal' and 'political' aspects of recognition,[43] or basic and optional aspects of relations,[44] continued to be used in support of claims that certain acknowledgements of an effective government's existence were obligatory.

Those who denied the existence of any duty to recognize were seldom explicit in their reasoning. Several pointed to governments' refusal to acknowledge any such duty.[45] O'Connell noted the logical problems in arguments claiming that a duty already exists, while Charpentier concluded that the lack of consensus on a set of criteria for recognition and on the idea that there is a binding duty to recognize once they are fulfilled meant that no duty could be assumed to exist.[46] Tripathi, responding to opponents' claims that changes of government were an entirely internal affair, argued that changes of government are acts of state open to the same sort of examination and comment as others.[47]

In the early Cold War era governments continued to assert wide discretion in recognition decisions. The United States government conceded only that duties to recognize might be created by treaty.[48] For all their readiness to recognize any government in effective control, the Swiss and Italian governments explicitly stated that no duty exists.[49] In 1959, the Soviet government took the same view,[50] though later maintained that the principle of peaceful coexistence means that all states have the right to participate in international affairs.[51] Latin American governments remained divided on the question. Organization of American States debates on recognition of governments in 1949 and 1950 showed that the Cuban and Uruguayan governments were the most eager to establish a duty while the Chilean was the most opposed.[52] The East German government devoted much energy to proving that both it and the state of which it was agent had a right to recognition (another way of saying others had a duty to recognize it) before other governments adopted a 'two Germanies' solution in 1972.[53] Yet it was equally willing to support the Brezhnev Doctrine and its consequence of refusing to recognize non-Leninist governments in Soviet-bloc states.[54] The British government declared acceptance of a duty to recognize new states in 1948,[55] and usually followed the policy of accepting any effective regime as a government. However, its practice was not entirely consistent. This would have become clear in 1974 if the Sampson regime in Cyprus had lasted more than a few days,[56] and did become clear when the British explicitly withheld recognition from the Heng Samrin government of Cambodia.

The discussion took a new turn during the late 1970s and early 1980s as a number of governments settled the issue not by accepting a duty to recognize but by claiming they were abandoning the practice of recognizing other governments. This generally moved the governments involved closer to accepting a duty in practice because they stated that it was now their policy to maintain diplomatic relations with any regime that effectively rules its state.[57] Yet in practice most of the governments claiming to have abandoned recognition made exceptions against accepting regimes maintained in power by foreign troops[58] or condemned as undesirable by the UN Security Council.[59] Thus even governments claiming to have dispensed with recognition of governments retained some basis for refusing to deal with particular new regimes as agents of their state.

THE REACH OF BINDING RULES

Though rejecting a duty to recognize, governments have not claimed unlimited discretion in making recognition decisions. In particular they have accepted that ability to provide actual administration (in the traditional phrase, 'exercise effective control') over all or almost all of the state is the necessary condition for recognizing a new regime as its government. This has two consequences: (1) recognition as a government should not be granted before that degree of control is attained, and (2) treatment as a government should not be continued after it has been lost. Legal scholars and governments alike thus accept that both premature recognition and prolonged recognition are illegal under international law.[60] The occasional violations do not detract from the high level of consensus linking effective rule over the state and acceptance as its government.

The Necessity of Effective Control

The consensus that effective rule is the one condition necessary for recognition stems from the very definition of a government as those who rule the state, maintain internal order, and carry out international relations on the state's behalf. Some policy-makers and legal scholars have added that a new government ought also to be 'stable' – that is, show real prospect of being able to continue ruling for an extended period. Leaving aside the thorny question of when one can be confident a new government controls 'most' of the territory while a civil war rages, the only real argument among legal scholars has been whether control should be the sufficient as well as the necessary condition for recognition as a government. The claim that it should be sufficient as well is often labelled 'defactoist' because it entails accepting whatever regime actually holds power regardless of its origins, ideology, or policies. However, the term 'defactoist' has sometimes been extended more broadly to any recognition policy that does not distinguish among new regimes by how they gained power or by ideology. To avoid ambiguity, the term 'effectivist' will be used to denote the belief that effective control is the sole criterion for recognition.

About half of the nineteenth-century[61] and interwar[62] scholars addressing recognition of governments argued explicitly that effective control should be the sole criterion. Post-1945 effectivists split into two groups. Only one insisted that control was sufficient for all recognition;[63] the other said it was sufficient for 'minimum recognition' but permitted use of additional tests for 'full recognition' or establishment of 'optional interstate relations'.[64]

In the nineteenth century, governments were most likely to follow an effectivist policy when new regimes arose in parts of the world where they had few interests at stake. Thus European governments usually allowed their diplomatic representatives in Latin America full authority to recognize whenever a new group took power. The United States government took a similar approach towards the smaller European states and most of Latin America until the 1860s.

Governments also perceived that effectivist rhetoric could blunt others' criticism of a particular recognition decision. The Swiss government found effectivist arguments very useful in preserving neutrality and avoiding trouble with the great powers. Tsar Nicholas I used effectivist arguments to explain his recognition of Dom Miguel as King of Portugal in 1828, though his interest in seeing the constitutionalists under Dona Maria defeated was obvious to all. The three-sided Spanish civil war among absolutists, constitutionalists, and republicans that raged between 1868 and 1875 was so confused and seemed so likely to attract outside involvement that all the great powers pursued effectivist policies. This also involved using a rather lax definition of 'control' at times; even insecure control of the largest part of the country sufficed for the moment.[65] The Austrian and Russian governments masked rival political ambitions behind effectivist explanations of their decisions to break with the other powers and recognize the Karageorgevich dynasty in Serbia after the 1903 coup.

Interwar state practice was quite similar. The British and Swiss governments used control as the sole test more often than others, but let other considerations guide policy towards the new Soviet government. Highly confused situations encouraged reliance on a loosely-defined effectivism to choose among rival factions in ongoing civil wars. No one government controlled all (or even most) of China between 1916 and 1928, but the extensive foreign treaty privileges and other relations required ongoing dealings with some Chinese partner. Most European governments, along with those of Japan, the USSR, and the USA, chose to regard whoever ruled in Beijing as 'the government of China' no matter how limited its area of control or how sharp the challenge from warlords and the Kuomintang in Canton. Only the USA dropped out, refusing to recognize any government in China between 1926, when it was apparent that Marshal Tuan could not fulfil his promise to organize a government including representatives from all provinces of China, and October 1928 when Kuomintang forces occupied Beijing.[66]

The only clear trend in state practice came in Latin America, where reliance on effectivist policies increased. Though it did not brand the use of other criteria illegal, the 1923 award in the Tinoco Claims Arbitration gave powerful support to effectivist doctrines with its reasoning for accepting effective control rather than foreign recognition as the real test of whether a regime is a government capable of engaging state responsibility.[67] The Mexican government shifted the terms of discussion further in 1931 by adopting the Estrada Doctrine, under which it claimed to abolish recognition of governments and maintain full diplomatic relations with whoever effectively ruled a state. That same year the Central American republics ended their second experiment in constitutional legitimacy by denouncing their 1923 Treaty of Peace and Amity and giving up concerted nonrecognition of regimes taking power by coup d'état.

Reliance on effectivist policies increased in the Cold War period for two reasons. First, there were more governments in the world professing to accept them if one considers governments following a policy of establishing diplomatic relations without formal comment on recognition[68] as well as those stating that control is the sole criterion for recognition, asserting that recognition of governments is unnecessary,[69] or claiming the question does not arise in a particular case because the change was not really extra- legal.[70] Secondly, there were more occasions for recognizing new governments because many Third World states remained politically unstable. The British, Swiss, and Mexican governments continued to favour effectivist policies, and were joined by the Dutch[71] and most former British colonies. The practice of these governments could be summed up by a 1964 Canadian statement that 'where there is no special consideration, the practice followed by Canada is to deal with the government that is in control'.[72] African governments generally followed effectivist policies among themselves, quickly accepting new leaders who came to power through coups. The few exceptions involved particularly shocking changes (the 1963 coup in Togo, which was Africa's first, and involved murdering the president) or upset some governments because a leftist regime was replaced by a non- or less leftist one (Algeria 1965, Ghana 1966, Uganda 1971).

Again effectivist rhetoric often proved politically convenient. Britain found the arguments quite handy in discussions of its decision to recognize the PRC government in 1950 at a time when its US ally adamantly opposed such a step. The Indian government cited lack of control to justify its refusal to recognize any government in the Congo (Zaire) to its communist and socialist critics eager to have it recognize the radical Gizenga regime in early 1961.[73] The same arguments could be used by allies or domestic opponents when faced with a government decision to delay recognition, as seen in Australian, Canadian, French, and US debates over policy towards the PRC government.

No government was entirely consistent in its adherence to an effectivist recognition policy. Effectivism was used when there was no particular reason to object to a new regime, when a government wanted to deflect domestic or allied criticism of a particular recognition decision, or when an opposition or allies wanted to criticize a particular failure to recognize. When, however, there was broad agreement on another approach, both governments and opposition leaders were ready to invoke other reasons for granting or withholding recognition.

Most post-Cold War practice has continued along effectivist lines, though there has been some interest in using recognition policy (and other actions) to promote democracy or at least discourage return to undemocratic forms of rule.[74] The majority of legal scholars writing recently have also endorsed effectivist over other types of recognition policy.

Disqualifications

The emphasis on control as a necessary condition for recognition implies two other obligations. The first is to avoid 'premature recognition', that is, recognizing a new government before it exercises sufficient control. The second is to avoid 'prolonged recognition', still recognizing a government after it has lost control. In legal theory, the second is easier to avoid than the first since recognition is regarded as lapsing when control ends. In practice, however, governments have managed the second as well as the first by maintaining contact and making agreements with leaders or diplomatic representatives of a defunct government.

There was little discussion of premature recognition of governments in the nineteenth century; legal scholars' attitudes often have to be deduced from their statements on relations with secessionists. Only Wheaton, writing in 1836 and influenced by memories of the USA's and the Latin American states' need for help in their rebellions, said that governments were free to take sides in civil wars and expressed no concern about the possibility of premature recognition.[75] A larger group did not condemn premature recognition as illegal, but did warn that anyone recognizing rebels as a government would face severe political complications if the previously-established government won the civil war.[76] The complications would depend, obviously, on the relative power of the states involved, but it was open to governments to view recognition of rebels as the government of the whole state (not simply as a 'local de facto government' ruling part of the state) as an act of war and respond accordingly. A few even held stronger views. Fiore argued that the established government must – not just may – regard premature recognition of a rebel government as an act of war.[77] Four others argued that foreigners must continue recognizing the previously-established government until the civil war is over.[78]

The preponderance of scholarly opinion thus leaned against premature recognition.

Governments generally avoided premature recognition in the nineteenth century. At most, there were cases of relatively early recognition that later proved to be mistakes. In view of the constitutionalists' eventual triumph in Portugal, both the Russian and US governments might be deemed guilty of premature action when they recognized Dom Miguel's rival government instead in 1828, but at the time the constitutionalists' control was confined to one offshore island and seemed unlikely to expand. There was no rush to recognize the many liberal or constitutionalist governments established in Europe during 1848 even though the British, French, and US governments and publics clearly sympathized with them.[79] The great powers' decision to consult, act together, and basically follow the results of the three-sided struggle as it developed meant there were no clearly premature recognitions of Spanish governments between 1868 and 1875.

Only when governments had decided to intervene in favour of one side did they depart from caution in granting recognition. Interventions were common between 1815 and 1830 as one or more of the great powers asserted a right to order affairs in smaller European states. They continued into the 1830s with British and French involvement in Spanish and Portuguese civil wars, and flared again in 1848. By mid-century, however, intervention in civil wars (though not in nationalist struggles against foreign rulers) was less common in Europe.

The greater instability of the interwar period increased the frequency of and the interest in problems of civil war. This meant, among other things, greater discussion of premature recognition. On the whole, however, more interwar writers cautioned against premature recognition[80] than condemned it as illegal.[81] Interwar writers were no more able than their nineteenth-century predecessors to formulate a clear distinction between 'premature' and 'early' (or 'hasty') recognition. The problem lay in the ambiguity of the traditional doctrine that a new regime control all or most of the territory of its state before being accepted as the government. A few tried to specify a dividing line. Baty required that the old government's area of control be very insignificant and rebel victory assured before recognition was extended, while Scelle required that recognition await acceptance of a new regime by plebiscite or vote of a specially-elected national assembly.[82]

Even allowing for a loose definition of 'control' in highly fluid situations, there was much premature recognition in the interwar period. The First World War Allies avoided premature recognition of Czech and Polish governments (and states) only by creating a 'co-belligerent' status not revived during World War II. The Russian civil war inspired several premature recognitions. The French dislike of the Bolsheviks led them to recognize both Kolchak's and Wrangel's regimes as governments of Russia despite very limited areas of control.[83] Not much later, the Russo-Polish War of 1920 produced the first of several Bolshevik experiments. A Polish 'government in exile' was formed in Russian-occupied territory and immediately recognized as the government of Poland by the Bolsheviks.[84] Stalin used a similar device, though the 'People's Government of Finland' had to be based on Soviet territory, at the start of the Russo-Finnish War in November 1939. Both expedients were dropped when Soviet arms were less successful than anticipated.[85]

The most famous instances of premature recognition occurred during the Spanish Civil War of 1936–9. The German and Italian governments recognized Franco's Nationalists as the government of Spain in October 1936 even though the established Republican government controlled most of the country and was not defeated until 1939. The link to their overall policy of assisting Franco is clear from their accord on the matter:

> The two Governments will recognize the Spanish National Government *de facto* as soon as possible. They will keep in touch with each other for the purpose of announcing *de jure* recognition subsequently. When they announce this, the two Governments will confirm the principles of nonintervention and respect for the integrity and territorial unity of Spain, her protectorates, and her colonies.
>
> The two Governments will jointly examine the question of when, after the *de facto* recognition, the time has come to declare the agreed arms embargo to be invalidated.[86]

World War II inspired additional uses of the technique. Though the Germans did not recognize the Japanese-sponsored Wang regime as the government of China in 1940, they occasionally set up friendly regimes rather than rule a conquered country through military occupation. The Allies also bent recognition to their purposes, but had the advantage of being able to assert the traditional law of war that there should be no disturbances in the status of established governments until war's end. This did not prevent the Soviets from substituting their own government in Poland in 1944 and getting US and British acceptance of their participation in a new coalition in mid-1945, nor was rapid German occupation of Italy and reinstatement of Mussolini allowed to interfere with continued Allied acceptance of the Badoglio government that had supplanted him in July 1943.

Distance from the theatres of combat permitted closer adherence to normal rules in other parts of the world. Thus the Guatemalan and Costa Rican governments refused to recognize a Salvadorian government-in-exile formed under the ousted first vice-president in 1944 until it managed to gain control of the country from those who had accomplished the initial coup.[87]

The weight of Cold War scholarly opinion shifted towards favouring a duty to avoid premature recognition in reaction against an increased tendency among governments to use aid to one faction in a civil war as a major form of international conflict. The arguments in favour of establishing such a duty were derived from a variety of general legal principles. Many cited the principle of nonintervention.[88] One Soviet specialist derived it from UN Charter obligations to settle disputes peacefully and generally develop friendly relations among states.[89] Others invoked the rights of established governments,[90] while a few argued from the rule that control is the necessary condition for recognition as a government.[91] Many stated no reasons for their conclusions.[92] A relatively small group still supported the older argument that premature recognition is risky but not illegal.[93] However, there was still no progress in forming consensus on when a grant of recognition is premature rather than hasty. Even the many scholars particularly concerned with civil wars came to no consensus.[94] The main change was that no one failed to denounce or at least warn strongly against premature recognition.

Even though the opportunities for premature recognition during the Cold War era were far more abundant than the actual occurrences, there were enough instances to make it a significant problem. Recognition of any government in the Congo (now Zaire) after the Kasavubu–Lumumba split probably would have been premature, but the UN General Assembly majority's decision to back the Kasavubu group's claim against their Lumumba–Gizenga rivals put the governments recognizing the latter[95] at a disadvantage. A similar split, minus the UN General Assembly's involvement, occurred when the Viet Cong formed a 'provisional revolutionary government of South Vietnam' in 1969. It was quickly recognized as the government of South

Vietnam by the Hungarian, Czech, Mongolian, PRC and Egyptian governments,[96] and enjoyed wider recognition by 1974. As in the Congo, the overall situation was vastly complicated by the nature of the civil war under way. Those who viewed the Vietnamese conflict as a civil war within a separate South Vietnam could regard the Viet Cong as puppets of an interfering North Vietnamese government. Those who viewed the conflict as a civil war within one Vietnam that had been temporarily divided could view the Saigon government of South Vietnam as a puppet of the USA. The depth of this uncertainty, plus the political advantages of having a local face, led the North Vietnamese to establish a separate government for South Vietnam after their triumph in May 1975 and formally reunify the country later.

The proclamation of a pro-Western 'Khmer Republic' under General Lon Nol in 1970, and the subsequent formation in Beijing of a 'Cambodian Royal Government of National Unity' led by the ousted head of state, Prince Sihanouk, produced obviously partisan reactions on both sides. Many Western governments managed to evade recognition issues by regarding the Republic as a legal change because the National Assembly endorsed it under the relevant provisions of the Cambodian Constitution.[97] When the exile government was proclaimed from Beijing the following May, the PRC, Albanian, North Korean, and North Vietnamese governments immediately recognized it as the government of Cambodia.[98] Thirteen other governments recognized it as such within a few months.[99] These recognitions were also clearly premature because the exile government's Khmer Rouge allies did not begin guerrilla operations on Cambodian territory for another few months, and the 'government' itself did not move onto Cambodian territory until the Khmer Rouge took the capital in April 1975.[100]

Events moved so quickly in both Vietnam and Cambodia in the spring of 1975 that any premature recognitions were not premature for very long. The Khmer Rouge offensive picked up momentum in March, and the Soviets, who withdrew their embassy from Phnom Penh in October 1973 but also avoided relations with either the exile government or the Khmer Rouge as much as possible,[101] decided it was time to endorse the winners and recognized the exile regime on the 28th.[102] Lon Nol's resignation a few days before the Khmer Rouge took Phnom Penh triggered what are best regarded as hasty recognitions of the Sihanouk government by India, Liberia, and Sri Lanka. French, Turkish, Australian, Iranian, and Portuguese recognition followed after Khmer Rouge troops entered Phnom Penh but before the new government was fully consolidated. Other governments waited until the new government was more securely established in the capital before extending recognition.[103] The end of the Vietnam conflict occasioned less confusion because the Thieu government did not resign, governments sympathetic to the Viet Cong and North Vietnamese had recognized the 'Provisional Revolutionary Government' long before, and other governments saw no reason to rush matters.

African regional quarrels provided other instances of premature recognition. In June 1965 the Sudanese government announced its intention to recognize a government-in-exile of Chad being formed on Sudanese territory by refugees. Discussions encouraged by the Organization of African Unity led to a settlement of Sudan's differences with Chad, and a Sudanese promise to expel the refugees and stop aiding oppositionist groups.[104] In September 1971 the Chad and Sudanese governments were again embroiled in disputes when the Libyan government decided to recognize the 'Chad National Liberation Front' even though it was then based entirely in Sudan. Again, the dispute was patched over and the Libyans went back to dealing with the Chad government in their efforts to take and keep the Aouzou strip.[105]

Not all civil wars or inter-bloc struggles inspired premature recognitions. The Greek communists' 'First Provisional Government of Free Greece' was not recognized as a government though the communists did receive significant aid from the Soviet bloc.[106] In 1961 the US government ordered Cuban exiles in Florida to disband their 'Government of Cuba in Arms in Exile' in the belief that tolerating its presence would constitute recognition of some sort.[107]

Post-Cold War writers have maintained the general condemnation of premature recognition. Those who commented at any length were also more likely to regard premature recognition as an interference in the affairs of another state.[108]

Trends in scholarly opinion are clearer than trends in state practice. Legal scholars have grown less tolerant of premature recognition, and generally regard its spread as another aspect of the broader breakdown of nineteenth-century rules requiring neutrality in civil wars. Most Third World and Western legal scholars have deplored the tendency of governments to trim the rules in their favour during ideological struggles. Governments failed to arrive at a consensus against any and all use of premature recognition during the interwar and Cold War eras because they could not come to consensus on the broader proposition that civil wars are matters properly involving only the population of the affected state. This was particularly true during the Cold War, when direct armed conflict between the superpowers and their European allies was too dangerous to contemplate. Both East and West sought to expand their circle of allies, clients, or friends by a wide variety of other means; encouraging, promoting, and aiding like-minded factions in civil wars was one of them. Some Third World governments also sought to guide the politics of their region through involvement in the factional fights or wider civil strife in neighbouring states, and this could easily extend to premature recognition.

Prolonged recognition has not been as prominent as premature recognition, though it has occurred. Governments have generally agreed that they must avoid continuing relations with representatives of a defunct government beyond a brief transitional period. Brief transitional periods were accepted for two reasons. First, the state of communications in the early nineteenth century meant that it could be weeks or months before governments even knew there had been a change of government in a distant state. Second, the new government most often kept in place the senior foreign ministry officials and diplomats appointed by its predecessor. Thus it was easier to continue dealing with the already-appointed diplomatic representatives unless the new government made clear it intended to replace them.

The issue of prolonged recognition arises when a government continues to deal with the diplomatic representatives or the political leaders of a defunct government even after the leaders have lost power and the diplomats have been replaced by the new government. At this point, an acceptable temporary expedient becomes a refusal to acknowledge the new government's authority and right to act for the state.

Prolonged recognition was not a major concern in the nineteenth century. Though ideological differences did lead to interventions, premature recognitions, and other forms of foreign involvement in some political conflicts, it did not yet inspire continued relations with a defunct government. The only time the issue arose in state practice was in arguments about when British bankers acting as financial agents for Chilean President Balmaceda should have stopped executing his orders to sell Chilean government-owned silver. The rival Congressionalist faction, who became the new government, argued that the sales should have stopped as soon as local newspapers reported his resignation. The English Court of Appeal ruled that the newspaper reports were too speculative to be relied upon, but the agents should have stopped when Balmaceda's resignation was reported in the official gazette even if British and other recognition of the Congressionalist regime came later.[109]

Prolonged recognition became a more prominent issue in the highly charged atmosphere of the early interwar period. New governments considering themselves to be fundamentally different from their predecessors came to power in several states. The Soviet government in particular aroused hostility and many governments refused to have any dealings with it. Some governments, including those of China, France, Italy, and the USA, went further and continued dealing with Tsarist envoys as representatives of Russia able to act in its name. The Chinese did so in part to maintain operation of the system of extraterritoriality under which Russians, like other foreigners, were handed over to their own consuls rather than tried in Chinese courts. When the Chinese began attacking the whole system of foreign privileges in 1920, they desisted.[110] Their attitude towards the Soviet government soon became more friendly, particularly after it proposed revising the old Chinese–Russian treaties. The French and Italians continued to deal with Tsarist-appointed consuls,[111] while the USA dealt with the Tsarist-appointed ambassador as well.[112]

Other governments avoided such dealings. The Swiss government admitted an informal mission from the Bolsheviks in 1918 while the British government first dealt with Soviet representatives in third capitals and then admitted a Soviet trade delegation in 1921.[113] British governments accepted as binding on Russia only acts of Soviet-appointed officials.[114]

Despite these early examples, few interwar writings explicitly condemned prolonged recognition.[115] Nor was the subject of much concern to Cold War era scholars.[116] The shift of opinion was indicated more indirectly, by greater support for ideas that any regime effectively ruling its state should be accorded certain forms of minimum respect. Continued relations with the Republic of China as government of all China were often criticized. However, the longest-running case of prolonged recognition of a government,[117] continued Mexican dealings with representatives of the Republican government of Spain displaced by Franco's Nationalists in 1939, attracted only occasional newspaper reports.[118]

State practice continued to divide. The Soviet and Yugoslav governments also refused to recognize the Franco government, but did not maintain any dealings with the Republicans.[119] The British government avoided prolonged recognition and even challenged the right of ROC representatives to sign multilateral treaties on behalf of China.[120] Soviet-bloc governments routinely did the same, but the British stance was more significant for being unconnected to the wider East–West competition. Meanwhile, many governments, including those of Australia, Canada, France, Italy, Nigeria, Senegal, the USA, and West Germany, continued to treat ROC representatives as able to act on behalf of China during varying periods of refusal to recognize the PRC government. However, the 1975 communist victories in South-east Asia did not produce new governments-in-exile or prolonged recognitions.[121] This was clear evidence of a wider tapering off in the practice.

The Cold War era tendency to expand the variety of relations undertaken with unrecognized regimes could also be used to maintain contacts with defunct ones. The Belgian government was still accepting travel documents issued by the Spanish Republicans and a Polish government-in-exile in 1968, but insisted that no recognition of either as government of its state was involved.[122] The various forms of informal contact maintained with rebels, such as establishment of 'information offices', were also allowed to members or appointees of defunct governments. These devices hardly change the facts of who rules; they are mainly ways to keep alive symbolically claims that a particular change of government is unwelcome.

With 'normalization of relations' between the PRC and other states in the 1970s, the whole subject of prolonged recognition lost prominence. The lack of highly publicized later instances together with a shift towards increased reliance on effectivist policies meant that the subject was not even discussed among the post-Cold War writers.

Proposed Duties to Deny Recognition

Proponents of some of the optional criteria sometimes went beyond claiming that their preferred criterion was a good one to saying that its universal application should be assured by creating a duty not to recognize a new government unless or until it was met.[123] There are two reasons none of these proposals have been adopted. First, even those sympathetic to the idea of obligatory nonrecognition have not been able to agree on what criteria should be adopted by the international community. Second, any such proposal faces strong objection by those who believe that the principles of sovereign equality of states and self-determination of peoples establish a right of each state to choose its own political institutions and rulers according to whatever standards it wishes to adopt.

Legal scholars agree that governments can create duties to avoid recognition through special agreements. There have been cases of ad hoc agreement directed against a particular claimant, such as the great powers' understanding to avoid recognizing the Kuomintang as the government of China between 1918 and 1928.[124] Proponents of additional duties are thinking in terms of general rules such as the Quadruple Alliance's agreement 'not to recognize in any way the governments formed by open revolt'[125] or the Central American treaties of 1907 and 1923 providing for refusal to recognize a new regime coming to power by coup or rebellion until it had been accepted by the national congress. So far, such agreements have been short-lived; they usually founder on political disagreements among the parties. In 1990–92 it appeared that notions of a 'right to democratic governance' would become the basis of wider agreements, but such ideas were turned aside by both proponents of the traditional formulations of national self-determination and state sovereignty and democrats who felt that imposing democracy from outside was inconsistent with democratic values.[126]

SUMMARY

The discussions of how far international law governs decisions about recognizing foreign governments constitute a multi-level debate between those (mostly legal scholars) wishing to limit discretion by extending the reach of unvarying legal rules and those (most often policy-makers) wishing to preserve discretion. At its most abstract level, the debate took the form of argument about whether recognition is a legal act governed entirely by rules or a political act adjustable to circumstances within broad guidelines. Because policy-makers believe the emergence of new governments can have important effects at the international level, or trigger or intensify ideological contention over forms of domestic organization, they have preferred treating recognition as a political act adjustable to particular circumstances. Even when their inclinations point in a very different direction, legal scholars have been forced to admit that though the effects of recognition can be expressed in legal rules, the decisions about recognizing remain political and only loosely rule-bound.

A less abstract level of debate involves efforts to prove that there now is, or ought to be, a duty to recognize any government that effectively controls all or most of its state. Such a duty would leave governments some discretion in determining when sufficient control exists, but proscribe applying other criteria in assessing whether a new regime deserves recognition as a government. Efforts to prove the existence of such a duty founder on the same rocks as efforts to prove that recognition decisions are legal acts: governments, the ultimate makers of international law, do not acknowledge such a duty. The refusal to accept such a duty has several roots. The first is policy-makers' general preference for maintaining areas of discretion in case special circumstances arise. Even governments that follow an effectivist policy nearly all of the time have not been willing to commit themselves to following it in every case. Second is the real clash of values among those who want to emphasize control and those who want to add other criteria. An emphasis on control affirms the autonomy of states: whoever wins the domestic political struggle automatically becomes the state's agent. Yet it can be seen as doing so at the expense of other widely-held values – such as democracy, human rights, or broad socio-economic justice – because there is no guarantee that the political struggle will produce rulers whose beliefs and policies advance these values. Thus not only reactionaries fearing new forms of government but also progressives believing in the importance of various 'human' or 'cosmopolitan' values could have good reason to eschew effectivist recognition policies in certain instances.

Policy-makers now appear to accept the proposition that recognition should not continue after a government has lost control of its state. Legal scholars hardly discussed this problem in the nineteenth century, since there were no real instances of prolonged recognition. They began to condemn prolonged recognition in the interwar period after some governments used it, and have continued to condemn it ever since. A few governments tried it in the interwar era, and again in the earlier part of the Cold War era, but it is currently out of fashion.

Reduced to essentials, legal scholars' views and governments' actions show that there has been only one binding rule regarding recognition decisions since 1815: control of all or most of the state is the necessary, but not sufficient condition for recognition as its government. Avoiding premature and prolonged recognition are simple logical derivatives of this rule. For this reason, there is a stronger case for arguing that legal duties to avoid both do exist, even if governments do occasionally violate them. The lack of a duty to recognize based simply on exercise of effective control has allowed persistent debate about what other criteria are permissible grounds for decision. Lack of a duty also opens room for the possibility of using recognition or nonrecognition for the extending government's own purposes.

4 The Main Criteria for Recognition

Any definition of criteria for recognition necessarily involves defining the values to be advanced by the institution of recognition of governments.[1] Defining effective control, no matter how acquired or maintained, as the necessary and sufficient criterion for recognition as a government affirms the sovereign autonomy of states in their internal affairs and bars international scrutiny of new regimes' political ideologies and means of gaining power. Governments' failure to agree on any such rule has opened up wider areas of discretion which have been used for two purposes: to claim that some other values should be promoted in the international system by specifying additional criteria as necessary for recognition, and to advance their individual interests by granting or refusing recognition or by trading it against concessions by a particular new regime. The first is the subject of this chapter, which discusses the most frequently used optional criteria, and of the next, which discusses the rest; the second purpose will be addressed in Chapter 10.

Efforts to promote particular values have taken two forms. The milder involves arguing that the lack of a duty to recognize permits governments to employ additional criteria. Those who agree on a particular value may therefore try to promote it through their recognition decisions regardless of what other governments do. The stronger involves arguing that there should be a duty to avoid recognizing any regime that fails to meet the additional criteria. In this version, advancing the particular value would be incumbent on all governments. So far, all efforts to promote particular values, whether by one or a few governments or more generally, have been very uneven for two reasons. Even single governments or small groups of governments attempting to promote a particular value have not done so with uniform energy because of internal disagreements or the perceived need to accommodate other concerns in particular cases. Collective mechanisms have been proposed as a way to avoid uneven implementation and the pressures to recognize that build when a large number of third governments accept a particular regime, but have attracted little support so far because of the lack of agreement on what values should be promoted.[2]

This disagreement is also reflected in the work of legal scholars. In all the eras under study here, a respectable portion of legal scholars have either advocated or accepted as legal the use of criteria additional to effective control, but the scholarly community, like governments, has not developed any consensus on the values to be advanced or the criteria to be used. This has encouraged governments' tendencies to employ various criteria, and even different criteria at different times. Legal scholars have often scorned the resulting inconsistencies, but have also been forced to admit the depth of the disagreements and the difficulties of maintaining consistency across situations and shifting political considerations.

POPULAR SUPPORT

Ability to elicit popular support is one of the most-discussed additional criteria for recognition as a government. It appeals strongly to those who believe that the people should have a say in determining their own political institutions. Yet efforts to include it as a necessary criterion for recognition as a government have been hobbled by the lack of an agreed definition. Minimally, 'popular support' can be defined as acquiescence in the new regime's rule. In this formulation it hardly forms a separate criterion because effective control is demonstrated by the absence of significant resistance to the new regime and its policies. Most advocates of requiring popular support have more demanding definitions in mind. Some insist that obedience must be voluntary rather than secured by intimidation or violence, while others insist it means organizing an election or plebiscite in which the people express their acceptance or rejection of the change. Using any of these more demanding definitions shifts the issue to the way control is exercised or the desirability of providing for expression of popular acceptance or nonacceptance of the new regime.

Few nineteenth-century writers included popular support among the additional criteria for recognition. This is not surprising in light of the narrow spread of democratic ideology and the state-centred cast of international legal doctrine at the time. Among the few who did, however, differences in defining what constitutes good evidence of popular support appeared early. The few writers of general texts who mentioned the criterion defined it as acquiescence and interpreted it as an aspect of control.[3] Others, including two studying civil wars, made popular support a distinct criterion by requiring some form of express popular endorsement.[4] They also brought into international law the wider political debate about whether popularly supported governments would be more stable and provide better rule than others.[5]

Early in the nineteenth century even governments upholding democracy at home treated acquiescence as a sufficient sign of support for recognizing new regimes in other countries. Thus the US Secretary of State told the British ambassador in 1833 that 'It has been the principle and the invariable practice of the United States government to recognize that as the legal government of another nation which by its establishment in the actual exercise of power might be supposed to have received the express or implied assent of the people.'[6]

By mid-century, however, provision for explicit popular acceptance was emerging as a separate criterion. The Swiss and United States governments waited for the plebiscite results before recognizing the Second Empire in France.[7] The Austrian, British, German and Russian governments waited for formal endorsement of the new constitution by a specially-elected National Assembly before recognizing the Third French Republic in 1871,[8] though the Swiss and US governments recognized this change as soon as the provisional Republican government was proclaimed.[9] Only the Brazilian government recognized the Portuguese Republic before the 1911 elections.[10] This time, to Portuguese disappointment, the US government followed the British in waiting because the new government initially styled itself 'provisional'.[11] Similar delays followed proclamation of the Chinese Republic in 1912,[12] though in this case the practical reasons for waiting to see if the republic had much support were fairly obvious.

The criterion of willing popular support was invoked more in the Western Hemisphere, particularly by the US government after 1865. Yet even here practice was inconsistent. The US government invoked popular support separately in recognizing changes of government in Bolivia (1868), Peru (1866 and 1868), Venezuela (1879), Peru (1880, 1883, 1885), Brazil (1889) and El Salvador (1890). It failed to do so in recognizing changes of government in Peru (1881), Colombia (1867, 1890), Costa Rica (1868), and Venezuela (1892).[13] The Brazilian change involved replacing the monarchy with a republic, but the other changes were shifts between fairly similar rulers within republican institutions. Latin American governments seldom invoked popular support separately in the nineteenth century, relying instead on acquiescence as evidence of control.[14] However, in 1907 the governments of Costa Rica, Guatemala, Honduras, Nicaragua, and El Salvador included willing popular support as a separate criterion in the Additional Convention annexed to their Treaty of Peace and Friendship.[15] The Additional Convention was intended to discourage coups by making unelected governments work harder for recognition, and was part of a project for promoting greater political integration of the region. The US government, though not a party, stated it would apply the rules in its own decisions about recognizing new regimes in those states.[16] This fitted nicely with contemporaneous US efforts to encourage constitutional government in Central America, the Caribbean, and Mexico.[17]

The questions of whether to require popular support, and, if so, in what form, attracted more comment in the interwar period. Encouraged by the spread of (at least nominal) republicanism after World War I, a number of legal specialists made popular support the main criterion for recognition and gave preference to express forms of approval.[18] Others, noting that plebiscites can be rigged or voters intimidated, put no emphasis on these formal expressions.[19]

Governments remained thoroughly inconsistent in their policies. Nearly every government asserted the need to be sure the Bolsheviks enjoyed willing support before accepting them as the government of Russia. The Swiss were still repeating this line in 1927.[20] Greek plebiscites accepting the return of King Constantine I in 1920, establishment of a republic in 1924, and re-establishment of the monarchy in 1936 elicited varying reactions. The British government awaited the results of all three before recognizing the change.[21] The US government recognized the 1924 provisional government before the plebiscite with the intriguing expedient of not specifying whether the head was king or president so that the recognition would cover whatever form was accepted.[22] The US government did, however, delay recognition until the new Portuguese president was confirmed in office by plebiscite in 1917.[23] The Mexican and Soviet governments cited lack of popular support separately from objections that the regime was fascist for their refusal to recognize the Franco government of Spain after 1939.[24] However, many changes of government inspired no such discussion. Two of the most momentous, Mussolini's accession to power in Italy and Hitler's in Germany, inspired no discussion at all because both dictators used constitutional forms to gain power and appeared to have real popular support.

Popular support was used as a separate test more often in Latin America. In most cases, this was part of the Central American treaty-based efforts to enforce republican legitimacy by insisting on a formal popular acceptance.[25] Other US invocations of popular support, after coups in Nicaragua (1924) and Argentina, Brazil, Chile, Peru, and Guatemala (1930–31), suggested some weakening of policy because recognition was extended after promises to hold elections by a certain date rather than after the elections themselves.[26]

Specialist opinion remained divided after World War II. Some criticized requiring express popular consent as a form of legitimism,[27] or as interventionism,[28] while others reverted to treating acquiescence as confirmation of control rather than as a separate test.[29] The argument that popularly-based governments are more stable or behave better was less often invoked in the literature on recognition,[30] though still circulated in discussions of world politics or particular cases. One leading commentator even argued that requiring national governments to have genuine popular support would not be possible until establishment of a world government capable of enforcing the rule.[31]

The spread of democratization in the 1980s[32] and the end of the Cold War encouraged ideas that popular support should be expressed through a plebiscite accepting a new constitution or, better, through genuinely competitive ('free and fair') elections of a new government. However, legal specialists continued to disagree on its role in recognition decisions. Though a few thought express popular consent would play a larger role,[33] most specialists continued to define 'popular support' as acquiescence,[34] to say it was not a separate criterion,[35] or to oppose its use.[36]

The expediency of government use remained equally obvious in the Cold War period. The Soviet government listed popular support as one reason for recognizing the PRC government one day after its establishment in Beijing, while the US and other governments invoked it as a reason to deny recognition.[37] East–West competition in other parts of the world also produced considerable discussion of who really had popular support and thus merited recognition.

Yet a few governments became more consistent in their practice. The Canadian and Swiss governments did not invoke popular support as a separate criterion after World War II.[38] The British government mentioned obedience only.[39] Governments de-emphasizing recognition or claiming to have abandoned it[40] also focused on obedience without reference to positive popular support.

The criterion of popular support was sometimes invoked in justification of nonrecognitions in Africa, most coming from leftwing governments reacting against rightwing coups. After the 1966 Ghanaian coup, governments of Guinea, Mali, and Zambia withheld recognition. Guinea appeared ready to invade to return Nkrumah to power, the Mali government expected that the Ghanaian population would rebel against the new regime, and the Zambians were still saying two years later that Nkrumah was more popular than those who overthrew him and would win re-election if the new rulers dared hold one.[41] The governments of Guinea, Somalia, Tanzania, Zaire, and Zambia all suggested a lack of popular support in their denunciation of the 1971 Amin coup in Uganda as the work of 'imperialists'. President Sekou Touré of Guinea even challenged Amin to specify when and how the Ugandan people had chosen him as president.[42] In general, however, African governments refusing to accept a new regime on that continent invoked other rationales.

Popular support was discussed and invoked as a separate criterion more often in the Western Hemisphere. The Mexican government invoked it in reaction to the 1960 Salvadorian coup, but usually went no further than citing a vague 'commitment to democracy' in explaining recognition decisions.[43] The OAS did endorse using 'whether the new regime will call elections within a short period of time' among the factors to be taken into account in 1965,[44] but interest in the idea soon waned. The 1965 US intervention in the Dominican Republic, which had been justified initially by the need to end conflict among the various factions, but resulted in selection among them, dampened Latin enthusiasm.

Replacement of military juntas by elected civilian governments in several Latin American states during the mid-1980s, the transformations of Eastern Europe and the USSR, and the spread of democracy elsewhere led to revived emphasis on popular support. However, it was subsumed under promotion of democracy rather than used as a separate consideration in recognition decisions.

LEGITIMACY

As a criterion for recognizing new governments, 'legitimacy' has taken various forms. All rest on a belief that one particular form of government is better than others, and should be promoted through recognition policy and possibly other means as well. The reasons offered for believing that one form of government is superior have varied; arguments have rested on practical considerations of efficiency, stability, or beneficence, metaphysical beliefs in divine, natural, or historical law defining the highest possible forms of human organization, or both. For legitimists the problem of political organization comes down to identifying the one best form of rule and spreading it around the world. This does not necessitate denying the existence of separate states; it only means insisting that all states should organize their domestic political systems in similar fashion.

This highly teleological approach to politics sometimes collides with and sometimes reinforces using popular support as a criterion for recognition as a government. In its monarchical form, legitimism ignores popular attitudes and concentrates on who has the best dynastic claim to the throne. In its democratic and communist forms, legitimism rests on an assumption that the people really desire the best form even if terror, false consciousness, or irrationality lead to temporary acceptance of other forms. Democratic legitimacy has also involved some conflating of legality and legitimacy. Legality involves insistence that any change of government, including change of form, be accomplished according to the constitution, basic law, or fundamental customs then in force, so focuses on the method of change. Democratic legitimacy is focused more on consent by the governed, so is compatible with any voluntarily accepted change.[45] Yet – despite occasional warnings from legal scholars[46] – democratic legitimists have often failed to disentangle the two.

Legal specialists have been less prone to legitimism than policy-makers. This may derive from the strong traditions of state autonomy in international law, which lead most legal specialists to argue against outside involvement in the internal politics of states.[47] Since World War I, it may also reflect the growing support for ideas of national self-determination and the right of each people to choose its basic institutions for and by itself. Policy-makers, particularly when faced with an ideologically divided world, have been willing to experiment with legitimism. This has extended to occasional armed interventions and many instances of supporting like-minded factions fighting civil wars in other states. In recognition policy, legitimism has most often taken the form of denying recognition when a favoured form of government is replaced by another, though there have also been some premature recognitions of like-minded factions in hopes of helping them establish themselves or to provide stronger legal justification for material aid to them.[48]

In the early nineteenth century, 'legitimism' meant monarchical legitimism. The Quadruple Alliance's usage shifted from Talleyrand's initial focus on protecting the historical claims of a particular dynasty to a broader defence of monarchical absolutism. Efforts to maintain absolutist principles even against monarchs willing to adopt constitutional forms of rule inspired Austrian interventions in Naples and Sardinia (1821), French intervention in Spain (1823), and Austrian interventions in the Papal States, Modena and Parma (1830). It also underlay Russian recognition of Dom Miguel as King of Portugal in 1828, Russian refusal to recognize Louis Philippe as King of France in 1830, and Austrian, Prussian and Russian refusals to recognize Doña Isabella as Queen of Spain in the 1830s.[49]

Most members of the small community of international law scholars tended to be more liberal than Austrian, Prussian and Russian policy-makers, and criticized monarchical legitimism. This is most apparent in the writings on intervention, where even those who permitted foreign intervention in some circumstances rejected its use to prop up or impose a particular ruler or form of government.[50] Political developments favoured the spread of their views to governments. The new German and Italian monarchies formed in mid-century took constitutional form, and constitutionalism of varying strength spread to the Low Countries and Scandinavia as well. By 1875 there were enough constitutional monarchies and republics among the great powers and there was enough republicanism and socialism among the populace to make absolute monarchy an obsolescent form in Europe.

Democratic legitimacy began to emerge out of British and French willingness to support constitutionalists against absolutists. This became clear in their policies toward Portugal and Spain during the 1830s and the Italian states in the 1850s and 1860s. Yet this policy was not as strikingly proclaimed as the Quadruple Alliance's absolutism. It was explicitly invoked only once in a recognition decision, when the Chilean Congress refused to recognize Maximilian as Emperor of Mexico in 1864 because of its belief that monarchy was contrary to the regional laws of the Americas.[51]

Democratic legitimacy resurfaced in Carlos R. Tobar's proposal that legality of origin be a criterion for recognition among the American republics.[52] His proposal was incorporated into Article 1 of the Additional Protocol to the 1907 Treaty of Peace and Amity among Guatemala, Honduras, Nicaragua, Panama, and El Salvador. The parties promised they 'shall not recognize any other Government which may come into power in any of the five Republics as a consequence of a coup d'état or of a revolution against the recognized

Government so long as the freely elected representatives of the people thereof have not constitutionally reorganized the country'.[53] This fitted with provisions in all five national constitutions that the congress must approve the accession to the presidency of anyone not previously elected to the office or not vice-president and succeeding to a vacancy and that the people or a specially convened constituent assembly must approve amendments to the constitution. Though focused on legality, the Tobar Doctrine was an expression of democratic legitimacy because few politically-active Latin Americans believed that a constituent assembly would approve a shift to non-republican institutions.

The parties' implementation of the treaty did not discourage coups. More problems arose when the US government shifted from simply applying the treaty and began a broader programme of promoting its own ideas of good government and protecting various US interests in Central America and the Caribbean. In 1909, the US government aided Nicaraguan rebels by landing Marines and then announcing that it would recognize no member of the former government as president of the country.[54] In 1912, the US Marines again landed to aid the new government against rebels. The Salvadorian government protested that this was illegal under the nonintervention clauses of the treaty, but the Nicaraguan government rejected the protest.[55] In 1911, the US government, invoking the spirit of the treaty, mediated between the government and rebels in Honduras and encouraged formation of a new coalition government.[56]

Woodrow Wilson began applying a stricter insistence on constitutional legality in 1913, but most instances also involved protecting US and US citizens' material interests to such an extent that Latin Americans and domestic US critics saw the policy as nothing but an excuse for meddling in other nations' affairs.[57] US refusal to recognize the Huerta government of Mexico from 1913 until 1916 provides the clearest example of the mixture of motives. Wilson initially justified nonrecognition with constitutionalist objections to Huerta's coup, then cited substantial opposition by rival factions, and then added objections to Huerta's programme of extensive nationalization of land and mineral resources.[58]

Interwar scholars, aware of the late nineteenth-century and World War I instances, began criticizing the various forms of constitutional legality and democratic legitimacy as unworkable and interventionary.[59] Criticizing legality was fairly easy, even for democrats, because its basic premise that changes of government should occur only according to procedures of the existing constitution, and its implication that foreigners could uphold the old constitution even when the people of the affected country did not, contradicted the older democratic belief that the people should always be free to change their government by any means. A few scholars thought democratic legitimacy might be possible under a world federation.[60] The European scholars accepting stipulation of democratic legitimacy by treaty all stated that such treaties may be applied only by and among the parties.[61]

US uses and abuses of the 1907 Central American Treaty continued in the early interwar period. The US government refused to recognize the Tinoco government of Costa Rica even though the 1917 plebiscite on a new constitution was regarded as satisfying the treaty requirements by the Guatemalan, Honduran, and Salvadorian governments.[62] It then refused to recognize the next president even though the Costa Rican Congress confirmed him in office, because it wanted an election held under the pre-1917 constitution. The Costa Ricans did not do this, but eventually followed other procedures Wilson specified.[63] Constitutionalism was again applied to deny recognition to De la Huerta as provisional president of Mexico on the grounds he had made deals with rival factions to circumvent the election laws.[64] This conveniently forgot the US role in promoting inter-faction deals in Nicaragua (1911), the Dominican Republic (1913), and Haiti (1914). Legal niceties were again forgotten in US promotion of inter-faction deals in Central American and Caribbean countries.[65]

Yet none of this was sufficient to destroy all Latin American interest in constitutional legality. The Brazilian government proposed denying recognition after the 1920 and 1930 Bolivian coups,[66] and a few raised the idea after the 1925 Ecuadorian coup.[67] In 1923, the five Central American republics concluded a new Treaty of Peace and Amity with an even more comprehensive set of rules about the treatment of new governments. Article II specified that:

> the governments of the contracting parties will not recognize any other government which may come to power in any of the five republics through a *coup d'état* or a revolution against a recognized government so long as the freely elected representatives of the people thereof have not constitutionally reorganized the country. And even in such a case they obligate themselves not to acknowledge the recognition [*sic*] if any of the persons elected as

President, Vice-President, or Chief of State designate should fall under any of the following heads:

(1) If he should be the leader or one of the leaders of a *coup d'état* or revolution, or through blood relationship or marriage be an ascendant or descendant or brother of such leader or leaders;
(2) If he should have been a Secretary of State or should have held some high military command during the accomplishment of the *coup d'état* or revolution, or while the election was being carried on, or if he should have held this office or command within six months preceding the *coup d'état*, revolution, or election.

Furthermore, in no case shall recognition be accorded to a government which arises from election to power of a citizen expressly and unquestionably disqualified by the Constitution of his country as eligible for election as President, Vice-President or Chief of State designate.[68]

The first sentence copied the 1907 treaty; the elaborations were meant to further discourage coups by making leaders and their near relatives ineligible for the presidency. Though ignoring female relatives,[69] the provisions could have disqualified large numbers of the politically active in all five countries since politics was generally the preserve of a small elite of families involved in frequent intermarriage.

Despite these problems, and others of interpreting the term 'leader', the treaty was applied among the Central American republics for the rest of the decade. The US government also applied it, and again exceeded the parties in enthusiasm. In the aftermath of a series of coups in 1930, disputes arose that led Nicaragua and then El Salvador to denounce the treaty. The other parties soon stopped applying it as well. The US government foreswore constitutional legality as part of Roosevelt's 'Good Neighbor Policy' in 1933.[70]

Neither democratic legitimacy nor constitutional legality were practised in other areas of the world. Even the US government only applied them twice in South America, to the 1919 Peruvian and 1920 Bolivian coups.[71] Any interest in that region ended in 1930, with a rash of coups triggered by the political tensions stemming from the Great Depression. Neither idea guided recognition policies by or towards European or Asian governments.

Cold War era assertions of legitimacy involved use of contending democratic and Leninist forms, but the majority of Cold War era writers condemned all legitimist recognition policies. Members of the minority accepting it varied in enthusiasm. Sibert accepted democratic legitimacy.[72] Frowein sought to accommodate both legitimism and effectivism by basing 'recognition as a de facto regime' on control and 'recognition as a government' on other criteria.[73] Verhoeven deplored abuses for individual state gain, but regarded legitimism as a way to increase the normative content of international law and place it in the service of particular values rather than of whatever status quo existed at a particular time.[74] A few, both Western and Soviet writers of general texts, allowed legitimism when established by treaty or regional custom.[75]

Most writers, including those making special study of recognition, condemned legitimism as bad policy[76] or as a form of interventionism.[77] Non-Marxist writers had little trouble rejecting the Soviet government's Brezhnev Doctrine[78] as interventionary (even without noting its legitimist implications); Marxists faced a tougher choice.[79] Some, regarding protection of the gains of the ongoing world socialist revolution as most important, defended the doctrine.[80] Others viewed it as a cover for Soviet unilateralism and disciplining of allied states.[81]

Though there were no new Central American experiments, legitimist notions did not entirely disappear from Western Hemisphere discussions. The Guatemalan government proposed that 'anti-democratic regimes' be denied recognition at the Eighth Interamerican Conference of 1945.[82] However, the Ninth Conference, in 1948, adopted a resolution calling for continuity of diplomatic relations among the American Republics that was widely interpreted as an endorsement of effectivism.[83] As the Cold War intensified, notions of democratic legitimacy were revived. The Tenth Interamerican Conference in 1954 declared that 'international communism' was a threat to the hemisphere that must be combatted jointly, though specifically stated that this should not impair the right of peoples to choose their own government.[84] After Castro's accession in Cuba, a number of other declarations, most notably the 1965 Punta del Este Charter, identified protection and advancement of democracy as goals of the Interamerican system.

Though Cuba was long excluded from Organization of American States activity,[85] formalized procedures for coordinated nonrecognition of Leninist or other nondemocratic governments were not adopted. The closest approach was Resolution 26 of the Second

Emergency Interamerican Conference in 1965, which established an optional consultations procedure.[86] Venezuela adopted the 'Betancourt Doctrine' of refusing to recognize governments that came to power through coup, and applied it to Peru (1962 and 1968), Brazil (1964) and Argentina (1967).[87] In some instances, governments did require a new regime to promise elections by a certain date before extending recognition. Between 1961 and 1963, successive Dominican and Honduran juntas tried to wriggle out of such pledges by playing on anti-communist fears, but other governments insisted on them.[88] A Peruvian junta seizing power just before the 1962 elections also got a chilly reception until it produced the required assurances. The reaction was summed up in the US government's attitude:

> The junta had decreed the restoration of constitutional guarantees of civil liberties in Peru. It has set the date of June 9, 1963 for the holding of free elections.
> Furthermore it has guaranteed that under the constitution all political parties will be afforded full electoral rights and that the results of free elections, whatever they may be, will be respected by the junta and the armed forces it represents.[89]

The Cubans joined in condemnation of the 1964 Brazilian coup by breaking off diplomatic relations and not resuming them until June 1986 after civilian rule again prevailed.[90]

The Dominican coup of 1965 inspired a US-led intervention to end the ensuing civil strife, prevent a feared Leninist takeover, and return the country to constitutional rule. OAS institutions were then invoked to substitute a mixed Latin American force for the US troops and provide international observers of the elections. Only the government chosen in these elections was recognized by the governments involved in the OAS action.

Though democratic legitimacy themes were sounded again in reactions to the 1966 Argentine and 1968 Peruvian coups,[91] Western Hemisphere interest in democratic legitimacy was clearly on the decline. In the USA, an effort to attach a rider to the 1966 foreign aid appropriation cutting off aid to any OAS member state experiencing an extra-legal change of government was defeated.[92] The US and Argentine governments tacitly abandoned using democratic legitimacy as a test for recognition; the new Venezuelan president formally disavowed the Betancourt Doctrine in 1969.[93] The violent coup ending Salvador Allende's presidency in Chile, which also marked a departure from the Chilean military's traditional uninvolvement in politics, occasioned few constitutionalist protests. Cuba and Mexico were among those refusing recognition or dropping the level of diplomatic contact,[94] while a larger number focused more on condemning the large US role in the coup and the new regime's persecution of leftists.

Democratic character was sometimes mentioned as a reason for granting recognition to new regimes in Asia and Africa, but in many of the cases it seems to have been a routine invocation unconnected to the actual reasons for recognizing. The Kennedy Administration in the US mentioned the criterion in recognizing new governments in Togo, Syria, and Iraq, but actually paid far more attention to the reactions of neighbouring states.[95] The Indian government cited democratic beliefs as a reason for supporting the King of Nepal against Rana family attempts to depose him, but the King was also more willing than his rivals to adopt a set of reforms the Indians were urging on the Nepalese government.[96] Though Western European governments condemned the 1980 Turkish coup, they did not resort to any form of nonrecognition.[97]

The shock of Africa's first coup, which toppled the government of Togo in 1963, led to a brief flurry of interest in some form of democratic legitimism. The Guinean and Nigerian governments both called on others to refuse recognition, and others proposed consultations on the matter. Most of the independent African governments did delay recognition until after elections, but did not agree to include this as a general rule when the Organization of African Unity was formed later in the year.[98] Other coups soon followed, and African regional recognition practice went in a mainly effectivist direction. There was a brief flurry of discussion after Doe's 1980 coup in Liberia, but majority sentiment among commentators favoured following an effectivist rule.[99]

In 1985 it would have been safe to conclude that effectivist policies had replaced democratic legitimism in all parts of the world. A decade later, the situation is more mixed. The mid to late 1980s saw not only one of the periodic swings from military to civilian rule in Latin America, but increased demand for and more frequent attainment of at least the forms of democratic rule in Eastern Europe, Africa, and other parts of the world.[100] The many efforts to negotiate an end to the civil wars in Angola, Cambodia, El Salvador, Guatemala, and Nicaragua also suggested the preferred programme: getting contending factions to negotiate a cease-fire, establishing some form of all-inclusive interim government where none of them had a preponderance of administrative control, writing a new democratic constitution for countries where none existed or the old was discredited for some reason, and holding elections with international observer teams present to ensure their fairness. In most cases, the effort proceeded without any use of recognition policy, but there were instances where it became relevant. Reaction to the 1980 Bolivian coup,[101] in which an interim government was displaced and the results of the June elections were declared void by the army, provided an early indication. Though some governments recognized quickly,[102] the OAS and the European Community condemned the coup, the US recalled its ambassador, and the Ecuadorians and Dutch broke off diplomatic relations.[103]

Public refusals to accept a government's attempt to annul election results were prominent after the 1986 Philippine elections. President Marcos, who had been pressured into holding elections and permitting opposition candidates to run, claimed he had won, but the claims were weakened by widespread complaint of fraud. Both he and opposition candidate Corazon Aquino claimed victory and each held rival inauguration ceremonies on 25 February. On 19 February the New Zealand government publicly noted the allegations of fraud and commended Defence Minister Juan Enrile and Chief of Staff Fidel Ramos for supporting Aquino.[104] Some Canadian members of parliament began demanding that Canada withdraw recognition from Marcos on the 24th and the next day criticized the government for waiting to see what the US did before committing itself. The government's spokesman said 'There is now a new Government in the Philippines which is in effective control of that country. I celebrate that development. Canada has welcomed the election of that Government which is in control of the Philippines.'[105] The US government, which had avoided public comment but used private channels to urge Marcos to step down, indicated its attitude soon after the inaugurals by issuing a press statement that it 'extends recognition to this new government headed by President Aquino'.[106] Other governments made no particular comment about recognition, but those who had instructed their envoys to stay away from Marcos's ceremonies saved themselves embarrassment.[107]

The US government mixed democratic legitimacy with other considerations in its relations with Panama during 1988–9. Though General Manuel Noriega ousted him in February 1988, the US government continued to recognize Delvalle as President. Attempts to recruit Japanese and European cooperation failed; the Japanese gave express recognition in June and the Western Europeans acted on their usual policy of avoiding recognition and dealing with whoever held control.[108] The situation grew more tense after Noriega annulled the opposition victory in the 1989 presidential elections and installed another henchman in power. The US government began with nonrecognition of Noriega's man,[109] then suggested that his domestic opponents should overthrow Noriega while cooperating with an OAS mediation effort that collapsed in late August. Tensions rose further in October after an indigenous coup attempt failed and in mid-December when Noriega reinforced his position by taking over as head of all the armed forces and declared war on the US. Incidents in Panama City led to a massive US intervention which installed Guillermo Endara, the victor of the 1989 elections, as president.[110] This aroused severe criticism from many governments, but only one clear refusal, by Cuba, to recognize.[111]

Yet neither the intervention nor the ironic elements involved in US action against Noriega[112] discredited the wider idea that democracy should be encouraged. Several times in 1990 the French government was willing to state its preference for settling political conflicts by holding competitive elections.[113] General Pinochet's resignation in favour of Patricio Alwin, the civilian victor of the December 1989 elections in Chile, led a number of governments to resume the diplomatic relations they had broken off earlier.[114] A number of joint declarations and international resolutions adopted in 1990 suggested that democratic legitimacy would become the norm.[115]

Two reactions to coups in 1991 suggested that nonrecognition (and other measures) to protect democracies from reversion to other modes of governance enjoyed wide support. The most dramatic involved the 'State Emergency Committee's' August 1991 attempt to take power in the Soviet Union. After a day of hesitation, Western governments began condemning the coup on the 20th, calling for restoration of Gorbachev, and preparing to reduce aid and contacts.[116] The European Community Council meeting demanded re-establishment of constitutional government and announced that $1,100 million worth of aid would be suspended.[117] An Extraordinary NATO Foreign Ministers' Meeting on the 21st agreed to a statement demanding Gorbachev's return to power, expressing support for all the 'democratically elected leaders' of the USSR and its republics, stating that member governments would do nothing that would be construed as recognition of the State Emergency Committee, suspending formal diplomatic relations with the USSR, suspending aid, and indicating that member governments would not attend the Conference on Security and Cooperation in Europe meeting on human rights scheduled for

Moscow in September if Gorbachev had not returned to power in the interim.[118]

The other instance was the reaction to the military coup ousting President Aristide of Haiti in October. Canadian members of parliament secured government assurances that Canada would not recognize or deal with the Haitian 'defactos'.[119] The OAS also condemned the coup, and agreed to impose trade sanctions until Aristide returned to power.[120] After three years of sanctions, the junta's refusal to implement a negotiated settlement, and one half-hearted US military action, the UN Security Council endorsed intervention to restore Aristide.[121] The junta backed down at this point and permitted Aristide to return home and resume the presidency.

Yet by 1994 the tide of democratic legitimism was receding. Though a few legal scholars advocated it,[122] most remained concerned that support for democratic rule should not become an excuse for massive interference in other states' domestic affairs.[123] The UN General Assembly expressed this concern by adopting Resolution 45/150, urging the principle of holding 'periodic and genuine elections', and Resolution 45/151, stating that this principle should not become the basis for interference in other states' affairs, on the same day.[124] Only the OAS adopted formal procedures for reacting to coups displacing elected governments,[125] though the European Union could do likewise through European political cooperation. Most extra-legal changes of government inspired no strong reaction; foreign governments generally settled down to dealing with those in power. The main exceptions involved countries where competing factions continued to battle it out with foreign assistance[126] or where political order collapsed and outside involvement was regarded as necessary to create the conditions for re-emergence of some coherent political structure.[127]

During the Cold War era the Soviet bloc developed its own form of legitimism. This communist or Leninist legitimism had its first trial in Hungary during the autumn of 1956. The issue was obscured at the time by Imre Nagy's attempt to withdraw Hungary from the Warsaw Pact, which gave the USSR ample reason to intervene, but the situation was blamed on 'imperialists' and 'reactionaries'. The Soviets were forced to explain their policy far more clearly after deciding to intervene to remove the Dubček government of Czechoslovakia even though there was no unrest and no effort to abandon the Warsaw Pact. The result was elaboration of the Brezhnev Doctrine that if events in one communist state threatened or actually led to overthrow of the government, all other communists have the right and duty to prevent this by any means necessary. Though used to justify armed intervention, the Brezhnev Doctrine could also support nonrecognition of a noncommunist successor government in a more distant state. This is suggested in one paragraph of the Soviet's August 1968 statement:

> Such [a formalistic] approach to sovereignty means that, for example, the progressive forces of the world would not be able to come out against the revival of neo-Naziism in the Federal Republic of Germany, against the actions of butchers Franco and Salazar, against the reactionary, arbitrary actions of 'black colonels' in Greece, because this is 'the internal affair' of 'sovereign' states.[128]

The USSR also cited an 'anti-Soviet terror campaign' as the reason for refusing to maintain diplomatic relations[129] with the Pinochet junta in Chile.[130]

Just as Leninist governments had no trouble condemning democratic legitimism as a bourgeois sham for keeping power, Western governments had no trouble condemning the Brezhnev Doctrine. More significant was the difference between other Leninists' reactions to the 1956 and 1968 Soviet moves. Only the Yugoslav government commented at length on the intervention in Hungary, while the intervention in Czechoslovakia elicited strong condemnations from the Albanian, Chinese, Romanian and Yugoslav governments.[131] None of the Leninist critics disagreed with the basic idea that Leninist governments were more progressive than others and hence deserving of protection, but they did object to Soviet claims of unilateral authority to decide who does and does not measure up as a good Leninist. The debate was ended in 1989 when the Soviet Union first indicated that its Eastern European allies could choose their own political arrangements[132] and then coordinated a formal renunciation of the Brezhnev Doctrine by the Warsaw Pact.[133]

ABILITY AND WILL TO FULFIL INTERNATIONAL OBLIGATIONS

This criterion has four aspects, two on each side of the verb. 'Ability' refers to physical and administrative capacity, 'will' to intentions and volitions. 'International obligations' cover both the duties prescribed by general and regional international law and the obligations contained in agreements with one or more other states. Governments invoking this test as a reason for nonrecognition have taken account of both general and specific obligations to varying degrees, and been concerned more with will than ability.

Nineteenth-century writers agreed that the existence of some agency able and willing to fulfil international obligations is a necessary attribute of statehood, and looked for a government able to do so before accepting a new state's existence. A few then extended the test to new governments of existing states, despite the doctrine of continuity of states.[134] Lorimer and Lawrence used the criterion in such a way as to exclude from full membership in the international community those states having governments too backward, too intolerant, or too insufficiently 'civilized' to participate in international relations;[135] the others provided no clear explanation for their position. Most legal specialists assumed, in contrast, that any government capable of controlling all or most of a state was also capable of carrying out international obligations, and will was considered irrelevant because it was required by the doctrine of state continuity to fulfil the state's duties and obligations.

This criterion was seldom mentioned in discussions of new governments coming to power in Europe, but was invoked in other parts of the world.[136] In Latin America, the US and British governments invoked it but were satisfied by a general reassurance. Where local rulers were bound by extensive treaty relations giving Europeans various privileges, as in Egypt, Morocco, the Ottoman Empire, and China, the great powers used it as a device to ensure perpetuation of the privileges. Yet the likelihood of use depended on the depth of the recognizing government's interests in seeing commitments maintained. The US government did not insist on particular assurances after the Honduran coup of 1903 despite the country's deep indebtedness; the debts were to European lenders.[137]

The close link to great power imperialism inspired serious contentions over the criterion's acceptability in the interwar period. A number of new governments, particularly in Mexico, China and Russia, challenged application of the test with some success. Though some Soviet sources sometimes credited Bolshevik resistance with ending use of the criterion,[138] the roles of the other resisting governments and a change in European opinion towards condemning the most blatant forms of imperialism deserve credit as well.

The controversies of the early interwar period forced legal scholars to pay attention and led most to take sides. A fair number approved of the general form of the test as necessary to ensuring respect for international law.[139] A larger number criticized all forms of the test. Some argued that it amounted to taking unfair advantage of the new government's need for recognition to extract concessions.[140] Others argued that 'ability' was already assured by requiring that governments be in actual control of the state before they were recognized and 'will' was already determined by continuity of the state.[141]

State practice continued to be mixed. Official British and US doctrine still included the test as a general standard. Actual US practice in Central America and the Caribbean involved using it as a club against new governments there. The Cuban 'Ferrara Doctrine' of 1932 allowed its use as a supplementary test, stipulating that failure to fulfil treaty obligations towards Cuba was good cause for nonrecognition,[142] and other Latin American governments occasionally invoked it. However, most opposed, and it was not included in the Pan American Union draft treaty on recognition in 1928.[143]

It was more difficult to insist on full respect for existing treaties with new governments in stronger states. Doubts about stability and actual administrative control conditioned other governments' policies toward the various Chinese factions in the 1920s. The need to deal with some Chinese authority led most to accept whichever faction ruled in Beijing as the government of all of China, but most waited to see strong administrative control before agreeing to end the nineteenth-century treaties giving foreigners wide privileges in China. While the Austrian, German, and Soviet governments renounced privileges early in the decade, the other European powers, Japan, and the USA did so only after the Kuomintang extended its rule from the south to Beijing in mid-1928.[144] Attempts to require the Soviet government and new governments in Mexico and Turkey to accept all the treaty obligations of their predecessors ended in compromises permitting many of them to lapse.

These interwar controversies did not settle the matter for legal scholars or governments. Some Cold War era scholars continued to include the test. Many of them seem to have listed it by rote,[145] but a few did argue for its importance.[146] The critics continued to split, some basing objections mainly on individual abuses[147] and others citing its redundancy.[148]

Government criticism of applying the test became more pronounced in the Cold War era. Soviet-bloc governments condemned it as an 'imperialist weapon' that no progressive state would use. They also resisted its use against them. The communist Hoxha government of Albania refused to assure the US government that it would reaffirm the validity of all treaties in force between Albania and the USA, but insisted on a right to review them consistent with Leninist doctrine that class revolution meant establishment of a new state. After some months, the US government decided not to press the matter or recognize the Hoxha government (a policy that persisted through March 1991).[149] Indian government statements argued both that the test was redundant and that it had been badly abused.[150] The Batista government of Cuba limited its assurances to written agreements and won recognition after a short delay.[151] In 1964 the new government of Zanzibar found a way simultaneously to give assurance and to maintain its self-respect by getting the US government to agree on a joint declaration in which both sides, not just the newly-recognized, reaffirmed respect for international obligations, the UN Charter, and each other's rights and duties as states.[152] This may or may not have been a conscious borrowing of the contemporaneous PRC practice of insisting that all agreements be phrased in reciprocal terms even when only one side is taking up a particular obligation.[153]

Yet the governments continuing to invoke the test were less regular in their practice. The British government moved to stressing control as the main criterion. The Canadian government listed the test in its formal statements,[154] but seems to have treated it as a routine matter.[155] The US government used it more during the Eisenhower administration than later. It came up in US debates about whether to recognize the PRC government, but that debate was so envenomed by domestic political controversy that it was not a good indicator of US policy in general.

By the mid-1970s international usage had bifurcated. General assurances remain part of diplomatic routine, and many new regimes give them spontaneously.[156] Assurances about specific obligations are another matter. Past abuses, in particular their association with efforts to extract concessions,[157] have made the giving and seeking of specific assurances unacceptable to most governments.

Neither governments nor legal scholars showed much interest in the criterion during the post-Cold War period. Most scholars failed to mention it, one reformulated it as 'capacity' to fulfil obligations[158] while others argued explicitly that the principle of state continuity makes it redundant.[159]

SUMMARY

International law creates two sorts of discretion in recognition decisions: in choice of the moment to recognize and in choice of the criteria other than effective control of all or most of the state on which to base decisions about whether to recognize. A strictly effectivist position limits governments to the first sort of discretion, and bounds it fairly narrowly in the vast majority of situations because power usually passes rapidly from the old to the new regime. However, policy-makers have always insisted that they possess both types of discretion. Though some legal scholars have criticized the resulting situation, most have accepted that discretion does exist and focused instead on the question of how it may be used.

Discussion of optional criteria is complicated by the fact they can be used for two very different purposes. A few governments have, for longer or shorter periods, maintained a consistency in the use of optional criteria that appears to reflect principled reasons for their application. Yet in many instances optional criteria have been asserted on an ad hoc basis appearing more to tailor decisions to the ideological or material interests of the recognizing state. Using recognition decisions for this purpose had been condemned by most legal scholars and many other observers of foreign policy.

There has been growing criticism of the use of any optional criteria since World War I, but this has not led all legal specialists to abandon them. At the same time, advocates of using optional criteria continue to disagree about which are permissible or desirable. 'Popular support' and 'ability and will to fulfil international obligations' have considerable support. However, it is not always possible to distinguish them from the basic criterion of control. Insisting on expressions of popular support through elections or plebiscites is distinct, but reliance on tacit acquiescence proven through lack of substantial opposition is not. Ability to fulfil international relations comes with effective rule, and the principle of state continuity makes will irrelevant because obligations must be fulfilled by any new regime in its function as agent of the state. Monarchical and Leninist legitimacy have disappeared because of the rarity of the type of government they seek to protect; democratic legitimacy remains the subject of lively debate.

In surveying the period since 1815 as a whole, it is clear that interest in invoking popular support as a separate condition for recognition and insistance on formal expressions of that support were higher in the interwar era than in the nineteenth century or the early Cold War period. Before 1914, many governments were monarchies unlikely to stress the idea, and the republics generally accepted that a diversity of forms would persist. After 1945, interest in spreading like ideologies was mixed with greater realization of how popular support could be manipulated to produce highly undemocratic results. Cold War discussions were also complicated by the very different meanings given to 'democracy' and 'popular support' by East and West. These became obvious in discussions about reorganizing Eastern Europe immediately after the war, and persisted as long as Leninism maintained a hold on governments and peoples. As the the Soviet bloc and then the USSR itself collapsed in 1988–91, interest increased yet again as part of a broader desire to promote democracy.

Similarly, stress on ability and willingness to fulfil international obligations waxed in the interwar period and waned in the Cold War era. The main nineteenth-century invocations came in the Americas, where governments of the often unstable Central and South American republics were routinely asked to declare their general readiness to accept obligations. It was less used in other parts of the world, in large part because the problem was often solved by formal incorporation into a European empire or informal sphere of influence. The greater interwar concern with specific obligations reflected several developments: continued US intrusion into the affairs of Mexico, the Caribbean, and Central American states, greater controversy about foreigners' property rights in the USSR and other countries nationalizing property or asserting greater control over its use, and the slow pace of dismantling the nineteenth-century treaty privileges in China. With general acceptance of the Soviet government, the shift of the US government towards a 'Good Neighbor Policy' of less intrusion in the Americas, and the end of the old treaty regime in China, these motives disappeared. Governments went back to focusing more on willingness to uphold the obligations stipulated in general and regional international law. As more countries shifted to an effectivist recognition policy in the 1960s and 1970s, interest in the criterion was confined to formulaic statements of general recognition policy or blanket statements of assurance by new regimes seeking foreign acceptance.

Governments have been more willing than legal scholars to consider legitimist criteria. New governments, particularly those of a new type, have used legitimist policies less than older governments. Some governments have shifted position after becoming established, particularly if challenged by newer regimes holding other ideologies. After the contrasting monarchical and constitutional legitimacy splurges of the early nineteenth century, most governments adopted a 'live and let live' approach accepting as a fellow government whoever ruled, without much concern about their ideology. Legitimism figured in reactions to the Bolsheviks, but otherwise was confined to Central America during the interwar period. The Cold War period was another matter: both blocs experimented with legitimist doctrines, showing greatest interest during the mid-1960s. Détente coincided with another receding of legitimism, but this trend was not disturbed when Cold War tensions increased again in the late 1970s. The notable revival of democratic legitimacy arguments in the late 1980s and early 1990s stemmed from the end of the Cold War. For a second time since 1918, there was only one legitimist doctrine in play. Thus arguments were not about whose version to follow, but about whether there was now enough agreement on the basic principles of domestic governance for international law to include rules specifying particular features of domestic political organization. The answer in the mid-1990s was 'no': the international principles of sovereignty, nonintervention, and self-determination remained strong enough to prevent incorporating rules about the institutions of domestic governance into international law despite greater consensus on rules limiting the way power could be wielded in the developing international law of human rights.

Today, as in the nineteenth century, an examination of actual state practice supports the conclusion that governments still insist on the right to select and use certain optional criteria even though they are now exercising that right less frequently and in favour of fewer criteria. The pattern also reveals that, despite the neatness of memoranda setting out general recognition policies, governments actually have a repertoire of policies and select among them as they feel the situation warrants. It is possible not only to identify the components of the repertoire and the occasions when a government will use each, but also to follow changes in repertoires over time.

In the nineteenth century, most governments pursued an effectivist policy in distant parts of the world and confined the use of optional criteria to areas closer to home. Thus European governments were generally content to accept any new government in Latin America even when they were most actively intervening in favour of absolutism or constitutionalism on their own continent. Similarly, the US government confined its interest in constitutionalism and democratic legitimacy to the Caribbean and Central America, while Latin American governments often linked their use of optional criteria to notions of a special regional law covering their immediate area or the Americas as a whole. In the Americas, optional criteria were applied more frequently after mid-century and the frequency of extra-legal changes of government remained fairly high. By the end of the century, local and US use of optional criteria was higher in the Caribbean and Central America than in South America. The difference in US use can be explained by the limits of the rapidly developing US informal empire; the difference in Latin use stems from the greater interest among Central American republics in various subregional integration schemes.[160]

The use of optional criteria increased in the interwar period more than would be expected from the small increase in the frequency of extra-legal changes of government (2.4 a year, compared to the nineteenth-century average of 2.3 a year). As in the nineteenth century, interwar practice in the Americas diverged from practice elsewhere. The early interwar period was marked by considerable use of constitutional legitimism. The US continued to use it as a cloak for protection of its particular interests, and the Central American experiments also continued. Even a few South American governments considered using the criterion. In the 1930s there was a general shift away from such ideas. The Mexican Estrada Doctrine asserted an effectivism so undiluted that it appeared to argue for abolition of the recognition of governments. The following year the Central American Republics dissolved their 1923 treaty. In 1933, Franklin Roosevelt made the US move away from democratic legitimism explicit in his 'Good Neighbor Policy'. However, the criteria of popular support and democratic legitimacy were soon revived in efforts to avert a spread of fascism to the New World during World War II.

Considering the increase in the number of independent states (UN membership went from 51 in 1945 to 154 in 1980) and the larger number of extra-legal changes of government as many of the new states in Africa and Asia proved politically unstable, the overall use of optional criteria continued to decline in the Cold War period. This was masked, however, by more prominent cases of using various of the optional criteria to recognize quickly or withhold recognition on the basis of ideology. The Franco government of Spain was denied recognition by some and ostracized by others for its fascism. Several of the Western powers and their clients held out against recognizing the PRC government for long periods.

Even in the Americas, where optional criteria remained more heavily used than elsewhere, their use declined after 1970. The few

Latin American governments that had adopted democratic legitimacy repudiated it, and use of other optional criteria declined as well. The Americas thus participated in the wider shift towards more strictly effectivist recognition policies. These were registered not only in practice, but in a series of government statements de-emphasizing the whole process of recognition. On the whole, and even allowing for continued discussion of democratic legitimism, recognition policy is more effectivist now than it has been at any time since the mid-nineteenth century.

5 Other Proposed Criteria

Popular support, ability and will to fulfil international obligations, and legitimacy do not exhaust the list of proposed additional criteria for recognition as a government. Legal scholars and policy-makers have also considered nondependence on foreign support in the exercise of control ('local origins'), respect for other states' rights, origins in conformity with international law, and respect for human rights. The first three were already discussed in the nineteenth century, and fitted comfortably with the prevailing view that states were the only entities having legal rights and duties, and legal capacity to act, under international law. The fourth is a twentieth-century development resting on newer beliefs that the protection of international law should extend to individuals and groups.

NONDEPENDENCE ON FOREIGN MILITARY SUPPORT

In most instances the leaders of a coup d'état or rebellion who succeed in taking power exercise it with the help of their domestic supporters. Sometimes, however, it becomes apparent even to casual observers that a particular regime would not be in power, or would be overthrown quickly, if it did not have support from foreign governments. The long tradition of permitting governments to request temporary assistance in maintaining order, and the frequency of foreign assistance to competing factions in civil wars, have meant that incidental foreign support, though cited as a reason for disliking a new regime, is not treated as a reason to deny that it effectively controls its state. More controversy arises when foreign support is more than incidental to seizing and maintaining power.

Nineteenth-century legal scholars generally repeated the principle that states are free to select their own governments, but did not adopt the possible corollary that regimes which result from or depend on foreign military involvement should be denied recognition. In the early part of the nineteenth century, the great powers accepted foreign intervention as a method of influencing the selection of government in weaker states. On two occasions in mid-century, however, some did cite foreign involvement as reason to avoid recognition. On the first there were British, French, and US objections to the Rivas government of Nicaragua (1854–6), which came to power with the help of a group of US nationals led by William Walker.[1] The other involved US objections to the French-sponsored Mexican Emperor Maximilian.[2]

In the interwar period, mild objections to foreign involvement were replaced by the more emphatic doctrine of self-determination of peoples. Foreign involvement was not merely unfortunate under this new doctrine; it was a direct assault on a people's basic rights. Yet writings on recognition did not immediately reflect this new idea. The first sustained discussion occurred in the London International Law Conference, an assembly of experts convened in 1944 to advise the Allies on organization of the postwar international order. It recommended that international law ban recognition of regimes created by, or wholly dependent on, foreigners[3] (the term 'puppet government' was already in wide use) – a tactic the Axis had often used. Such considerations also underlay objections to Soviet efforts to impose particular governments on Austria, Hungary, and Poland in 1945–6, but these cases were discussed as violations of the Yalta Accords. The neutral Swiss did label the Hungarian regime a puppet and refuse to recognize it until after the December 1945 elections.[4]

The criterion was more popular in the Cold War era. Several legal scholars advocated it,[5] and governments did invoke it on some occasions. The US government announced an intention to deny recognition to puppet regimes, but actually invoked the theme only with the PRC.[6] The Soviet government used it to explain continued nonrecognition of the Franco government in Spain.[7] Many communist and Third World governments invoked it against Lon Nol's Republican Government in Cambodia,[8] while the Central African Republic initially invoked it against Amin's coup in Uganda.[9] The issue also surfaced in the wake of Cuban military presence in Angola, Tanzanian intervention in Uganda, Vietnamese intervention in Cambodia, and Soviet intervention in Afghanistan. The Angolan and Ugandan situations inspired only fleeting discussion. Though OAU member governments were trying to broker a negotiated settlement among the MPLA, UNITA, and FNLA and initially holding back recognition, the Nigerian decision to recognize the MPLA in late 1975 led most others to do likewise.[10] Senegal, the only regional holdout in 1980, recognized in 1982.[11] Other governments delayed recognition as well, but usually based this on more than the Cuban presence.[12] While Tanzanian involvement in Uganda was acknowledged, other governments did not regard it as making the new Ugandan government a puppet.[13] Cuba refused to recognize the Endara government of Panama established after the December 1989 US intervention.[14]

The Afghan and Cambodian cases inspired far more controversy. Both involved an outside power's settling political struggles by backing one faction and providing it with most of the military force needed to maintain its power against active domestic opposition. Western governments quickly condemned the Soviet intervention in Afghanistan: reactions easily discounted as Cold War politics. All dropped their diplomatic representation in Kabul to the chargé level,[15] the US imposed trade embargoes and other measures against the USSR, but only some explicitly denied recognition. The British government told Parliament in 1981 that it was not recognizing the Karmal government,[16] and explained in 1985 that it would not maintain normal diplomatic relations because Karmal 'depends on an occupying army of over 115,000 Soviet troops'.[17] Yet Third World reaction was also strong, and took the Soviets and others by surprise. Though a few states allied to or seeking closer relations with the USSR accepted the Karmal government,[18] the majority did not. They first expressed their opinion in UN General Assembly Resolution ES-6/2 calling on the Soviets to withdraw,[19] and reiterated this each year until Gorbachev reversed Soviet policy in 1988.

The Cold War divide was relevant, but less central, to the Cambodian case. When the communist government of Vietnam replaced the murderous regime of Pol Pot in Cambodia with another set of communists led by Heng Samrin, Cold War and Sino-Soviet rivalries affected some governments' attitudes. However, most governments refusing to deal with the new regime cited the fact that it depended entirely on foreign troops to remain in power against Pol Pot and two other factions. Some governments, like the Indian, which recognized in July 1980,[20] did not concern themselves with this. Those unready to accept Heng Samrin's regime found themselves in a difficult position because Pol Pot's supporters appeared to offer the only organized local opposition. Thus the Australians, British, and French all combined refusal to recognize or deal with Heng Samrin with equal refusal to accept Pol Pot.[21] Even the organization of a coalition among the three main opposition factions, led by Prince Sihanouk, Sonn San, and Pol Pot in 1983[22] did not affect nonrecognizing governments' attitudes because they felt Pol Pot's was the most powerful element of the coalition and feared he would use it to return to power.[23] Only in September 1990, after the balance had shifted within the coalition and it and Heng Samrin agreed to form a joint transition government, until elections were held under UN supervision, did these governments see a Cambodian regime meriting acceptance.[24]

Despite these contentions, the question of dependence on foreign military support received little attention in post-Cold War legal writings. Only Oppenheim addressed the question, and concluded that dependence on foreign troops allows (though does not require) denying recognition.[25] Nor have governments had to face the issue in this period.

RESPECT FOR OTHER STATES' RIGHTS

A few nineteenth-century writers proposed that governments unwilling to respect the rights of other states, in particular those actively seeking to undermine the international order or subvert foreign governments, should be denied recognition.[26] Proponents were aware of the potential for abuse. They tried to limit this application by requiring that the undermining or subversion involve actions rather than words and that the action appear capable of causing immediate and severe damage. Only a very few interwar[27] and early Cold War era[28] scholars mentioned this criterion, and it is absent from post-Cold War texts.

The criterion was occasionally discussed by governments. Some had raised it in regard to France under the Terror in the 1790s.[29] Quadruple Alliance rhetoric included some reference to the dangerous nature of non-absolutist governments but legitimist rhetoric took pride of place. Opponents of recognizing the Bolsheviks mentioned the idea, but objections based on lack of popular support and nonfulfilment of international obligations were more frequent. Though the Soviet government did proclaim and act on subversive intent, its later shift towards greater attention to domestic affairs, the impracticality of ignoring a state as powerful as the USSR, and others' desire for trade and other contact combined to make most governments accept the USSR as a tolerable, even if not desirable, member of the international community within a few years.[30] The Nazis avoided recognition issues by winning elections before imposing their dictatorship, but even if they had not, subversion was not then a major concern. This is clearest in a Soviet reaction:

> Then followed the revolution which brought a new party to power in Germany preaching the most extreme anti-Soviet ideas. . . . But

> perhaps these people, on coming to power and occupying responsible posts, would disown these ideas. We understand very well the difference between doctrine and policy. It does happen that an opposition on coming to power tries to forget the slogans used in the fight against its political opponents. But in the given case this did not occur.[31]

Subversion was one of many reasons for denying recognition to the PRC government invoked in the United States, but hardly exhausted the arguments against recognition.[32]

ABSENCE OF UNDUE VIOLENCE IN THE SEIZURE OF POWER

The notion that recognition ought to be refused when a new government came to power through excessive violence has been raised on a few occasions. It was first applied after the 1903 Serbian coup, which involved killing the king and queen, several members of the cabinet, and a number of the queen's relatives. The British government refused recognition until 1906 when the new king agreed to retire the officers who had been directly involved.[33] The Dutch, French, German, Italian, and US governments also delayed recognition to indicate disapproval of the violence, but the Austrian and Russian governments did not.[34] The objections were not to the number killed – equally, or more, violent political activity on other occasions was accepted without comment – or inspired by any deep sympathy for a king who had suspended the constitution and further alienated his subjects by marrying his mistress and seeming to accept the influence of her politically ambitious family. They were more expressions of dismay at night-time murders in the palace living quarters and their occurrence in 'civilized' Europe.

The world became accustomed to higher levels of violence after 1914. However, the British withheld recognition from the newly-installed King George II of Greece to protest about executions of the former premier, foreign minister, and military commanders for treason (failure to prevail in the war against Turkey) in 1923.[35] Undue violence was also asserted in 1946 to justify Brazilian nonrecognition of the new Bolivian junta after its centre–left supporters killed most of the members of the deposed rightwing dictatorship and hanged their bodies in the streets.[36] Ghanaian and Nigerian objections to the 1963

Togo coup were intensified by the fact that the president had been shot while seeking refuge in a foreign embassy. The new regime was recognized, but the draft OAU Charter was altered to include a condemnation of using assassination in political struggles.[37] Some communist members of the Indian parliament suggested withholding recognition from the Sukarno government of Indonesia because of the massive violence involved in the coup and ensuing roundup of Indonesian communists. The Indian government refused, saying that inquiry into the regime's mode of accession would constitute interference in Indonesia's domestic affairs.[38] Nor did the British alter policy after Rawlings had three former heads of state executed in Ghana, though they condemned the shootings as 'repugnant'.[39] A French commentator noted, after President Sankara was killed during a coup in Burkina Faso, that ruptures in diplomatic relations are caused by grave incidents in relations between states, not bloody changes of regime.[40]

High levels of political violence, whether in civil wars, government suppression of opponents, resistance movements against governments, or the more diffuse forms of armed activity labelled 'terrorism', did not entirely extinguish policy-makers' sensitivities. His record of mass murder led many governments to oppose the return of Pol Pot to leadership in Cambodia. Many African governments hesitated after Sergeant Doe had members of the previous government executed in 1980 after their appeals for clemency.[41] However, such considerations have not been invoked with any consistency.

Legal scholars expressed scant interest in the criterion.[42] This reflects their awareness that coups, insurrections, and civil wars are likely to remain common methods of changing governments. Different instigators may prefer different tactics, but in many cases the level of violence employed depends as much on others' responses as on their own plans.

ORIGINS IN CONFORMITY WITH INTERNATIONAL LAW

The notion that new governments should be recognized only when their composition and ascent to power conform to international law overlaps with a number of other proposed optional criteria, particularly indigenous origins. It is distinct, however, because it can refer to any aspects of the new regime's composition or mode of accession. Yet it is hard to determine just what this criterion would mean since there is so little consensus among its advocates on what norms of composition and accession international law should include. Thus Feldman's advocacy of refusing recognition to any regime coming to power in violation of 'a fundamental norm of international law' in 1969[43] attracted little support because it was so closely linked to controversial Soviet conceptions of the fundamental norms.[44] In addition, most current formulations of fundamental norms do not include any rules about how governments come to power or who can be included in them; rather, most lists emphasize nonintervention, self-determination, and the right of states to choose their own political, economic, and social institutions. About the only means of gaining power that could be described as violating fundamental norms of international law today would be imposition by a foreign armed force.

The only clear effort to articulate a criterion of form violating international law appeared in the Chilean Congress's decision that Maximilian should not be recognized as Emperor of Mexico in 1863 because monarchy was contrary to the regional law of the Americas.[45] However, this was a somewhat aspirational statement of the regional law because Brazil was still a monarchy. Governments and legal scholars alike have preferred to rely on other criteria that more directly address their concerns about a particular new government.

The Stimson Doctrine of nonrecognition, enunciated in 1933, suggested a negative application of the criterion by stating a duty to avoid recognizing any situation brought about by violation of the League Covenant. This was first applied to establishment of states or alterations of boundaries brought about by use of armed force contrary to the Covenant or the Kellogg–Briand Pact. However, it would be easy to extend the idea to new regimes owing their position to foreign intervention. Thus the state of 'Manchukuo' was not recognized because its creation was part of Japanese aggression against China. However, the Stimson Doctrine is irrelevant to regimes coming to power through domestic action.

RESPECT FOR HUMAN RIGHTS

Though widespread interest in using international law to advance human rights is a recent development, some isolated voices proposed including a new government's attitudes towards human rights as a criterion for recognition even before World War II. The Italian scholar Pasquale Fiore included 'respect for the rights of man' in his

1885 list of criteria that could be applied in deciding whether to recognize new governments,[46] while the German scholar Heinz-Carl Arendt took up the idea in the late 1930s.[47] Some post-World War II scholars thought it could and should be applied immediately;[48] Lauterpacht was more cautious and felt application would have to be deferred until a world government capable of making and enforcing common standards existed.[49]

Governments were slower to take up the idea. Yet as the Cold War continued, they devoted more and more attention to human rights, violations of human rights, and verbal exchanges on the subject. The only sustained discussion of the possibility during the Cold War era occurred among the American Republics. In 1953, Cuban and Uruguayan proposals sent to the Inter-American Council of Jurists listed respect for human rights as a precondition for recognition as a government. Yet neither proposal was adopted.[50] Resolution 26 of the 1965 Second Emergency Interamerican Conference suggested only that a new government's attitude towards human rights was one factor that merited consideration in any consultations on how to react to its accession.[51]

Even the post-Cold War discussions of promoting democracy have not raised failure to respect human rights as a separate ground for nonrecognition. In part this reflects confidence that democratic governments will respect human rights. But it is more directly the result of shifts toward effectivist policies or decisions to dispense with recognition of governments altogether. These were partly a product of complications faced in the late Cold War period when the popular tendency to equate recognition with approval and rising concern with human rights led to severe domestic debates about recognition of several new regimes.[52]

SUMMARY

The optional criteria of respect for other states' rights, origins in conformity with international law, absence of undue violence in the takeover, and respect for human rights have not been invoked by governments very often, and have received only occasional attention from legal scholars. Nondependence on foreign origins has received greater attention, particularly in 1975–90.

The criterion of respect for other states' rights is redundant. International law already requires this, and governments are mere agents responsible for ensuring, among other things, that obligations are in fact met. Certain rules of international law, such as non-succession to a previous regime's debts incurred for purposes of fighting a civil war,[53] that permit relief from certain obligations, exist but are exceptions proving the general rule.

As long as international law includes no rules stipulating limits on the methods used to attain power, it is hard to apply the criteria of undue violence or of origins in conformity with international law. Even the late twentieth-century version of the later criterion, origin that does not violate a fundamental norm of international law (*jus cogens*), offers little additional guidance. It might suggest, following lines suggested by the Stimson Doctrine, that it is proper to avoid recognizing regimes that are brought to power by foreign troops engaged in an illegal intervention. However, either the 'undue violence' or the 'origins in conformity with international law' criterion could be used to deny recognition to regimes that hack their way to power by mass murder or genocide.

Despite greatly increased interest in international protection of human rights, the idea of making recognition dependent on respect for human rights has not caught on. The Belgian government suggested one possible reason in 1979 when explaining that it maintained low-level diplomatic relations with the Pinochet junta so it could engage the junta in discussion of the issue and try to persuade it to modify its policies.[54] There is another: a new regime does not have a human-rights record at the time of accession. Individual members may have a good or bad reputation, but in many cases it is difficult to determine just how a new regime will behave, particularly in countries wracked by civil war or having weak traditions of human rights. In addition, the international community has developed a set of institutions for dealing with these issues more likely to be effective than one or a few governments' recognition policies because they apply to new regimes and established governments alike.

6 The Forms of Recognition

Governments ready to recognize a new regime face two subsidiary questions. The first, common to all, is how to convey that decision to the regime concerned. International law provides for a choice between express and tacit ways of conveying the decision. The second question, faced only by governments that accept the distinction between '*de facto*' and '*de jure*' recognition, is which degree of recognition to accord. They might proceed immediately to the full '*de jure*' form, or they might decide to start with the more limited or provisional '*de facto*' form and await further developments before according '*de jure*' recognition. Governments choosing to start with '*de facto*' recognition have to convey that decision expressly because the legal scholars and governments using the distinction have agreed that recognition is '*de jure*' unless otherwise specified.

EXPRESS AND TACIT RECOGNITION

Legal scholars and diplomats alike have devoted considerable attention to the way in which governments convey their decision to recognize a new regime as the government of its state. The discussion has always proceeded from agreement on the two basic ways of conveying decisions. Legal scholars have often argued for preferring one over the other, and governments have sometimes adopted clear preferences. In principle, however, both remain available and may be used as a government thinks best in particular circumstances.

In the nineteenth century, there were four common methods of express recognition. The first was returning a formal reply to a new regime's notice that it had assumed power. The most explicit included a statement that the receiving government recognized the other, but actual use of the word 'recognition' was not necessary. Any written response addressed to the head or foreign minister of the new regime using that title and all the standard diplomatic greeting and closing phrases established that the responding government accepted the new regime as a fellow government and would conduct the full range of bilateral relations with it.[1] Express recognition could also be communicated by a diplomat's oral statement to the head or foreign minister of a new regime, a treaty provision,[2] or a joint declaration with other governments.[3]

As public interest in and media coverage of foreign affairs increased in the twentieth century, parliamentary or press conference statements about recognition became more common. Generally these simply repeated the terms of a note or diplomat's statement previously communicated to the new regime concerned. Yet they sometimes did more. Though most governments preferred communicating recognition decisions directly to the regime concerned, the pressure of domestic political debate sometimes forced them to state attitudes publicly first.[4] Public statements were also used to clarify positions when governments began expanding the range of relations they undertook with unrecognized regimes.[5] After the mid-1970s public statements were also used by governments de-emphasizing or abandoning formal recognition to indicate the extent of their willingness to deal with a new regime.

Tacit recognition occurs when a government performs an act regarding, or establishes a contact with, a new regime that is inconsistent with nonrecognition. All legal scholars' treatments of tacit recognition began with a statement that recognition is to be inferred when a government's actions show that it intends to deal with the new regime as a government. Yet scholars have often failed to agree on what acts provide reliable indications of such intention. The basic list has remained the same since 1815: establishment of formal diplomatic relations, establishment of formal consular relations, and conclusion of a bilateral treaty.[6] However, the variety of activities regarded as comprising 'formal diplomatic relations', 'formal consular relations', and 'conclusion of a bilateral treaty' has narrowed considerably since the nineteenth century.

Though agreed that express and tacit recognition are equally valid, legal scholars and diplomats have long debated their respective advantages and disadvantages. Express recognition – particularly in forms including the phrase 'recognize as the government' – does have the advantage of maximum clarity. It is less subject to confusion if a change of government coincides with a routine transfer of diplomatic personnel. The military junta that ousted President Goulart of Brazil in 1964 was confused when the Mexican government recalled its ambassador shortly afterwards. It was some weeks before they knew, from dispatch of a successor, that this was a routine personnel transfer and not an expression of disapproval or a refusal to recognize.[7] Yet tacit forms have several attractions. As British Foreign Secretary

Canning argued early in the nineteenth century, tacit forms are less conspicuous and hence less damaging to the new regime's dignity.[8] They also permit governments to adjust policy more incrementally in confused situations or where rivals contend for control. The Canadians at least believe they are also less likely to inspire accusations of interference in another state's internal affairs.[9]

The use of tacit forms spread in the twentieth century. The Mexican government used arguments very much like Canning's to explain its 'Estrada Doctrine' of indicating recognition through maintenance of diplomatic relations, saying that formal declarations of recognition are 'an insulting practice and one which, in addition to the fact that it offends the sovereignty of other nations, implies that judgment of some sort may be passed upon the internal affairs of those nations by other governments...'.[10] During the later Cold War era several governments, including the Australian, Belgian, British, Canadian, French, and Swiss, went further and stated that they were abandoning the practice of recognizing governments altogether.[11] Yet tacit forms did not become universal. Contenders for power frequently sought express statements of recognition to gain political advantage over rivals. Thus the PRC government, which used tacit modes with others, insisted on express recognition of itself.[12] Recognizing governments might use express forms to influence a situation[13] or because a lack of diplomatic relations prevented use of tacit forms.[14]

Yet the greater reliance on tacit forms of recognition or on substituting maintenance of diplomatic relations for recognition did not end public or parliamentary discussion of whether recognition or its equivalent had occurred. A government's attitudes towards a particular new regime were the subject of public and parliamentary interest, and press or parliamentary statements became even more common. Officials of governments claiming to have eliminated recognition of governments constantly repeat 'we recognize states, not governments',[15] but the public and parliamentarians have persisted in discussing 'recognition' and understanding the government's posture with traditional categories.

If there were consensus about which acts necessarily imply recognition of a new regime as the government of its state, there would be no need to discuss whether explicit disclaimers can override such inferences. Governments would know how to convey their intentions and interpret others' conduct. However, the persistent interwar and Cold War era disagreements about which acts necessarily imply recognition encouraged policy-makers and legal scholars in a different direction.

Legal scholars tracked changing government practice and occasionally argued about whether greater emphasis should be placed on the character of the act or on the intention behind it. Policy-makers used the lack of agreement to widen the range of contacts maintained with unrecognized regimes.

The issue of how to interpret actions hardly arose in the nineteenth century. Most nonrecognitions were short-lived, the level of private activity that would benefit from uninterrupted intergovernmental contact was not very high, and most governments did subscribe to a common definition of the actions indicating recognition. The situation was very different in the twentieth century. Not only were there instances of prolonged nonrecognition, but the range of issues requiring some degree of inter-government contact expanded. The growth of the welfare state, a vast expansion of state trading and enterprise in many states, the expansion of cooperation in technical and administrative realms, and the growth of multilateral relations to include political as well as technical questions created strong new pressures to maintain intergovernmental contact. At the same time, the level of ideological contention prevented adoption of what would have been the simpler doctrine – an effectivist one of treating as a government any political organization capable of winning (or extracting) obedience in all or most of its country.

The result was great confusion in legal doctrine. Governments following an effectivist policy sought to maintain the nineteenth-century definitions of relations implying recognition, perhaps as a way of discouraging others from trying to combine having relations with a new regime and refusing to accept it as a government. Governments withholding recognition for political purposes sought to expand the possibilities. Disclaimers were important to this process for two reasons. First, they covered activities in new areas where precedents were genuinely lacking. Second, they permitted the more innovation-minded to pay some regard to the views of other governments or of their own more traditionalist colleagues – at least until there were enough examples of emulation for them to argue that the relation in question was compatible with nonrecognition.

Among the first clear departures from nineteenth-century doctrines were German and French relations with General Adolfo de la Huerta, who claimed to be President of Mexico after helping lead a rebellion against Carranza in 1920. Both governments' envoys in Mexico responded to his notice of entry into office but tried to conceal the fact. The Germans asked that their note be published only after the

US or another European power had recognized, while Belgian and Mexican press reports of the French response led the French foreign ministry to issue disclaimers.[16] The US government felt obliged to make disclaimers when a new Chilean junta acted on requests made to the preceding government, that the US then attempted to withdraw, and issued exequaturs – formal notices acknowledging their appointments – to newly-arrived US consuls.[17] US policy in the 1920s and early 1930s was particularly contradictory because of strong arguments between traditionalists and others over whether particular contact that might be interpreted as implying recognition should proceed. The problem receded after 1933 because the US government finally ended its long nonrecognition of the Soviet government and the traditionalists had lost influence. By 1940, the US government was asserting that 'recognition is essentially a matter of intention',[18] not something to be inferred automatically from particular actions.

The British solution to the problem of combining nonrecognition and wider contact with new regimes was somewhat different. Foreign Office legal advisors continued to maintain that recognition flowed automatically from certain acts, but the government wanted to establish broader contact with certain regimes it did not yet wish to accept as the legitimate government of their states. It escaped the dilemma by reviving the distinction between *de facto* and *de jure* recognition used in the early nineteenth century with the new Latin American republics. This enabled it to receive accredited 'diplomatic agents' from Franco's nationalists while continuing to recognize the rival Republicans as the government of Spain.[19]

Only a few interwar writers commented on governments' contradictory uses of disclaimers. Williams argued that since intention was the key, it was unwise to list a long set of acts whose commission always implied recognition. Briggs focused on intention to support British and French contacts with Franco before 1939.[20] Accioly and Baty strongly supported nineteenth-century doctrine that certain acts always imply recognition,[21] and the Institute of International Law was sympathetic to that position.[22]

The strength of precedent in favour of allowing most of the newer forms of low level intergovernment contact to proceed regardless of recognition reduced the need for disclaimers in the Cold War period. Most were made in the context of relations with rival Leninist and non-Leninist contenders for power. Thus the US government routinely issued disclaimers when undertaking bilateral contacts with the PRC government. Some were attached to acts, like the 1955 agreement on repatriation of prisoners, regarded as not implying recognition even in the nineteenth century, while others accompanied new departures, such as US President Nixon's 1972 state visit to Beijing. The British and Soviet governments equally regularly issued disclaimers when UN activities involved co-participation in multilateral treaties or conferences including the ROC government.[23] The records of the 1954 Geneva Conference on Korea and Indochina, the 1962 Geneva Conference on Laos, and the 1973 Paris Conference on Vietnam were full of statements disclaiming any recognition of some participants by others. There were so many of these at the 1973 Conference that Article 12 of the Paris Accord stated, '...Signature of this Act does not constitute recognition of any Party in any case in which it has not previously been accorded.'[24]

Yet a few governments did hold to earlier traditions and issue disclaimers even when the bulk of opinion accepted that a particular action did not imply recognition. The British government stated that its participation in UN meetings with Taraki-appointed delegates 'should of course in no way be taken to imply that the United Kingdom Government recognizes the new regime in Afghanistan as the Government of that country'.[25] The Australian government issued disclaimers when agreeing to ship relief supplies to Cambodia in 1979[26] and when allowing its counsellor of embassy to attend a meeting between the entire diplomatic corps and Colonel Rabuka after his second coup in Fiji.[27]

The range of governmental views on the effect of disclaimers is indicated in contrasting Chilean and US formulations. In 1950 the Chileans proposed that a projected OAS treaty on recognition include a provision that 'Tacit recognition is any act that indicates without ambiguity the willingness or intention of a state to grant recognition.'[28] In 1963 the authoritative US guide stated that 'whether these or any other acts may be construed as recognition depends, of course, upon the intent to recognize in the attendant circumstances'.[29]

Many postwar scholars accepted broad use of disclaimers,[30] while others accepted certain uses.[31] However, a strong minority preferred maintaining the nineteenth-century view that certain acts unambiguously signal recognition. Lauterpacht argued that establishing formal diplomatic relations, grant of consular exequatur, and conclusion of a general bilateral treaty always imply recognition.[32] Shao, Fenwick and Ross took similar positions.[33] Akehurst even warned that international law sometimes attaches consequences to acts regardless of intentions.[34]

Verhoeven's 1975 treatment of the subject reflected the depths of confusion governments had created by their inconsistent practice. He rejected the idea that intent alone determines recognition because of the difficulty of identifying intent in the absence of explicit statements. Yet he also concluded that the great variations among different governments' practices made it impossible to list a set of acts whose commission always meant recognition.[35] While Verhoeven avoided stating any firm general rules,[36] most other scholars agreed that recognition could safely be inferred from formal diplomatic relations and grant or acceptance of a consular exequatur. Agreement that conclusion of a bilateral treaty meant recognition was less solid because of differences in the definition of the agreements that fell within the term 'bilateral treaty'.

Yet even those governments most prone to using disclaimers to cancel inferences accepted the general view that establishment of formal diplomatic relations and signature of bilateral agreements on major political questions or requiring ongoing diplomatic contact for their implementation amounted to recognition. Governments were more united than scholars on the proposition that leaving diplomats in place did not of itself amount to recognition, though the Libyan government attempted to claim that it did in 1969.[37] The strength of this consensus is shown best in the actions of governments de-emphasizing or claiming to eliminate recognition of governments. They could not have indicated their willingness or unwillingness to deal with new regimes without building on the idea that formal diplomatic relations are established only after or with recognition as a government.

'DE JURE' AND *'DE FACTO'* RECOGNITION

Recognition of governments, like other forms of recognition, has been cast in binary form: a new regime is recognized as the government of its state or it is not. Yet there have been efforts to escape binary reasoning. The most frequent argument, particularly strong in Britain and the Commonwealth, is that recognition decisions involve choice among three possibilities: 'nonrecognition', '*de facto* recognition', and '*de jure* recognition'. Another version involves acceptance of various sorts of 'limited recognition'.

Legal scholars began exploring these ideas in the mid-nineteenth century. Holtzendorff discussed a vague notion of 'partial recognition' in his warning that new regimes would resent continued respect given to those they had deposed. Though the warning was directed mainly at criticizing partiality towards defunct governments, he also noted that any such respect amounted to incomplete acceptance of the new regime's claim to rule its state.[38] Lorimer distinguished several degrees of recognition based on a new regime's ability and will to fulfil the rights and obligations of international law developed among 'civilized' states.[39] Klûber distinguished between a 'provisional' and a 'definitive' recognition, the latter occurring only after the new regime had completely defeated all internal opponents.[40] Yet Le Normand, who studied the matter more deeply, specifically rejected the notion of different types of recognition.[41]

Governments did not use the terms '*de jure* recognition' or '*de facto* recognition' in the nineteenth century. If a change in the form of government (from a monarchy to a republic, for example) accompanied or followed a change in personnel, governments might recognize the new regime as the '*de facto* government' of its state, according a separate recognition as the '*de jure* government' after a constituent assembly or a plebiscite had approved the change in form.[42] They might also use the qualifier '*de facto* government' if they doubted a new regime's staying power.

However, a few government statements provided material for establishing distinctions among types of recognition. British representatives to the Congress of Verona in 1822, meeting to address the Spanish civil war, were told that their government made distinctions 'rather as to the Mode of our Relations, than as to whether they shall or shall not subsist, to the extent, in the matter of Rights, as regulated by the Law of Nations'.[43] The ambassador in Vienna was informed in June 1848 that 'In point of fact, the British Govt. has fully acknowledged the French Republic, and Diplomatic Intercourse is daily carried on between the two Govts. The only thing that remains to be completed is the form of an exchange of credentials.'[44] US President Harrison's comments on the establishment of the Brazilian Republic were equally unclear:

> Towards the end of the past year the only independent monarchical government on the Western Continent, that of Brazil, ceased to exist and was succeeded by a republic. Diplomatic relations were at once established with the new government, but it was not completely recognized until an opportunity had been afforded to ascertain that it had popular approval and support.[45]

Interwar scholars showed greater interest in distinguishing types of recognition, but came to no consensus on how to do so. Most of those discussing *de facto* and *de jure* recognition used the terms to distinguish between a provisional, revocable form of recognition and a definitive, irrevocable one.[46] A smaller group used the terms to distinguish acceptance of a limited competence and of full competence.[47] Others decided the distinction was between entering into limited relations and entering into full relations.[48] Yet others used the terms in more than one of these senses.[49] Confusion only increased with some scholars' view that the distinction was between an express and a tacit grant of recognition,[50] or that '*de facto* recognition' described any sort of contact with an unrecognized regime.[51]

All of this confusion led others to criticize the making of such distinctions. Baty argued in 1922 that the distinction between *de jure* and *de facto* recognition implied an unwarranted distinction between governments more and less legitimate under international law. Though accepting the well-established distinction between a 'general government' ruling all or most of the state and a 'local *de facto* government' ruling a rebel-held portion, he argued that all general governments deserved the same degree of respect.[52] Others argued that distinctions suggested that only some recognition decisions were guided by legal rules and had legal effects.[53] Others saw the distinction as an effort to cover situations when a government chose to deal simultaneously with rival regimes in the same foreign state,[54] with some fearing it was a way to give rebel regimes more respect than had traditionally been accorded to them through recognition of belligerency.[55]

Interwar state practice gave credence to the suspicion that the distinction resulted from misapprehensions and careless use of language. The First World War precedents cited by advocates as establishing the distinction did not do so. The Czechoslovak National Council was recognized by the French government as 'the supreme organ of the Czecho-Slovak Movement in Entente countries', and by the US government as a '*de facto* belligerent government'.[56] The British government stated that it recognized the Estonian National Council as a '*de facto* independent body' in 1919.[57] The Polish army was deemed 'autonomous and co-belligerent under the supreme political authority of the Polish National Committee'.[58] In all of these instances, the adjective '*de facto*' qualified the entity being recognized, not the recognition. The Allies were treading carefully here because, with the exception of the Estonian National Council, the entities being recognized controlled no territory and were acting only outside the countries they claimed to lead. The Allies were fully aware that they could not be recognized as governments of states, so resorted to a new 'co-belligerency' status until victory permitted facts to catch up with aspirations. Scholars mistaking the precedents may have been encouraged by the short interval between aspiration and reality, but the governments involved were not attempting to create a new type of recognition.

However, confusion was again promoted by later contradictory government statements. After Carranza was killed and De la Huerta chosen as provisional President of Mexico, the US government refused to deal with him because it regarded the choice as an inter-faction deal intended to circumvent the election laws. The US chargé in Mexico City was instructed that he 'should therefore be cautious in any necessary dealings with the parties now in possession, not to permit any imputation that the present regime has been even *de facto* recognized by the Government of the United States'.[59] Yet later the same year the US minister in Bolivia was told that 'the President has determined to recognize the Government of Bolivia, as soon as a provisional President is elected, as the *de facto* Government of Bolivia. Formal relations with the Bolivian Government will be entered into when it is permanently established.'[60] The diplomats stationed in Beijing in 1924 attached the qualifier '*de facto*' to relations rather than to recognition or to the new government. In their joint statement they declared that 'they have entered into *de facto* relations with [the Tuan government] on the understanding that this provisional government has been constituted with the concurrence of the nation for the purposes of taking charge of the affairs of the Chinese Republic pending establishment of a formal government representing all the provinces and parties in the Republic'.[61]

Yet in some instances the qualifiers were attached to the recognition rather than to the status of the entity recognized. The Danish government accorded '*de facto* recognition' to the Soviet government in 1923 and '*de jure* recognition' the following year.[62] In 1925 the British used the term 'provisional recognition' regarding Reza Khan's government in Persia before the Constituent Assembly formally named him Shah.[63] The US government used the term '*de jure* recognition' in response to the Franco government's inquiries about the state of relations in April 1939.[64] The Swiss government was consistent in defining a revocable '*de facto* recognition' used when a new regime's staying power was doubted.[65] Smith identified a clear pattern in British practice:

> The development of a particular situation frequently passes through three stages. First comes 'belligerent recognition'.... Secondly, there is '*de facto*' recognition, which means that official relations are established with the new state or government but are not conducted through regular diplomatic agents. Thirdly, there is '*de jure*' recognition, which involves the mutual exchange of fully accredited diplomatic agents and the observance of all the ceremonial courtesies incidental to normal relations between friendly states.[66]

Yet the reality was not as clear. British courts had trouble interpreting Foreign Office certificates that added to the confusion. In the case of *The Gagara*, the Court of Appeals interpreted the government statement about the Estonian National Council as meaning that Estonia enjoyed *de facto* recognition as an independent state.[67] In *Luther* v. *Sagor* the court was informed that 'His Majesty's Government recognizes the Soviet Government as the de facto government of Russia', and read it as *de facto* recognition.[68] In *Princess Paley Olga* v. *Weisz*, the Foreign Office said that the Soviet government 'had been recognized by the British Government as the *de jure* Government' in 1924, and 'in 1918 – or the end of 1917 – as the *de facto* Government'. In *The Arantzazu Mendi*, the Foreign Office stated that the Republican government was still recognized as the *de jure* government of Spain, and the competing Nationalists as 'a government which at present exercises *de facto* administrative control' in a large part of Spain.[69] Yet the judgments in both led legal scholars and other courts to believe that they involved *de facto* recognition rather than *de facto* status.

Confusion continued into the early Cold War era. Most scholars who discussed the distinction used it to differentiate between provisional and final recognition.[70] Yet even they did not agree on whether it was revocable or an irrevocable preliminary to a later *de jure* recognition.[71] Three scholars pursuing extended studies of the subject treated the distinction as one between limited and unlimited relations.[72] A few used it to denote recognition of limited or of full competence.[73] A few used it to distinguish tacit from express recognition.[74] Hsiung thought '*de facto* recognition' was a good term for describing relations with sympathetic deposed or rebel regimes while recognizing a rival as government of the state,[75] while some others also used it for distinguishing between factions involved in a civil war.[76] Another group, mainly writers of general textbooks, used combination definitions.[77] Finally, a few used the phrase '*de facto* recognition' to cover any sort of contact with an unrecognized regime.[78]

Criticism of making any sort of distinction continued as well. Some scholars rejected the notion that any distinctions applied to recognition as a government.[79] Others acknowledged that the distinction had been made but regarded it as an inappropriate political expedient.[80] An overlapping group argued that the phrase '*de facto* recognition' was a sloppy way to say 'recognition as a "*de facto* government"'.[81]

By the mid-1970s the critics outnumbered the advocates, particularly among scholars treating recognition issues at length. However, arguments did not end. Continued British and Commonwealth discussions were sufficient to keep the distinction alive. Though some general texts stated clearly that '*de facto*' and '*de jure*' qualified the government's status,[82] others noted that they could qualify the type of recognition.[83] Only a few went on to note that the distinction was erroneous or irrelevant.[84]

Early Cold War era state practice provided more examples of ambiguous language. The British government said it was '*de facto* in relations with the Egyptian government' on 30 June 1953.[85] On the 28th, further questions elicited the statement that 'if Her Majesty's Government had not been satisfied that the Government of Egypt were in sufficient control of the country to justify the step taken, *de facto* recognition would never have been extended'.[86] Indian scholars had considerable trouble interpreting Indian government statements. Misra interpreted them as calling any contact with an unrecognized government '*de facto* recognition'.[87] Mehrish interpreted the same statements as a policy of extending '*de facto* recognition' first and following it later with '*de jure* recognition'.[88] Tripathi thought '*de facto*' referred to a type of recognition[89] but also described India's policy before 1977 as one of indicating support for Third World nationalists by maintaining various sorts of contacts while following a very strict rule of avoiding recognition as a government until the nationalists in question actually ruled their state.[90] Hsiung interpreted PRC policy as avoiding any distinction when granting recognition,[91] but one Chinese source did distinguish between 'formal recognition' covering express or tacit recognition as a government and establishment of formal diplomatic relations, and '*de facto* recognition' covering trade and 'people-to-people contacts'.[92]

Even those governments with a consistent practice did not share a consensus on the best approach. The Swiss government distinguished between partial and full relations with a new government.[93] The US and Canadian governments settled on distinguishing between *de facto* and *de jure* governments rather than between types of recognition.[94]

The high levels of confusion led most policy-makers to avoid the terms. In 1964, Belgian Foreign Minister Spaak noted that 'we live in a peculiar epoch as regards matters of international law . . . one does not declare war and one does not make peace. No one pays attention in practice to the distinction between de jure and de facto recognition that I learned from my professors.'[95] Even the British, who devoted more attention to the distinction than anyone else, gave up using the term '*de facto* recognition' in the late 1940s.[96] The reduction in governmental usage led Brownlie to conclude in 1986 that the distinction was 'three decades out of date as a matter of the ordinary description of state practice'.[97] His summary ignored some isolated uses in public statements,[98] but did indicate the main trend of state practice.

Growing awareness among scholars that policy-makers were not employing distinctions between *de facto* and *de jure* recognition[99] was not sufficient to settle the question. Continued discussion among British and Commonwealth writers[100] will keep the scholarly debate alive by suggesting this is a question that must be covered in any complete treatment of recognition.

Though the *de facto–de jure* distinction attracted most attention, some scholars elaborated notions of 'partial recognition' or of other statuses that might be recognized. Many Soviet-bloc writers, influenced by the continuing Western nonrecognition of certain states or regimes in the bloc, advanced the notion that any form of contact with a regime amounted to a 'partial' or 'limited' recognition.[101] Others preferred defining other statuses to which a new regime in the process of formation might aspire,[102] notions encouraged by Organization of African Unity and United Nations practice of granting certain national liberation groups observer status in the organizations' forums.

SUMMARY

The broad outline of legal doctrine relating to methods of conveying recognition has remained quite stable: the choice was defined as a binary one between express and tacit forms. A longterm view of legal scholarship and state practice also permits the conclusion that underlying the great debate about which acts constitute tacit recognition there was also persisting agreement that the most significant forms of direct contact – establishment of formal diplomatic relations, formal notification of consular status, and conclusion of a written bilateral agreement on political questions or a general framework for bilateral relations – conveyed acknowledgement that a new regime was indeed the international agent of its state.

The erosion of nineteenth-century consensus on when recognition can be inferred by acts had two distinct sources. The first was the widening agenda of intergovernmental relations, which came to include multilateral as well as bilateral diplomacy and to cover a wider range of issues as development of the welfare and administrative state led to an expansion of the concerns regarded as proper spheres for government activity or regulation. The second was the effort to persist in nonrecognition of particular regimes for lengthy periods of time despite these developments. Disclaimers against inferring recognition from particular contacts were used not merely with the new forms of intergovernmental contact but with some older forms that had been included within the nineteenth-century definitions of formal diplomatic relations or conclusion of bilateral treaties. When the debates finally died away in the Cold War era, the result was a reaffirmation of the nineteenth-century categories with narrower definitions of what they included.

Confusion about the implications of particular actions and the need to guide wider audiences including the public, administrative agencies, and national courts forced governments into supplementing their communications to new regimes with public explanations. Thus for much of the interwar and Cold War era, tacit grants of recognition were rapidly overtaken by express statements. Yet the distinction did not disappear, and was available when governments sought to de-emphasize or abandon formal recognition of new regimes by stating whether they maintained diplomatic relations rather than whether they recognized.

Confusion about what acts amounted to tacit recognition was increased by failure of legal scholars and governments alike to distinguish carefully between nonrecognition motivated by political hostility and nonrecognition motivated by real doubts about the extent or stability of control, between longer and shorter intervals of nonrecognition, and between situations where there was only one and situations where there were rival contenders for power. By their very nature, the hostile nonrecognitions (which were also the long ones), and the rivalry situations produced the largest number of acts that could be drawn upon as legal precedent. Failure to make distinctions among situations encouraged disarray and loosening of the nineteenth-century definitions of acts implying recognition. Yet this was not the only source of change; virtually all diplomatic usage became less formal in the twentieth century than it had been in the nineteenth.[103]

The attempt to create two distinct degrees of recognition as a government by distinguishing between *de facto* and *de jure* forms represented one solution to the problem of indicating that a new regime effectively ruled its state without thereby appearing to endorse its political orientations. Had it succeeded, there would have been less need to narrow the categories of acts implying recognition because there would have been a way to indicate reluctance to accept a particular new regime. However, it collapsed under its own internal confusions. Advocates never managed to agree on whether the terms '*de facto*' and '*de jure*' qualified the status being accepted or the recognition being accorded; nor did they agree on the effects of according '*de facto*' rather than '*de jure*' recognition. Legal scholars' efforts to curb the impact of government refusals to recognize effective regimes by promoting notions of 'minimum', 'partial', or 'functional' recognition or by developing a distinction between 'political' and 'legal' recognition enjoyed no more success. As the twentieth century wore on, governments either returned to treating recognition of governments as a binary distinction between recognized governments and unrecognized regimes or else sought to end the discussion by abandoning recognition of governments entirely.

7 Recognition in Bilateral Relations

Recognition or nonrecognition of a new regime as government of its state has its most immediate effects on bilateral inter-government relations. In most legal scholars' work and governments' summaries of practice, information about the impact of recognition or nonrecognition is presented in two discussions: one on the effects of recognition or nonrecognition, and the other on which acts may be interpreted as conveying tacit recognition. This chapter relies on both discussions to trace the evolution of scholars' and governments' definitions of the sorts of bilateral relations regarded as possible only with recognized governments and those regarded as possible with unrecognized regimes as well. Any such analysis must pay attention to two sorts of differences among instances when recognition is an issue. First, it is essential to determine whether nonrecognition of a new regime rests on doubt that it meets the minimum criterion of controlling its state, on other criteria (particularly when motivated by political hostility), or on a legal obligation to avoid recognition.[1] Nonrecognition motivated solely by doubts about control is likely to produce fewer problems of reconciling nonrecognition with a need for contact because control is usually consolidated or lost fairly quickly. Nonrecognition for other reasons is more likely to persist and raise the sharpest dilemmas of balancing the desire to pursue political points with the pressures for relations stemming from increased interconnection among states. Obligatory nonrecognition requires quite strict limitations of contact, so also raises dilemmas for those who want to ensure that the population within the affected state does not suffer unduly. Secondly, nonrecognition of a sole claimant to power is less complicated than pairing nonrecognition of one or more contenders for power with recognition of another. In these situations, nonrecognizing governments will tend to, or be pressed by the recognized claimant to, limit their contacts with the unrecognized rivals.

Though the range of contacts and relations undertaken with unrecognized regimes has changed over time, the reason for allowing them has not. Today as in the nineteenth century legal scholars and policymakers alike realize that private cross-border activities of various kinds, and ongoing political concerns, require governments to maintain some degree of contact. This was clear not only from discussions about recognition of governments; international law also permitted treating rebels who had a clear political organization and actually administered a definable portion of a state's territory as a 'local *de facto* government' in charge of that area.

THE IMPACT OF RECOGNITION

Recognition of a new regime as government of its state operates on the legal plane as an estoppel; a recognizing government cannot then fail to treat the recognized as a government unless it loses control of its state. On the political plane, recognition removes all barriers to bilateral inter-government relations. The way is cleared for establishing or resuming formal diplomatic relations, establishing or resuming full consular relations, and concluding any sort of bilateral agreement on any subject. Yet recognition is no guarantee that the full range of bilateral relations will be, or will remain, established.[2] No government maintains embassies or legations in every other capital of the world.[3] In addition, governments have long maintained the practice of breaking off diplomatic relations or suspending other forms of bilateral contact to indicate strong objections to some aspect of another government's policy or conduct. However, the rule that recognition is irrevocable means everyone understands that no challenge to the other's legal status as a government is involved in such interruptions of diplomatic contact.

The only invariable effect of recognition occurs in situations where rivals contend for power or a recognizing government has continued to maintain relations with representatives of a defunct predecessor. In these situations, recognition means an end to any formal diplomatic or formal consular relations maintained with the predecessor or rival. However, informal relations of various types can persist.

The persistence of various forms of bilateral contact is currently a sore point between the PRC government and a number of others recognizing it as the government of China but maintaining contacts with the ROC government on Taiwan. In earlier decades, when many governments still recognized the ROC as the government of China and it was still seeking acceptance, the PRC often had to abide by various forms of dual relationships.[4] Once most governments had recognized it, the PRC began exerting more pressure on them to limit contacts with ROC authorities. In 1983, it demanded that Western governments maintaining embassies in Beijing close their informal consular offices on Taiwan. Some complied; the US and Japanese governments did not.[5] In 1995–6 the PRC criticized and threatened retaliation for US decisions to allow ROC President Lee Teng-hui to come to the US for his college reunion, and to permit ROC Vice-President Li Yuan-zu an overnight stop on a trip from Taipeh to attend the new Guatemalan president's inauguration.[6]

THE IMPACT OF NONRECOGNITION

Nonrecognition limits the extent of bilateral inter-government contacts, but the extent of the limitation has been a matter of considerable debate in the twentieth century. Discussions have focused mainly on diplomatic contact, consular relations, conclusion of agreements, reception of nondiplomatic offices, administrative contacts, and inter-government aid or sales.

The Form and Content of Diplomatic Contacts

The need to remain in contact with new regimes has promoted development of the custom that foreign diplomats stay at their posts when there is an extra-legal change of government and continue to carry out many of their duties. John Basset Moore summarized nineteenth-century doctrine, still accepted today, in writing that 'the sending of a new minister, or the retention of an old one, while it implies continued recognition of the state, does not constitute a recognition of the new government, so long as there is no formal presentation of credentials and communications bear only an unofficial character'.[7] Thus informal relations could be carried on by ambassadors or ministers who remained at their posts, by chargés d'affaires if the ambassador or minister was recalled or transferred, or by newly-sent diplomatic agents. Newly-sent agents were not formally accredited to the new government, but were usually allowed to use their state's embassy or legation building and given the customary diplomatic immunities. However, either government could decide to end the informal relations at any time.[8]

Defining the activities falling within the permissible 'informal' relations relied partly on the form of contact and partly on the substance of matters discussed. Nineteenth-century legal scholars and diplomats paid great attention to form: communications with unrecognized governments were conveyed by oral messages, letters addressed to members of the new regime by name rather than title, or third-person memoranda omitting the usual opening and closing courtesy phrases. Other formal marks of respect, such as attendance at receptions or naval salutes, were also avoided.

Scholars and diplomats also agreed that matters immediately affecting the sending state's rights or interests, or the security of its nationals and their property in the other state, could be taken up with unrecognized governments. In nineteenth-century doctrine, bilateral discussions with unrecognized governments were confined to routine or urgent questions relating to protection of nationals or of the state's rights. However, there were instances of wider discussions, particularly when recognition was being withheld to secure concessions from a new government. For instance, the new Sultan of Morocco was required to accept a scheme for settlement of foreigners' claims for damage, provisions for repayment of the Moroccan debt, renewal of the 1906 Act of Algeciras and its provisions for French and Spanish exercise of police powers in the country, and protection of foreigners before the great powers recognized his position.[9] In 1914, the US government required agreement on protecting foreigners' rights, financial reform, and non-alienation of land before recognizing new Haitian governments in 1914–15.[10]

Nineteenth-century definitions of informal relations did not include contacts between diplomats of a new regime and diplomats of a nonrecognizing government stationed in the same third country. Such interaction was avoided except when the diplomatic corps as a group needed to present its views on some matter of diplomatic privilege. These restrictions posed few problems in the nineteenth century because most nonrecognitions persisted for only a short period. Even then, the conventions about form allowed diplomats to get highly political messages across. British participation in joint Austro-British-Russian warnings to governments of Balkan states against increasing tensions in 1905 provides a good example of how the form but not the substance of messages differed. British diplomats co-signed the formal communications to the Bulgarian and Greek governments, but conveyed their views to the Serbian government separately because their government had not yet recognized the Serbian king.[11]

Governments also adjusted the expression of informal relations to indicate their opinion of a new regime. If a government was only waiting to satisfy itself that the new regime would prove reasonably stable, it would instruct envoys to carry on in almost normal fashion, and even to attend receptions and ceremonies in their personal capacity.[12] Disapproval was indicated by sharply restricting informal contacts. The US minister was instructed to avoid Napoleon III's receptions entirely until after the plebiscite approving his assumption of the imperial title in 1851.[13] When the Austrian Archduke Maximilian visited London, Brussels and Paris between his selection to and acceptance of the Mexican throne, the US government instructed its minister in Paris that 'If the Archduke Maximilian appears in Paris only in his character as an imperial prince of the house of Hapsburg, you will be expected to be neither demonstrative nor reserved in your conduct towards him. If he appears there with any assumption of political authority or title in Mexico, you will entirely refrain from intercourse with him.'[14] The less hostile British government received him in London as an Austrian Archduke and permitted him to negotiate loans with private bankers, but did not promise recognition.[15] In Paris, Napoleon III, sponsor of the whole project, received him as Emperor.[16] Similarly, in 1906 the British minister in Belgrade was first told to avoid all ceremonies welcoming the new king from his exile in Switzerland, and then recalled to London before he arrived.[17]

Here, as in other areas of diplomatic practice, the formalities weakened in the interwar era. In the nineteenth century, heads of unrecognized regimes and of nonrecognizing governments did not communicate directly with each other; in the interwar period this happened a number of times. Mexican President Obregón wrote to US President Harding two years before US recognition of his government.[18] In early 1933, US President Roosevelt included Soviet President Kalinin among addressees of two messages sent to heads of all states participating in the League of Nations disarmament and economic conferences.[19]

Contacts between diplomats stationed in third countries became an accepted method of informal contact, particularly when there were no direct channels available because of prior rupture of diplomatic relations. German and Soviet diplomats discussed German recognition and initiation of diplomatic relations in between sessions of the Genoa Conference. The British discussed prisoner exchanges with the Bolsheviks in Copenhagen and various issues with the new Hungarian government in Belgrade and Vienna.[20] The Dutch began their talks with the Soviets in Berlin,[21] and Swiss and Soviet diplomats sought to settle the problems arising from the Vorovsky Affair in the same city.[22] US practice provided many other examples of such third capital contacts because of the frequency with which it engaged in lengthy nonrecognitions.[23] In most cases these negotiations were begun by the parties themselves, yet there were instances of a third government helping arrange the meetings in its capital.[24]

In at least two cases, relations with the rival factions involved parallel formal and informal relations. Building on traditional rules about relations with rebels who formed 'local *de facto* governments' controlling part of a state's territory, the British and Dutch governments agreed to exchange 'agents' enjoying most diplomatic privileges with the Franco regime in 1938 though still recognizing the Republicans as the government of Spain.[25]

Both established governments and new regimes sometimes refused to permit a full range of informal contact. The Peking governments in China accepted Soviet agents but did not permit them to use the Russian legation until after the Soviets agreed to recognize the Tuan government in 1924.[26] The Tinoco government of Venezuela expressed its unhappiness over US refusal to recognize by refusing to deal with the US minister in Caracas.[27] The US government refused to accept an agent from the new Liberian government in 1931 while waiting to see how it responded to the report from a League of Nations investigatory commission concluding that slavery and forced labour were prevalent in that country.[28]

Bolshevik reactions to nonrecognition and foreign intervention in the Russian civil war created several controversies about diplomatic immunities. In July 1918, they reacted to Allied support for White factions by arresting all Allied nationals living in Petrograd and Moscow. Protests from the governments secured release of the diplomats, consuls, and members of military missions; the others were released only after additional negotiations.[29] In August 1918 Red Army troops pillaged the British embassy and killed the naval attaché after he had shot three of the intruders.[30] The Swiss encountered trouble later that year. They accepted a Bolshevik mission in early 1918 but expelled all of its members in November for revolutionary agitation. The Bolsheviks then sent troops to pillage the Swiss legation (killing the counsellor of the legation in the process), and to hold the staff under house arrest until February 1919.[31] As their hold on power at home became more secure, as they began to accept that revolution in Europe was not imminent, and as some governments moved toward fuller relations, the Bolsheviks began to adopt traditional diplomatic practices.

Diplomatic niceties also suffered in wartime. In January 1945 the US government's wartime censorship office began opening mail to or from the Bolivian and Salvadorian legations in Washington because it felt nonrecognition of their governments suspended their correspondence privileges. The State Department took the opposite view, and secured orders instructing the censorship office to desist.[32] However, extreme exigencies could make recognition or nonrecognition irrelevant. The British government subjected all diplomatic correspondence to censorship in May–June 1944 as preparations for the Normandy invasion accelerated.[33]

A few interwar writers, including the Italian Gemma and the German Schlüter, continued to maintain very restrictive definitions of informal relations, in large part to increase the occasions for inferring some form of recognition from extended contacts with a new regime.[34] However, such views did not gain wide acceptance. Most legal scholars followed governments in accepting a wider array of informal diplomatic contacts.

The subjects taken up in informal relations also broadened in the interwar period. The imperial Austro-Hungarian and German governments believed they had recognized the Bolshevik government of Russia by concluding the peace treaty at Brest-Litovsk. Yet the post-armistice Republican governments of Austria and Germany took the opposite view.[35] The US government continued its practice of working out debt-repayment schedules, administrative reforms, and other political arrangements before recognizing new governments in the Caribbean and Central America. The Chinese, Italian, Japanese and US governments all carried on extensive negotiations with the Soviets before recognizing them as the government of Russia. In some cases, as with US discussions with the Mexican, Turkish, and the Chinese Nationalist governments, recognition was extended simultaneously with conclusion of the treaties being negotiated. In others, the failure of negotiations meant continuing nonrecognition. In 1924 the Dutch–Soviet negotiations on a treaty of commerce, friendship, and navigation broke down over differences on the question of most-favoured-nation treatment, and no government treated the negotiations as meaning that the Dutch had recognized the Soviet government.[36]

Yet some governments held to nineteenth-century practices. The French deferred all negotiations with the Bolsheviks, even on the debt questions of great interest to many French citizens, until recognizing the Soviet government in 1924.[37] The British seem to have deferred discussion of revising the Britain–El Salvador commercial treaty in 1932 until after recognition of the new government.[38]

State practice in the Cold War and post-Cold War periods continued along the same lines. Direct communications with leaders of unrecognized regimes were more common.[39] The increase in multilateral meetings of various sorts provided even more opportunity for diplomatic-level contacts in third capitals. Improvements in air transportation made it much easier for high officials to meet each other. Allowing or refusing such meetings could be adjusted to the degree of hostility between a nonrecognizing government and a new regime. The British refused to grant visas to any official of the Vietnam-supported Heng Samrin regime in Cambodia.[40] In 1986 they not only allowed an Afghan opposition leader to visit as a government guest but returned the Taraki government's protest without a reply.[41] Recognition of one rival claimant might mean refusing to meet with officials of other factions. The British government said in 1989 that allowing British officials to meet with ROC counterparts on Taiwan was incompatible with recognition of the PRC.[42] The Australian government has instructed its officials that they may not visit Taiwan and must even avoid taking flights that have scheduled stopovers there.[43]

The state of government opinion on the custom of informal relations with unrecognized regimes was revealed in negotiation of the Vienna Convention on Diplomatic Relations. In its 1958 draft, the UN International Law Commission included a provision that nonrecognition of a state or government is no obstacle to sending or receiving special diplomatic missions. It was deleted by the General Assembly's Sixth (Legal) Committee because the convention was intended to cover only permanent missions, not because anyone disagreed with the substance of the provision.[44]

Agreement that informal relations were permissible did not mean agreement on what activity they included. In the 1960s the British government was still relying on Satow's 1932 formulation:

> During the continuance of a civil war or revolution the diplomatist on the spot may often have to intervene on behalf of his own countrymen with the insurgents in possession, but he will do this personally and unofficially until his government recognizes the new power which has been set up.[45]

Canadian instructions for similar situations were to (1) continue informal relations on routine and non-postponable matters, (2) refrain from discussion of political questions, and (3) carry out all acts and exchanges as informally as possible.[46] This caution was also reflected in British and Commonwealth practice. In 1966 the Canadian government made public statements urging the PRC government to adhere to the Nuclear Test Ban Treaty, but refrained from any direct communication on the matter.[47] It also said it could not invite PRC participation in the Montreal Expo '67 because the convention on world's fairs required that invitations be forwarded through diplomatic channels.[48] In 1976, the situation was reversed: this time it was the ROC which could not be invited to the Olympics.[49] The US adopted a different approach. In the early 1960s the US Foreign Service Manual cautioned about the form of communications but said nothing about substance in its advice that 'Formal diplomatic contact with the [unrecognized] foreign government shall be suspended and no formal written communications transmitted to it. Formal communications from the government may be accepted, but shall not be acknowledged.'[50]

Yet most of the variation in informal relations stemmed less from differences in standing instructions than from greater elaboration of ways to indicate nuances of attitude towards a new government. Western governments could do little about the Soviet intervention in Hungary in 1956 except express disapproval and successfully challenge the new government's delegates' right to represent Hungary in the UN General Assembly. The actual state of relations was kept ambiguous for some time, as indicated in a 1958 British statement that 'Her Majesty's Government have never taken any special step to recognize the Kadar government; but neither, for that matter, have they taken any special step to break off relations.'[51] The US government indicated disapproval of the 'break in the continuity of the democratic constitutional order' after the 1967 Argentine coup by instructing its envoys to avoid all contact with members of the military junta until it extended recognition about two weeks later.[52] The Mexican government also varied its reactions depending on its attitudes towards a new government. In most cases, recognition was not long delayed and informal relations proceeded in the interim. However, strong disapproval of the 1947 Nicaraguan, 1963 Dominican, and 1963 Honduran coups meant a longer delay and suspension of all diplomatic contacts.[53]

The complications attendant on dealing with a rival faction while recognizing another as government of its state appear most vividly in US relations with the PRC and ROC governments. Continued nonrecognition of the PRC, despite its actually controlling most of the country, involved the US government in a wide-ranging set of political discussions via the US and PRC ambassadors in Warsaw,[54] visits by top leaders in 1971–2, and even adoption of legislation specifically extending diplomatic privileges and immunities to the PRC's agents in 1973 while leaving the ROC mission in possession of the Chinese embassy.[55] Since 1979, US relations with the ROC have involved many of the same expedients, with diplomatic privileges and property rights stipulated in the Taiwan Relations Act.[56]

Strictly bilateral discussions continued to range into political matters in the Cold War period, though a few governments preferred avoiding such topics until after recognition. As it had with the Soviets, the French government avoided discussions of debt repayment with the PRC until after recognizing it as the government of China in 1964.[57] The British initially refused to undertake any bilateral dealings with the Yemeni republicans.[58] An unrecognized regime could also adopt the same line if that served its purposes. The PRC government cited continued nonrecognition by the US government as a reason to avoid disarmament conferences, nuclear test-ban talks, and discussion of other possible commitments it wanted to avoid.[59] Yet it was perfectly willing to engage in political discussions when its interests would be advanced, as exemplified in the 1972 Shanghai communiqué[60] and a 1973 joint communiqué reaffirming the usefulness of the 'liaison offices' that had been established earlier in the year.[61]

Nonrecognition, even in some cases of strong hostility, was ignored in efforts to mediate between rival factions in one country or between regimes they did not recognize and governments they did. Though refusing to recognize either as government of Yemen, the British indicated in April 1964 that they were ready to make a second attempt to persuade the sides in the Yemeni civil war to accept a 'neutral zone' between them.[62] The French government let leaders of the rival Cambodian factions meet in Paris in 1987 despite nonrecognition of the Heng Samrin regime.[63] The US participated actively in the negotiations among Angola, Cuba, and South Africa which led to the 1988 agreement under which South Africa conceded Namibian independence in return for Cuba's withdrawing its troops from Angola even though it did not recognize the Angolan government until May 1993.[64]

The question of how obligatory nonrecognition of a government might affect diplomatic contacts was not clearly addressed until the middle of the Cold War era, after the UN Security Council mandates that member states should not recognize continued South African administration of Namibia. In an Advisory Opinion, the International Court of Justice stated that nonrecognition required that the scope of special or resident diplomatic missions accredited to South Africa not extend to Namibia and that states must make clear to the South African government that continued diplomatic relations with it did not imply acceptance of its continued administration of Namibia.[65]

Cold War and post-Cold War scholars continued to follow rather than lead government practice. Only one, Hingorani, suggested that leaving diplomats in place was incompatible with nonrecognition.[66] This was a lonely position; even those arguing that recognition of governments should be de-emphasized or abolished did not question the diplomatic tradition of maintaining missions in place as long as both sides agreed.

Bilateral Agreements

Legal scholars and governments have long agreed that conclusion of 'a bilateral treaty' was inconsistent with refusal to recognize a new regime, but have not come to consensus on just what agreements are included within that term. The only consensus relates to when an agreement can be said to exist. Both governments and the overwhelming majority of legal scholars define this moment of 'conclusion' as signature of the agreement, not subsequent ratification or entry into force.[67]

The question was perhaps simpler in the nineteenth century because form and content tended to overlap. The term 'treaty' was reserved for the most formal agreements, and these tended to address major political questions like ending wars, settling boundaries, or establishing alliances. But governments also made less solemn but equally binding agreements in a whole range of other written documents variously labelled 'agreement', 'accord', 'protocol', 'declaration', or 'exchange of notes'. Only a few legal scholars suggested that implications of recognition could be avoided by using the less formal types of agreement[68] or avoiding agreements covering general and political questions.[69] For their part, governments generally believed that making agreements on political questions was incompatible with nonrecognition. This was Bismarck's attitude towards concluding a formal armistice with the Third French Republic in 1871.[70] Similarly the French concluded a 'modus vivendi' on trade matters with the provisional republican government of Portugal in 1911 rather than the customary treaty of commerce.[71]

Interwar scholars, faced with a larger number of prolonged nonrecognitions, discussed the matter in greater detail. Some maintained the ambiguities of nineteenth-century discussion by saying that bilateral agreements could be made with unrecognized regimes if they were 'temporary' or addressed 'non-political' questions.[72] A few claimed that conclusion of any bilateral agreement constituted recognition.[73] Another small group claimed that form could override content, and that even general and political agreements could be compatible with continuing nonrecognition if a less formal type of agreement was used.[74] They, like governments, were not particularly concerned with the apparent inconsistency of refusing to accept a new regime as a government while making political agreements with it.

The long nonrecognitions of the interwar period required governments to pay considerable attention to the issue. The British government initially maintained a restrictive view of the possibilities. Though accepting that a 1920 agreement on prisoner exchange was compatible with refusal to recognize the Soviet government, it decided that concluding the 1921 trade agreement involved at least *de facto* recognition.[75] By the end of the period the British had aligned with the prevailing view that only peace treaties, alliances, and general treaties of commerce, friendship, and navigation (which serve as framework treaties for relations on a wide variety of issues) required or implied recognition of the other government involved.

Yet the distinction between 'temporary' agreements dealing with particular matters and political agreements was not always strong. The Franco-Soviet and Hungarian–Soviet prisoner-exchange agreements of 1920 contained nonintervention and nonaggression clauses respectively.[76] The Austrian and German Republics both took the view that their predecessors' conclusion of a peace settlement with Russia in the Treaty of Brest-Litovsk did not mean that they had recognized the Bolshevik government.[77] This did not stem from any Austrian or German claim that they were new states; it appears more likely to have been inspired by the voiding of Brest-Litovsk in the Treaty of Versailles.[78]

Cold War era scholars usually divided bilateral treaties into those consistent and those inconsistent with nonrecognition of the other government involved. Commercial, economic, humanitarian, technical, and temporary agreements were generally put in the former category, perhaps reflecting the influence of practice that allowed co-participation in multilateral treaties on such subjects. Only a few scholars – all but one writers of general textbooks – suggested that nonrecognition prevented conclusion of any sort of bilateral treaty.[79] Kelsen's more considered conclusion rested on his distinction between optional 'political' and mandatory 'legal' components of recognition; in his view all bilateral agreements establish optional relations and hence involve 'political' recognition. The others offered no rationale for their views. Two scholars, Zivier and Gorus, went to the opposite extreme and argued that there was no sort of treaty necessarily inconsistent with nonrecognition.[80]

The scholars' shift away from older views regarding recognition as necessary for the conclusion of bilateral agreements was encouraged by Cold War developments in state practice. Both analogies from multilateral relations, where becoming co-parties to the same agreement stemmed more from the nature of multilateral activity than from individual policy choice, and use of informal types of agreement for a wider range of matters encouraged this trend. The 1954 Geneva settlement on Indochina was an 'accord', while the 1962 Laos settlement was embodied in a 'declaration' with attached protocols. US–PRC agreements between 1973 and 1979 were 'joint communiqués' and 'agreed announcements', and the US State Department admitted in 1974 that the latter form was developed specifically to avoid inferences of recognition.[81] While most of these agreements covered minor issues, the February 1972 Shanghai Communiqué contained a US promise not to hinder peaceful unification ('reunification' in the text) of Taiwan and the mainland.[82] Individual governments might maintain policies regarding conclusion of a particular type of agreement or conclusion of an agreement on certain subject-matters as requiring or carrying recognition, but there was no consistency in the definitions of type or subject-matter.

Legal scholars' discussions also showed little convergence of opinion. While all agreed that some bilateral agreements can and some cannot be made with unrecognized regimes, there was no consensus on how to define the categories. Some used the temporary–permanent distinction,[83] some the formal–informal,[84] some the political–nonpolitical.[85] Several gave no clear definition[86] while others argued that proper disclaimers could cancel any inferences of recognition.[87]

Continuity of the state meant that changes of government did not affect the validity of existing treaties. Yet lengthy periods of rivalry could complicate the situation. In 1947 the Chinese Communists announced that they would not be bound by any agreements made by the Nationalists unless they were approved by the Political Consultative Committee, an assembly of representatives from all major parties seeking a negotiated end to the civil war. Later, Article 55 of their Common Programme indicated that the PRC would 'recognize, abrogate, revise, or renegotiate' them as desired.[88] When they recognized the PRC in 1966, the Canadians accepted not only terminating all treaties signed with the ROC after 1949 but also the 1946 Commercial Modus Vivendi.[89] The Japanese conclusion that recognition of the PRC ended the Japan–China Treaty of Peace signed with the ROC in 1952,[90] and the US conclusion that recognition required ending the US–ROC Mutual Defense Treaty,[91] accorded more clearly with traditional views that agreements made with a regime after it loses control do not bind the state.

The Namibia Advisory Opinion suggests that obligatory nonrecognition would require very strict limits on treaty relations. The International Court of Justice advised that states must avoid making any new treaties in which South Africa claimed to act 'on behalf of or concerning' Namibia and must avoid continued application of existing treaties to Namibia if that application required 'active intergovernmental co-operation'. Yet the population was to be protected by continued application of 'certain general conventions, such as those of a humanitarian character, the non-performance of which may adversely affect the people of Namibia'.[92]

Consular Relations

Nineteenth-century legal doctrine and practice permitted consular relations to continue on an informal basis despite nonrecognition. Governments could continue to deal with consuls sent by the former government, or accept the presence of replacements sent by the new regime. The only clear rule was that requesting an exequatur from a new regime or issuing one to its appointee was incompatible with nonrecognition. As with diplomats or other agents, these informally tolerated consuls could function only as long as the receiving government permitted.

Nineteenth-century legal scholars did not indicate how shifting to an informal basis affected consular activity; that was illuminated by state practice. If new consuls had to be appointed by either side, the US government sent or received them as 'commercial agents' without formal accreditation.[93] Continuing consuls were instructed to limit their contacts with the new authorities as much as possible. Instructions issued to the US consul in Santo Domingo during the brief nonrecognition of the new Dominican government in 1889 were typical:

> In the meantime... you will continue to maintain intercourse with it, so far as may be necessary for the transaction of consular business, explaining, however, to Señor Ferraro that you will do so provisionally and subject to the formal action to be taken by the United States diplomatic representative.[94]

The Swiss government sent its consuls very similar instructions after proclamation of the Brazilian Republic in the same year.[95]

The British government had to deal with a more complicated question in 1873. It had a consul resident in Fiji even though acknowledging the government there only as a *de facto* ruler. Foreign Office experts' debate over whether leaving him in place implied any greater recognition of the Fiji government was complicated by the fact that he had been instructed to deliver some diplomatic messages to the government as well as continuing his consular duties. After some debate, they decided that his continued residence did not amount to any greater acknowledgement of the government.[96]

Interwar practice continued along the lines developed in the nineteenth century. Consuls were still permitted to stay at their posts and continue their work despite extra-legal change of either the receiving or sending government as long as their presence was tolerated. Newly-appointed consuls sent by an unrecognized government were not given exequaturs, but subordinate officials and local authorities were notified informally and asked to allow consular work to proceed.[97]

There were some exceptions to the nineteenth-century rule that new regimes could dismiss consuls sent by a predecessor government. The Swiss accepted the Bolshevik government's decision to dismiss the Russian consul in Geneva because he failed to swear allegiance to the new regime.[98] However, the French and US governments continued to accept the authority of consuls appointed by the Tsarist government until they recognized the Soviet government in 1924 and 1933 respectively, even though the Soviets wished to replace them. In the US case, this led to a complicated situation in which the Soviets expelled all US consuls in 1923, while both Tsarist-appointed Russian consuls and Soviet-appointed agents doing consular-type work without any acknowledgement by the US government were active in the USA.[99] This situation ended only when the US government revoked the exequaturs of the Tsarist consuls on the day it recognized the Soviet government.

The prolonged nonrecognitions of the interwar period affected consular practice in a number of ways. First, they increased the number of occasions when consuls made up for the lack of resident diplomatic staff by carrying out diplomatic tasks informally. Secondly, they made it impossible for some governments to continue avoiding sending new consuls or transferring consular personnel from one consulate to another within a country during nonrecognition of its government.[100]

Disputes between the new PRC government and a number of foreign consuls in 1949–50 gave a particularly clear view of the state of the rules early in the Cold War era. The Shanghai Military Committee expelled the Spanish consul for 'contempt' of the PRC and continuing his consular work. Dutch, French, and US consuls were also denied continued toleration after it became clear that their governments were not going to recognize the PRC authorities very soon. The PRC and the US governments were also locked in a dispute about PRC confiscation of some US-owned property. The US government insisted it was consular premises; the PRC insisted it was military property and never claimed any right to confiscate consular premises.[101]

Cold War era practice accentuated the tendency to regard consulates, consulates-general, and diplomatic missions as different levels of contact, and only a few scholars dissented.[102] Though diplomatic and consular relations had been regarded as beginning and ending together, the 1963 Vienna Convention on Consular Relations codified the possibility of separating them.[103] This reinforced the existing trend towards indicating different degrees of willingness to maintain contact by sending, or accepting the continued presence of, both diplomatic and consular missions, or consular missions only, or neither.[104] Thus the Soviets indicated a modification of their refusal to deal with South Korean authorities by exchanging 'consular sections' in 1990.[105] Such differences were particularly common when governments were maintaining contact with rival authorities at the same time.[106] In only one case, the Khmer Rouge's April 1975 announcement they they would expel all foreign diplomats and consuls once they consolidated power, did a government suggest reversion to the older tradition.[107]

Situations involving rival claimants inspired some controversies. A number of governments recognizing the PRC continued informal consular offices on Taiwan. The British government maintained a consulate-general on Taiwan communicating with provincial authorities rather than with the Nationalist government after recognizing the PRC in 1951.[108] The US government continued to maintain consular activity on the island, but the Australians, British, French and

Germans all shifted it to Hong Kong in the 1980s.[109] The British government demanded explanations after the Panamanian ambassador, another Noriega partisan on the embassy staff, and four private security guards ran a Land Rover through the door of the Panamanian consulate in London and ousted the consular staff loyal to deposed President Delvalle.[110]

The Namibia Advisory Opinion suggests that consular relations would have to be tightly circumscribed during obligatory nonrecognition. It stated that new consuls should not be sent to Namibia and those already there should be withdrawn. In addition, the South African government should be informed that continuing consular relations with it did not imply any acceptance of its continued rule over Namibia.[111] Yet the various methods of maintaining informal consular agents would be possible,[112] as would serving Namibians through consulates in neighbouring countries.

Trade, Information, Travel, and Cultural Offices

Government trade delegations are a product of the command economies set up in the USSR and other countries after 1917. During their first years in power, the Bolsheviks claimed that trade delegations should be treated as diplomatic offices and that accepting them meant recognizing the sending government. This was motivated partly by a hope of speeding others' acceptance,[113] but also by desire that any official representing the Soviet government abroad should have diplomatic immunities. However, other governments rejected this approach. The British government refused diplomatic status to the trade delegation admitted under the 1921 Anglo-Soviet trade agreement even though it regarded accepting the delegation as being at least *de facto* recognition.[114] The Italian government also denied diplomatic status to the Soviet trade mission until 1924, when the Italo-Soviet Treaty of Commerce and Navigation stipulated Italian recognition of the Soviet government.[115] The US government admitted Soviet trade delegations on ordinary visas and tolerated their activity.[116]

Though trade delegations sometimes gained partial immunities after 1945, their presence was regarded as compatible with nonrecognition. Governments recognizing one claimant sometimes found it expedient to maintain trade-delegation-level relations with the other. This was particularly true if, like the PRC, the unrecognized claimant centralized international trade in government agencies.

Government information, travel, and cultural offices separate from diplomatic or consular missions developed during the Cold War era as a result of greater government efforts to promote tourism or present themselves and their countries in a favourable light abroad. They were seldom discussed by legal scholars, but state practice indicated a tendency to tolerate their activity even during periods of nonrecognition.

Many governments even permitted rival factions in a foreign civil war to maintain separate information offices. The Australian government has allowed a wide variety of governments and political factions to maintain information offices.[117] The Danish, Finnish, French, Norwegian and Swedish governments all allowed the Viet Cong to maintain information offices in their capitals.[118] The Dutch government refused on the grounds that 'it would be contrary to international custom to recognize simultaneously the agencies of a counter-regime'.[119] Yet allowing information offices can be a way of accommodating realities while maintaining nonrecognition for symbolic purposes. The Mexican government allowed the Franco government of Spain to open cultural and information offices in Mexico City even though it persisted in recognizing and maintaining diplomatic relations with the Republican government-in-exile.[120]

Direct Government Aid or Sales

Even before the advent of extensive state trading in the twentieth century, governments purchased or sold various items, most often surplus military equipment, to one another. The short periods of nonrecognition in the nineteenth century meant that the question of whether such deals were compatible with nonrecognition was not raised because the transactions could easily be delayed until recognition had occurred. Matters became more complicated in the interwar period because of the greater volume of government trading and the lengthier periods of nonrecognition. The US government was initially cautious, undertaking transactions with unrecognized governments only when they involved no papers signed by officials of both sides.[121] Such concerns about form were soon set aside. Once a government decided it was willing to engage in a particular trade transaction with an unrecognized regime, it usually went forward without difficulty. One exception was British government insistence that the Yemeni Republic acquire the surplus blankets it wished to purchase through a private intermediary rather than directly in 1962.[122]

An extra-legal change of government may delay aid programmes. Yet decisions to start, increase, reduce, suspend or terminate military, economic, technical, humanitarian, or budgetary aid depend far less on recognition or nonrecognition of the recipient government than on the overall political attitude towards it. The US government suspended all but humanitarian aid after the 1962 Peruvian and 1967 Argentine coups ousting elected governments, but allowed aid to continue without interruption after the 1961 Guatemalan coup because of greater sympathy with the leaders' goals.[123] The French government suspended budget subsidies for Dahomey after the 1968 coup, restored some after selection of a civilian cabinet, and restored the rest after a referendum endorsed the new government.[124] The Belgian, Danish, Dutch, Swedish and West German governments all suspended aid after the 1973 Pinochet coup in Chile, and continued to deny aid even after recognizing his government.[125] By 1990 denial or increase of aid was often used to bolster efforts to mediate negotiated solutions to civil wars or to encourage democratization. Any regime subject to a general or specific obligation to avoid recognition would not be regarded as eligible for aid, though the population of the territory it ruled could be regarded as meriting various forms of humanitarian assistance. The difficulty here is that unless humanitarian aid is accompanied by strong outside intervention, its provision will depend on cooperation by the regime.

Use of Private Intermediaries

The long periods of nonrecognition common in the interwar and Cold War eras greatly encouraged the use of actual or ostensible private intermediaries by governments desiring to maintain some form of contact despite nonrecognition. In some instances, these are simply analogous to the state entity–private firm relation common in international trade between centrally planned and market economies. Thus, for example, Japan–PRC trade was organized through special trade promotion bodies that were government agencies in China and associations of private businesses operating with government encouragement in Japan.[126] Similar arrangements have dealt with repatriation of individuals and families,[127] and with relief operations involving government surplus property or provision of transport.[128]

Private intermediaries are often used when a government is trying to maintain simultaneous contact with rivals, particularly if the faction in power controls a major country. Japan–ROC relations have been run on the Japanese side through the Association for Interchanges and on the ROC side by the Association on East Asian Relations.[129] The Anglo-Taiwan Trade Committee performs similar functions in British–ROC relations.[130] Such channels suffice for trade and other economic exchanges, though cannot substitute for inter-government contact if political matters need attention.

SUMMARY

The rule that informal diplomatic relations can be maintained with unrecognized regimes has been a constant of legal doctrine and state practice. Allowing for the general decrease in diplomatic formality, the ways of distinguishing 'informal' from 'formal' diplomatic relations have also remained fairly consistent. Written communications used less elaborate forms, public ceremony was reduced or eliminated, and credentials were not presented. Yet the substantive matters taken up in these informal discussions expanded considerably. Even the more cautious governments undertook clearly political discussions with unrecognized regimes after World War I.

Though a few governments still avoided concluding agreements with unrecognized regimes, others exploited the possibilities of form to package important political understandings as a 'modus vivendi', 'joint communiqué', 'accord' or other type used in the nineteenth century for temporary or minor agreements. This was particularly true when nonrecognition was prolonged for political reasons. Governments which stuck more closely to the facts of control faced fewer situations where they needed to make agreements with the unrecognized.

The realm of consular relations remained largely undisturbed, though some new governments chose to limit consular relations with nonrecognizing governments. Yet even they found it difficult to eliminate consular contact entirely because of its role in facilitating travel, trade, and other private activity. The expedients of channelling consular work through neighbouring countries, 'consular sections', or other offices were all responses to this reality. The development of trade, cultural, tourism, and information offices stemmed from active government efforts to promote exchange, travel, and interest, but could be used as an alternate channel of diplomatic contact, particularly with rival contenders for power. Direct government aid, a rarity in the nineteenth century, became important in the twentieth and offered additional possibilities for expanding or narrowing contact with an unrecognized regime.

The reduced difference between relations with recognized governments and with unrecognized regimes derived in part from the tendency to perceive many of the new issues entering the agenda of inter-government relations as 'technical' or otherwise 'nonpolitical'. Yet it also reflected greater willingness to ignore the logical implication that nonrecognition of a regime indicates doubt about its ability to act as agent of its state. This readiness to ignore logic was particularly strong when political hostility was being expressed through nonrecognition or persistence of simultaneous relations with rival factions.

Legal scholars inadvertently encouraged expansion of relations with unrecognized governments by failing to distinguish consistently among different situations. In many works, particularly general textbooks, all instances of recognition were treated as alike and part of a common pool of precedent. Lengthy nonrecognitions were not distinguished from short ones. Withholding recognition out of political hostility or a sense of legal obligation was not distinguished from withholding out of doubt about a new regime's hold on power. Situations involving two or more rival factions were not distinguished from situations where only one group claimed power except in discussions of the international law regarding civil wars and recognition of belligerency or insurgency.

Digests of government practice sometimes gave more sense of context, but their compilers – whether foreign ministry legal staff or outside scholars given access to relevant documents – generally failed to compare actions taken in different types of situations. Thus reports of government practice also encouraged treating all examples derived from state practice as a relatively undifferentiated pool of precedents.

Virtually all governments were inconsistent in their actions, though some – like the British and French – kept inconsistency to a narrower range. The US government was steadily among the most inconsistent, in large part because of its predilection for using nonrecognition to express political hostility even to effective regimes. A combination of high international prominence (particularly after 1945) and longer-standing willingness to publish summaries of current practice and diplomatic documents assured its actions of widespread attention. This contributed considerably to broadening the array of precedents because the US government was often seeking the advantages of simultaneously expressing hostility through nonrecognition and dealing with whoever was actually in control. Its relative insulation in the nineteenth century and the interwar period and its great power after 1945 meant it was less subject to counter-pressures for greater consistency in behaviour than other governments.

Yet the US government was not the only source of inconsistency. Enough other governments were acting inconsistently often enough to prevent those seeking greater consistency from determining the broad trend of legal development. The strain put on traditional rules from expansion of the international agenda into economic, social, and technical concerns and the development of multilateral diplomacy was strong. The search for ways to continue nonrecognition of effective regimes ensured that those strains became so strong that older understandings broke down. Scholars and foreign office lawyers interested in greater consistency were forced in one of two directions: to affirming the need for a stricter adherence to an effectivist policy or towards abolition of recognition of governments. Both involved bids to end the laxity of practice by eliminating the possibility of expressing hostility through nonrecognition.

8 Recognition in Multilateral Relations

From modest beginnings in the nineteenth century, multilateral relations have grown to involve nearly every state in the world in at least some of the large array of global and regional organizations dealing with just about every conceivable political, economic, social, cultural, and technical issue. These relations involve inter-government contacts of various types: regional heads of government meetings, the foreign ministers' meetings of the Concert of Europe, the League of Nations Council, or *ad hoc* conferences, ambassadorial-level assemblies and conferences, and gatherings of lower-level administrators and experts in the public international unions of the nineteenth century or the UN specialized agencies of today. Multilateral activity is now so widespread that it is impossible to examine all of it here. This chapter will concentrate on examples from the League of Nations, the United Nations, and some of the larger regional organizations.

In many ways multilateral activities are similar to the familiar forms of bilateral contact. Yet they differ in one important respect: while each government determines its bilateral contacts itself, admission to multilateral activity is decided by the group of participating governments. Only if such decisions must be made unanimously can a government be sure of avoiding contact with a regime it does not recognize. Whenever a simple or qualified majority of the participants decides, matters are somewhat more complicated. If enough others do not recognize, then a new regime's request for participation is likely to be refused. If only a few refuse recognition while a sufficient majority accept the new regime's participation, then the nonrecognizers have to accept the new regime as a co-participant for the multilateral activity involved unless they want to withdraw themselves in order to avoid all contacts.

The question of participation by unrecognized regimes was not particularly urgent in the nineteenth century because most nonrecognitions lasted fairly short periods of time and the extent of multilateral relations was not very great. Yet even then it arose because of the wider controversy about whether participation should be open to any state, or require an invitation by a majority of those organizing a new activity or already participating in an existing one. They were matters of concern because they were linked closely to a more general controversy about how the right to participation should be determined. This controversy had several parts, each relating to one of the forms of multilateral relations: co-participation in a single-occasion multilateral conference, concurrent acceptance of a multilateral agreement, and co-participation in a standing intergovernmental organization.

CO-PARTICIPATION IN MULTILATERAL CONFERENCES

In the early nineteenth century multilateral conferences consisted of the various diplomatic congresses of the great powers and other single-occasion meetings. While the Congress of Vienna involved just about all European states, the later congresses of the Concert period included representatives of the great powers and such others as they chose to admit. This allowed the great powers joint control of entrée. The mid-century conferences on technical and administrative matters were organized as diplomatic gatherings with participation by invitation of the sponsoring government. That government would often consult others in forming the invitation list, but it was clear that participation was by invitation; there was no notion that statehood or status as a government conferred any right or presumption of participation. Nonrecognition was not a bar to participation if the sponsors chose to ignore it. Thus the Russian government sent the French 'Government of National Defence' a notice of its intention to denounce the ban on Russian naval activity in the Black Sea established in the 1856 Treaty of Paris ending the Crimean War. Though not yet recognizing that new regime, the Russians argued that France was too important a power to be ignored in any discussions about the Black Sea.[1]

Most interwar writers treated multilateral negotiations as roughly analogous to bilateral ones, and regarded co-participation as compatible with nonrecognition.[2] Governments generally accepted the same rule, even when co-participation required sending their own representatives to a place ruled by an unrecognized regime.[3] Lengthy nonrecognition for political reasons might mandate another policy. The US government absented itself from the Genoa Conference of 1922[4] to avoid co-participation with the Soviets. Later it did participate in both political and technical conferences with them,[5] though hedged its participation with statements that the co-participation did not imply recognition of all the other governments involved.[6]

The related problem of issuing invitations to unrecognized regimes was handled in various ways depending on how the particular conference was convened. In the interwar period there were three possibilities: convocation by the League of Nations Council or Assembly, convocation by a government on behalf of one of the public international unions (a continuation of nineteenth-century practice), and convocation by one or more governments acting in their own name. With League-convened conferences, the recognition or nonrecognition of new regimes in member states was irrelevant because member states had a right to attend. The League Secretariat kept track of who was ruling each member state, and issued invitations to the effective ruler. This would only cause controversy in two sorts of situations: if the new regime was not recognized by a large number of other governments and they objected to its participation, or if more than one set of delegates claimed to represent the same state. The nonrecognition of a new regime in a non-member state seeking inclusion might be relevant, but was only one possible reason for denying an invitation. The public international unions also had a strong presumption that the host government should invite all member states regardless of its own recognition or nonrecognition of particular governments. This was clear in the Universal Postal Union, where members shared a consensus that UPU activities were 'administrative' and hence compatible with nonrecognition.[7] When the US government, initially named to host the 1929 UPU Postal Congress, proved reluctant to invite the Soviet government, the other members moved the Congress to London.[8]

Conferences convened outside the framework of an intergovernmental organization were organized according to nineteenth-century rules. This left host governments free to act on or to ignore their own nonrecognition of particular regimes. This was clear in organization of the San Francisco Conference to perfect and adopt the UN Charter. The US, as host government, omitted Poland from the list of invited states because of concern that an invitation would intensify competition between the Soviet-sponsored Union of Polish Patriots and the British and US-supported London government-in-exile for influence in the projected coalition government.[9]

A very small group of Cold War era scholars argued that co-participation in a multilateral conference meant recognition of the other governments involved.[10] Postwar practice has consistently favoured regarding co-participation as not affecting individual states' recognition policies,[11] regardless of whether the conference was held under the auspices of an intergovernmental organization or a particular government. As in the interwar period, controversy was most likely when more than one set of delegates claimed to represent the same state, or when a large number of members did not recognize the regime in a non-member state seeking a special invitation. In UN-sponsored conferences, the controversies reflected debates in the General Assembly and, when involving delegations of member states, were settled as specified in General Assembly resolution 396(V),[12] by following General Assembly decisions on seating.[13] Conferences called by one or more governments mediating an international or civil conflict would necessarily ignore recognition questions to get all of the relevant participants to the table; however, some were delayed as participants argued over the symbolism of seating arrangements and other procedural details.[14]

CO-PARTICIPATION IN MULTILATERAL TREATIES

Co-signature of or later accession to a multilateral treaty inspired more controversy. In early nineteenth-century practice, multilateral treaties were 'closed': a state could become party only through inclusion in the initial conference or after approval of later accession by all states that had accepted the treaty. Thus any government, not just an unrecognized one, had to gain the unanimous acceptance of those already party to the agreement. Any one which chose to treat non-recognition as a bar to participation could do so. Some disclaimers issued at mid-century show that multilateral treaties on technical or administrative issues were coming to be treated as equivalent to their bilateral counterparts and regarded as open to unrecognized governments. Governments not yet recognizing the unified Italian state (and hence its government) let the Italians sign the 1863 Scheldt Convention, the 1865 Act creating the European Danube Commission, and the 1865 International Telegraph Convention subject only to disclaimers that co-signature did not imply a grant of recognition.[15] By the end of the century, multilateral treaties addressing administrative and technical matters became 'open' conventions to which any state could accede by notifying the depository government.[16] Nonrecognition thus became irrelevant to a growing range of multilateral treaties.

More occasions for working out the implications of co-participation in multilateral treaties arose during the interwar period. Most legal scholars[17] and all governments agreed by the end of the period that co-participation was generally consistent with nonrecognition. All agreed that a new regime's accession to an open convention could not affect another government's nonrecognition since it had no say in the matter. Accession to a closed convention was treated as analogous to conclusion of a bilateral treaty since the consent of all parties was necessary. Thus, closed conventions on political matters might remain shut to a government not recognized by one of the participants. Participants could, however, choose to ignore nonrecognition. The US government made such an exception for Soviet accession to the Spitzbergen Treaty in 1924. The Treaty stipulated that Russia could accede when it had a government recognized by all other parties, and in 1924 the US was the only one still refusing to recognize. It agreed to permit Soviet accession on condition that this was not regarded as affecting its nonrecognition.[18]

Long nonrecognitions of several governments plus strong internal arguments about how far the US should enter into relations with any of them created strong inconsistencies in US practice. The US government took the precaution of adding disclaimers against inferring recognition of any co-participant when ratifying the 1926 International Sanitary Convention, the 1929 Convention on Safety of Life at Sea, the 1930 International Load-Line Convention, and the 1931 Convention on Control of Narcotic Drugs.[19] No disclaimers were issued when ratifying the 1923 Lausanne Convention on the Regime of the Straits, the 1929 Convention for the Suppression of Counterfeiting Currency, the 1932 International Telecommunications Convention, and the 1932 International Air Sanitary Convention.[20] No disclaimers were added when ratifying the 1924 and 1929 Universal Postal Conventions on grounds that the sponsoring Universal Postal Union was an association of postal services rather than of states.[21]

By the early 1930s the US had developed a more consistent policy. Instructions issued to delegates in 1931–2 state that (1) later adherence to a multilateral treaty by an unrecognized regime does not disturb US nonrecognition, (2) US nonrecognition is not disturbed if the US later accedes to a multilateral treaty already ratified by an unrecognized regime, (3) in most cases co-signature of a multilateral treaty does not mean recognition, though US delegates should issue a disclaimer to be safe, and (4) co-signature does suggest recognition if the treaty establishes direct and reciprocal obligations to accept other parties' official acts as valid, so US delegates must issue a disclaimer that the treaty will not create any relations between the US government and another it does not recognize.[22]

The small group of clearly political multilateral agreements inspired additional discussion. The US government was interested in having the Soviets participate in the Kellogg–Briand Pact, but asked the French government to relay the invitation.[23] Chen argues that the US government reversed itself by inviting the Soviets to participate in the 1933 League of Nations disarmament and world economic conferences,[24] but mistook messages to participants for the actual invitations, which were issued by the League.

After World War II, governments distinguished more clearly between multilateral conventions on administrative, technical, and other nonpolitical matters, and multilateral conventions on political matters. Co-signature and accession to the former were regarded as compatible with nonrecognition no matter the extent and intensity of interaction involved. This was encouraged by the fact that virtually all such treaties came out of meetings organized by intergovernmental organizations where members had to accept majority decisions on who could sign. Co-signature of multilateral agreements on political matters carried disclaimers that no recognition was intended if they involved inter-government contacts for implementation. Agreements involving peacekeeping or truce-supervision, such as the 1954 Indochina, 1962 Laos, and 1973 Vietnam agreements,[25] were all accompanied by disclaimers. The 1954 Interamerican Convention on Diplomatic Asylum even codified the rule in Article 10, which provided that 'The fact that the territorial State is not recognized by the State granting asylum shall not prejudice the application of this Convention, and no act carried out by virtue of this Convention shall imply recognition.'[26] Otherwise, nonrecognition of other governments involved need not affect matters. A few issued disclaimers, but most participants accepted unrecognized regimes (including some in nonrecognized states) as co-participants in the 1963 Partial Nuclear Test Ban Treaty, the 1968 Nuclear Nonproliferation Treaty, and the 1967 Outer Space Treaty.[27]

Like their interwar counterparts, Cold War era legal scholars followed and reported on state practice in this area more often than suggesting any ideas of their own. More discussed multilateral treaties after 1945 because they had the advantage of being able to draw on more state practice. The majority of Cold War era scholars accepted co-participation in multilateral conventions as consistent with nonrecognition, though a minority sought to differentiate between multilateral treaties implying and not implying recognition. Hyde and Oppenheim did so on the basis of whether the treaties required direct official contact between governments.[28] Chen combined the political–nonpolitical and direct contact–no direct contact distinctions to argue that only political treaties requiring direct contacts are inconsistent with nonrecognition.[29] Bot used the open convention–closed convention and contact–no contact distinctions to argue that only closed conventions requiring direct contacts are inconsistent with nonrecognition.[30] Others suggested, without clear definition, that some do involve recognition.[31]

The lengthy contentions between rival regimes brought up an additional problem in the Cold War era: the status of multilateral treaties signed by one faction but not accepted by the other. The PRC government maintained that it should not be regarded as automatically succeeding to all the UN-sponsored and other multilateral treaties signed by the ROC after 1947.[32] Other governments were willing to concede the point regarding multilateral treaties signed after October 1949, when the Communists gained control of most of the country.[33] Thus several governments notified the International Civil Aviation Organization (ICAO) secretariat that they did not accept as valid either the ROC denunciation of the ICAO Convention effective on 31 May 1951 or the ROC re-accession effective from 1 January 1954.[34]

By the end of the Cold War era governments were also facing the question of how to handle co-participation in multilateral treaties in cases of obligatory nonrecognition. UN Security Council-mandated nonrecognitions of the Smith regime in Rhodesia and of South African control of Namibia led to strict limitations on their participation in multilateral treaties. The International Court of Justice provided some guidelines in the Namibia Advisory Opinion in suggesting that states avoid allowing South Africa to sign or accede to any new multilateral treaties on behalf of Namibia and apply only those 'of a humanitarian character' benefiting the inhabitants.[35]

CO-PARTICIPATION IN INTERGOVERNMENTAL ORGANIZATIONS

The question of how co-participation in meetings of an intergovernmental organization related to individual governments' recognition decisions became acute after establishment of the League of Nations. Unlike the earlier public international unions, the League dealt with political questions. It also had a more intensive schedule of meetings; the Council assembled four (after 1929, three) times a year while the Assembly gathered each autumn. At the same time, participation did not depend on unanimous invitation. Territorial entities[36] could be admitted to membership by two-thirds of the Assembly, and delegations seated by a simple majority.[37] These features soon raised two related questions: whether admission of a territorial entity claiming to be a state to membership implied its recognition as a state by every other member, and whether seating of a particular delegation implied recognition of the regime sending the delegation by every other member.

There was some support for the view that admission or seating should mean recognition by all other members. The Commercial Tribunal of Luxembourg, though not the Luxembourg government, even adopted that view in 1934 following the USSR's admission.[38] Some legal scholars proposed using the League to make recognition decisions that would bind all member governments.[39] Initial precedents suggested different outcomes depending on whether status as a state or as a government was involved. The British and French opposed admitting the Baltic Republics in 1920 on the grounds that conditions were still 'too unsettled', but shifted position after deciding to recognize the new states. Yet at the same time they supported admitting Albania to League membership and seating an Albanian delegation in 1920 though they did not formally recognize the Albanian government until the following year.[40] Before long, however, admission to membership or seating of a delegation were regarded as incompatible with nonrecognition only by those voting in favour. Since governments were unwilling to give up their discretion to a multilateral body, this was the only way to reconcile the right of a new state or government accepted by the requisite majority of members to participate in the organization with the insistence of other governments on their right to determine their own bilateral relations.[41]

The United Nations took up where the League left off, with neither admission to membership nor seating of delegations requiring unanimous consent.[42] In 1949–50, controversies over who should represent

China inspired debate over criteria for seating delegations and the relation of such decisions to members' individual recognition policies. The Cuban government proposed that seating of delegates should depend on their government's having effective control of the state, enjoying general consent from the people, being able and willing to fulfil the purposes and obligations of the Charter, and respecting human rights.[43] Others objected that this would mean imposing some very subjective tests, and argued for making decisions depend solely on whether the sending regime was the effective ruler of the state.[44] Resolution 396(V) left the question open by declaring that 'whenever more than one authority claims to be the government entitled to represent a Member State in the United Nations and this question becomes the subject of controversy in the United Nations, the question should be considered in light of the Purposes and Principles of the Charter and the circumstances of each case'.[45] Resolution 396(V) also settled the question of how UN decisions affect individual recognition policies by declaring that 'the attitude adopted by the General Assembly or its Interim Committee shall not of itself affect the direct relations of individual Member States with the State concerned'.[46] This leaves governments free to decide whether supporting the seating of a delegation amounts to recognition,[47] supporting is compatible with continued nonrecognition of the sending government,[48] recognition means a state must support that government's delegates against seating any sent by rival factions,[49] or nonrecognition should be accompanied by efforts to challenge a government's right to send delegations.[50]

It also raised the question of how far an organization's decision to accept a new regime affects the policies of nonrecognizing states among the membership. Decisions by the competent plenary organs bind the members for the purposes and activities of the organization. For the state where the organization maintains its headquarters, those decisions also mean permitting delegations of regimes they do not recognize but which have been accepted by the organization to enter the country and enjoy the usual diplomatic status.[51] Though it is not always easy to determine where multilateral relations end and bilateral ones begin, the broader rules that 'technical', 'administrative', and 'humanitarian' relations can proceed despite nonrecognition mean the issue arises less often than it would if stricter rules about contact with unrecognized regimes prevailed.

In most instances, the seating of delegations from new regimes causes little controversy. Arguments are more likely when rival delegations appear. The longest-running controversy involved China, with the ROC delegates maintained in place after 1950 by a US-led majority, and PRC delegates seated in 1971. In 1960, the Congo situation provided a particularly confusing situation. The Congo was admitted to membership in September, but the General Assembly postponed seating a delegation because both President Kasavubu and Prime Minister Lumumba sent delegations. The USSR, Lumumba's leading foreign supporter, urged seating his delegation on the grounds that the Congolese *loi fondamentale* gave the prime minister wide power in foreign affairs. Majorities in the Credentials Committee and the full Assembly decided in favour of Kasavubu's delegation, invoking the formal grounds that a head of state's right to appoint delegates prevails over a head of government's.[52] After the Imam of Yemen died in September 1962, civil war broke out between supporters of his son and supporters of Brigadier El Sallal, with the latter soon controlling most of the country. In October each side's foreign minister sought to be seated in the General Assembly. After some debate, the Credentials Committee supported by 6 votes to 3 the Guinean motion to seat El Sallal's appointee, and the General Assembly followed suit.[53]

Though most Cold War and post-Cold War legal scholars accepted that abstaining or voting against admitting a particular state or seating a particular delegation was compatible with nonrecognition, some still argued that a vote in favour was not.[54] Several continued to propose that admission of a state or seating of a delegation should be regarded as recognition by all UN members, though they admitted that governments thought otherwise.[55] Yet some doubted that any such rule would cure the arbitrariness that seemed endemic to Cold War era recognition decisions.[56]

Separating seating of delegates from individual recognition policies permitted the development of some additional ways to vary expressions of political attitudes towards new regimes. Some indicated scepticism about the new Iraqi government in July–August 1958 by challenging its decision to appoint a new delegate to the Security Council.[57] China and others proposed in 1973 and 1974 that delegates from the Cambodian government-in-exile be seated in place of those sent by Lon Nol, but this was postponed in 1973 and defeated in favour of a resolution endorsing UN mediation efforts in 1974.[58] A number of governments acknowledged that the Vietnam-supported Heng Samrin government actually ruled Cambodia after 1979, but voted in favour of seating delegates sent by the rival 'Royal Government of National Unity' led by Prince Sihanouk (even though it included the Khmer Rouge) to express disapproval of Vietnamese involvement.[59] Feelings were strong enough that an Indian proposal to leave the Cambodian seat open was rejected.[60] Challenging the seating of delegates also became a way to indicate disapproval of a government clearly in control of its state.[61] This was done in the mild form of 'taking no decision' on credentials of the Kadar government of Hungary between 1956 and 1962[62] and the stronger form of refusing to accept credentials of South African delegates between 1974 and 1994.[63] Rhodesia was refused admission, and hence denied any place, until the formation of a black majority government in 1979.

A similar separation of seating delegates and recognizing governments for purposes of bilateral relations spread to other international organizations as well. Subsidiary organs of the General Assembly, such as UNCTAD, UNDP, and UNICEF, follow the General Assembly.[64] The more autonomous bodies like the specialized agencies may follow the General Assembly closely or seek separate confirming votes of their own memberships. The variety of practice was shown in decisions regarding ROC and PRC delegations in the 1950s and after 1971. Though a PRC delegation was seated at the 1950 Universal Postal Union Executive Board meeting, a mail ballot of the membership shifted representation back to the ROC after the General Assembly vote to continue seating the latter. After the General Assembly's decision to seat PRC delegates in 1971, another mail ballot brought UPU practice into line.[65] The World Meteorological Organization also polled members before inviting a PRC delegation.[66] The International Labour Organization Governing Board invited a Chinese delegation itself, rejecting a US proposal that there be a mail poll of the membership on the grounds that the ILO should be guided in such matters by 'the central political body of the international community'.[67] UNESCO and the World Health Organization reacted in similar fashion.[68] In the Food and Agriculture Organization, the Council first invited China to apply for membership. Later, this was revised into an invitation to 'resume membership' after the legal staff advised that the ROC decision to withdraw in 1951 was not really effective.[69] In both the World Bank and the IMF, formal notice of the General Assembly's decision was presented to the Executive Directors,[70] but actual PRC participation was deferred. In GATT, where the PRC had been an observer since 1965, the parties agreed to treat the PRC as representing China in line with long practice of following General Assembly decisions.[71]

Regional organizations make their own rules, but converged on similar practices. The Pan American Union resembled the nineteenth-century public international unions in having periodic conferences rather than a standing plenary body. This left some room for excluding participation by new regimes if they did not enjoy much recognition at the time the conference was convened. Thus the Governing Board decided against inviting Nicaragua to send a delegation to the next conference in 1947. The change to a new institutional structure as the Organization of American States altered the situation. The original OAS Charter, which retained the idea of periodic conferences, defined the members as 'All American States that ratify the present Charter',[72] thus avoiding the need for decisions on admission to membership. However, the 1967 amendments, which established standing plenary bodies, included a procedure requiring a two-thirds vote in both the new Permanent Council and the General Assembly to authorize membership.[73] Article 34 of the 1948 Charter, drawn up when Western Hemisphere states were in one of their effectivist moods, sought to prevent seating disputes as well by stipulating that 'All member states have the right to be represented at the Interamerican Conference.'[74] This was continued in 1967.[75] Though the original Charter included no provision on expulsion or suspension, the members added the possibility in a 1962 resolution defining adherence to Marxism–Leninism and extra-hemispheric powers as grounds for suspension of rights and providing for suspension by a two-thirds majority. This was promptly applied against Cuba. The 1990 amendments reflected the mood of the time by stipulating that participation could be suspended as part of efforts to encourage a return to democracy.[76]

Despite the large number of coups in Latin America, the OAS was not often roiled by controversies over participation. In most cases, the coup had succeeded and other members settled down to relations with the new regime before the next OAS meeting. Thus, delegates appointed by General Pinochet represented Chile at meetings of the special commission for restructuring the OAS held in November–December 1973[77] and the Tlatelolco Foreign Ministers' Conference in February 1974.[78] Yet other governments might stay away from a conference to avoid contacts with another. The Venezuelan government sent no one to the Second Special Interamerican Conference at Rio in November 1967 because it was then refusing to recognize the military junta ruling Brazil.[79]

Changes of government caused controversy at the Organization of African Unity on some occasions despite a 1965 resolution that members had a right to be represented. Delegates from a number of nonrecognizing governments walked out in protest after Ghanaian delegates were seated at the 1966 foreign ministers' meeting,[80] but the Liberian and Nigerian governments supported seating them though only formally recognizing the new government later.[81] In 1971 delegates from neither the ousted Obote nor the new Amin government of Uganda were admitted to the foreign ministers' meeting, while the Amin government avoided controversy by boycotting the June heads of state and government meeting.[82] The new Comoros regime was explicitly excluded from the summer 1978 meeting of the Council of Ministers because it had come to power with the help of mercenaries.[83]

Full membership and seating in plenary and other organs is not the only way new regimes can participate in multilateral relations. The UN and some other intergovernmental organizations also maintain an 'observer status' – permitting attendance and participation in debate but not voting – open to non-member states, other territorial entities, and 'national liberation movements'. Political groups claiming to be the legitimate government of a state have often sought, and occasionally received, such status. Such decisions clearly reflect the amount of support a particular group enjoys around the world. After the UN General Assembly terminated South Africa's mandate over South West Africa (Namibia) in 1966, it both established a UN Council for Namibia with rights to act for the territory within the UN and granted observer status to the South West Africa People's Organization as the 'authentic representative' of the Namibian people. The communist Provisional Revolutionary Government of South Vietnam sought observer status at the UN in 1973, which would have brought it to parity with the Saigon government, but this effort withered under US opposition. It was allowed to establish a liaison office in Geneva in January 1975 for the purposes of consulting on humanitarian aid being provided by UNICEF and the High Commissioner for Refugees and related matters, but not for ongoing contact with the other UN agencies in Geneva.[84] Only in May, after the communists had taken Saigon, was it granted observer status *vis-à-vis* the Economic and Social Council, and invited to send a delegation to the UN Conference on Women in Mexico City later in the year.[85]

Changes of government and nonrecognitions of particular regimes can pose problems for the operational activities of intergovernmental organizations. Where the activities involve technical matters or humanitarian relief, the contacts cause little controversy. This was shown quite early in UN history, in operations of the UN Relief and Rehabilitation Administration. It had some initial problems in establishing a relief program for Albania in June 1945 because only one of its 44 members – the USSR – then recognized the Hoxha government. Initial proposals that UNRRA make agreements with the commander of the Albanian National Army of Liberation were rejected as insufficient. Members accepted a UNRRA–Hoxha government agreement because Resolution 1 of the UNRRA Council referred to 'authorities exercising administrative control over an area' rather than to 'governments'.[86]

International secretariats generally try to maintain the continuity of activity, and deal with the effective ruler of a country unless clearly instructed otherwise by the member states. This can be seen with particular clarity in IMF dealings with South Vietnam in April–May 1975. Two days after Thieu resigned as president, but before the communists took Saigon, the South Vietnamese government asked the IMF for a hard currency loan of about $20 million against Vietnam's 'gold tranche' and cash for its $20 million of Special Drawing Rights. A majority of the Executive Directors supported honouring the requests if they could be confirmed; a minority wanted to refuse for fear of angering North Vietnam. The IMF was spared a serious internal argument when neither the old nor the new South Vietnamese government responded to the IMF cable requesting confirmation. In early May its spokesman said the IMF was still ready to honour the requests if the newly-victorious Provisional Revolutionary Government desired.[87]

Yet difficulties can arise if there is strong political competition between rival factions. After having its delegates seated in the UN General Assembly, the PRC insisted that all UN agencies end all contacts with and assistance to the ROC. In January 1972, the PRC protested about UNDP and Office of Technical Cooperation decisions to fulfil any commitments made before September 1971 on the grounds that they violated the General Assembly decision that ROC delegates be expelled. It also pressured the Secretariat into revoking the press credentials of two ROC journalists on the grounds that they worked for an official news agency, dropping all statistics on 'the ROC' or 'Taiwan' from UN compilations, and removing from UN Headquarters a plaque presented by the ROC. The Japanese were also persuaded to exclude ROC nationals from any training institutes in Japan receiving UN budget support.[88]

Obligatory nonrecognition also means strict limits on a new regime's participation in international organizations. Rhodesia was not admitted to any international organization as long as the Smith regime remained in power. The UN General Assembly established a Council for Namibia after revoking the South African mandate, and permitted it to represent Namibia in UN-sponsored conferences and the specialized agencies,[89] though did not admit Namibia to membership until after the establishment of a freely elected government in April 1990.

SUMMARY

A combination of relatively short nonrecognitions and infrequent multilateral dealings on political issues encouraged development of distinctive traditions in bilateral and multilateral diplomacy. The fact most nineteenth-century multilateral conferences and activity involved technical and administrative questions such as connecting telegraph systems, standardizing railway gauges, or coordinating quarantine regulations encouraged governments to regard co-participation in multilateral relations as separate from their bilateral recognition policies. This impulse was strengthened as multilateral treaties became open rather than closed conventions and intergovernmental organizations made decisions on participation by majority vote.

The few hesitations about dealing with political issues in the interwar era soon eroded, and governments were prepared to separate just about every multilateral activity from recognition. The only exceptions involved efforts to express support or hostility by favouring or opposing a particular regime's participation in some multilateral conference or treaty. Yet these were aimed less at affecting multilateral relations than at trying to show that a particular new regime did or did not command wide support or acceptance among the other governments of the world.

Though recognition policies marginally affect multilateral relations, multilateral relations affect recognition policies in significant though unobtrusive ways. Multilateral conferences and intergovernmental organizations provide channels through which nonrecognizing governments and new regimes can maintain informal contact. Their existence thus reinforces the interwar and Cold War era understanding that contact between diplomats in third countries does not disturb nonrecognition, and thereby governments' ability to indulge in lengthy nonrecognitions while simultaneously accommodating to the facts of actual rule.

Multilateral treaties provide an alternative for organizing many aspects of inter-state and inter-government relations. Increasingly in the twentieth century, multilateral treaties are the source of the rules governments apply in the conduct of bilateral relations. For instance, the GATT provides participating states with a multilateral answer to the basic questions of organizing international trade; they need not rely on bilateral commerce, friendship, and navigation treaties to enjoy most-favoured-nation treatment or access to each others' markets. As the trade example implies, the substitution is far from complete, but in the areas where multilateral institutions prevail, governments can address a host of important issues without raising questions about recognition of a particular regime. Contrary to the hopes of some legal scholars, this alternative channel has also given governments greater leeway to indulge in politically motivated nonrecognition policies by providing another way they could maintain the contacts needed for cooperation in technical realms.

9 Recognition in Domestic Administration and Law

While most relevant to inter-government relations, the legal status of foreign regimes has some implications for the conduct of internal administration and the disposition of lawsuits by national courts. Whether a regime is recognized as the government of its country can affect cooperative activity among counterpart government agencies, taking cognizance of official acts or certificates, and lawsuits that involve a foreign regime as party or private activities proceeding under its law. This chapter will examine three broad sets of activity: administrative cooperation, international trade, and lawsuits before domestic courts.

Most of the problems discussed in this chapter arise because governments frequently withhold recognition for reasons unrelated to a new regime's lack of ability to rule effectively. In these instances, particularly if the nonrecognition persists for a long time, national administrative agencies and courts have had to balance the foreign policy concerns inspiring nonrecognition with the functional needs to maintain administrative contacts and protect private rights.[1] Though the current trend towards de-emphasizing or abandoning recognition of governments is reducing the number of instances when such balancing is needed, the need to find a balance will never be eliminated entirely for two reasons: the existence of civil wars in which rival factions each rule different parts of the state while the conflict continues, and the possibility that treaty obligations, new developments of legal doctrine regarding criteria for recognition, or binding decisions of international organizations will require nonrecognition of a particular regime. The civil war situations could be handled by building on the nineteenth-century rules about relations with 'local *de facto* governments'; mandated nonrecognition would require more explicit attention to striking a reasonable balance.

ADMINISTRATIVE CONTACTS

The growth of multilateral relations in various 'technical' realms was the most visible part of a wider practice of contacts between counterpart administrative agencies in different countries. These hardly existed in the nineteenth century, but grew in importance and intensity through the twentieth. Because they addressed various shared concerns relating more to the well-being of citizens rather than the policies of state, governments were willing to continue such contacts with any regime that governed territory with enough regularity and stability to have counterpart agencies. This was shown with particular clarity during the long US nonrecognition of the Soviet government in 1917–33. US agencies included Soviet ones on their mailing lists of counterparts receiving routine notices, Soviet trademarks were registered, Soviet government-employed agronomists and zoologists were allowed to visit the US, and cooperation in public health matters continued.[2] The long nonrecognitions of the Cold War era meant continuation and elaboration of such contacts.

Establishing that government agencies should accept certificates relating to civil status or ownership of property issued by foreign counterparts regardless of recognition took somewhat longer. The US government initially accepted marriage certificates and other documents signed by Soviet officials only when their status as officials was certified by the Tsarist-appointed consuls still received by the USA.[3] In 1929 the Civil Tribunal of Liège upheld the city registrar of marriage's refusal to accept as valid a divorce notice attested by the Odessa city registrar.[4] Authorities in Berne were reluctant to accept Soviet notorization of a declaration renouncing an inheritance, though avoided the issue by rejecting it on the grounds that it was dated 1907 but notorized only in 1922.[5] In 1936 the Cámara Federal of Rosario decided that Argentine officials had acted correctly in refusing to accept Soviet attestations of nationality, but permitted naturalization when applicants could prove by other means that they were not already Argentine citizens.[6]

By the end of the interwar period, there were no hesitations in accepting certification of civil status (such as birth, marriage, divorce, and death) or of private transactions when issued by an officer of an effective government. This change paralleled national courts' greater readiness to accept any effective government as capable of making laws governing the civil status, daily life, and ordinary transactions of the population.[7]

Direct inter-agency cooperation was another matter. Even after 1945 some governments imposed limits on administrative contacts. In 1961, the French government concluded that inter-agency dealings should be restricted to 'urgent matters of a strictly administrative character'.[8] Administrative cooperation dependent on having diplomatic relations or a bilateral treaty in place was much more likely to be affected by nonrecognition because it was seen as more intimately related to matters of public policy. Thus, for example, the PRC Ministry of Justice denied a US court's 1957 request for help in securing evidence on the grounds that there was no treaty on judicial assistance in force between the two countries.[9] Many governments were reluctant to accept travel documents issued by an unrecognized regime. At least in the early 1980s British immigration rules permitted refusing entry to anyone using a passport or travel document issued by an unrecognized regime.[10] They might be admitted, however, on the basis of accepting the documents as evidence of identity if they could be regarded as nationals of a recognized state with a recognized government.[11]

The effect of nonrecognition on administrative cooperation could vary depending on whether cooperation required face-to-face meetings, activity followed from a previously-established cooperative arrangement, or the nonrecognition was motivated by political concerns rather than the new regime's lack of effective control. All of these possibilities were reflected in the 1962 version of the US State Department's standing instructions to missions abroad:

> Immediately upon the interruption of relations . . . representatives of other civilian agencies of the United States government are permitted to continue routine functions on an informal basis. However, no new programs may be initiated during the period when relations are suspended. If in his judgment circumstances warrant, the chief of mission of the United States may instruct personnel of civilian agencies and of armed services missions to suspend all contact with the foreign government pending instructions.[12]

The range of administrative contact was likely to be narrower when nonrecognition was mandated by an international organization rather than decided unilaterally. In 1971, the International Court of Justice was asked for an advisory opinion outlining how states should implement the 1970 decision[13] that UN member states must not recognize continuing South African rule over Namibia. It concluded that 'active intergovernmental cooperation' with South African authorities regarding Namibia should be avoided, but specifically urged application of multilateral treaties when nonapplication would 'adversely affect the people of Namibia', and acceptance of South African-issued certificates of civil status and other acts 'which can be ignored only to the detriment of the inhabitants'.[14] The European Court of Justice took the concerted nonrecognition of the 'Turkish Republic of Northern Cyprus'[15] as requiring that EU members accept only certificates of origin issued by officials of the Republic of Cyprus because the closeness of administrative cooperation involved meant that accepting them from TRNC-appointed officials (even if purporting to act for the 'Cyprus Customs Authorities' rather than the TRNC) would be inconsistent with nonrecognition.[16]

LAWSUITS

National courts have considered two sets of questions when hearing lawsuits involving unrecognized regimes or their acts. The first is how to determine whether a particular regime is or is not a government for the matter at hand. This raises questions of the extent to which courts must accept executive branch decisions on recognition and nonrecognition as determining a regime's status, and of the rules of evidence to be applied if they are not obliged to follow the executive branch. The second is how to decide the particular matter. The lawsuits that arise can be divided into four broad categories: (a) those initiated by an unrecognized regime, (b) those initiated by another party against an unrecognized regime, (c) those involving an unrecognized regime's claims to its state's property located within the court's jurisdiction, and (d) those involving a private dispute that cannot be resolved without reference to laws or administrative actions of an unrecognized regime.

There have been strong divergences among national legal systems in this area because the results depend not only on international law, but also on national constitutional doctrines defining the relation of courts to the executive branch, national law, and national traditions of interpreting the rules of private international law (conflict of laws, as it is more generally known today). Three broad families of legal practice have had the most influence internationally in this field: the civil law traditions of Western Europe, the common law traditions of the United Kingdom, and the somewhat different common law traditions of the United States.

Legal scholars' writings on these issues have tended to fall into one of two types: brief summary discussions of the various effects of recognition for national courts or more extended discussions following, commenting on, and urging particular further developments of legal doctrine in particular states. National courts have usually led in these areas, so this discussion will focus mainly on their decisions.

Determining Who is a Government

Both civil law and common law systems start from the common presupposition that recognition is a foreign policy decision within the authority of the executive branch. The foreign ministry is the authoritative source of information about the government's policy towards a particular foreign regime[17] and a significant source of information about the extent to which a particular foreign regime controls and seems likely to continue controlling its state.

Courts in both types of legal system have also developed mechanisms for securing statements of executive branch views on these questions. In civil law states, guidance comes in an *avis* from the foreign ministry. In principle, judges are supposed to follow executive guidance but they have considerable authority to interpret the *avis* and weigh its value as evidence.[18] In United Kingdom and Commonwealth common law, guidance is supplied by a Foreign Office certificate.[19] The practice of seeking certificates arose in the UK during the early nineteenth century, and judges had come to regard them as conclusive on both the government's own policy and the political situation abroad by the early 1920s.[20] This did not end judicial consideration of the matter, however, because many certificates were vague and required considerable interpretation. In the USA, executive branch guidance can take the form of a State Department statement, an *amicus curae* brief, or executive branch appearance as an intervenor.[21] Both UK and US courts continue to accept the basic premise that the judiciary should not contradict executive policy, but base this on very different reasoning. In the US judicial deference rests on the constitutional doctrine of separation of powers, whereas in the UK and Commonwealth states it rests on the judge-made doctrine that courts and executive should 'speak with one voice'[22] on recognition matters. However, the courts do assert their own authority within the sphere of law application.[23]

The shift towards de-emphasizing or abandoning formal recognition of governments, and the consequent avoidance of the term 'recognition' in any executive certificate or statement provided to courts in common law states, forced a general reconsideration of how courts should determine who governs a particular foreign state. As several scholars have concluded, the change gives the courts greater independence from executive guidance.[24] The executive still provides its views when asked, and often explains either its policy or its preferences in a particular case, but the net result has been to separate determination of who is a government for purposes of international relations and foreign policy from determination of who provides effective administration for purposes of domestic law and conflict of laws issues.[25] The change also puts decisions about each in the hands of different decision-makers. Though courts still work to avoid direct conflict with executive policy,[26] the change increases the likelihood that an unrecognized regime will be accepted as an effective administrator for private law questions even when the executive branch refuses it recognition.[27]

Initiation of Lawsuits

In the nineteenth century most unrecognized governments did not last long enough to initiate lawsuits, so the question seldom arose. Edeson argues that the doctrine that unrecognized governments could not initiate lawsuits was well established in England by 1815, and '*de facto* recognition' was invented as a way for the new Latin American republics and their supporters to get around the known hostility of Lord Eldon.[28] Verhoeven concludes that the doctrine was established in Europe during the 1890s, when it was applied first by French courts and then by courts in other countries.[29] It remains the general consensus among legal scholars and national judges that an unrecognized government does not have a right to sue in the courts of a nonrecognizing state.

Though they have no right to sue, a court might permit an unrecognized regime to sue, particularly when executive branch statements or actions indicate no objection.[30] Japanese courts have entertained suits by the ROC since Japanese recognition of the PRC in 1972 if the matter dealt with property claims or other economic activity. This led the German scholar Heuser to conclude that when a government permits an unrecognized regime to participate in economic activity the courts of that country must permit it to sue over matters related to that activity.[31] US courts have permitted suits by corporations owned by unrecognized regimes.[32] In civil law states, unrecognized regimes have occasionally been allowed to sue on 'private law' matters.[33] The US government pre-empted challenges to the

ROC's right to sue after shifting recognition to the PRC by establishing statutory provisions for it in the Taiwan Relations Act of 1979.[34]

The shift to de-emphasizing or abandoning formal recognition separated judges' decisions from foreign policy much more clearly. This did not mean that courts suddenly had an easier time appreciating the situation regarding a particular regime. The executive's comments on the extent of dealings with a new regime could still require careful interpretation, and resort to traditional doctrines about which acts amount to tacit recognition in assessing whether executive branch dealings with a new regime indicate full government-to-government relations. A particular foreign situation might be confused enough to require assistance from expert witnesses or use of media reports.[35]

Immunity from Lawsuits

Unlike allowing initiation of lawsuits, which is a matter of comity rather than strict obligation, immunity from lawsuits and related measures of execution is a clear right of states and their governments under international law. The extent of those immunities has changed considerably, however, because of the more general shift from nineteenth-century doctrines of 'absolute immunity' covering every sort of government act to contemporary doctrines of 'restricted immunity' under which states and governments can be sued over the wide variety of commercial activities. Thus even a recognized government enjoys less immunity from suit today than a century ago; but the question remains whether an unrecognized regime should also enjoy the same immunity.

Despite the persistence of states and the doctrine of state continuity, the weight of scholarly opinion in the nineteenth century and much of the interwar period favoured allowing only recognized governments immunity from suit. Advocates of extending immunity to any new regime that is a 'general government' controlling all or most of its state became more numerous.[36] Here, too, the legal scholars were following changes in state practice. In most civil law states, the courts were according immunity in the interwar period. French courts were the major exception; they made the shift only in 1971.[37] A US court accorded the Soviet government immunity in 1923.[38] UK and Commonwealth courts were slower to adopt the rule. British courts were prepared to accord immunity to the Nationalist government of Spain because it was recognized '*de facto*' by the British government,[39] but generally denied immunity to the unrecognized.[40]

Since the 1970s, national courts' decisions on immunity have been affected by two developments: de-emphasis or abandonment of formal recognition of governments and increasing regulation of immunity by statute in common law states.[41] De-emphasis or abandonment of recognition means leaving the decision about immunity to the courts. The recent British, Canadian, and US statutes encourage according immunity to unrecognized regimes because they define the term 'foreign state' without reference to recognition of the government. The courts are further encouraged to apply the statutes using the normal rules of evidence and statutory interpretation rather than seeking executive guidance. At the same time, the statutes are likely to decrease the number of attempted suits against unrecognized regimes because of rules making it difficult to serve writs to or otherwise establish jurisdiction over a foreign government.[42]

Possession of State Property Located within the Court's Jurisdiction

Local law protects their rights wherever foreign states or governments are permitted to own real estate and other forms of property. Thus in leasing out the former Cambodian embassy in 1986, the Australian government included a provision that the lease could be broken with 28 days' notice in the event of a resumption of diplomatic relations with that country.[43] Similarly, British courts ordered some $2 million in Somalian funds put into escrow in 1991 because there was no government to whom they could be paid.[44] The US Protection of Diplomats Act, which covers diplomatic premises as well as personnel, defines a foreign government as 'the government of a foreign country, irrespective of recognition by the United States'.[45]

There is more controversy about whether an unrecognized regime should be allowed possession of such state property. Legal scholars and courts alike have generally agreed that state property should be turned over only to recognized governments. In situations where rival regimes claim to rule, courts in the UK and Commonwealth states using the distinction have usually given preference to the faction recognized as the *de jure* government. Courts in other states have reached the same result by differentiating between the recognized government and unrecognized rivals.[46] US law stipulates that the Federal Reserve Bank and any federally-insured private bank should turn over funds held for the account of a foreign state only to persons certified by the Secretary of State as having the right to act for that state.[47] Use of diplomatic and consular premises involves a partial exception. Under long-established diplomatic usage, embassies and consular staffs can continue to use their state's diplomatic premises even if the new government is not recognized,[48] as long as the receiving government tolerates their presence.[49] Here, too, a recognized government will prevail over unrecognized rivals and temporarily empty premises must be protected until there is again a diplomatic staff permitted to use them.[50]

Rival factions have tried to use lawsuits in other countries to contend for possession of state property located abroad. British courts declined to get involved in Nationalist–Republican disputes about ship requisitions in the case of *The Arantzazu Mendi.*[51] Yet Norwegian courts upheld the right of the Spanish Republicans to Spanish property in Oslo.[52] Foreign courts may be particularly open to such suits if the executive branch has a clear preference among the factions. In 1988 US courts accepted suits initiated by supporters of deposed Panamanian President Delvalle, still recognized as president by the US government, and ruled that only Ambassador Sosa, a Delvalle supporter, had authority to draw on Panama's accounts in US banks.[53] US authorities also assisted Sosa's efforts to have all money owed to Panama by companies or individuals in the US paid into special accounts established at the Federal Reserve Bank of New York.[54]

Rival factions with a secure territorial base can acquire property and have certain ownership rights protected even against the recognized government of their state. In assigning ownership of Chinese state property in 1972, the Japanese government distinguished between properties used for sovereign and representative functions and those used for commercial or cultural purposes. All of the former were turned over to the PRC regardless of when acquired; the ROC was permitted to retain any of the latter it acquired after 1952.[55] PRC commentators criticized this,[56] but other governments have adopted similar decisions. The US State Department was unable to persuade Congress to invalidate the ROC's last-minute transfers of the Chinese embassy, procurement and services mission office, and consulates to already established private US–ROC friendship groups, but fully supported the PRC's suits to secure possession.[57] At the same time, the US government stated its view that financial assets acquired by the ROC after 1949 should not be transferred as they had been 'earned by the people of Taiwan' and should accrue to them.[58] Provisions protecting the ROC's right to hold property acquired between 1949 and 1979 and after 1979 were also included in the Taiwan Relations Act.[59]

Giving Legal Effects to Laws and Administrative Acts

By far the largest part of jurisprudence relating to unrecognized regimes involves decisions on whether and how far to give effect to their laws and administrative acts. As with immunity from suit, decisions on these points are affected by other legal rules. On these matters, recognition or nonrecognition serves as a particular qualification to the operation of normal conflict-of-laws rules about when and how far courts should give effect to a foreign state's laws and acts. Two distinctions are particularly important here: between 'public law' and 'private law', and between domestic and extraterritorial effect laws and other government acts.

As in other areas, there is a paucity of nineteenth-century jurisprudence. Some of the few indications suggested that private law acts having effect within the territory actually ruled by a particular faction should be given effect. US courts, which had to face the question after the American Civil War, generally favoured giving effect to private law acts while nullifying public law ones.[60] Similarly, in the Dreyfus Case, an arbitral panel based its award on accepting the acts of an effective but unrecognized regime.[61]

In much interwar practice, recognition of a foreign authority was regarded as necessary for courts to give any effect to laws and administrative acts – even those involving private law matters and affecting persons, property, or transactions within the territory controlled by the unrecognized regime. This was most clear in Britain after the Court of Appeal ruled in *Luther* v. *Sagor* that giving effect to Soviet decrees depended on recognition. However, it was true of French jurisprudence as well.[62] German courts gave effect to Bolshevik acts before 1922, but their judgments do not make clear whether they based this on their existence or assumed that the recognition accorded by the Treaty of Brest-Litovsk still applied.[63] Dutch and US courts did give effect to some Soviet acts involving property located in the USSR despite nonrecognition.[64] If the property confiscated was outside Soviet territory such acts were not given effect until the Soviet government was recognized.[65]

The trend towards giving effect to laws and actions of unrecognized governments relating to private business transactions or the day-today life of persons within their territory gathered momentum after 1945. Japanese courts began inquiring into the effectiveness of a foreign administration rather than relying on recognition in order to deal with a large number of cases involving acts of the two Korean states and the two rival Chinese governments.[66] Dutch and Swiss courts also continued to apply conflict-of-law rules and inquire only into whether a regime held control.[67] French and Italian courts began applying the private law acts in the mid-1970s.[68] US courts reached very mixed results, sometimes giving effect to and sometimes denying effect to acts of unrecognized regimes.[69]

British scholars had been urging similar changes in their country for some time[70] when UK courts began moving in the direction of giving effect to private law acts of unrecognized regimes in the *Carl Zeiss* and *Hesperides Hotels* cases.[71] Though they both involved an unrecognized state, Lord Denning's preference in *Hesperides Hotels* for giving effect to 'the laws which regulate the day to day affairs of people' was taken up by other judges.[72] Though British decisions in cases involving the Ian Smith regime in Rhodesia have been cited in arguments about how far courts should give effect to acts of unrecognized regimes,[73] Allott cautions that they also involved matters of British colonial law so have limited relevance for general discussions of nonrecognition.[74] Both the British government's abandonment of formal recognition in 1980 and recent statutes encouraged the courts to consider whether a regime exercised administrative control and whether its acts should be enforceable in the UK under normal conflict-of-laws rules.[75] The UK Foreign Corporations Act, 1991, settled one question by allowing treatment of foreign companies as legal persons if they are incorporated under a definite corporation law administered through 'a settled court system'. The courts are left to determine this on their own, not through requesting executive certificates.[76]

By the early 1990s, the preponderance of national jurisprudence agreed with the District Court of Kyoto, which stated in 1956 that 'private international law is designed to find the most appropriate law . . . and is not concerned with adjusting the mutual relationship of sovereigns. Therefore, foreign law applied under private international law principles should not be limited to the law only of a recognized State or Government; effectiveness of foreign law should not depend on recognition.'[77]

Recognition still affects the extent to which courts give effect to public law acts because they are more directly linked to acknowledgement of sovereignty. Though dealing with an unrecognized state, the US court's judgment in *Carl Zeiss Stiftung* v. *V.E.B. Carl Zeiss* suggested that public law acts of unrecognized regimes would not be given effect in the USA.[78] British courts suggested the same in 1982.[79] However, nonrecognition is not the only reason for refusing to give effect to the public (or even private) law acts of a foreign regime. The conflict-of-laws doctrines of most national legal systems permit courts to deny effect to foreign laws and actions violating the local principles of public policy. In some legal systems, the courts can also refuse to give effect to acts violating international law. Most legal systems also follow the rule that local courts will not enforce foreign public law, including criminal statutes and tax laws.

There is some evidence that courts would be more rigorous in denying effect to acts of regimes refused recognition because of a mandate from the UN Security Council under Chapter VI of the Charter or other international legal obligation. Though there has been no clear case of mandated nonrecognition of a new government, court decisions relating to the South African 'homelands'[80] and Northern Cyprus[81] suggest a strict approach. Though the Namibia Advisory Opinion[82] took care to separate private law acts, it did make clear that obligatory nonrecognition required governments to limit their application of the public law acts of the target regime.[83]

INTERNATIONAL TRADE

International trade is not the only sort of cross-border activity affected by relations between governments, but it is one of the most prominent and long-standing. It may serve, then, as an example of how nonrecognition can affect private transactions as well as indicating how governments handle their 'commercial' relations with unrecognized regimes. In the nineteenth century, international trade was almost exclusively in the hands of private firms, so the actual conduct of trade did not involve inter-government contacts. Commercial treaties and consular relations provided a framework within which trade occurred, and they were usually continued even during periods of nonrecognition. Some governments regarded nonrecognition as preventing the conclusion of a new or revised trade treaty, but others were willing to conclude temporary trade arrangements like the Franco-Portuguese 'modus vivendi' of 1911.[84] In all, the tradition that trade is not affected by nonrecognition (though it might be disrupted by continuing disorder) was strong.

Questions of recognition or nonrecognition appeared more relevant to trade when governments were directly involved. Beginning just before the turn of the century, but receiving considerable impetus from the spread of socialist, nationalist and Leninist ideas after 1917, governments began gathering international trade into their own hands. In the early interwar period, eagerness for recognition inspired the Soviets to claim that the conclusion of any sort of trade agreement was an act of recognition. This led the British, Dutch and Italian governments to defer the making of any sort of commercial treaty until after recognition.[85] Later they dropped this insistence. This enabled the Swiss to reverse the sequence, consenting to a commercial treaty in 1941, but not recognizing until 1946.[86] It also enabled the US to tolerate the presence of trade missions well before recognition in 1933.

Nonrecognition did not necessarily mean interruption of all trade transactions though it did sometimes mean imposition of special rules. French regulations about trading with the USSR in 1920 provided that (1) trade was not prohibited, (2) traders acted at their own risk because the government could not provide either diplomatic or consular assistance, (3) goods en route to or from Russia would be treated according to the general trade laws and regulations, (4) export of arms and munitions to Russia was banned, and (5) trade via the Black Sea would be under the control of Allied naval authorities.[87] The failure of trade treaty negotiations in 1924 did not discourage Dutch firms involved in Soviet trade, and the government left them to their own devices.[88] The various interruptions of trade that occurred, such as the reciprocal Soviet–Swiss boycotts of 1923–7,[89] were signs of special hostility or the result of particular disputes, not a general practice regarding unrecognized governments.

In the Cold War era, the prevalence and importance of market economy states in international trade meant that they defined the general rules. State trading came to be treated as 'non-sovereign' or 'commercial' activity governed by norms very similar to those prevailing among private firms. The Soviets resisted these developments, but ended up accepting them as part of the price for resuming broader East–West trade in the 1970s.[90] Thus trade transactions were separated from recognition and other political matters unless the governments involved specifically chose otherwise. As the Australian foreign minister put it in 1968, 'Nonrecognition does not, of course, in itself prevent trade being carried on by other agencies or by individuals with the countries concerned.'[91] Governments even let their state trading entities deal with counterpart agencies of unrecognized governments.[92] The Egyptian government exchanged 'commercial bureaus' with the PRC in August 1955, a year before extending recognition.[93] The French sent an 'economic mission' in 1956 when Franco-Chinese trade resumed, but did not recognize until 1964.[94] The Australians were reluctant to make trade agreements with the PRC (or other unrecognized regimes),[95] while the governments of Chile, Belgium, France, Japan, Italy, and West Germany allowed trade to resume in 1952 within the framework of an agreement between private firms and the Chinese.[96] The Japanese were sufficiently interested in trade to accommodate a number of Chinese political demands in order to get it.[97]

Unless they have accepted particular obligations in a treaty or must respect a trade embargo declared under Chapter VII of the UN Charter, governments are at liberty to permit or restrict trade with states ruled by regimes they do not recognize. Italian refusal to shift negotiations from a 'private' to an intergovernmental level limited the early growth of trade with the PRC.[98] Western European trade with China also got caught up in arguments with the more restrictive-minded US about how much trade in what goods should occur. After Pinochet's coup in 1973 Cuba cut off trade to Chile, including shipments of sugar for which payment had already been received.[99] Improving relations can be reflected in trade, as with improvements in Sino-US relations in 1972–3.

SUMMARY

The development of administrative contacts with agencies of unrecognized regimes and of trade with private or state firms in states ruled by unrecognized governments reflected the division between 'public' or 'sovereign' and 'private' or 'routine' activities developed in bilateral relations. In both areas governments were able to build on nineteenth-century traditions separating these from the flow of foreign policy, though trade issues were complicated for a time during the interwar era by the Soviet government's decision to monopolize foreign trade. Here as in other areas, governments had to decide how to treat a relatively new type of governmental activity.[100]

Settling questions of how to treat unrecognized regimes and their laws or acts in national courts took longer. Many of the issues raised questions of sovereignty and so carried considerable political symbolism. Courts in all countries began by treading carefully and following executive suggestions about who constituted a government. Yet they soon began to accept certain possibilities: that any effective government should enjoy immunity from suit, that it should be able to sue when its interests were directly affected by private activity, and that private law acts should be given effect under ordinary conflict-of-laws rules. The second and third were clearly elaborations of the public–private distinction already established in other parts of legal doctrine on recognition. The first was not, but seemed to derive fairly directly from the independence of other states and the mutual respect to be granted to any effective ruler of territory. Giving effect, particularly extraterritorial effect, to public acts such as confiscations of property and granting possession of state property, was far more closely tied to sovereignty and continued to be affected by recognition.

The speed with which national courts accommodated to these new developments depended on two things, whether they functioned in a common or a civil law system and whether the government of their country engaged in or avoided lengthy nonrecognitions. On the whole, civil law systems accepted giving effect to administrative and private law acts more quickly than did common law systems. Yet in each the pioneers in giving effect – the US and Swiss courts – operated in states where the executive engaged in lengthy nonrecognitions of the Soviet government and courts had to find ways to accommodate both politics and reality. Courts in other states had fewer occasions for using those skills because their governments were more effectivist in their recognition policies.

Administrative contacts and trade were hardly affected by the shift towards de-emphasizing or abandoning formal recognition of governments, but the relations between courts and the executive branch were affected significantly. Courts can no longer rely on recognition to determine a regime's status; they have had to shift focus to the effectiveness of administration. They still solicit and receive executive guidance. But most executive branch statements now avoid discussing recognition and focus instead on the extent of inter-government relations with a new regime, the general political situation in a foreign state, or stating whether there are international legal or national policy reasons the court should take into account while considering its decision.

10 Political Uses of Recognition

International law encourages, but does not require, governments to follow a strictly effectivist recognition policy. The resulting discretion in the timing and reasons for them creates the possibility of using recognition decisions for political purposes. Most legal scholars have paid some attention to this activity, mainly to condemn it as introducing elements of arbitrariness that do not belong in a well-ordered recognition process. Students of the foreign policy or the expansionist impulses of individual states have paid more attention, but they generally focus on one particular government's activity rather than on comparison across governments or historical eras.

The political goals sought through recognition policy can be divided into two main types: efforts to promote global or regional standards for accession to power, conduct afterwards, or both; and efforts to express individual opinion or secure unilateral advantages. In some instances, the two sorts of efforts overlap. This ought not to be surprising; governments – particularly those of great powers – seek to establish an international order that is conducive to maintenance of their domestic beliefs and ways of life.[1] The real difficulties occur when an effort to build global or regional consensus on some set of values is exploited for unilateral advantage by one of the partners or by an outside state. Then, as manifest in both US use of Central American constitutional legitimism and Soviet application of the Brezhnev Doctrine, the wider effort is likely to be undermined as governments object to the unilateral advantage-seeking.

In the abstract, any recognition policy can be viewed as 'politically motivated'. A strictly effectivist policy endorses and perpetuates a particular understanding of international order as based on the mutual coexistence of independent states with full discretion in the choice and revision of their domestic arrangements. Clearly, governments do gain from having such an order accepted as the norm. Here, however, the 'political uses' of recognition to be analysed are those occasions when a government uses a non-effectivist policy to secure some unilateral end. These are most likely to appear in premature recognition of a new regime, prolonged nonrecognition of a new regime that has demonstrated clear control over its state, and prolonged recognition of a defunct government. The political goals sought with such policies can take any of three forms: (1) expressing approval or disapproval of a particular new regime or its methods of taking power, (2) influencing the new regime's policies by trading recognition for concessions, and (3) affecting the choice of government in another state by encouraging or discouraging the new regime or different factions in an ongoing civil war.

The first form is simple: a government need only grant or withhold recognition outside the parameters of an effectivist policy. No extended interaction with the target regime is required, and very little in the way of material action – the dispatch or withdrawal of diplomatic representatives, some amount of public explanation of the policy, and perhaps urging or opposing the target's inclusion in multilateral activity. The second and third forms are more complicated because their success depends on more than the desire of the goal-seeking government. They involve interaction between the goal-seeking government and the target regime carried out before a more or less attentive and potentially mobilizable set of third government spectators, all operating in a context defined by the contemporaneous shape of the international system. This interaction means that efforts to gain concessions or to influence the choice of government are usually accompanied by other measures, such as military involvement in a foreign civil war, providing or denying financial assistance, and allowing or discouraging private contacts.

EXPRESSING APPROVAL OR DISAPPROVAL

Recognition or nonrecognition can be used to express an opinion of the new regime without seeking any influence on its future, policies, or actions. The linking of nonrecognition with disapproval is natural since extended nonrecognition of an effective government is unusual. The linkage was even stronger and came to mind more naturally after politically motivated nonrecognition became common in the interwar and Cold War eras. Once evoked, the link became very strong, even in the minds of people in countries where the government usually followed an effectivist recognition policy. Thus the British and Dutch, as well as the Australian and US governments cited the need to break the link between recognition and approval as one of the reasons for de-emphasizing or dispensing with recognition of governments in the 1970s and 1980s.[2]

Approval is most clearly conveyed through hasty or even premature recognition. Since the penalties for premature recognition are usually weak, it is an inexpensive and relatively safe policy. It may even yield benefits if the regime thus recognized succeeds in taking and holding power. Yet the main significance of hasty or premature recognition is not in the statement itself, but in the material benefits that can be conveyed in bilateral relations or internal law and administration.

Governments generally avoided premature recognition in the nineteenth century. Dona Maria's eventual triumph in Portugal makes Russian and United States recognitions of Dom Miguel's government seem premature in retrospect, but at the time Dona Maria's supporters controlled only one offshore island and appeared unlikely to gain additional ground.[3] The British, French and US governments did not rush to recognize any of the liberal governments established in 1848 although their sympathies were clear. Outside governments also based recognition on control during the three-sided struggle among absolute monarchists, constitutional monarchists, and republicans in Spain in the late 1860s and early 1870s.

Even on loose definitions of 'control over most of the state', there were many cases of premature recognition in the interwar period. Most were linked to interventions in foreign civil wars, but a few were simply statements of opinion. Some of these were occasioned by the need to have some negotiating partner despite ongoing turmoil in China. On a strictly effectivist rule, no faction was the government of all of China between World War I and 1928. The Soviets followed a two-prong policy of recognizing whoever ruled in the Beijing area as government of China but supplying far more support to the Kuomintang (KMT) in the south, and promoting a political alliance between the KMT and the Chinese Communists. The British, Japanese, and US governments were far more passive, sometimes not recognizing anyone as the government and establishing extensive relations with the Kuomintang only after its armies entered Beijing in 1928.[4]

The most famous interwar instances of premature recognition involved Franco's Nationalists in Spain, who began their revolt in July 1936 but did not rule most of the country until early 1939. The governments of El Salvador and Guatemala were the first to recognize, doing so on 10 November 1936. The Nicaraguan government recognized on the 27th, giving 'solidarity with Guatemala and El Salvador against communism' as its reason.[5] The Albanian government, by then a virtual Italian protectorate, recognized on the 26th.[6] Unlike the German and Italian recognitions on the 17th, which were linked to active intervention, these governments' actions were symbolic only.

A few of the instances when rival regimes claimed to rule the same state inspired premature recognitions during the Cold War period. Recognition of any government in the Congo right after Kasavubu and Lumumba split would have been premature, but the UN General Assembly majority's decision to back Kasavubu against Lumumba put supporters of the latter – including the Soviet, Chinese, Czech, Hungarian, Polish, North Vietnamese, North Korean, Egyptian, Malian, Guinean, Indonesian, Cuban, East German, and Yugoslav governments – at a disadvantage in justifying their recognition.[7] Those regarding Vietnam as divided into two states between 1954 and 1975 would also count the Hungarian, Czech, Mongolian, Chinese, and Egyptian decision to recognize the Viet Cong's 'Provisional Revolutionary Government of South Vietnam' in 1969 as quite premature.[8] Even the sympathetic Indians waited until the Viet Cong took Saigon in 1975.[9] Proclamation of the Khmer Republic by Marshal Lon Nol in 1970 and formation of a 'Cambodian Royal Government of National Unity' (GRUNK, from its name in French) inspired hasty endorsements of both. Western governments argued that because the National Assembly had accepted the change under provisions of the constitution then in force, the change was legal and no issue of recognition arose.[10] When the GRUNK was proclaimed in Beijing the following May, the PRC and 16 other governments quickly extended recognition even though the Khmer Rouge did not begin guerrilla operations until later or the GRUNK establish itself within Cambodian territory until April 1975.[11] The Soviets, who had recognized the Lon Nol government and avoided relations with the GRUNK, shifted position just ahead of events and recognized it on 29 March 1975 as the Khmer Rouge drive on the capital gained irresistible momentum.[12] The Indian, Liberian and Sri Lankan governments recognized on 1 April, just before the Khmer Rouge entered Phnom Penh. The French, Turkish, Australian, Iranian and Portuguese governments recognized as they were establishing themselves in the capital. Other governments waited until they were clearly in control of the country.[13]

African regional quarrels provided some additional instances, the largest number involving the long Chad civil war. In June 1965 the Sudanese government announced its intention to recognize the 'government-in-exile' founded on its territory by refugees from Chad. OAU mediation prompted a settlement of differences between Chad and Sudan, including Sudanese promises to expel the refugees and stop aiding their organizations.[14] Renewed Sudan–Chad disputes and continuing political division in Chad encouraged the Libyan government to recognize the Chad National Liberation Front as the government until a further OAU mediation patched up the conflict.[15] Libya also supported the claims of others against Hissene Habre in the 1980s, recognizing Habre's government only in 1990.

Expressing disapproval of a new regime can involve not only refusal to recognize it but also the clearly illegal step of prolonging recognition of a former regime by continuing to treat with its diplomatic representatives after its loss of control is obvious. Though the slowness of communications sometimes meant that governments continued to deal with defunct regimes, there were no cases of using prolonged recognition in this way during the nineteenth century. Conscious prolonged recognition first appeared in the interwar period. China (motivated mainly by the need to maintain contact with some official representative of Russia to implement the extraterritoriality treaties), France, Italy and the USA continued to deal with diplomats and consuls appointed by the Tsarist or Kerensky government after November 1917.[16] The Mexican government continued to recognize the Republican government of Spain after Franco's triumph in 1939, despite the Estrada Doctrine. The Mexicans finally recognized Franco's successor, the constitutional monarchy under King Juan Carlos, in March 1977.[17]

Nearly all of the instances of prolonged recognition after 1945 involved China. A large number of governments, among them the Australian, Canadian, French, Nigerian, Senegalese, US, and West German, continued to recognize the Republicans under Chiang as government of China for anywhere from 10 to 30 years after the PRC triumph. A multilateral variant appeared after 1979 when the majority of members agreed to allow Pol Pot's delegates to remain in the UN General Assembly as representatives of Cambodia, even though several of the governments supporting this decision explicitly stated that they were not maintaining any bilateral relations with Pol Pot's faction.[18]

In the vast majority of cases, governments have respected the rule that recognition cannot persist beyond control. Thus most expressions of disapproval involve refusals to recognize the new regime without continuing to recognize the old. Such delayed recognitions began in the nineteenth century. The combination of desire to defend monarchical institutions with inability to intervene inspired Russian refusal to recognize the liberal July Monarchy of Louis Philippe from 1830 until 1832 and Austrian, Prussian and Russian refusal to recognize the constitutionalist Isabella II as Queen of Spain later in that decade.[19] The violence of the coup bringing the Karageorgevich dynasty to power in Serbia in 1903 inspired a British nonrecognition lasting three years, and shorter periods of nonrecognition by the Dutch, French, German, Italian and US governments.[20] Chilean refusal to recognize Maximilian as Emperor of Mexico[21] involved disapproval of the monarchical form; US nonrecognition remained a sign of disapproval only until Union victory in the US Civil War permitted more forceful threats of counter-intervention.

Nonrecognition to express disapproval continued in the interwar period. Many governments refused to recognize the Bolsheviks as the government of Russia (USSR after 1922) without intervening in Russian affairs or continuing to deal with Tsarist diplomats and consuls. Most European governments had relented by 1925; the US, Swiss, Portuguese, Saudi, and many Latin American governments persisted longer in refusal to recognize.[22]

Using nonrecognition to indicate disapproval continued sporadically in the Cold War era. The PRC victory in 1949 inspired the largest number of such responses. Several states avoiding continued dealings with the ROC government nevertheless withheld recognition of the PRC for a year or more.[23] The USSR and Yugoslavia never recognized the Franco government of Spain.[24] Pinochet's coup in Chile inspired nonrecognition by Cuba and the USSR. In Africa, a few coups triggered particularly strong reactions. The 1963 Togo coup (the first in sub-Saharan Africa), the 1966 Ghanaian coup ousting Nkrumah, Idi Amin's 1971 coup in Uganda, and Doe's 1980 coup in Liberia inspired some refusals to recognize.

Using nonrecognition to indicate disapproval of a new regime may begin with its accession, or may replace an unsuccessful attempt to prevent its coming to power. It involves inconvenience in bilateral relations and some hobbling of access to courts and assets located in the nonrecognizing state. The extent of the inconvenience depends on which government or governments deny recognition, but in most cases the new regime can get by. The effect of nonrecognition as disapproval in multilateral relations depends on the number and influence of governments refusing to recognize. If only a few are denying recognition, multilateral relations are hardly affected. The US ability to keep the PRC government from representing China at the UN after the early 1960s is exceptional and depended on adroit invocations of rules permitting a shift from simple to two-thirds majority for approving a change in the Chinese seating. When, as in the case of the Heng Samrin regime in Cambodia between 1979 and 1991, refusal to recognize is far more widespread, the accumulation of individual nonrecognitions also limits multilateral activity.

Governments pursuing recognition or nonrecognition as expressions of opinion about the new regime can easily maintain their policies. Even a strong target state will have trouble altering them. The USSR was able to extract recognition from the initially reluctant Danes,[25] but the Swiss avoided recognition until 1946 despite some early Soviet efforts to extract it.[26] Equally, the US was unable to keep major allies from recognizing the PRC government in the 1950s and 1960s, or to discourage their quick recognitions of the new Leninist governments in Cambodia and Vietnam in 1975.[27]

The expansion of multilateral relations and inter-government contact after 1919 did not affect governments' ability to persist in nonrecognition because most of the contacts regarded as following from or likely to arise because of those activities were defined as compatible with nonrecognition. This disappointed the hopes of legal scholars and others who expected that increasing levels of interconnection among states would force governments to give up lengthy refusals to recognize an effective regime.

Yet a government can express hostility towards a new regime without resorting to refusal to recognize. Diplomatic contact can be restricted to low-level missions, representation through a third state, or use of temporary rather than resident missions. The making of agreements can be delayed and limited to the most pressing issues. Aid can be decreased or ended, trade and travel can be banned or discouraged. In the wider landscape of disapproval, nonrecognition is an additional measure available when the disapproved happens to come to power through extra-legal means. The essentially incidental character of recognition is best shown through comparison of US relations with two Leninist governments in the mid-1970s. Though the US had recognized the Castro government of Cuba in 1959, diplomatic relations were handled by third 'protecting powers' – Switzerland for the USA in Havana and Czechoslovakia for Cuba in Washington until 1977 when the US and Cuba agreed to exchange 'interests sections' operating out of the protecting powers' embassies.[28] Travel to and most trade with Cuba was banned. Though not yet recognizing the PRC government in 1973, the US conducted diplomatic relations directly through 'liaison offices' in Washington and Beijing, travel was permitted, and some trade beginning.[29]

INFLUENCING THE NEW REGIME'S POLICIES

Using recognition to influence a new regime's general policies or specific actions requires withholding recognition until the new regime either performs as required or promises to do so. Many legal scholars added considerable confusion to the discussion of these policies by using the term 'conditional recognition' in two very different ways. The first is a more political one of referring to efforts to secure concessions before recognition as the attaching of conditions. The second is the legal usage defining 'conditions' as uncertain future events which must occur for a legal act to take or retain legal effect. Legal usage divides these into 'conditions subsequent' (or 'suspensive conditions'), which specify circumstances in which a prior legal act will lose effect, and 'conditions precedent' (or 'resolutory conditions'), which specify circumstances that must exist before a prior legal act takes effect.

Conditions in this legal sense have not been attached to recognition of particular governments.[30] It is reasonable to view actual control of the state as a general condition precedent for recognition and loss of control as a general suspensive condition ending recognition. Yet neither legal scholars nor policy-makers have proposed invoking any doctrine of condition precedent to deny effect to premature recognitions even within the internal law and administration of the recognizing state. Any government whose actual rule over a state is ignored by a premature recognition may regard this as a hostile act, but it is unclear what it may do in consequence if the other does not link that premature recognition with armed intervention or other meddling.

Nineteenth-century legal scholars agreed that legal conditions, whether resolutory or suspensive, were not useful or necessary in recognition of governments. Most also accepted extraction of promises, though late in the century a few warned that tolerating this practice opened the door to external meddling in states' affairs.[31] Governments resorted to extracting promises fairly frequently. Most related to the new regime's treatment of foreigners, usually the nationals of the recognizing state. A few addressed the new regime's conduct toward all or some of its own people, such as the British offer to recognize Dom Miguel as King of Portugal in 1828 if he would grant amnesty to Dona Maria's supporters.[32] The Juarez government of Mexico resisted giving promises demanded by Britain, France and Spain after its establishment in 1860, exacerbating the conflicts over claims and treatment of foreigners that had become acute in the late 1850s. This helped bring on the French intervention supporting creation of the empire under Maximilian. When French intervention ended in 1867, the Juarez government was able to resist more strongly because of US support and the ability to make counter-claims arising out of the intervention.[33]

By the end of the century the US government was the most active seeker of promises, but confined this activity to Central America and the Caribbean. Typical was the US decision to help rebels against the President of Nicaragua by sending the Marines in 1909, announcing after the president resigned that no member of his government would be recognized as his successor, and sending Marines again in 1912 to help the new government against its opponents.[34] In 1911, the US pressured both government and rebels in Honduras into forming a coalition government, which it promptly recognized.[35] Yet this US activity reflected less a distinct approach towards recognition than a particular approach towards exerting influence abroad that favoured indirect methods over formal colonization.

Though most promises were sought by single governments, there were instances of joint efforts. Parallel concerns about treatment of foreigners and repayment of public debt led the British, French and Spanish governments to coordinate policy towards successive Mexican governments between 1857 and 1863. This broke down when the French decided to extend intervention from securing repayment of claims to support of a new monarchical government set up with connivance from Mexican monarchists and other conservatives.[36] A more successful great power effort occurred in 1908. The British, Dutch, French, German, Italian, Spanish and US governments, which had all guaranteed Moroccan independence in return for Moroccan undertakings about future policy in the 1906 Act of Algeciras, secured acceptance of a fairly wide set of promises in return for recognizing Mulai Hamid as Sultan.[37]

These collective uses must be seen in context. They occurred when several powers agreed on the policy to follow towards a considerably weaker state, and an extra-legal change of government provided the opportunity to link recognition and concessions. These were less an aspect of recognition practice than a special form of great power management of other countries' affairs. The great powers often settled situations jointly and imposed their preferences on smaller powers if they could develop a common approach on a shared concern.

Legal scholars became more critical of using recognition to extract promises in the interwar era. Dennis regarded the practice as a crude form of imperialism; Goebel, Baty, and Scelle argued that the practice was inappropriate to the essentially routine function of recognition, and Anderson regarded it as improper.[38] The Inter-American Council of Jurists proposed that the 1927 draft inter-American treaty on recognition include a provision that 'recognition is unconditional and irrevocable'.[39] Kunz and Brown sought to restrict the practice by arguing that it should be allowed only in certain circumstances;[40] Scelle argued that promises could be required by an international conference.[41] Yet rejection was not universal. Individual scholars defended the practice,[42] while the Institute of International Law's 1936 resolution on recognition permitted, though did not encourage, it.[43]

Interwar attempts to extract promises before recognition can be divided more sharply into the successful and the unsuccessful. Success was most likely when several great powers acted together, though a single one could often prevail in regions close to home. Failure was likely in two sorts of circumstances: with new regimes in strong states, and with new regimes in weak states able to muster popular support at home or abroad in the rising tide of anti-imperialist sentiments.

The great powers had the easiest time securing promises in the wake of both world wars. In November 1919 the British and French required the Huszar government in Hungary not only to prove its ability to maintain internal order, but also to hold elections without delay, forswear territorial claims against neighbouring states, and guarantee civil liberties.[44] When a plebiscite endorsed creation of a monarchy, the further stipulation was added that no Habsburg be chosen as king.[45] The French made clear that they would accept no Hohenzollern as King of Finland in the period when the form of government was being debated.[46] Similar concerted efforts occurred during the late stages of World War II. The Badoglio government of Italy had to promise to include all 'democratic' (non-fascist) political groups and cooperate fully with the Allies. The British and US governments used threats of nonrecognition to secure broadened Austrian, Hungarian and Polish provisional governments. The Yalta Declaration was a series of stipulations that new governments in Axis-occupied countries be governed by broad coalitions until the early holding of elections.[47]

The Bolsheviks resisted stipulations from a favourable position given the size, location, and power potential of their country. The German Weimar Republic, anxious to break out of its diplomatic isolation, recognized them in 1920 on the basis of a mutual write-off of the huge claims on both sides. The British, French, Italian and Japanese recognitions of 1924–5 were accompanied by agreements in principle on particular disputes, but no one-sided promises. The French government did attach some 'reservations' in its statements to the National Assembly,[48] but these were not regarded as promises given in the traditional sense.[49] The Litvinov agreements made concurrently with US recognition in 1933 were not linked formally to the recognition. As Secretary of State Hull explained to the Senate Foreign Relations Committee, 'Although the agreements of November 16, 1933 between the two Governments were concluded simultaneously with the establishment of diplomatic relations between them, the maintenance of diplomatic relations has not been made "wholly contingent" ... on the fulfillment by the Soviet government of the obligations set forth in these agreements.'[50] Later disagreements about Soviet support for Communist activity in the USA did not lead to a severance of relations.

Once recognized by most of the major powers, the Soviets were able to take a very tough stance against others' attempts to extract promises. Their attitude was clear in a 1925 statement that

> Recently we refused to conclude an agreement with Hungary because we saw no need to buy the recognition of Hungary and of countries like Hungary, at the cost of concessions which might one way or another conflict with the interests of our Union. The other states will have to take into account that the later they are, the worse it will be for them.[51]

Their underlying power even allowed the Soviets to extract at least one recognition. They told the Danish government in 1923 that if it wanted to conclude a commercial treaty with terms as favourable as those being granted to other countries it had to recognize the Soviet government *de jure* by 15 February 1924.[52] Though making a 'preliminary' agreement with them in April 1923, the Danes did not proceed to *de jure* recognition until June 1924.[53] A 1926 attempt to extract recognition from the Swiss by insisting on establishment of diplomatic relations before resolving the Vorovsky affair failed when the Swiss insisted on handling the issue in isolation.[54]

Turkish and Chinese experience showed very clearly the influence of anti-imperialist sentiment and the effects of competition among the great powers – including the USSR – for influence. The Turkish Republic under Mustafa Kemal (Kemal Ataturk) secured recognition and assistance from the USSR in March 1921. The Italians and French dealt with Kemal though the Sultanate was still in existence, and gave up territorial claims that summer and autumn. When the Republic was definitively established in November 1922, it won acceptance from all the great powers. The Turks then moved on to a more difficult enterprise, ending the Capitulations under which foreigners enjoyed various privileges, including trial by their own consuls, in the former Ottoman Empire. The Soviets had renounced Capitulations in 1921, and the other powers did likewise at the Lausanne Conference in 1923.[55] The Chinese Republic laboured under the additional difficulty of severe factional divisions that kept anyone from forming a government that could be said to rule the whole country until 1928. Yet it, too, made progress on treaty revision because the Germans in 1921 and the Soviets in 1924 unilaterally renounced their old treaty privileges. The Western powers and Japan realized they could not maintain the old system, and were ready to adopt alternatives, but had trouble agreeing on a common approach and let things drift until the Nationalists under Chiang took control and provided a more coherent Chinese policy.[56]

Requiring promises remained common in the Caribbean area, with the US government again the leading user. However, the targets were becoming more assertive. The Théodore government of Haiti (November 1914–March 1915) refused to sign the agreements on rights of foreigners, financial reform, and non-alienation of territory being demanded by the US because it realized these would be very unpopular at home. The US then shifted to insisting on promises to hold elections and provide information to the commission investigating the country's financial situation preparatory to proposing reforms.[57] After the Théodore government was overthrown, the US went back to the first set of demands, but that regime was in turn overthrown before any agreement could be reached. Only with a third regime were the desired agreements concluded.[58] The Obregón government of Mexico balked at making promises or signing treaties in return for recognition for two years, saying that doing so would injure Mexico's dignity as an independent state and that some of the promises would be contrary to Mexican law. Yet it ended up making certain promises before receiving US recognition.[59] France used a threat of nonrecognition to secure extension of the Franco-Salvadorian commerce treaty in 1931.[60]

Though stipulations were used heavily early in the interwar period, even great power enthusiasm for them waned. This was part of the wider waning of enthusiasm for the 'gunboat diplomacy' that had sometimes supported stipulations and more often supported extraction of agreements from recognized governments in weaker states. The Soviet challenge was important to stiffening resolve in some target states, but the rise of local nationalism and a greater willingness of socialists and other domestic critics of European and US imperialism to challenge their own governments' policies were more important. The Franklin Roosevelt administration in the US made the most obvious break with older practice in declaring its 'Good Neighbor Policy'. It even signed the Montevideo Convention on Rights and Duties of States, which provided in Article 6 that 'The recognition of a State merely signifies that the State which recognizes it accepts the personality of the other with all the rights and duties determined by international law. Recognition is irrevocable and unconditional.'[61] This statement of regional law on recognition of states was quickly carried into recognition of governments.

Postwar writers were generally critical of unilateral attempts to extract promises. Several scholars, primarily but not exclusively those arguing that use of any criterion but control was illegal, opposed the practice in all circumstances.[62] A few maintained the less stringent criticism that promise-securing transforms what should be a routine act into a controversy and creates resentments.[63] Others condemned the practice as poor policy while not excluding the possibility of conditions in the strict legal meaning of the term.[64] Others allowed the practice with optional relations but not the basic acknowledgement of existence.[65] Most scholars accepting the practice were writers of general texts.[66] Most justified it with the narrow argument that the practice is a consequence of the discretion left in recognition decisions, but Starke identified a deeper reason:

> Professor Lauterpacht considers such mutual bargaining to be obnoxious and contrary to the true function of recognition, but he overlooks the fact that the international society of states is still an imperfect community, which makes it impossible for recognition to be as perfect a diplomatic institution as he conceives it to be.[67]

Yet these were minority views. Early in the period, Latin American jurists resumed their campaign to ban the practice in the regional law of the Americas. This resulted in two articles for a draft convention on recognition of governments in 1949:

ARTICLE 2

Recognition shall not be granted as a means of securing any advantage from the *de facto* government, nor shall it be made subject to the acceptance of special demands by the recognizing State or become the object of negotiation or compromise.

Pre-existing diplomatic disputes may be submitted through customary diplomatic channels after recognition.

ARTICLE 3

Recognition shall not be withheld as a sanction or reprisal.[68]

The Soviet government, now joined by its Leninist allies, continued to condemn the use of stipulations as an imperialist device. New regimes in weak states continued to resist. The Leninist Hoxha government of Albania rejected a US request that it reaffirm the validity of all treaties in force between the US and Albania on 7 April 1939 (the date of Italian occupation). It was willing to reaffirm the multilateral treaties, but wanted to leave the bilateral conciliation, extradition and naturalization treaties suspended pending a post-recognition revision. The US government rejected this solution, refused recognition, and withdrew its diplomatic mission.[69]

New regimes in stronger countries were able to turn the tables on other governments. The French initially believed that they would be able to maintain some sort of diplomatic relations with the ROC on Taiwan after recognizing the PRC government in 1964. The Chinese made clear that all such relations would have to end before establishment of diplomatic relations, and the French complied.[70] This was their general practice with all recognizing governments, and became more demanding as years passed. Even the US government gave up its Mutual Defense Treaty as well as formal diplomatic relations after recognizing the PRC government in 1979, though has persisted in a level of 'private' and informal inter-government relations that elicits occasional protest from Beijing.[71] In one case, a group of Third World countries turned the practice on an old colonial power. Many Third World governments deferred recognition of the Spinola government of Portugal until after it acknowledged that Portugal's African colonies were independent states.[72]

Extracting promises in return for recognition declined during and after the Cold War. Most post-Cold War writers did not even mention them, and those who did opposed their use,[73] warned that they were not particularly effective,[74] or reminded readers of the traditional rule that nonfulfilment does not permit retracting the recognition.[75]

INFLUENCING THE NEW REGIME'S SURVIVAL

A government has the greatest chance of influencing a new regime's prospects for taking and keeping power through recognition policy when that new regime is still trying to consolidate control. While most common in actual or incipient civil wars, quick recognition may also occur when there is only one claimant, if the recognizer feels its support will help the new regime establish itself *vis-à-vis* third governments. Italian recognition of the Albanian monarchy in 1928,[76] Soviet recognition of the PRC government in October 1949, and Western acceptances of the Khmer Republic in March 1970 were all examples of this sort of effort.

Combining recognition with other forms of intervention was most common in the interwar period. Allied intervention in the Russian civil war was combined with recognition of Kolchak's regime as the government of Russia, and the French continued this with Wrangel's regime.[77] The Bolsheviks for their part recognized the Finnish 'Red Guards' as the government of Finland at the start of their ultimately unsuccessful rebellion in 1918,[78] and a Polish 'government-in-exile' formed under Julian Marchlewski on Russian territory until military stalemate forced them to negotiate with the Polish Republic in 1920.[79] The German and Italian governments recognized Franco's Nationalists as the government of Spain on 17 November 1936, as they began their unsuccessful first attack on Madrid, and soon supplied them with massive aid. The USSR recognized a 'People's Government of Finland' formed in the Soviet-occupied area just after the start of the Russo-Finnish War until stalemate forced it to begin peace negotiations with the established Republic in March 1940.[80] World War II involved considerable imposition of regimes in occupied areas. Yet the weakest of them did not even enjoy recognition from nominal allies. The Japanese-sponsored Wang government of China was not recognized by the other Axis states.[81]

Yet recognizing some faction as the government of its state is not a prerequisite for aiding it. The British and French aided constitutionalist movements in Portugal and Spain without recognizing them as governments until they met effectivist criteria in the 1820s and 1830s. Though the French justified their intervention in Mexico after 1863 as support for Maximilian's imperial government, they had been pressuring that country for several years. Most aid to factions during the Cold War was not accompanied by recognition as a government. Nor were efforts to influence political choice confined to instigating or taking advantage of extra-legal changes of government. Both sides channelled money into propaganda and election campaigns.

Outside aid is helpful, but will not determine the outcome unless massive in comparison with the resources of local competitors. Most factions' ability to gain power rests on ability to garner local support; ability to maintain power depends even more crucially on it, as the US experiences in South-east Asia and the Soviet experience in Afghanistan demonstrated. Thus it behoves factions who want to remain in power over a politically-aware population to avoid appearing to be the puppet of any foreign power even when they receive foreign assistance.

Outside governments hoping to hinder a new regime obviously withhold recognition, stating publicly that they are doing so and why. Where elements of a deposed predecessor still exist, nonrecognition of the new regime may be accompanied by prolonged recognition of the former government. Such prolonged recognition puts a sharper point on the policy, but is not necessary to discouraging a new regime and may earn the prolonged recognizer considerable criticism.

SUMMARY

Looking at the most obvious unilateral political uses of recognition – premature recognition, prolonged nonrecognition, and prolonged recognition – reveals some clear shifts in their incidence in different eras. Premature recognition and prolonged recognition were rare in the nineteenth century; the deviations from effectivism generally involved prolonged nonrecognition. Premature and prolonged recognition became much more prevalent in the interwar period, and then declined – premature more quickly – in the Cold War era. Prolonged recognition largely died out as the major governments continuing to recognize the ROC shifted their recognition to the PRC in the mid to late 1970s. Prolonged nonrecognition was used in all three eras, though rose somewhat in the interwar and early Cold War periods. It, too, declined considerably after 1975.

The propensity to pursue individual political ends through recognition policy also depends on the relative power of initiating and target governments and on the sort of advantage being pursued. For purposes of analysis, states can be divided into three groups defined by their capability relative to others: great powers, middle powers, and weak states. This produces nine possible combinations of initiating and target government as shown in the matrix grid below:

		target	
	great	*middle*	*weak*
initiator *great*			
initiator *middle*			
initiator *weak*			

Comparing political uses of recognition by both the relative power of initiator and target and the goal sought reveals some strong continuities among the four periods. In all four eras, expressing opinions was open to any government sufficiently far away from the target to avoid its strongest pressures. Yet in the nineteenth century weak states did not indulge themselves in this way very much. This is consistent with both the generally effectivist cast of recognition policy at the time and the strong elements of hierarchy differentiating small and great powers. In the interwar and Cold War periods, large numbers of weak states did engage in using recognition policy – most frequently prolonged nonrecognition but occasionally premature recognition and prolonged recognition – to express opinions. There were no instances of weak states using recognition as a means of securing concessions. The few instances of weak states coupling recognition policy with unilateral involvement in a foreign civil war or other effort to influence the choice of government elsewhere came in the Cold War era, and involved regional politics in Africa or the Middle East. Middle powers acted much like weak states, even though their position did allow them greater leeway in relations with weak states.

Great powers account for most of the political uses of recognition, with sharply different tendencies among them. Most of the great powers engaged in political uses of recognition policy for relatively brief periods. Most of these occurred during or immediately following major wars. However, the USA was engaged in political uses of recognition fairly constantly from the late nineteenth century until the 1970s, and the USSR likewise during most of its existence. By 1980, even those two were shifting away from political use of recognition as part of a wider shift towards de-emphasizing or even abandoning the practice altogether.

There was also a notable shift in the goals sought. Use of recognition to extract concessions was far more prevalent in the nineteenth century than later. Efforts to extract promises began meeting serious resistance in the interwar period. Attempts to extract concessions from the Bolsheviks foundered on an imprudent choice of target, but even weaker states like Turkey and Mexico summoned resources for successful resistance in divisions among foreign powers and rising anti-imperialist sentiment at home or in initiating states. Concession-seeking was not continued in the Cold War era, when political uses of recognition were occasionally linked to efforts to influence the choice of government and more often to expressions of opinion.

Adding up the number of instances indicates that use of premature recognition was highest in the interwar period while use of prolonged recognition and prolonged nonrecognition was about equal in the interwar and Cold War eras. Yet this should not be allowed to leave the impression that extra-legal changes of government were more likely to inspire political uses of recognition in the twentieth century than in the nineteenth. If all the possible occasions for adopting such policies are taken into account, by considering both the increased number of extra-legal changes of government and the increasing numbers of independent states making their own recognition decisions, the proportion of recognition decisions reflecting political calculations actually fell. There were some 227 extra-legal changes of government (an average of 2.3 a year) in 1815–1914, 74 (an average of 2.4 a year) in 1915–45, 181 (an average of 3.68 a year) in 1946–91, and 11 (an average of 2.75 a year) in 1992–5.[82] The number of states also increased markedly after 1945, going from approximately 60 to approximately 200. Taking these increases in both the occasions for recognition and the number of entities making such decisions into account, the relative portion of extra-legal changes of government inspiring unilateral political uses of recognition decreased even more than the absolute number of instances.

Yet it is accurate to perceive the importance of political uses of recognition as waxing and waning in the twentieth century. The actual instances attracted considerable attention from policy-makers and legal scholars alike, and influenced discussion of recognition of governments far more than any thought that the number of instances was falling as a proportion of total recognition decisions. Here, as in many aspects of politics, the most vivid activity, not the most typical, created the strongest impressions.

11 Altering the Institution of Recognition of Governments

Occasionally in the nineteenth century, but with greater frequency as the twentieth century passed, legal scholars and policy-makers proposed basic alterations in the institution of recognition of governments. Proponents have advanced four main arguments in favour of change. A few have claimed that complications arising when some governments extend while others refuse recognition are severe enough that individual discretion in the matter must be curbed to secure greater uniformity of treatment. A wider circle of legal scholars have argued that eliminating individual governments' discretion in recognition decisions would increase global order by ending use of recognition for unilateral political advantage. Cold War and post-Cold War scholars and policy-makers have argued that the progressive reduction in the differences of treatment accorded to recognized governments and unrecognized regimes permits abolishing the institution. Others argue that recognition of governments is superfluous in the contemporary world because the rapid and extensive dissemination of information about events in other parts of the world permits courts, administrative agencies, and the public to determine on their own who rules where.

Nineteenth-century scholars and policy-makers were aware of the possibility that different governments might react to a new regime in different ways, but were not troubled by that possibility. Even when unaware of the informal coordination of responses through diplomatic consultations, they tended to assume that any regime demonstrating effective rule over its state and a reasonable prospect of remaining in power more than a short time would be recognized fairly quickly. They could also tolerate differences in treatment because the fairly narrow agenda of intergovernmental relations in the nineteenth century meant few issues would be affected.

The need for change began to be felt in the interwar period. Some governments persisted in extremely lengthy nonrecognition of certain regimes, most prominently of the Bolsheviks in Russia. At the same time the pace of diplomacy was accelerating and the agenda of intergovernmental relations expanding with the spread of government administration to more areas of life. The general desire to avoid a repeat of World War I also inspired efforts to institutionalize international relations more clearly.

The Council and Assembly of the League of Nations were intended to serve as central coordinating forums for the adjustment of political differences and the avoidance of war. Increased institutionalization of international relations in other spheres was promoted by establishment of League organs dealing with social and economic affairs and by greater activity in the public international unions founded in the late nineteenth century. This general interwar interest in greater institutionalization was expressed as well in proposals to change the basic rules regarding recognition of governments. Two sharply contrasting proposals have dominated discussions since 1918. The first would preserve the institution but remove its individualistic character by entrusting recognition decisions to an international body acting on behalf of all governments. The second would abolish the institution altogether.

COLLECTIVIZING DECISION

Even in the nineteenth century, governments frequently consulted one another as they considered whether to recognize a new regime, and sometimes even concerted their decisions. Public and scholarly awareness of these processes was limited to occasions when a conference of the great powers led to publicly announced positions. Thus the consultations following the advent of the July Monarchy in France in 1830, the various rebellions of 1848, the ousting of the Ottoman Sultan in 1876, accession of a new Sultan of Morocco in 1908–9,[1] proclamation of the Portuguese Republic in 1911,[2] and proclamation of the Chinese Republic in 1912[3] reached public awareness at the time. The much more extensive practice of consultations among the diplomatic corps during Latin American changes of government was not widely known. A few legal scholars also added confusion by using the term 'collective recognition' to cover both consultations involving only exchanges of views and concerted decisions.[4]

Both consultations and occasional joint decisions continued in the interwar period. The Supreme Allied Council coordinated responses to political changes stemming from World War I, and the Japanese,

US, and major European governments sought to concert recognition policy in China during the 1920s.[5] The six states involved in mediating the Chaco dispute between Paraguay and Bolivia also coordinated recognition of the new Paraguayan military government in 1936.[6]

Establishment of the League of Nations and its standing political organs created the possibility of establishing a formal mechanism of joint decision. Thus a few interwar scholars proposed that votes on whether to seat a particular government's delegates should be the procedure by which member states make their recognition decisions.[7] In 1943 the London International Law Conference, a gathering of legal scholars and practising lawyers advising the Allies on legal issues relating to organization of the postwar world, recommended a two-step procedure:

> A new government to which recognition *de jure* has been granted by a certain number of governments shall be allowed to apply for general recognition before an international authority having competence for that purpose, such decisions to be binding on all States.[8]

Some Cold War era scholars returned to the idea of using majority votes in the UN General Assembly to determine recognition[9] even though a few argued that using an intergovernmental body would not reduce the influence of political calculations.[10] One sought to balance governments' reluctance to accept a collective procedure with the need to curb abuses by proposing that recognition and nonrecognition decisions be reviewed by an international body acting much like an administrative court in domestic law.[11]

These ideas were not taken up in either the League or the UN. Though some of the diplomats in Geneva supported using admission to the League as joint recognition of statehood,[12] there was no effort to use either admission of a state to membership or seating of delegates sent by a particular regime as a mechanism for joint recognition of governments. Albania was admitted before all the great powers had recognized the Albanian government, and both Belgium and Switzerland continued to withhold recognition from the Soviet government despite admission of the USSR in 1934. League practice was the basis of UN Secretary-General Lie's conclusion in 1950 that decisions about seating delegations and decisions about recognizing governments were two different matters handled by different entities.[13]

In the Cold War era governments occasionally formalized consultation within regional groupings. Members of the European

Community consulted regularly and included recognition decisions among the items to be handled through European political cooperation.[14] In Africa a number of subregional groupings developed strong habits of consultation.[15] The OAU had no procedure for joint decision or consultation and OAU meetings generally accepted whatever delegation a member sent.[16] However, the meetings of foreign ministers or heads of state and government became a forum for discussing recognition questions when members so desired. The majority decision to seat MPLA delegates as representing Angola in 1975 was followed shortly by recognition from most member states.[17] Consultations were infrequent in Asia until 1975, when Leninist victories in Cambodia, Laos, and Vietnam inspired consultations among ASEAN states.[18] After 1979 they effectively concerted positions on the successive Pol Pot, Heng Samrin, and Sihanouk regimes in Cambodia after 1979.

In the OAS a 1948 proposal to concert decisions foundered on opposition from the Mexican and other governments who felt it put too much stress on recognition and would encourage outside interference in a state's internal affairs.[19] A less ambitious 1949 proposal to formalize consultations without committing members to concerted decisions failed for the same reason.[20] Even the 1962 OAS resolution condemning 'international communism' as a threat to the hemisphere and urging joint action against it included no provision for consultations about recognition and even carried a caveat that it should not be interpreted as permitting interference with each state's right to choose its own government.[21] Yet soon after coups replaced relatively long-lived democratic governments of Argentina and Peru in 1962, OAS members were ready to address the issue again. This time, they accepted a proposal that members should consult after any extra-legal change of government in the hemisphere, but only with the proviso that each member retained the right to make its own recognition decision.[22] In the mid-1960s a combination of reaction against US intervention in the Dominican Republic and a shift towards more effectivist recognition policies by a number of governments led members to avoid OAS-wide consultations. Only in 1990, after almost all Latin American republics were ruled by civilian governments, did OAS members endorse a new programme of consultations.[23] However, regional sentiment remains opposed to collectivizing decisions.

The obverse notion of collective nonrecognition, decision in an international organization requiring members to avoid recognizing a particular regime, has attracted greater interest. Williams proposed in 1929 that the League adopt a procedure for concerted nonrecognition of any new regime that appeared to threaten the security of the international community as a whole.[24] The US government proposed, and the League accepted, a programme for concerted nonrecognition of the Japanese puppet state of Manchukuo in 1933. This 'Stimson Doctrine' applied to territorial changes brought about in violation of the League Covenant, but the idea of concerted nonrecognition of changes resulting from violations of international law was easily extended to new regimes.

Even here, however, no general rules have been developed. The Pan American Union's wartime efforts to concert nonrecognition of any Axis-influenced government that arose in the Western Hemisphere were halting, and abandoned in late 1946.[25] On occasion, a coalition of members has been able to have another's delegates excluded from meetings because of objections to a new regime or to a foreign intervention. Panamanian delegates were excluded from a meeting of the subregional Rio Group soon after the 1989 US intervention.[26] A Comoros delegation was excluded from the 1978 OAU summit because of mercenaries' prominence in the coup bringing it to power.[27] Delegates sent by Sgt. Doe were excluded from the 1980 OAU Economic Summit and the May 1980 ECOWAS summit.[28] However, none of these decisions involved telling member states how to conduct their bilateral relations.

There are only three clear cases of international organization instructions regarding bilateral relations with particular regimes. The first was concerted refusal to accept continued South African rule over Namibia after 1966. This acquired sharper focus in 1985 when the South Africans attempted to set up a white-dominated 'interim government' to prevent the likely SWAPO victory in any fully free vote.[29] The second was refusal to accept the white minority regime of Ian Smith in Rhodesia. In both cases, the Security Council defined the situation as a 'threat to international peace' and invoked Chapter VII to mandate nonrecognition of the regime involved.[30] The third was condemnation of the military coup deposing Haitian President Aristide and bringing the 'defactos' under General Cedras to power, which culminated in UN endorsement of armed intervention to restore Aristide in 1994.[31] However, these decisions may not amount to endorsement of a generalizable doctrine of collective nonrecognition because each was hedged with statements about the uniqueness of the case.[32]

ABOLISHING RECOGNITION OF GOVERNMENTS

Interest in abolishing recognition can also be traced back into the nineteenth century. Liszt, borrowing the maxim 'silence implies assent' from domestic law, argued that recognition should be assumed unless a government objected within a certain interval of receiving the customary formal notification of the accession of a new government in another state.[33] Rivier argued for outright abolition on the grounds that recognition of governments is unnecessary:

> It results from the principle of the permanence of identity of the nation, which subsists and remains the same regardless of the changes occurring in the form of government, that a recognition of the new state of affairs, of the transformation of the constitution, by other nations does not appear at all necessary.[34]

After World War I, Louter and Huess advocated abolition and agreed with Rivier that the principle of state continuity makes recognition of governments superfluous.[35] Yet abolition competed for attention with other reforms, particularly proposals to establish a duty to recognize any regime in effective control.[36] Abolition was also criticized by those who thought that some institution of recognition was needed to deal with the great variety of situations that arose,[37] or was too deeply engrained in state practice and popular understanding to be eliminated.[38]

The Mexican government was the first to express serious interest in abolition. Recalling its own experiences and surveying the scene after the many Latin American coups of 1930–1, Foreign Minister Estrada indicated that:

> [T]he Mexican Government is issuing no grants of recognition, since that nation considers that such a course is an insulting practice and one which, in addition to the fact that it offends the sovereignty of other nations, implies that judgment of some sort may be passed upon the internal affairs of those nations by other governments, inasmuch as the latter assume, in effect, an attitude of criticism, when they decide, favorably or unfavorably, as to the legal qualifications of foreign regimes.
>
> Therefore the Government of Mexico confines itself to the maintenance or withdrawal, as it deems advisable, of its diplomatic agents, and to the continued acceptance, also as it may deem advisable, of such similarly accredited diplomatic agents as

> the respective nations may have in Mexico; and in so doing it does not pronounce judgment, either precipitately or *a posteriori*, regarding the right of foreign nations to accept, maintain, or replace their governments or authorities.[39]

Other governments showed little interest; many were soon using recognition policy in the intensifying fascist versus anti-fascist ideological struggles. Even Mexican diplomats were ambivalent about whether abolition was actually intended.[40]

Early in the Cold War era, a number of writers became confident that increasing interconnection among states would force governments to adopt effectivist recognition policies,[41] ending the political abuses that inspired calls for abolition. Several scholars still advocated explicit abolition[42] while some others continued to argue that abolition of recognition of governments would not satisfactorily address the problem of deciding who, if anyone, deserves to be regarded as government of a state beset by civil war.[43] Nor had the balance of scholarly opinion shifted much by the end. In the 1980s and early 1990s one group of scholars supported abolition[44] while others continued to argue that recognition performed useful functions.[45]

More governments indicated interest in abolition. In April 1945, Ecuadorian delegates presented a proposal for abolition to the Eighth Interamerican Conference:

> 1. The custom of recognizing *de facto* governments in the system of reciprocal relations of the American Republics is abolished.
> 2. The establishment of a *de facto* government in any of them shall not affect the normality or continuity of pre-existing diplomatic relations between the State where the change of regime has occurred and the other States.[46]

The Conference referred the proposal to the Inter-American Council of Jurists, where even those initially sympathetic to the idea weakened it by accepting a procedure for choosing among rival regimes during civil wars. Additional discussion soon showed that even in the American regional context governments were not yet prepared to accept abolition.[47]

They were, however, prepared to de-emphasize it. Resolution 35 of the Ninth Interamerican Conference (Bogota) endorsed a Mexican proposal recommending continuity of diplomatic relations, in terms strongly resembling Estrada's 1931 pronouncement:

1. That continuity of diplomatic relations among the American States is desirable;
2. That the right of maintaining, suspending, or renewing diplomatic relations with another government shall not be exercised as a means of individually obtaining unjustified advantages under international law;
3. That the establishment or maintenance of diplomatic relations does not imply any judgment upon the domestic policy of that government.[48]

Though neither global nor regional organizations endorsed abolition, a number of governments began shifting their policy in that direction in the 1960s. The French government was probably the first to claim publicly that it had dispensed with recognition of governments. Statements made after Thieu's 1963 ousting of Diem in South Vietnam included the claim that France recognized only states, not governments.[49] The French, Belgians and Senegalese used the same phrase in announcing their reactions to African coups in 1965.[50] By 1975, the Kenyan, Swiss, Soviet, US and Spanish governments had also invoked the idea at least once.[51]

More significant were later announcements that a particular government had adopted a general policy of dispensing with recognition of governments. These first became common in Western Europe. The Belgians adopted the rule without fanfare in 1974.[52] Commenting on relations with the new Islamic Republic in Iran in 1979, the Italian foreign minister said not only that Italy adhered to the rule, but that it was 'the dominant rule of international law and practice, which is followed by a majority of the states of the European Continent and by all members of the European Community, with the exception of Great Britain'.[53] The British government announced their shift in April 1980 with ministerial declarations to both Houses of Parliament.[54] The Swiss had also adopted it by 1982 when a government spokesman said that 'According to a constant practice... Switzerland recognizes only States.'[55] The Dutch announced their adherence in mid-1990.[56]

The British adoption prompted many Commonwealth governments to consider their position. Dugard says the South African government adopted the policy sometime in the 1980s.[57] The Australians[58] and Canadians[59] both announced adoption of a similar policy in 1988. The New Zealand government's move was first publicly stated in a Foreign Ministry certificate to the High Court in 1989.[60] The Australians showed particular fidelity to the new line during the 1991

Soviet coup attempt. Though instructing its ambassador to 'convey formally' concern that Gorbachev's foreign policy be preserved, it stated publicly that the question of whether the 'State Emergency Committee' would be recognized as the government of the USSR 'simply does not arise in those terms'.[61]

In actual implementation, a 'recognize only states' policy looks much like the more widely shared practice of employing only tacit forms of recognition. Both proceed on the assumption that effective control of the state will be the main consideration in deciding how to treat the new regime. Both involve very similar action by the foreign ministry and diplomatic corps. Thus the actions of governments simply de-emphasizing recognition of governments look very similar to those of governments claiming to have abandoned it. In the late 1940s, the Swiss had given their diplomats abroad authority to continue formal diplomatic relations with whatever regime effectively controlled the state where they served, though leaving open the possibility of a different decision by the Federal Council.[62] While still following its older policy in 1975, standard Canadian instructions to diplomats abroad were that any extra-legal change of government triggered a 'technical suspension' of diplomatic relations, which would end when they were instructed to inform leaders of the new regime orally that they were now ready to continue diplomatic relations and that this amounted to Canadian recognition.[63] West German practice was very similar in the early 1980s.[64] Similarly, the US government's standard instructions were that 'recognition will be implied by the United States Government continuing to deal with the new government'.[65]

The main difference has come in statements explaining the policy to legislators, the public, or national courts faced with lawsuits involving or affected by acts of unrecognized regimes. These avoided the word 'recognition' – and frequently reminded the audience of the 'recognize states only' policy – but did have to indicate the types of contact undertaken with the new regime and whether these amounted to 'normal government-to-government relations'.

Even those governments claiming to have abandoned recognition of new governments have not given up the possibility of refusing to deal with a particular new regime. This is evident in a number of the general policy statements. The British qualified their policy by saying it applied to regimes 'able of themselves to exercise effective control'.[66] The Australians, whom one commentator regarded as giving themselves less discretion than any other government,[67] said that they 'will conduct relations with new regimes to the extent and in the manner which may be required in each case'.[68] The Australian opposition publicly stated its view that the new policy did not preclude refusals to deal with a new regime as the government of its state,[69] and the government promised that the new policy would not lead to establishment of diplomatic relations with the Heng Samrin government of Cambodia or the Taraki government of Afghanistan.[70] The Canadians[71] and Dutch[72] made similar qualifications.

Particular decisions bear out the relevance of these escape clauses. The Mexicans refused to have diplomatic relations with the Franco government of Spain during its entire existence from 1939 to 1977. The French expressly recognized the Gouvernement de Union Nationale de Tchad under Goukoune as 'the legitimate government of Chad' despite stiff competition from other factions.[73] Its defeat by Hissene Habre's forces allowed the French to shift back to avoiding statements about recognition while supporting Habre against Libyan-supported rivals.[74] The British dusted off traditional language to indicate nonacceptance of Iraq's conquest of Kuwait in 1990 by saying 'We continue to recognize the legitimate government of Kuwait.'[75] Britain, France and Germany all made unilateral statements condemning the 1991 Soviet coup attempt and refusing to deal with the 'State Emergency Committee' as well as joining in joint NATO and EU condemnations.[76]

Therefore it is impossible to conclude that any government has entirely dispensed with the institution of recognition of governments. Governments have dispensed with making express positive statements in most cases, but they need not claim to have abolished recognition to do so. Some have also dispensed with making negative statements, though not with refusal to have inter-government relations with a new regime. Yet even some of those claiming to have abandoned recognition have kept the possibility of making positive or negative statements in reserve and used it on occasion.

SUMMARY

The idea of replacing the inherited institution of recognition of governments gained attention among legal scholars well before it engaged policy-makers' minds. The scholars far more than the governments were interested in the possibilities of using the League of Nations and the United Nations for centralizing recognition decisions.

Governments were ready to consult one another and sometimes to decide jointly in smaller groups, but resisted handing decisions about their bilateral relations over to some global body. They were prepared at most to accept the possibility of concerted nonrecognition. UN-sponsored collective nonrecognition was an exceptional measure, applied against Rhodesian independence as long as the Ian Smith regime remained in power, and against continued South African rule over Namibia after 1966. The UN General Assembly's decision to exclude South African representatives from 1974 until 1994 had less effect because many governments (not just in the West) continued to maintain bilateral diplomatic relations with it. The one clear case of UN-based collective nonrecognition of a new government, refusal to accept the 'defactos' under Cedras as the government of Haiti in 1994, came late in the process and after regional decisions to squeeze them out by measures short of military intervention.

By the mid-Cold War era, a growing number of governments were expressing interest in abandoning recognition of governments. Like the legal scholars who had been criticizing the practice for years, they concluded that the relation between recognition and approval that had been encouraged by flagrantly ideological refusals to recognize fully effective governments in the interwar and early Cold War years had created an inconvenient situation. While some sought the solution in shifting to a more strictly effectivist recognition policy conveyed through maintenance of diplomatic relations, others went further and announced they would abandon recognizing governments. Borrowing ideas from the scholars, they argued that the doctrines of state continuity, self-determination, and a state's right to choose its own government made recognition of governments unnecessary, illegitimate, or both.

In the late 1980s and early 1990s, notions of abandoning recognition of governments competed with notions of using nonrecognition as a weapon in the global effort to promote democracy. This effort, which peaked with the formal intergovernmental endorsements of democracy in 1990–1, amounted to revival of a legitimist approach to recognition resting on belief that one form of government is better than all others and deserves to be promoted through concerted international action. Though the tide of democratic legitimism has receded somewhat from its 1990 high, it remains a significant force. It is still strong enough to ensure that even if positive recognition of governments is abandoned, the possibility of nonrecognition will be retained.

So long as nonrecognition remains a possibility, it is impossible to conclude that the legal institution of recognition of governments has been abolished entirely. Retaining the possibility of nonrecognition leaves open the possibility of developing doctrines of obligatory nonrecognition, whether based on some generally-applied criterion, embodied in regional or more local treaties, or mandated in particular cases by the UN Security Council or a competent regional intergovernmental body.

12 The International System and Recognition of Governments

In the Westphalian system of independent states that was spread from Europe to the rest of the world, recognition of governments is the legal institution through which the human agents with authority to act on behalf of each state are identified. It is one area in which international law is closely linked to national law. A government succeeding to power according to the constitution, basic law, or established domestic custom is assumed to succeed as well to its predecessor's status as international agent of the state. Only if there is legal discontinuity at the domestic level because a new government comes to power in some other way, as by coup d'état or revolution, is its status as international agent of the state open to question. The main features of the process by which questions of agentship are settled – individual decision by the government of every other state and legal rules permitting choice not only of the moment but of the criteria for deciding whether to recognize the new government as international agent – flow directly from the basic organizing principles of the Westphalian system of states. There is no world government, so no single agency or office registering changes of government and issuing globally-valid certificates of agentship.

The principle that states are autonomous in their choices, accountable to other states only as specified in general or regional international law and their particular treaties with other states, plays out in two contradictory ways when the time comes to recognize a new government. Domestic autonomy, expressed in the doctrines of sovereign equality of states, self- determination of peoples, and nonintervention in domestic affairs, means that each state has a right to determine its own political, economic, and social organization and to select its own rulers in its own way. International autonomy, also expressed in the doctrine of sovereign equality, means that each state is free to undertake or avoid relations with any or even with all other states. This tension between the domestic and international aspects of state autonomy has been at the root of the most serious contentions over the actual and proper meaning of the institution of recognition of governments. On one side range the advocates of an effectivist rule requiring acceptance as international agent of any government providing effective administration of a state and enjoying obedience from its population. In their view, the tension should be resolved by treating recognition as a strictly routine process of ascertaining and acknowledging the observable fact of presence or absence of effective rule; the right to avoid relations would then be confined to post-recognition choices of maintaining or severing diplomatic and other relations. Among legal scholars, this solution has been favoured by those positing a duty to recognize any regime that provides effective rule and those seeking to distinguish between 'legal' and 'political' aspects of recognition. On the other side range advocates of using recognition of governments to impose some additional international-level qualifications for the status of international agent. Though often motivated by concern for the maintenance of some minimum standards of conduct, their position has the consequence of permitting states to subordinate others' domestic autonomy to their own international autonomy.

The weight of policy-makers' opinion has shifted between effectivist and non-effectivist positions several times since 1815. These shifts are influenced by scholarly argument, but also by changes in the system of states itself. Not only do individual states grow stronger or weaker, emerge into or lose independence, remain united or fall apart. The system as a whole evolves as the patterns of great power conflict change, the concerns inspiring cooperation or conflict shift, various social groupings become politically aware and influential, technology changes, processes of production and consumption change, and different ideas gain sufficient currency to shape policies and action. Both sorts of change affect how the various institutions of the international system are understood and used.

Yet any one international institution is more directly affected by some changes than by others, depending on the area of international life it helps regulate. Recognition of governments involves a matter of the political organization of the states system so more quickly reflects changes in norms and beliefs about how that political organization should be structured at the domestic and the international levels. This means that changes in the patterns of great power competition and the ideas shaping efforts to organize national and international governance affect the institution quite directly. Changes in technology and patterns of production or consumption have a more indirect effect, influencing recognition of governments only as they affect political organization or what people can accomplish. Similarly, the impact of shifts in social group mobilization and political influence are felt only when they produce striking changes in political organization. Changes in the concerns that inspire cooperation or conflict seldom affect recognition of governments as an institution (though can easily affect readiness to recognize or not recognize a particular government) since recognition is focused on identifying the agents with whom cooperation or conflict can occur, not the substance or means of maintaining cooperation or conflict.

CHANGING PATTERNS OF POLITICAL USE

The influence of changes in the international system on the institution of recognition of governments can be seen most clearly in the shifting patterns of political use of recognition. Political use involves rejecting fully effectivist conceptions of recognition and consciously using the freedom to avoid accepting a new government as international agent of its state to express support or hostility, extract some concession, or attempt to affect its prospects of survival. Such political uses of recognition reveal the underlying normative contradictions because they cut so clearly across recognition's functional purpose of providing clear identification of those properly acting as international agents of states. The contentions between advocates of effectivist and other conceptions of the rules on recognition are expressed most clearly in debates over the propriety of political uses, and the extent of political use is the clearest indication that governments have not accepted an effectivist approach.

A survey of the political uses of recognition of governments attempted since 1815 bears out the observation that the institution of recognition is affected most directly by changes in the international system relating to modes of political organization, and only indirectly by other sorts of change. The pattern of political use has been most sensitive to changes in the pattern of great power conflict and the level of international competition among adherents of rival political ideologies. Yet it has also responded to the twentieth-century increase in interconnection among national societies brought about by new technologies and new patterns of production and consumption.

Understanding how the pattern of great power competition affects the institution of recognition of governments requires looking at each of its components: the number of great powers, the disparity of resources between great powers and other states, the disparity of will between great powers and other states, and the flexibility of alignment among great powers.

The important difference in the number of great powers is between one, and two or more. This proposition cannot be tested at the global level. Though Britain in the nineteenth century and the US after 1945 were clearly the centres of the international economy, this economic position was never sufficient for the exercise of an overall predominance. However, some instances of regional predominance do bear out the claim. Where local states were independent, recognition policy could be part of the arsenal of informal empire whenever their internal politics were troubled. In the late 1850s and early 1860s, successive governments of Mexico came under considerable pressure from the British and French, which was unrelieved because no other great power took any interest in the situation. Though the British dropped out when the French moved from nonrecognition to intervening on behalf of a newly-installed regime, the French had a clear field for a time. Only in late 1865, when its civil war was over and it possessed great-power-sized forces for the only time in the nineteenth century, did the US provide the effective counterweight that induced the French to abandon their venture. Similarly, the US government was able to maintain strong pressure on the Tinoco regime in Costa Rica during 1917 because neither Britain nor France was willing to offer Tinoco the loans he needed or the recognition as president that he wanted. In contrast, US efforts to impose stipulations on three new Haitian governments in 1914–15 were impeded by French and German recognitions of the target regimes.

Alliances of great powers occasionally functioned as cohesive blocs, as in the immediate aftermath of the Napoleonic Wars, World War I, and World War II. However, all three experiences show that a predominant coalition is not the functional equivalent of a single predominant power. The Napoleonic and World War II coalitions both fell apart after a few years, and members resumed competition with each other. The World War I coalition also suffered the same fate, but never included all of the great powers anyway. Thus the Bolsheviks began their escape from diplomatic isolation by making agreements with the German government in 1920, and China and Turkey could use relations with both Germany and the USSR to counterbalance other powers.

The ability of weaker states to pursue their own recognition policies depends partly on the presence of multiple great powers and partly on ability to de-link regional affairs from great power concerns. Central American efforts to define a regional recognition policy were hobbled by US efforts to use that policy in its own way. The newly-independent states in Africa were able to develop their own recognition policies after 1960 with less outside involvement because Cold War competition between East and West allowed steering a neutralist course between the two blocs. The Sino-Soviet rift expanded the area of choice for Eastern European states during the Cold War by providing competing definitions of the proper Leninist reaction to particular new regimes.

Disparity of resources does not prevent using recognition or non-recognition to express support or hostility, though clearly the expressions of a great power cast a larger shadow than those of a weak state. Disparity of resources is far more crucial to the success of efforts to secure particular commitments from a new regime or to affect its chances of survival. This was well understood in the nineteenth century: all attempts to use recognition for either of these two purposes involved a stronger state exerting pressure on a notably weaker one. In many cases, the initiating government also had reason to believe no other power would counterbalance its efforts. This basic prudence was briefly forgotten in the early interwar period, but Soviet ability to resist provided a sharp reminder, and post-1945 practice was again more attentive to disparities in resources.

Interwar instances also showed that disparity of resources might be countered by reduced disparity of will, particularly if weak state will increased and great power will eroded simultaneously. Greater emphasis on the doctrine of self-determination had just this effect: the rulers and articulate publics of weak states in and outside Europe gained a rallying call while a significant segment of elite and public opinion in the great powers also accepted the principle and began modifying their diplomatic practice accordingly. This simultaneous strengthening of will among the weak and erosion of will among the strong was furthered in the Cold War era as decolonization proceeded and the sorts of 'gunboat diplomacy' endured in the nineteenth century were increasingly de-legitimated and labelled intervention in others' affairs.

Yet it is hard to identify the full effects of these normative changes because in particular cases weaker states' resistance was also aided by rivalry among great powers. The efforts of the new Turkish Republic and the various Chinese factions of the 1920s to secure recognition, and abolition of the nineteenth-century treaty privilege regimes, were significantly aided by German and Soviet decisions to grant concessions. The normative effects seem clearer after 1955, when the anti-colonial majority in the UN General Assembly extended recognition as states to a range of 'mini-states' and former colonies with weak domestic political and social organization, and brought them within the protection of UN membership.[1]

Though the broad pattern of changes in the flexibility of alignment established an important part of the context, particular situations were often determined by the degree to which the great powers could act in concert after a particular extra-legal change of government. The clearest examples of working in concert involved Morocco in 1907–8, activities of the Supreme Allied Council (Britain, France, Italy, and the USA) in 1917–18, and cooperation among the 'Big Three' (Britain, the USSR, and the USA) in 1943–5. The second and third involved reorganizing the states system in the immediate aftermath of major war, the first was one of several instances of co-operation among the powers outside Europe despite the hardening of alliances.

Whenever inflexibility of alignment was great enough, weaker states lost room to manoeuvre between the great powers. It is difficult to imagine a set of circumstances in Cold War Europe resembling the events precipitating acceptance of the Albanian monarchy in 1928. The Italian government (which was encouraging the monarchical project) recognized the monarchy as soon as it was proclaimed in September. The Yugoslav government, which had intervened in 1925 to maintain the republic against its internal enemies and saw the change as part of a wider increase in Italian influence, was in a quandary. It wanted to avoid entirely alienating the Albanian government (the new king had been prime minister in the republican government that received Yugoslav help in 1925) but also did not want to accept the change before knowing how Britain and France would react. The US government, probably unaware of all the complications involved, recognized the monarchy a week later. This led the Yugoslavs first to consult the British and French and then to accept the monarchy, though they did not recognize the change until later.[2] Even the Soviets, in whose Leninist ideology the change was retrogressive, came around to recognizing the monarchy in 1934 to better counter German and Italian efforts to gain influence throughout the Balkans.[3]

Changing intensity of international ideological competition had more effect on the pattern of political uses of recognition than shifts in the pattern of great power competition. This is shown most clearly by changes in the frequency and duration of expressions of opinion or attempts to affect a new regime's chances of survival. These were far more prominent during the periods of high ideological contention – 1815–30, the interwar period, and the Cold War. During the relatively nonideological periods between 1830 and 1914, almost all political uses of recognition involved attempts to extract concessions from a new regime or to express disapproval of how it had come to power. The one exception was in Central America, where democratic legitimacy, in the form of upholding constitutional over extra-constitutional methods of gaining power, was tried after 1907. Before 1830 and after 1914, expressing approval or disapproval of a new regime's character and attempting to affect a new regime's chances for survival predominated among the political uses. Premature recognition and prolonged nonrecognition were both known in the early nineteenth century; prolonged nonrecognition was frequent after 1917, though declined considerably after 1970. The change in patterns of political use of recognition is particularly striking in the Cold War period: while political use increased after 1945 and included two competing forms of legitimist recognition policy, attempts to trade recognition for concessions disappeared.

Not only were there more political uses of recognition in ideological eras, withholdings of recognition lasted far longer. The longest cases of refusal to recognize between 1830 and 1914 – US nonrecognition of Maximilian in Mexico and British nonrecognition of the new Karageorgevich king of Serbia – lasted three years. In both the interwar and Cold War eras, three years was a relatively short delay. The Bolsheviks received their first great power recognition about two and a half years after taking over, and their last 15 years later. Several governments, strongly encouraged by the US example, withheld recognition of the PRC for more than 20 years. A few other regimes, particularly those of Heng Samrin in Cambodia and Pinochet in Chile, were also targets of nonrecognitions lasting more than five years.

The late nineteenth-century increase in interconnection did not inhibit persistent nonrecognition because governments found ways to meet the need for minimal contacts in elaborations of the older traditions of 'informal' bilateral relations or in the growing network of multilateral activities and organizations. Private activities were sheltered by the growing separation of acceptance as the *de facto* ruler of a particular territory for administrative purposes and for settling private lawsuits, from acceptance as international agent of the state. The regimes affected by prolonged nonrecognition occasionally chafed at the refusals, but tended not to press matters in the expectation that sooner or later other governments would accept the reality of their existence. The renewal of increases in interconnection after the disruptions of World War I, the Great Depression, and World War II also failed to affect political uses of recognition in the early Cold War era.

Yet increased interconnection did underlie the shift away from using recognition of governments for political purposes after 1970. Changes in technology, the increasingly complex network of trans-border production and consumption patterns, and greater political mobilization of social groups around the world affected recognition policy in two ways. First, they permitted developing more ways to express political approval or disapproval, extract promises, or affect a regime's survival prospects. Inter-government loans and other forms of aid provided new, non-military ways of exerting real pressure on regimes in most developing countries and trade or investment embargoes could be used even against regimes not needing aid but desirous of participating in the increasingly global economy. Increased political mobilization of individuals and social groups in all parts of the world made it possible to influence the course of politics elsewhere by supporting some faction or movement even while accepting those in power as the government. Leninists and fascists both engaged in this sort of activity during the interwar period, with the Leninists developing a particularly elaborate (even if usually transparent) distinction between 'inter-party' and 'inter-state' relations. Similar efforts were pursued by both blocs and even by regional powers during the Cold War. Development of a new status as a 'national liberation movement' provided a way to endorse or aid a faction fighting against colonial or other alien rule without using recognition of governments. Thus the decreased acceptance of military pressure did not mean that the more powerful states were left without ways of influencing others.

Secondly, interconnection after 1945 involved growing coordination or cooperation on a wider range of issues as governments became responsible for a wider array of services in domestic politics. Governments read the Great Depression as a lesson in the baneful effects of managing national economies without wider cooperation to cope with the strong connection between the domestic and the international economy. The rise of environmental concern in the late 1960s suggested another range of concerns where each state's uncoordinated domestic efforts would not solve the problems at hand. These developments brought government administrative organs into greater contact with counterpart agencies in other countries either directly or through co-participation in the increasing number of 'technical' multilateral organizations, and created yet another level of interest in maintaining cross-border interactions.

In this new situation, not only legal scholars but also a growing number of policy-makers and attentive citizens began to regard as illogical the combination of refusing to recognize a particular regime as the international agent of its state and yet maintaining a wide array of bilateral and multilateral dealings with it. This shift of view is most clearly documented for the United Kingdom, where the government adopted a largely effectivist recognition policy in the late 1940s under the influence of Sir Hersh Lauterpacht's arguments that there is a duty to recognize any regime that effectively rules its state.[4] More governments shifted to an effectivist policy later, though their public statements suggested that they were motivated less by concerns about functional necessities imposed by growing interconnection than because political use of recognition had created problems by encouraging the public to equate recognition with approval of a new regime. This added new levels of complication to domestic debates about policy towards particular countries, shown most vividly in the hesitancy of Democratic Party politicians in the USA to advocate recognition of the PRC in the 1960s (it took Richard Nixon, whose record as an anti-communist was second to none, to carry conservatives along with the change), and the occasional proposals in other countries that some government be 'derecognized' because of ideology or policy. By 1960, the link between recognition and approval of a new regime was so strong that it affected public opinion not only in countries where the government indulged in political uses, but also in several where the government did not. Governments first sought to sever the link by shifting to tacit recognition and accepting new regimes before domestic debate became too clamorous. In the mid-1960s a few went further and began claiming they had abandoned the practice of recognizing new governments.

This return to greater effectivism was not significantly affected by the reduction of East–West tensions during the détente of the early to mid-1970s or the sharp renewal of tensions in the late 1970s. Most of the refusals to recognize the PRC government ended in this period, and relatively few new politically-motivated nonrecognitions were initiated. The most prominent political uses of recognition between 1970 and 1985 were not unilateral efforts, but the concerted nonrecognitions of the Heng Samrin government in Cambodia, continued South African administration of Namibia, and the Ian Smith government in Rhodesia.

The renewed discussion of and some action on notions of democratic legitimacy in the late 1980s and early 1990s suggest that graphing the relation between effectivist recognition policies and the level of international ideological competition yields a V-shaped curve, with high interest in legitimist criteria at both low and high levels of international ideological competition. At the high end legitimist policies are a weapon in ideological conflict; at the low end they serve as a mechanism for maintaining the consensus on design of domestic institutions. On this analysis, the prevalence of effectivism in the nineteenth century reflected an intermediate situation where ideological differences among states were great enough to prevent consensus on any one way of organizing domestic political systems but not felt so strongly or so urgently that adherents of different ideologies felt impelled to subvert political arrangements in other states. In the abstract, a principle of free choice (hedged only by a requirement to respect other states' rights) appears to be a logical necessity for maintaining a system of independent states. In practice, however, the logic of state autonomy in the choice of domestic political arrangements may be eroded not only by efforts to overturn the Westphalian system and create a global empire or other world government, but also by consensus that even in a system of independent states international and domestic governance are sufficiently intertwined[5] that all states need to adopt similar principles of domestic rule even if they retain some choice in how to interpret and implement them.

Any shift from the current understanding of state autonomy as choice in the principles as well as the details of domestic organization would occur partly for material and partly for ideational reasons. The material reasons are the improvements in technology and changes in patterns of production and distribution that have made possible a highly interconnected and mutually-aware set of domestic societies. The ideational reasons are the demands for application of democratic norms of governance in both domestic and international politics and their spread to other areas of life as well. The Westphalian system emerged in the seventeenth century with an alignment of international and domestic norms of governance: monarchs ruled domestically with scant consultation of their subjects, and dealt internationally with each other as fellow members of an elite club. The norms diverged as the application of democratic norms was progressively expanded in domestic governance but foreign affairs were still considered a special realm. Efforts to organize democratic control of foreign policy did not of themselves challenge the idea that foreign policy required patterns of decision and action different from those prevailing domestically. That challenge arose later, as wider groups of citizens perceived the effects of interconnection and drew the conclusion that the old traditions of separating domestic and foreign policy no longer met the practical needs of an interconnected world or the normative requirements of late twentieth-century concern with group rights, individual rights, and accountability in all forms of social organization.

EVOLUTION OF THE INSTITUTION

The insistence on maintaining political uses of recognition demonstrates once again that what might be suggested by the functional logic of an international institution can be overridden by decisions to use the institution for other purposes as well. Yet it also demonstrates the corrosive effects of using an institution for such incompatible cross-purposes that the underlying contradictions of those purposes are exposed for all to see. The institution of recognition of governments is more discredited today than it would otherwise have been because the political uses of the interwar and early Cold War eras so vividly exposed the contradictions between the international function of assessing whether a particular regime can serve as the international agent of its state and individual states' foreign policy goals.

If governments had been less insistent on using recognition for individual foreign policy ends, it is likely that increasing interconnection among states would have inclined policy-makers more steadily towards an effectivist application of the institution. If that had happened, it is likely that recognition of governments would look much the same today as it did in the nineteenth century. The practice of continuing informal inter-government relations prior to recognition would have remained a convenience for getting through short periods of uncertainty. There would have been little need to expand the substantive content of 'informal relations' to address political questions or maintain the general framework of economic and other contacts for years at a time. Nor would domestic administrative agencies and courts have faced the problem of how to treat the acts, certifications, or counterpart agencies of an unrecognized regime anywhere near as often because in most instances recognition would have settled matters before the agency or court had to decide what to do.

Had the effectivist path been taken, there would have been little need to consider how to mesh the distinct streams of bilateral and multilateral relations. Increasing interconnection inspired development of a growing range of multilateral relations in administrative and technical fields during the twentieth century. The potential for separating them from bilateral relations had been established in the nineteenth century by drawing on established diplomatic traditions distinguishing between the 'high politics' of military security and general relations and the 'low politics' of everything else (particularly among economic liberals assuming that markets and the gold standard could operate with a minimum of government interference). This permitted distinguishing matters that were 'foreign policy questions' from matters that were simply intergovernmental coordination. It was therefore quite natural to bring multilateral relations within the category of 'informal relations'. Under an effectivist recognition practice, multilateral relations would have been an additional temporary bridge of uncertainty but not an alternate track for maintaining some degree of contact during periods of prolonged nonrecognition.

There was never any significant likelihood that new or continued participation in multilateral cooperation would depend on prior recognition by all the other participants because of the move from unanimous to majority decision about participation. Decision by a qualified majority rather than unanimity was already the usual rule even before the League of Nations was established. The League's innovation consisted in extending majoritarian decision to participation in the explicitly political organs. Majority decision meant that one or a few nonrecognizing governments could still find themselves in the position of having to accept participation by a regime they did not recognize because they were outvoted – unless they wanted to go to the extreme of quitting the multilateral activity or organization altogether. Yet multilateral relations did offer a new mode of concerting recognition or nonrecognition. The idea of using intergovernmental forums for coordinated recognition decisions gained little currency, but the idea of using them to concert nonrecognition of particularly objectionable situations, including certain types of new regimes, did win wider following. This raised the possibility of developing a whole new set of non-effectivist recognition practices – political uses in the interest of maintaining widely-shared interests or normative standards.

The significant number of governments which refused to adopt effectivist recognition practices during the interwar period and the first half of the Cold War period burdened themselves with the problem of balancing the need for continued contact to cope with growing interconnection, and their desire to treat some clearly ineffective regimes as governments or avoid accepting some clearly effective ones as such. Had these governments been a small minority ruling weak states, their actions would not have had as great an effect on the development of legal rules. However, they were a fairly large group and included several great powers; this gave them enough weight in the decentralized process of international law-making to pull the evolution of rules on recognition of governments in the non-effectivist direction they wished to go.

Yet they were ultimately caught in the coils of inconsistency created by their own expedients. Some felt that de-emphasizing recognition of governments by shifting to tacit forms and acting relatively quickly would solve their problems; others decided that the popular tendency to link recognition with approval was so strong that the only way to escape the inconsistencies was to abandon recognition of governments altogether.

Outright abandonment seemed feasible in the late twentieth century because of the vast increase in the timeliness and volume of information about events in other parts of the world. Policy-makers could more confidently dispense with recognition because domestic courts and administrative agencies, and even private citizens, groups and firms, were better able to determine for themselves who ruled with what prospect of stability in another state. In the nineteenth century, foreign offices usually did have significant advantages over others in the acquisition and analysis of information, and it was not unreasonable for courts and other government agencies to follow their guidance. By the 1930s, however, courts in several states were confident that they could appreciate the situation in other countries using other sources of information and applying their normal rules of evidence to evaluate what they revealed. This new confidence was partly the result of practice dealing with politically motivated recognitions or nonrecognitions, but was later encouraged by developments in other areas of domestic law. Starting in the 1970s with new legislation redefining the scope of state immunity from suit and legal execution, then expanding into other areas, governments adopted statutes that turned particular decisions over to the courts by defining what constitutes 'a government' or an action eligible for respect without reference to recognition.

By narrowing the effects of nonrecognition compared with nineteenth-century practice, the interwar and early Cold War evolution of the institution left more room for continuing disagreement about the criteria for recognition. This permitted extending the wider debate about whether the older principle of free choice or some conception of universally-relevant principles of domestic governance should be maintained into discussions of the law on recognition of governments. It also allowed proposing that recognition be used to help enforce common standards through concerted nonrecognition, whether to discourage continued colonialism or institutionalized racism or to advance notions of a right to democratic governance.

THE FUTURE OF THE INSTITUTION

The confusions stemming from political uses of recognition decisions and the reactions against those confusions demonstrate quite strongly that legal institutions are not 'givens' imposed by some supernatural force or teleological unfolding of history, but are social constructs assembled and reassembled by human actors as they contend over the proper organization of life together. A particular regime's effective administration of the state it claims to rule and its enjoyment of obedience from most of the population are readily observable phenomena. There may be some room for question in particular cases, but such uncertainty usually lasts a relatively brief period of time. However, the debate about what to make of the observable phenomenon of control is a more enduringly contentious matter of attributing meaning.[6] In the nineteenth century, the observable facts of effective administration and securing obedience were usually translated into the meaning 'the new regime is a government'. Yet the exceptions provided openings for experimenting with other meanings in the interwar and Cold War eras. These persisted until the point was reached where it was unclear that there was any relation between effective rule and enjoyment of obedience on one hand and having or not having acceptance as a government on the other. Significant numbers of legal scholars and policy-makers were profoundly unhappy about the resulting degree of confusion, and sought to reduce ambiguity in various ways. Yet none of these proposals has won the unanimous support of states, so governments and legal scholars still face the question of what should be done with the institution of recognition of governments.

At the most basic level, what is done will depend on whether the international system develops more centralized modes of governance. If it does, the current institution of recognition of governments will be replaced by a process looking far more like administrative issuance of birth certificates or papers of incorporation in national law. If, however, the international system remains a decentralized one of autonomous states, the current pattern of each government determining the status of new regimes on its own will persist.

In the absence of such a centralization of international governance, three possible solutions are most frequently discussed. The first consists of abandoning the institution of recognition of governments altogether. The second involves expanding current patterns of multilateral activity to establish some procedure for collective recognition by majority vote in a global intergovernmental organization. The third involves establishing effectivism as the policy that will normally prevail, while allowing the possibility for exceptions stipulated in general international law or mandated by decision of an intergovernmental organization. In legal language, effectivism would be a rebuttable presumption; in computer jargon, it would be an overridable default.

A growing number of governments claim to be adopting the first alternative. They claim the right to decide whether to have full diplomatic relations and conclude agreements with a new regime, but no longer comment on its qualifications to act as the international agent or the domestic ruler of its state. While ready to supply information about events abroad or the extent of their own dealings with a new regime, they leave courts, subordinate administrative agencies, and private entities or individuals to determine whether the new regime deserves to be treated as a government for their particular purposes. Doctrines of state continuity and greater availability of information combine to provide both the framework of legal principle justifying assumption of smooth transfer of title to rule even when acquired unconstitutionally, and the practical ability to appreciate when transfers have occurred.

The advocates of abandoning recognition of governments are right that in most cases a new regime consolidates rule quickly, and that it is possible to determine when power has been transferred using information available in the news media. In these cases, all the information will point to the same conclusion: courts, administrative agencies, and private citizens will agree that the new regime is a government. An equivalent to the British 'speak with one voice' doctrine would be superfluous because shared information would lead to the same conclusion no matter what agency or court was involved.

However, such unanimity of view is less likely when two or more active rivals contend for control. It is in these situations that some agreed rules remain necessary. One possible response involves treating all factions as local *de facto* governments in the part of the state they rule and accepting none as representing the state in multilateral relations. The first half of this possibility does not depart far from existing precedent; the second half is a greater departure though has been used in regional organizations on occasion. Another possible response involves treating whichever faction holds the largest portion of territory as the general government of the state, with rights to represent it in multilateral affairs, and the others as local *de facto* governments. This follows current practice, and would be appropriate in periods when one faction did have a clear advantage in the ongoing struggle. A third possibility, also compatible with recent practice, involves active international promotion of a negotiated settlement involving an interim coalition government and elections to determine who will rule.

The second possibility, establishing a collective procedure in which a majority vote commits all, has the attraction of reducing individual arbitrariness by subjecting decisions to prior deliberation. This does not, as the practice of the UN General Assembly shows, guarantee an end to arbitrariness; it means simply that the forms of arbitrariness allowed will be those acceptable to a majority of the members. Unlike the first alternative, collective decision also offers the possibility of adopting criteria other than control of the state as prerequisites for treatment as a government because these could be defined and applied jointly. The impact of nonrecognition on a new regime would depend on how the collective process was structured. There would be little room for inching along to wider recognition if the new regime had to apply directly to the intergovernmental organization; there would be more if the new regime could apply for endorsement once a certain number of members had extended recognition. Yet there appears little prospect of adopting any sort of collective process very soon. States still prefer a range of discretion in the ordering of their bilateral relations.

The third alternative of overridable effectivism most resembles the actual direction of state practice today. A careful look at their practice shows that none of the states claiming to have abandoned recognition of governments has forsworn the possibility of nonrecognition in particular instances. Some claim a discretion to refuse recognition if in their individual view a new regime fails to meet some basic criterion, and have variously invoked dependence on foreign military intervention, antidemocratic character, and massive violations of human rights as justifying refusals to recognize. Others claim less individual discretion, but accept the propriety of concerted nonrecognition mandated by the UN Security Council under Chapter VII of the Charter or by a regional body.

Leaving open the possibility of overriding the effectivist presumption that any new regime controlling its state will be accepted as the state's international agent has strong appeal for those who believe that the international community should not endorse regimes which hack their way to power by committing atrocities or rely entirely on foreign military support. Massive election fraud or a small group's use of force to eject an elected government that has not forfeited popular support through its own misgovernment also offend many sensibilities today. Thus there is a respectable body of opinion regarding unvarying effectivism as a tacit endorsement of a norm that any small group who can grab power, extract obedience, and provide something resembling regular administration will be accepted as a government. Yet others rightly fear that admitting exceptions to effectivism opens up possibilities for abuse. The possibilities of abuse for individual states' ends could be reduced by requiring a collective decision, but that is no guarantee against inconsistent reactions to similar seizures of power or great power arm-twisting to secure acceptance of particular standards.

Any policy of collective nonrecognition would also face the problem of balancing efforts to discourage certain regimes with the need to maintain those forms of international cooperation that benefit the population of the country involved. Any collective nonrecognition that ignored the functional consequences for the population of an effective regime would be imposing inconvenience and possibly harm on the most vulnerable rather than on the most responsible. The dilemmas involved would be particularly acute when nonrecognition was accompanied by economic embargoes and other measures of isolation. The International Court of Justice attempted to define a reasonable balance in the Namibia Advisory Opinion, but the Haitian case suggests quite strongly that embargoes and other measures could easily hurt the population far more than the target regime. The existence of these dilemmas is not necessarily an argument against using collective nonrecognition, but it is an argument for care in its application.

Whether an overridable effectivism becomes the basic norm for recognition of governments will depend on how the international community – policy-makers, legal scholars, and attentive publics alike – answers the key question of how domestic governance relates to regional and global governance. The Westphalian tradition of state autonomy has the attraction of allowing the people of each state to determine their own future the best they can, free from outside meddling (though not without foreign advice and examples). Yet it suffers from the flaw of permitting small groups to monopolize domestic governance and use all the technologies of rule to abuse the rest of the population. The Westphalian principle of full autonomy in domestic affairs has been compromised many times as other considerations gained sufficient appeal;[7] an overridable effectivism would permit responsiveness to changing perceptions of how those other considerations should be taken into account.

Notes

1.THE INSTITUTION OF RECOGNITION OF GOVERNMENTS

1 Scelle, *Manuel* (1948): 98, argued that both are forms of recognizing governmental jurisdictions (*compétences gouvernementales*); Baty, 'Abuse of Terms' (1936): 377, and Chatelain, 'La reconnaissance' (1950): 717, argued that the two are so intertwined that they cannot be fully separated.
2 Most forcefully argued in recent years by Brownlie, 'Recognition in Theory and Practice', (1986).
3 For theoretical discussions of these problems, see e.g. Kratochwil, *Rules, Norms, and Decisions* (1987); Onuf, *World of Our Making* (1989); Franck, *The Power of Legitimacy among Nations* (1990); Koskenniemi, *From Apology to Utopia* (1989); Goldstein and Keohane (eds), *Ideas and Foreign Policy* (1993); Wendt, *Social Theory of International Relations* (forthcoming). For efforts to trace particular foreign policy choices, see Reisman and Willard (eds), *International Incidents* (1988); Khong: *Analogies at War* (1992).
4 Though sharing common canons of legal reasoning, these scholars did not have sufficient consensus on policy goals and means to form a transnational 'epistemic community' as defined by some international relations theorists. E.g. Haas (ed.), *Epistemic Communities and International Policy Coordination* (1992).
5 Exceptions include Kaplan and Katzenbach, *The Political Foundations of International Law* (1961), who focus on the distribution of capability, and Hoffmann, 'International Systems and International Law' (1965), who focuses on level of inter-state ideological competition.
6 Waltz, *Theory of International Politics* (1979).
7 E.g. Morgenthau, *Politics among Nations* (1948); Carr, *The Twenty Years' Crisis* (1947); Wolfers, *Discord and Collaboration* (1962).
8 Buzan, Jones, and Little, *The Logic of Anarchy* (1993).
9 E.g. Cox, *Production, Power, and World Order* (1987); Gill, *American Hegemony and the Trilateral Commission* (1990).
10 E.g. Wallerstein, *The Capitalist World-Economy* (1979); Chase-Dunn, *Global Formation* (1989).
11 What Jowitt called 'the Leninist extinction' in *The New World Disorder* (1992).
12 E.g. George, *Presidential Decisionmaking in Foreign Policy* (1980).

2. LIMITS TO RECOGNITION OF GOVERNMENTS

1 Weisse, *Le Droit international* (1898): 237–8; Le Normand, *La Reconnaissance internationale* (1899): 138; Oppenheim, *International Law* (4th edn, 1928), vol. 1: 151–2; Accioly, *Traité* (1940): 170; Scelle, *Manuel* (1948): 126; Berber, *Lehrbuch* (1960): 234; Chaudhari, *Public International Law* (1962): 97.

2 Holtzendorff, *Handbuch* (1885), vol. 2: 86.
3 Smith, *Great Britain and the Law of Nations* (1932), vol. 1: 172; Hackworth, *Digest*, vol. 1: 309.
4 Raestad, 'La Reconnaissance' (1936): 301–2, provided the most detailed scheme. Oppenheim, *International Law* (4th edn, 1928), vol. 1: 151–2, offered brief suggestions.
5 Hackworth, *Digest*, vol. 1: 463–4.
6 Hackworth, *Digest*, vol. 1: 306–7.
7 Hackworth, *Digest*, vol. 1: 231, 243, 269 and 295
8 Letter of President Obregón to President Harding, 11 June 1921, *FRUS, 1921*, 2: 419 (1936).
9 *FRUS, 1931*, 2: 919–21 (1946).
10 *FRUS, 1931*, 2: 921 (1946).
11 Berber, *Lehrbuch* (1960), vol. 1: 234; Menon, 'Some Aspects, III' (1990): 158.
12 Lauterpacht, *Recognition* (1947): 92; Fenwick, *International Law* (3rd edn, 1948): 159; Feldman, 'Recognition' (1969): 204; most Chinese scholars according to Hsiung, 'China's Recognition Practice' (1972): 36. The Chinese seem to have defined this more broadly than the Leninist sense of change in the class composition of the government.
13 *FRUS, 1948*, 4: 733–55 (1974).
14 Whiteman, *Digest*, vol. 2: 466.
15 Whiteman, *Digest*, vol. 2: 458, and *Current Notes on International Affairs*, 24: 540 and 604 (1958).
16 *British Practice in International Law, 1967*: 43; *Australian YBIL*, 1967: 239; *Canadian YBIL*, 4: 262 (1968); *Department of State Bulletin*, 56: 750 (1967).
17 *Australian YBIL*, 10: 505 (1987).
18 Noted in *Canadian YBIL*, 233 (1966).
19 The British reacted similarly to the 1967 coup in Sierra Leone because the new military leaders simply took the powers of the Governor-General into their own hands without explicitly saying the Queen was no longer head of state. Bundu, 'Recognition' (1978): 29. The clearer break in Fiji, where a republic was proclaimed in 1987, led them to conclude that continuity had been disrupted. *British YBIL*, 58: 514 (1987).
20 Undersecretary of State for Commonwealth Affairs to the House of Commons, 27 April 1967, in *British Practice in International Law, 1967*: 43.
21 Bundu, 'Recognition' (1978): 30.
22 Bundu, 'Recognition' (1978): 31–2.
23 *Current Notes on Foreign Affairs*, 32: 660 (1951) reported this as Australian, British, and US reaction. Whiteman, *Digest*, vol. 2: 466, says the US dispensed with recognition.
24 F. Vali, 'The Hungarian Revolution and International Law', *Fletcher Review*, 2: 9 (1959), quoted in Whiteman, *Digest*, vol. 2: 399–400.
25 Hsiung, 'China's Recognition Practice' (1972): 37.
26 *Current Notes on International Affairs*, 37: 146 (1966).
27 *Ann. française*, 1965: 1068; *British Practice in International Law, 1965*: 20–1.

28 *British Practice in International Law, 1965*: 21.
29 Rousseau, 'Chronique', *RGDIP*, 75: 479–80 (1971).
30 Rousseau, 'Chronique', *RGDIP*, 75: 1096 (1971).
31 Rousseau, 'Chronique', *RGDIP*, 75: 158–9 (1971).
32 Hsiung, 'China's Recognition Practice' (1972): 36.
33 Radio Kampala report of 15 April 1971, quoted in *Africa Contemporary Record*, 4: C79 (1971–2).
34 The Swiss began following a policy of recognizing whoever held power with regard to Latin American states right after World War II, but did not begin extending this to other parts of the world until after a more general policy review in 1949. Ando, 'The Recognition' (1985): 37.
35 Opposed: Rivier, *Principes* (1896): 60; Holtzendorff, *Handbuch* (1889), vol. 2: 31; Oppenheim, *International Law* (2nd edn, 1912), vol. 1: 31. Favouring: Lorimer, *The Institutes* (1883), vol. 1: 132–3.
36 Moore, *Digest*, vol. 1: 141, 147 and 149; *FRUS, 1913*: 728–9 (1920).
37 Williams, 'Recognition' (1929): 67; Baty, *The Canons* (1930): 212; Strupp, *Éléments* (2nd edn, 1930), vol. 1: 84; Møller, *International Law* (1931): 100; Bustamante y Sirven, *Droit international public* (1934), vol. 1: 173; Arendt, *Die Anerkennung* (1938): 165–7.
38 Liszt, *Das Völkerrecht* (12th edn, 1925): 92; Kunz, *Die Anerkennung* (1928): 134; Rolin, 'Observations' (1936), vol. 38: 353; Schlüter, *De-facto Anerkennung* (1936): 4.
39 Oppenheim, *International Law* (4th edn, 1928), vol. 1: 156; Spiropoulos, *Traité* (1936): 50. Wheaton, *Elements of International Law* (4th English edn, 1929), vol. 1: 45, also allowed revocation in circumstances other than a diplomat's error.
40 *FRUS, 1944*, 7: 1106–7 (1967).
41 Chen, *Recognition* (1951): 102; Kozhevnikov, *International Law* (1961): 121. By treating the incident as incidental to recognition of Finnish statehood, Erich, 'La Naissance' (1926): 448, and Verhoeven, *La Reconnaissance* (1975): 660, n. 107, concluded that no revocation was involved.
42 See page 168.
43 Note from Foreign Minister Molotov to the Polish ambassador in Moscow, 17 September 1939, in Degras (ed.), *Soviet Documents on Foreign Policy, 1917–1941* (1951), vol. 3: 374. Re-establishment of relations is discussed in Whiteman, *Digest* (1963), vol. 2: 407.
44 Recognition aspects are discussed in Whiteman, *Digest*, vol. 2: 407–8.
45 Chen, 'American Recognition and Non-recognition Policies in China' (1963): 104–7 and 118–22.
46 *FRUS, 1933*, 5: 342 (1952).
47 Letter from Secretary of State Hull to Senator Pittman, chairman of the Senate Foreign Relations Committee, 9 February 1935, in Whiteman, *Digest*, vol. 2: 45. Hull also insisted that recognition is an executive prerogative.
48 Bindschedler, 'Die Anerkennung' (1962): 376; Chaudhari, *Public International Law* (1962): 95; American Law Institute, *Restatement, Second* (1965): 396.
49 Lauterpacht, *Recognition* (1947): 338; Mugerwa, 'Subjects of International Law' (1968): 279–80; Oppenheim, *International Law* (8th edn, 1958): 139;

Dahm, *Völkerrecht* (1958), vol. 1: 147; Guggenheim, *Traité de droit international public* (1953), vol. 1: 198; Verdross, *Völkerrecht* (4th edn, 1959): 186; Berber, *Lehrbuch* (1960), vol. 1: 235; Cavaré, *Le Droit* (3rd edn, 1961), vol. 1: 324; Tandon, *Public International Law* (10th edn, 1965): 152; Tunkin, *International Law* (1982): 115; Loudwin, *Konkludent* (1983) Starke, *Introduction* (9th edn, 1984): 132; Dahm, *Völkerrecht* (new edn, 1989): 212.

50 Kozhevnikov, *International Law* (1961): 121; O'Connell, *International Law* (1965), vol. 1: 173; Hingorani, *Modern* (1984): 97–8.

51 Fenwick, 'Recognition De Facto' (1964): 966–7. Dhokalia, *International Law* (1963): 234; Jhabvala, 'The Credentials Approach' (1979).

52 Kapoor, *International Law* (1992): 161; Umozurike, *Introduction* (1993): 65; Menon, 'Some Aspects, V' (1991): 36–7.

53 Oppenheim, *International Law* (9th edn, 1992), vol. 1: 176–7.

54 Inter-American Council of Jurists (1953): 65–6.

55 Retraction of a 'hasty' grant of recognition to the Boumédienne government of Algeria in June is noted by Rousseau, 'Chronique', *RGDIP* (1965), 69: 1098, note 8.

56 Response to questions, 2 August 1965, in *British Practice in International Law, 1965*: 124.

57 The Dahomean government established diplomatic relations with the Republic of China (ROC) in January 1962, the PRC in April 1965, and the ROC again in April 1966, *China Handbook, 1966*: 197–8. The Central African Republic's government established diplomatic relations with the ROC in April 1962, the PRC in November 1964, the ROC in May 1968, the PRC by October 1971 and the ROC in May 1972, *China Handbook, 1968*: 365–6; Rousseau, 'Chronique', *RGDIP* (1972), 76: 494; and *China Handbook, 1972*: 391 and 510. The Senegalese government established diplomatic relations with the ROC in 1960, the PRC in 1964, the ROC in July 1969, and the PRC in December 1971, *China Handbook, 1972*: 391 and 510.

58 The Australian government opted for the latter view. Statement by the Minister of External Affairs to the House of Representatives, 9 April 1964, in *Current Notes on International Affairs*, April 1964: 52.

59 *Dade Drydock Corp. et al.* v. *The M/T Mar Caribe et al.*, US District Court for the Southern District of Texas, 1961, *F. Supp.* 199: 871; *International Law Reports*, 32: 70 (1966); *Republic of Cuba* v. *Mayan Lines, SA et al.*, US District Court for the Southern District of Louisiana, 1961, reversed by the Circuit Court of Appeals in 1962, *So. 2d* 145: 679; *International Law Reports*, 33: 36 (1967).

60 Australian statement on 'derecognition', 14 February 1981, *Australian YBIL*, 10: 286–7 (1987) and additional comments on pp. 287–91; British government statement of 6 December 1979, noted in Warbrick, 'Kampuchea' (1981): 240–1; and of 2 March 1988, *British YBIL*, 59: 437 (1988).

61 Credentials Committee debates about whether to admit a South African delegation to the UN General Assembly's resumed 35th session in March 1981, as reported in *UN Chronicle*, April 1981, p.5. Records of the meeting in General Assembly Official Records, 35th Session, Annexes, Agenda item 3, Doz. A/35/484/Add.2 (2 March 1981) report delegations challenging

the South African government's right to participate or to issue credentials but not saying that their governments have withdrawn recognition.

62 Eighteenth-century legal scholars did distinguish between 'public treaties' and 'private treaties' regulating purely dynastic or family matters. See, e.g., the discussion of 'real' and 'personal' treaties in Vattel, *Droit des gens* (1758), book 2, chapter 12, para. 188, and Martens, *Précis de droit des gens moderne de l'Europe* (1788), book 2, chapter 1, para. 60.

63 Larnaude, 'Les Gouvernements de fait' (1921): 457.

64 Kelsen, 'Théorie générale' (1932): 333; Livonius, *Die völkerrechtliche Anerkennung* (1934): 67–72. In *Principles of International Law* (1952): 413–16 Kelsen accepted the doctrine of state continuity.

65 See Taracouzio, *The Soviet Union and International Law* (1935): 21. Though the Polish scholar Marek, *Identity and Continuity* (1954): 33–8, argued that Soviet writers never really challenged the doctrine, the Soviet scholars Kozhevnikov, *International Law* (1961): 125, and Feldman, 'Recognition' (1969): 213, were still asserting discontinuity after class revolution.

66 Hsiung, 'China's Recognition Practice' (1972): 36.

67 April 1975 statement reprinted in Rousseau, 'Chronique', *RGDIP*, 79: 1107 (1975).

68 Lécharny, *La Validité* (1929): 57.

69 E.g. *Peruvian Guano Company* v. *Dreyfus*, Court of Appeals of Brussels, 1888, in *Revue générale de droit international privé (Clunet)*, 16: 716 (1889); *Dreyfus Frères et Cie.* v. *Chile*, Franco-Chilean Arbitral Tribunal, 1901, in Despagnet and Renault, *Recueil, Année 1901*: 180.

70 Wharton, *Digest*, 3: 840.

71 Tinoco Claims Arbitration (*Great Britain* v. *Costa Rica*), 1923, *UN Reports of International Arbitral Awards*, 1: 370 (1948); George W. Hopkins' Claim (*USA* v. *Mexico*), US–Mexico General Claims Commission, 1926. This doctrine was strongly enough established for Menon, 'Some Aspects III' (1990): 173–4, to treat the Dreyfus cases as affirming the same point.

72 See pages 130–6 and 111–14 respectively.

73 See pages 139–50.

74 Le Normand, *La Reconnaissance* (1899): 267–8; Wegner, 'Über Anerkennung' (1931): 201; Bindschedler, 'Die Anerkennung' (1962): 387.

75 Klüber, *Droit des gens* (2nd edn, 1874): 78; Weisse, *Le Droit international appliqué aux guerres civiles* (1899): 237; Liszt, *Das Völkerrecht* (9th edn, 1913): 112. Le Normand's protest may have been triggered by inclusion in earlier editions than consulted here.

76 Including Rougier, *Les Guerres civiles* (1903): 499, who expressed an intermediate view that capacity existed but could not be exercised before recognition, and Funck-Brentano and Sorel, *Précis* (3rd edn, 1900): 203, who took a purely constitutive view.

77 Liszt, *Das Völkerrecht* (12th edn, 1925): 91; Oppenheim, *International Law* (4th edn, 1928), vol. 1: 143–5; Spiropoulos, *Traité* (1933): 6, Sastry, *International Law* (1937): 34.

78 Goebel, 'The Recognition Policy of the United States' (1915): 66–8; Podesta-Costa, 'Règles à suivre' (1922): 52; Gemma, 'Les Gouvernements

de fait' (1924): 333; Anderson, 'De facto Government' (1925): 517; Oppenheim, *International Law* (4th edn, 1928), vol. 1: 151; Lécharny, 'La Validité' (1929): 16–17; Politis, 'La Théorie de la reconnaissance' (1929): 186–90; Anzilotti, *Cours* (3rd edn, 1929), vol. 1: 161; Baty, *Canons* (1930): 205; Jaffe, *Juridical Aspects of Foreign Relations* (1933): 120–4; Williams, 'La doctrine' (1933): 205–35; Livonius, *Die völkerrechtliche Anerkennung* (1934): 34; Rolin, 'Observations' (1934): 325; Bustamante y Sirven, *Droit international* (1934), vol. 1: 172–3; Huess, 'Zum Probleme' (1935): 10; Institut de droit international, 'La reconnaissance' (1936): 300; Verdross, *Völkerrecht* (1937): 115–16; Arendt, *Die Anerkennung* (1938): 103–9; André-Vincent, 'La problème' (1938): 411; Buza, 'Die juristische Natur' (1940): 80; Philip Brown, 'The Effects' (1942): 106–8.

79 Spiropoulos, *Die de facto Regierung* (1926): 11; Kunz, *Anerkennung* (1928): 158–9; McKittrick, 'Recognition of Changes' (1917): 38; Raestad, 'Le Reconnaissance internationale' (1936): 257; Fauchille, *Traité* (8th edn, 1921), vol. 1: 306–7; Hershey, *The Essentials* (rev. edn, 1927): 199; Møller, *International Law* (1931): 98; Accioly, *Traité* (1940), vol. 1: 143–4.

80 Raestad, 'La Reconnaissance' (1936): 270; Brown, 'Effects of Recognition' (1942): 106–8; Hatschek, *Völkerrecht* (1923): 146–7.

81 Chatelain, 'La Reconnaissance internationale' (1950): 725; Lador-Laderer, 'Recognition' (1957): 65–7; Jovanovič, 'Dualism' (1961): 136–7; Asamoah, 'Recognition' (1968) 128–9; Corbett, *Law and Society in the Relations of States* (1951): 60–2; Kaplan and Katzenbach, *The Political Foundations of International Law* (1961): 109–10; O'Connell, *International Law* (1965), vol. 1: 140; Frowein, 'Völkerrecht' (1985): 8; Brownlie, 'Recognition' (1986): 634–6.

82 Charpentier, *La Reconnaissance international* (1956): 230; Frowein, *Das de facto Regime im Völkerrecht* (1968): 15–21; Mugerwa, 'Subjects' (1968): 268; Kelsen, *Principles* (1952): 265–9; Dahm, *Völkerrecht* (1958): 133; Verdross, *Völkerrecht* (4th edn, 1959), vol. 1: 181–4; Kozhevnikov, *International Law* (1961): 119; Chaudhari, *Public International Law* (1962): 94–5; Tandon, *Public International Law* (1965): 149; O'Connell, *International Law* (1965), vol. 1: 139–40; Mookerjea, *International Law* (2nd edn, 1968), vol. 1: 122; Visscher, *Theory and Reality in Public International Law* (3rd edn, 1968): 239; Akehurst, *A Modern Introduction* (1970): 68; Reuter, *Droit international public* (1983): 21; Hingorani, *Modern* (1984): 97; Starke, *Introduction* (9th edn, 1984): 128–9; Cruz, *International Law* (1984): 79; Chen, *An Introduction* (1989): 41.

83 Teuscher, *Die vorzeitige Anerkennung im Völkerrecht* (1958): 81–5; Patel, *Recognition in the Law of Nations* (1959): 19; Gorus, *Manuel* (1980): 73; Loudwin, *Konkludente* (1983); Dahm, *Völkerrecht* (new edn, 1989): 188–90.

84 Lauterpacht, *Recognition* (1947): 61–6; Sibert, *Traité* (1951): 190–1; Guggenheim, *Traité* (1953), vol. 1: 189–91; Oppenheim, *International Law* (8th edn, 1958), vol. 1: 124–8.

85 Chen, *Recognition* (1951): 386–7; Azevedo, *Aspects généraux* (1953): 97–8; Shao, *Die Anerkennung* (1967): 26; Verhoeven, *La Reconnaissance* (1975): 724; Bierzanek, 'La Non-reconnaissance' (1962): 122; Bindschedler, 'Die Anerkennung' (1962): 387; Fuhrmann, 'Die Anerkennung' (1965): 423;

Feldman, 'Recognition' (1969): 206–7; Kato, 'Recognition' (1970): 301–2; Ross, *A Textbook of International Law* (1947): 116; Scelle, *Manuel de droit international* (1948): 121; Berber, *Lehrbuch* (1960), vol. 1: 229; Cavaré, *Le Droit* (1961), vol. 1: 327; Brierly, *The Law of Nations* (6th edn, 1963): 138–40; Delbez, *Les Principes généraux* (3rd edn, 1964): 159–60; Salonga and Yap, *Public International Law* (3rd edn, 1966): 98–9; Brownlie, *International Law* (1966): 82–4; Bastid, *Droit international public* (1970): 167; Coquia and Santiago, *Public International Law* (1984): 113; Verdross and Simma, *Universelles Völkerrecht* (1984): 560–1; Verhoeven, 'Relations internationales' (1985): 25; Menon, 'Some Aspects, I' (1989).

86 Umozurike, *Introduction* (1993): 61–2.

87 Detter, *International Law* (1992): 95; Oppenheim, *International Law* (9th edn, 1992), vol. I: 129; Kindred, *International Law* (1993): 250.

88 Foreign Minister Lamartine's circular of 4 March 1848, *Répertoire française*, 3: 33.

89 Speech of 5 April 1921, quoted in *Répertoire française*, 3: 82.

90 Bonfils, *Manuel* (7th edn, 1914): 445; Chen, *Recognition* (1951): 207.

91 Since treaties do not bind nonparties, they would have no right to do so unless implementation of the agreement prejudiced their rights in some way.

92 *United Nations Treaty Series*, 119: 3.

93 Tinoco Claims Arbitration (*Great Britain* v. *Costa Rica*), 1923, *UN Reports of International Arbitral Awards*, 1: 370 (1948).

94 *Certain German Interests in Polish Upper Silesia*, 1926, PCIJ Series A, No. 7.

95 See discussions of decisions by the US Supreme Court, and of some interwar Czech and German decisions, in Whiteman, *Digest*, vol. 2: 24–5.

96 See pages 148–50

97 See pages 180–2.

3. LEGAL RULES GUIDING RECOGNITION DECISIONS

1 Lorimer, *Institutes* (1883), vol. 1: 104–5; Bluntschli, *Das moderne Völkerrecht* (3rd edn, 1878): 75–6.

2 Grenard, 'Principes de la reconnaissance' (1931): 81–2.

3 Kelsen, 'Recognition in International Law' (1941): 605.

4 Borchard, 'Recognition and Nonrecognition' (1942): 108.

5 Arendt, *Die Anerkennung* (1938); Baty, 'Abuse' (1936): 377; Møller, *International Law* (1931), vol. 1: 64.

6 Lauterpacht, 'Recognition of Governments' (1950): 5.

7 Scelle, *Manuel* (1948): 123.

8 Brown, 'The Legal Effects' (1950): 617; Kelsen, *Principles of International Law* (1952): 269–73; Dahm, *Völkerrecht* (1958), vol. 1: 122–32; Brownlie, *Principles of Public International Law* (1966): 80–90; Coquia and Santiago, *Public International Law* (1984): 113–15; American Law Institute, *Restatement, Third* (1989): 84; Brownlie, 'Recognition' (1986): 637–8; Henkin, 'International Law' (1989): 31–3 (while advocating abolition of recognition).

9 Frowein, *Das de facto Regime* (1968): 17.
10 O'Connell, *International Law* (1965), vol. 1: 137–8.
11 Lauterpacht, *Recognition* (1947): v; Kunz, 'Critical Remarks' (1950): 716; Berber, *Lehrbuch* (1960), vol. 1: 225–6; Whelan, 'The United States and Diplomatic Recognition' (1961): 62; Alexandrowicz, 'The Quasi-Judicial Function in Recognition' (1962): 631; Bindschedler, 'Die Anerkennung' (1962): 393; Fenwick, *International Law* (1965), vol. 2: 578; Morrison, 'Recognition' (1966–7): 863; Bot, *Non-Recognition and Treaty Relations* (1968): 1–3; Verhoeven, *La Reconnaissance internationale* (1975): 581–2 and 617–27.
12 Patel, *Recognition* (1959): 57.
13 American Law Institute, *Restatement, Second* (1965): 203. As noted above, the *Third Restatement* gave a different view.
14 Ruda, 'The Law' (1991): 457; Arbour, *Droit international* (1992): 177.
15 Umozurike, *Introduction* (1993): 65.
16 Letter of the Canadian Secretary of State for External Affairs, 23 July 1971, in *Canadian YBIL*, 10: 309 (1972).
17 Rougier, *Les Guerres civiles* (1903): 488–9; Klüber, *Droit des gens* (1874): 85; Phillimore, *Commentaries* (3rd edn, 1879), vol. 1: 271; Martens, *Traité* (1883): 409; Gareis, *Institutionen des Völkerrechts* (2nd edn, 1901): 100–1; Despagnet, *Cours* (1905): 93.
18 Bluntschli, *Das moderne Völkerrecht* (1878): 75–6 and 116; Lorimer, *Institutes* (1883), vol. 1: 104–5 weakened his argument by allowing various exceptions to the duty.
19 Le Normand, *La Reconnaissance* (1889): 184.
20 Holtzendorff, *Handbuch* (1889), vol. 2: 86.
21 Funck-Brentano and Sorel, *Précis* (3rd edn, 1900): 209; Merignhac, *Traité* (1907): 295.
22 Fiore, *Nouveau droit international public* (1885), vol. 1: 297; Hall, *A Treatise* (3rd edn, 1890), vol. 1: 87; Westlake, *International Law* (2nd edn, 1910), vol. 1: 59.
23 E.g., Heffter, *Le droit international* (4th Fr. edn, rev., 1883): 118; Davis, *Elements* (1908): 42; Oppenheim, *International Law* (2nd edn, 1912), vol. 1: 426.
24 See pages 158–9.
25 Williams, 'Recognition' (1929): 77; Baty, 'Abuse' (1936): 377; Borchard, 'Remarks' (1942): 110–11; Scelle, *Précis* (1932), vol. 1: 101.
26 Louter, *Le Droit* (1920), vol. 1: 219–20; Bustamante y Sirven, *Droit international public* (1934), vol. 1: 176–7.
27 Baty, 'So-called' (1921–2): 469; Stowell, 'Remarks' (1931): 178; Louter, *Le Droit* (1920), vol. 2: 6; Liszt, *Das Völkerrecht* (9th edn, 1925): 92.
28 E.g., Raestad, 'La Reconnaissance' (1936): 309–11; Kelsen, 'Recognition' (1941): 315.
29 Quoted in Inter-American Council of Jurists, 'Recognition of de facto governments' (1953): 8.
30 *League of Nations Treaty Series*, 94: 57.
31 Note from Commissar for Foreign Affairs Litvinov to the French ambassador in Moscow, 13 August 1928, quoted in Jaffe, *Juridical Aspects of Foreign Relations* (1933): 147.

32 Lauterpacht, *Recognition* (1947): 158–61.
33 Azevedo, *Aspects généraux* (1953): 95–7.
34 Kozhevnikov, *International Law* (1961): 117–18; Feldman, 'Recognition' (1969): 209. Though these discussions dealt with both new states and new regimes, Soviet specialists regarded the rules on each as identical except on certain points clearly identified in their writings.
35 Higgins, *The Development of International Law* (1963): 137.
36 Charvin, 'La République démocratique allemande et le droit international général' (1971): 1022–3.
37 Sibert, *Traité* (1951), vol. 1: 199; Wright, 'Recognition, Intervention, and Ideologies' (1958): 97; Bindschedler, 'Die Anerkennung' (1962): 384.
38 As indicated by reference to the concept of *jus cogens* in Article 64 of the Vienna Convention on the Law of Treaties, *United Nations Treaty Series*, 1155: 347.
39 O'Connell, *International Law* (1965), vol. 1: 146.
40 Kato, 'Recognition' (1970): 304–5.
41 K'ung Meng, 'A Criticism' (1974): 246.
42 Oppenheim, *International Law* (8th edn, 1958); American Law Institute, *Restatement, Second* (1965): 303; Verhoeven, *La Reconnaissance* (1975): 575 and 581–2.
43 Chen, *Recognition* (1951): 129; Brown, 'Legal Effects' (1950): 639; Mugerwa, 'Subjects' (1968): 277; Ross, *Textbook of International Law* (1947): 121; Kelsen, *Principles* (1952): 282–3; Dahm, *Völkerrecht* (1958), vol. 1: 136–7; Berber, *Lehrbuch* (1960), vol. 1: 230; Tandon, *Public International Law* (1965): 150–1; Brownlie, *Principles* (1966): 85; American Law Institute, *Restatement, Third* (1989): 84.
44 Coquia and Santiago, *Public International Law* (1984): 637–8; Brownlie, 'Recognition' (1986): 637–8; Henkin, 'International Law' (1989): 31–3.
45 Verhoeven, *La Reconnaissance* (1975): 581; Starke, 'Recognition' (1950): 19; Fuhrmann, 'Die Anerkennung' (1965): 434–5; Asamoah, 'Recognition' (1968): 126; Kato, 'Recognition' (1970): 304; Hingorani, *Modern International Law* (1984): 83–4; Starke, *Introduction* (9th edn, 1984): 129; Dahm, *Völkerrecht* (new edn, 1989): 196–7.
46 O'Connell, *Principles* (1965), vol. 1: 142–4; Charpentier, *La Reconnaissance* (1956): 285–6.
47 Tripathi, *India's Foreign Policy* (1990): 38.
48 Whiteman, *Digest*, vol. 2: 7.
49 Wolf, 'Le Gouvernement de fait' (1956): 124, for Switzerland; Indian government statement quoted in Whiteman, *Digest*, vol. 2: 16.
50 Foreign Minister Gromyko's statement to the Geneva Foreign Ministers' Meeting of 12 May 1959, quoted in Whiteman, *Digest*, vol. 2: 13–14.
51 Mainly in discussions of the UN Special Committee on Principles of International Law concerning Friendly Relations and Cooperation among States. See e.g. remarks of Soviet delegate in UN Doc. A/AC. 119/SR. 35 (24 Sept. 1984), p. 18.
52 Statements quoted in Inter-American Council of Jurists, 'Recognition of De Facto Governments' (1953): 61–2.

53 Frenzke, 'Völkerrechtliche Anerkennung' (1967): 185 summarizes the arguments.
54 This was indicated before the event in the joint Soviet–Bulgarian–East German–Hungarian–Polish letter condemning the course of Czechoslovak reform in July 1968, quoted in *Keesing's Contemporary Archives*, 1968, p. 22887.
55 British statement to the International Law Commission, quoted in International Law Commission, *Report*, 1949 session (UN Doc. A/925): 186.
56 See discussion in *The Times* (London), 20 July 1974, p. 6, col. 5.
57 Arbour, *Droit international* (1992): 177 argued that such a policy 'tends subtly to substitute' a duty by reducing or denying opportunities to debate recognition policy.
58 See pages 181–2.
59 See page 177.
60 'Premature recognition' is a generally-used term; 'prolonged recognition' is my phrase for what is sometimes called 'continued recognition' and sometimes described with other phrases.
61 Martens, *Précis* (3rd edn, 1883): 410; Mackintosh, 'Speech' (1824); Le Normand, *La Reconnaissance* (1898): 191; Heffter, *Le Droit* (1883): 117; Martens, *Traité* (1883): 410; Neumann, *Éléments* (1886): 54; Holtzendorff, *Handbuch* (1889), vol. 2: 87; Merignhac, *Traité* (1907), vol. 2: 295; Pessoa, *Draft of a Code* (1911): 37; Lawrence, *Principles* (4th edn, 1913): 90–1; Bonfils, *Manuel* (1914): 445.
62 Goebel, 'Recognition Policy' (1915): 207; Louter, *Le Droit* (1920), vol. 1: 5–6; Baty, 'So-called' (1921–2): 469; Hatschek, *Völkerrecht* (1923): 80; Hershey, *Essentials* (1927): 209; Kunz, *Die Anerkennung* (1928): 123–4; Oppenheim, *International Law* (4th edn, 1928): 152; Williams, 'Recognition' (1929): 64; Strupp, *Éléments* (1930), vol. 1: 90; Grenard, 'Principes de la reconnaissance' (1931): 81; Møller, *International Law* (1931), vol. 1: 99; Scelle, *Précis* (1932): 101; Spiropoulos, *Traité* (1933): 52; Huess, 'Zum Probleme' (1935): 11; Raestad, 'La Reconnaissance' (1936): 309–10; Verdross, *Völkerrecht* (1937): 100–2; Arendt, *Die Anerkennung* (1938): 84; Hyde, *International Law* (2nd rev. edn, 1945), vol. 1: 159.
63 Ross, *A Textbook* (1947): 197; Viret, *La Portée* (1951): 18; Chen, *International Law of Recognition* (1951): 104; Alexandrowicz, 'Quasi-Judicial' (1952): 635; Teuscher, *Die vorzeitige* (1954): 115–21; Schwarzenberger, *A Manual* (1960): 69; Bindschedler, 'Die Anerkennung' (1962): 384; Brierly, *Law of Nations* (6th edn, 1963): 146; Dhokalia, *International Law* (1963): 213; Delbez, *Les Principes* (1964): 256.
64 Kelsen, *Principles* (1952): 297–8; Verdross, *Völkerrecht* (4th edn, 1959): 251 (a shift of position); Frowein, *Das de facto Regime* (1968): 321–2; Feldman, 'Recognition' (1969): 205; Blix, 'Contemporary Aspects' (1970): 644; Coquia and Santiago, *Public International Law* (1984): 113–15; Brownlie, 'Recognition' (1986): 637–8; Henkin, 'International Law' (1989): 31–3.
65 As made clear in British statements about recognition of the 1875 restoration. Smith (ed.), *Great Britain and the Law of Nations* (1932), vol. 1: 205.
66 *FRUS, 1928*, 2: 179 (1943).

67 Tinoco Claims Arbitration (*Great Britain* v. *Costa Rica*), *UN Reports of International Arbitral Awards*, 1: 369.
68 'Diplomatic Recognition', *Department of State Bulletin* (1979).
69 Discussed pages 178–82.
70 See pages 13–16.
71 This was a significant shift for a government that had not recognized the Soviet one until 1942.
72 Statement by the Secretary of State for External Affairs to the House of Commons, 22 September 1964, in *Canadian YBIL*, 4: 234 (1966).
73 Misra, *India's Policy* (1966): 107–16.
74 Discussed in more detail pages 58–67.
75 Wheaton, *Elements* (1836): 93.
76 Klüber, *Droit des gens* (1874): 37; Woolsey, *Introduction* (1883): 67; Holtzendorff, *Völkerrecht* (1889), vol. 2: 86; Merignhac, *Traité* (1907), vol. 1: 322.
77 Fiore, *Nouveau droit* (1885), vol. 1: 274.
78 Gibbs, *Recognition* (1863): 41–3; Weisse, *Le Droit international appliqué aux guerres civiles* (1898): 97–9; Le Normand, *La Reconnaissance* (1899): 268–9; Despagnet, *Cours* (1905): 95. Rougier, *Les Guerres civiles* (1903): 491–3 recommended this policy without arguing that there is any obligation to follow it.
79 Goebel, 'The Recognition Policy' (1915): 169–70 notes the strong public pressures on the US government.
80 Baty, 'So called' (1922): 481–2; Stinson, 'Recognition of De Facto Governments' (1923–4): 16; Fauchille, *Traité* (1924), vol. 1: 54; Spiropoulos, *Die de facto Regierung* (1926): 25–9; Anzilotti, *Cours* (1929), vol. 1: 169; Scelle, *Précis* (1932), vol. 1: 100; Bustamante y Sirven, *Droit* (1934), vol. 1: 169–70; Sharp, *Nonrecognition as a Legal Obligation* (1934): 182; Kunz, *Anerkennung* (1938): 135.
81 Gemma, 'Les Gouvernements' (1924): 334–7; Pollock, 'De Jure Recognition' (1924); Williams, 'Recognition' (1929): 64; Wheaton, *Elements* (6th Eng. edn, 1929), vol. 1: 54.
82 Baty, 'So-called' (1922): 486, who even considered a state to be divided until one contender fully extinguished all resistance; Scelle, *Précis* (1932), vol. 1: 100.
83 Azevedo, *Aspects généraux* (1953): 39. The other Allies provided aid but treated them as local de facto governments of the territory they held.
84 Grzybowski, *Soviet Public International Law* (1970): 74.
85 Degras, *Soviet Documents on Foreign Policy, 1917–1941* (1951), vol. 3: 405–7.
86 General protocol of 23 October 1936, *Documents on German Foreign Policy, 1918–1945*, Ser. C, vol. 5, no. 624.
87 *FRUS, 1944*, 7: 1108–12 (1967).
88 Azevedo, *Aspects généraux* (1953): 39, Charpentier, *La Reconnaissance* (1956): 303–7; Patel, *Recognition* (1959): 678–9; Schwarzenberger, *Manual* (1960), vol. 1: 63; Bindschedler, 'Die Anerkennung' (1962): 383–4; Asamoah, 'Recognition' (1968): 129; Menon, 'Some Aspects, III' (1990): 159.
89 Feldman, 'Recognition' (1969): 208.

90 Kelsen, *Principles* (1952): 282; Verdross, *Völkerrecht* (4th edn, 1959): 253; American Law Institute, *Restatement, Second* (1965): 318; O'Connell, *International Law* (1965), vol. 1: 179; Starke, *Introduction* (9th edn, 1984): 134.
91 Verhoeven, *La Reconnaissance* (1975): 553–5 and 571–4.
92 Ross, *Textbook* (1947): 199; Dahm, *Völkerrecht* (1958), vol. 1: 136–7; Wright, 'Recognition' (1958): 97–8; Berber, *Lehrbuch* (1960), vol. 1: 230–1; Fuhrmann, 'Die Anerkennung' (1965): 435; Mugerwa, 'Subjects' (1968): 277–8; Gorus, *Manuel* (1980): 73; Green, *International Law* (1988): 145; Dahm, *Völkerrecht* (new edn, 1989): 200; Chen, *An Introduction* (1989): 44.
93 Hornbeck, 'Recognition of Governments' (1950): 185; Kopelmanas, 'La Reconnaissance' (1957): 15; Cavaré, *Le droit* (1961), vol. 1: 320; Brierly, *Law of Nations* (6th edn, 1963): 146; Delbez, *Les Principes* (1964): 165; Tandon, *Public International Law* (1965): 162; and Salonga and Yap, *Public International Law* (1966): 107.
94 See, for example, the various opinions expressed in Rosenau, *International Aspects of Civil Strife* (1964); Falk, *International Law and the Vietnam War* (3 vols, 1968–72); Falk, *The International Law of Civil War* (1971).
95 They included the PRC, Czech, East German, Hungarian, Polish, North Vietnamese, North Korean, Soviet, Egyptian, Mali, Guinean, Indonesian, Cuban, and Yugoslav governments. Misra, *India's Policy of Recognition* (1966): 107–8.
96 *Ann. française*, 1969: 974–51.
97 The French and US governments publicly stated this conclusion the next day, Rousseau, 'Chronique', *RGDIP*, 75: 158–9 (1971), and the Australian the following week, *Current Notes on International Affairs*, 41: 603 (1971). Other Western governments simply maintained diplomatic relations without any public comment.
98 *Keesing's Contemporary Archives*, 1970: 24127.
99 Algeria, Congo, Cuba, Egypt, Guinea, Iraq, Libya, Mauretania, Romania, South Yemen, Sudan, Syria, Yugoslavia. *Keesing's Contemporary Archives*, 1970: 24127.
100 Though Barnes, 'US Recognition Policy and Cambodia', pp. 155–6, suggested that exile regimes should be considered a continuation of the former government comparable to the Allied governments-in-exile of World War II. Sihanouk's delay in establishing the government-in-exile makes such arguments less plausible on the legal plane.
101 *Ann. française*, 1973: 1104. The Soviets allowed the Lon Nol government to maintain an embassy in Moscow until they recognized the Sihanouk government.
102 *Washington Post*, 29 March 1975, p. A10, col. 5. The Soviets were still cautious, however; Prince Sihanouk announced the recognition and the Soviets made no comments on either his announcement or the Lon Nol government ambassador's claim that his expulsion from Moscow did not involve recognition of the rival regime.
103 Rousseau, 'Chronique', *RGDIP* 79: 1106–7 (1975). *Washington Post*, 18 April 1975, p. A15, col. 1; 19 April 1975, p. A15, col. 1; and 2 May 1975, p. A13, col. 7.

104 *Ann. française*, 1965: 1084–5.
105 *Ann. française*, 1971: 1124. It mentions no Sudanese recognition.
106 Whiteman, *Digest*, vol. 2: 394 includes a US warning against such recognitions but no notes that any actually occurred.
107 Whiteman, *Digest*, vol. 2: 354.
108 Ruda, 'The Law' (1991): 456; Seidl-Hohenveldern, *Völkerrecht* (1992): 164.
109 *Republic of Chile* v. *The London and River Plate Bank*, English Court of Appeal, 1894, in *British International Law Cases*, 2: 65 (1965).
110 Woodhead (ed.), *China Yearbook*, 1921: 623–6.
111 *Répertoire française*, 3: 85 (France); comment on *Nonis* v. *Federation of Seamen*, Court of Appeals of Genoa, 1930, in *Annual Digest, 1929–30*, Case No. 23, pp. 45–6 (Italy).
112 Houghton, 'Policy of the United States' (1929): 96.
113 See pages 106 and 117.
114 *Herzfeld* v. *Russian Volunteer Fleet*, High Court of Justice, King's Bench Division, 1928, in *Annual Digest, 1927–28*, Case No. 125.
115 The exceptions are Arendt, *Die Anerkennung* (1938): 159; Dickinson, 'The Unrecognized' (1923–4): 129; Pollock, 'De Jure Recognition' (1924). Dickinson was particularly insistent because he was a fierce critic of US refusal to recognize the Soviet government.
116 Exceptions include Lauterpacht, 'Recognition' (1950); Chen, *Recognition* (1951): 129; Guggenheim, *Traité* (1953), vol. 1: 197–8; Blix, 'Contemporary Aspects' (1970): 645 (in most situations); Falk, *International Law of Civil War* (1971): 14; Verhoeven, *La Reconnaissance* (1975): 387, note 113; Dahm, *Völkerrecht* (new edn, 1989): 201; Ruda, 'The Law' (1991): 456.
117 Western refusal to formally recognize incorporation of Estonia, Latvia, and Lithuania into the USSR persisted from 1939 until 1991.
118 E.g. Riding, 'Franco's Old Foes Gather in Mexico', *New York Times*, 15 April 1974, p. 13, col. 1.
119 *New York Times*, 15 April 1974, p. 13, col. 1.
120 E.g., objections to ROC adherence to the convention creating the International Atomic Energy Agency, Erdmann, *Nichtanerkannte* (1962): 85.
121 Speculation that South Vietnamese in the USA might form one inspired a journalist's question that elicited a statement from Secretary of State Kissinger that the US would not recognize any government-in-exile of South Vietnam. *US Practice*, 1975: 26.
122 Verhoeven, *La Reconnaissance* (1975), vol. 1: 99, note 123.
123 Chen, *International Law of Recognition* (1951): 429; Patel, *Recognition in the Law of Nations* (1959): 111; and Wright, 'Recognition' (1958): 97, on nonrecognition of puppet regimes. Feldman 'Recognition' (1969): 205 on nonrecognition of new governments whose composition or method of gaining power violates fundamental norms of international law.
124 Iriye, *After Imperialism* (1965): 192.
125 Troppau Memorial of 1820, quoted in Sharp, *Nonrecognition* (1934): 182.
126 See pages 66–7 for further discussion.

4. THE MAIN CRITERIA FOR RECOGNITION

1 Aristodemou, 'Choice and Evasion' (1994) supplies a Critical Legal Studies version of this argument, but any legal scholar studying recognition in any depth is aware of the underlying problem.
2 See pages 174–6.
3 Martens, *Traité* (1883), vol. 1: 410; Woolsey, *Introduction* (1883): 113.
4 Weisse, *Le Droit international* (1898): 236; Rougier, *Les Guerres civiles* (1903): 501; Lawrence, *The Principles* (1913): 88.
5 Yes: Weisse, *Le Droit international* (1898): 236; Rougier, *Les Guerres civiles* (1903): 501; Lawrence, *The Principles* (1913): 88. No: Mackintosh, 'Speech' (1824); Le Normand, *La Reconnaissance* (1899): 191.
6 Quoted in Wharton, *Digest* (1887), vol. 1: 530.
7 Moore, *Digest* (1906), vol. 1: 125–6.
8 Smith (ed.), *Great Britain and the Law of Nations* (1932), vol. 1: 144, who notes that the British waited because the government called itself 'provisional'; Bruns (ed.), *Fontes Juris Gentium, Series B* (1933), Sec. 1, vol. 1, pt. 1, no. 529.
9 Wharton, *Digest* (1887), vol. 1: 544 (US); Bruns (ed.), *Fontes Juris Gentium, Series B* (1933), Sec. 1, vol. 1, no. 503 (Swiss).
10 Accioly, *Traité* (1940), vol. 1: 182–3.
11 Hackworth, *Digest* (1940), vol. 1: 291–2.
12 Chen, 'American Recognition' (1963): 50–2.
13 Moore, *Digest* (1906), vol. 1: 137–64.
14 E.g. Mexican recognition of the new Guatemalan government in 1887. See correspondence in *FRUS, 1887*, 749 (1888).
15 *FRUS, 1907*, 2: 696 (1910); and *AJIL*, 2: Supplement, 229–30 (1908).
16 The Treaty had resulted from discussions promoted by Mexican and US mediation. See correspondence and conference records in *FRUS, 1907*, 2: 606–81.
17 See pages 59–60.
18 Larnaude, 'Les Gouvernements' (1921): 475–6; Stinson, 'Recognition' (1923): 1; Stowell, 'The Doctrine' (1931): 302, who also condemned accepting rule by terror.
19 Goebel, 'The Recognition Policy' (1915): 207; Kunz, *Anerkennung* (1928): 123–4.
20 Federal Councillor Motta's response to questions from the National Council, 26 June 1927, quoted in Zellwenger, 'Die völkerrechtliche Anerkennung' (1954): 21.
21 Smith (ed.), *Great Britain and the Law of Nations* (1932), vol. 1: 259.
22 Hackworth, *Digest* (1944), vol. 1: 290.
23 Hackworth, *Digest* (1944), vol. 1: 293. This may have been a reaction to his pro-German stance.
24 Soviet delegate statement in the UN General Assembly, 12 December 1946; *General Assembly Official Records, 1st session*, part 2, pp. 1212–13; McChesney, 'International Law and Mexican Foreign Policy' (1969): 63–4.
25 See pages 58–61.
26 Hackworth, *Digest* (1944), vol. 1: 223, 232 and 248.

27 Chen, *Recognition* (1951): 123–4;
28 Irizarry y Puente, 'The Doctrine' (1954); Menon, 'Some Aspects, III' (1990): 165–6.
29 Fenwick, *International Law* (3rd edn, 1948): 159–60; Cruz, *International Law* (1984): 85; Menon, 'Some Aspects, III' (1990): 162.
30 The Inter-American Council of Jurists's comments on their 1949 draft convention on recognition of *de facto* governments, quoted in Inter-American Council of Jurists (1953): 17–18, was one of the few general assertions.
31 Lauterpacht, *Recognition* (1947): 156.
32 See, e.g., Diamond and Plattner (eds), *The Global Resurgence of Democracy* (1993).
33 'Democracy and Legitimacy' (1991); Detter, *International Law* (1992): 67 and 105–9.
34 Kapoor, *International Law* (1992), 163.
35 Oppenheim, *International Law* (9th edn, 1992), vol. I: 151.
36 Ruda, 'The Law' (1991): 458; Seidl-Hohenveldern, *Völkerrecht* (1992): 164; Arbour, *Droit international* (1992): 175.
37 Soviet note, quoted in Hsiung, 'China's Recognition Practice' (1972): 21; Speech of US Assistant Secretary of State for Far Eastern Affairs, 18 May 1951, *Department of State Bulletin*, 24: 746 (1951).
38 Binavince, 'Canadian Practice in Matters of Recognition' (1974): 168; Wolf, 'Le gouvernement de fait en droit suisse' (1956): 115.
39 E.g., Written answer to questions in the House of Commons, June 1979, *British YBIL* 50: 294–5 (1979).
40 See pages 178–82.
41 Guinean and Malian reactions noted in *Keesing's Contemporary Archives*, 1966: 21275; later Zambian statements noted in *Africa Contemporary Record* (1968–9), vol. 1: 498.
42 *Africa Contemporary Record* 4: C61–C64 (1971–72).
43 McChesney, 'International Law and Mexican Foreign Policy' (1969): 346.
44 Resolution 26 of the Second Special Interamerican Conference (Rio, 1965), English text from *AJIL* 60: 398 (1966).
45 Compare Verhoeven, *La Reconnaissance* (1975): 598–607, who distinguishes between 'democratic legitimacy', as insistence on popular support for any change, and 'constitutional legitimacy', as insistence that any change be accomplished according to procedures stipulated by the constitution then in force. He further distinguishes between 'political legitimacy', focusing on the form of government, and 'ideological legitimacy', focused on the values it professes to serve. All forms of legitimism combine concern with form and values because they regard form as an expression of underlying values.
46 Rougier, *Les Guerres civiles* (1903): 484, note 1; Spiropoulos, *De facto Regierung* (1926): 43; Verhoeven, *La Reconnaissance* (1975): 587–8.
47 Note the caution of scholars who clearly prefer democratic modes of governance in 'Democracy and Legitimacy' (1991): 141; Crawford, 'Democracy in International Law' (1993): 18–23.

48 By taking advantage of the traditional rule that recognized governments may request foreign assistance for suppression of civil disorder not amounting to a full-blown political insurgency or rebellion.
49 Holbraad, *The Concert of Europe* (1970); Schroeder, *The Transformation of European Politics* (1994), chapters 13–15.
50 See, e.g., Carnazza-Amari, *Traité* (1880), vol. 1: 463–4; Funck-Brentano and Sorel, *Précis* (3rd edn, 1900): 34–6; Gareis, *Institutionen* (2nd edn, 1901): 102. Compare John Stuart Mill's argument that a people must attain democracy by their own efforts, in 'A Few Words on Nonintervention' (1859).
51 Mirkine-Guetzévitch, 'Droit international' (1931): 338.
52 March 1907 letter from Tobar, formerly foreign minister of Ecuador, to a friend, printed in *RGDIP*, 21: 482–5 (1914).
53 English translation in *AJIL*, 2: Supplement, 299 (1908).
54 Sharp, *Nonrecognition as a Legal Obligation* (1934): 43–5.
55 Sharp, *Nonrecognition as a Legal Obligation* (1934): 46.
56 Sharp, *Nonrecognition as a Legal Obligation* (1934): 45–6.
57 Whether this reflected Wilson's original intentions is immaterial. He did not curb the tendency in any way.
58 See Gilderhus, *Diplomacy and Revolution* (1977).
59 Larnaude, 'Les Gouvernements de fait' (1921): 476 and 498; Podesta-Costa, 'Règles' (1922): 51; Spiropoulos, *De facto Regierung* (1926): 42–6; Kunz, *Anerkennung* (1928): 150–1; Baty, *Canons* (1930): 219; Dennis, 'Revolution' (1930–1): 208–12; Dickinson, 'Remarks' (1931): 132; Scelle, *Manuel* (1943): 99–100.
60 Strupp, *Éléments* (1930), vol. 1: 89–90; Scelle, *Précis* (1932), vol. 1: 117–18.
61 Gemma, 'Les Gouvernements' (1924): 335; Wolgast, 'Völkerrecht' (1935): 792; Arendt, *Die Anerkennung* (1938): 175–7. The American Brown also adopted this view in 'The Recognition of New Governments' (1932): 336.
62 Sharp, *Nonrecognition as a Legal Obligation* (1934): 47.
63 McMahon, *Recent Changes* (1933): 37.
64 Hackworth, *Digest*, vol. 2: 261.
65 Including the Dominican Republic (1922 and 1930), Nicaragua (1924), Honduras (1924), and Haiti (1930).
66 *FRUS, 1930*, 1: 417–18 (1945).
67 Hackworth, *Digest* (1944), vol. 1: 244.
68 English translation in *AJIL*, 17: Supplement, 118 (1923).
69 Whose possible political significance became clearer in postwar Argentina, where Juan Peron's first wife Eva was a pillar of the regime and his second wife Isabella served as vice-president and succeeded to the presidency when he died.
70 See Sharp, *Nonrecognition as a Legal Obligation* (1934); McMahon, *Recent Changes* (1933).
71 Hackworth, *Digest*, vol. 2: 224 (Bolivia) and 274–5 (Peru). Initial thoughts of applying it after the 1925 Ecuadorian coup were not followed up. Hackworth, *Digest*, vol. 2: 244.
72 Sibert, *Traité* (1951), vol. 1, note on pp. 198–202.
73 Frowein, *Das de facto Regime* (1968): 229–32.
74 Verhoeven, *La Reconnaissance* (1975): 588–9 and 595.

75 Schwarzenberger, *A Manual* (1960), vol. 1: 69; Kozhevnikov, *International Law* (1961): 114–16; Berber, *Lehrbuch* (1961), vol. 1: 225; Delbez, *Les Principes* (1964): 257–8.
76 Neumann, *Recognition of Governments* (1947): 24–5; Chen, *Recognition* (1951): 111–13; Irizarry y Puente, 'The Doctrine of Recognition' (1953–4): 317; Briggs, *The Law of Nations* (2nd edn, 1952): 129–30; Marek, *Identity* (1954): 51–6; Dinegar, 'Some Aspects' (1963): 270–1; O'Connell, *International Law* (1965), vol. 1: 149–50; Dozer, 'Recognition' (1966): 322; Mugerwa, 'Subjects' (1968): 271–2; Gorus, *Manuel* (1980): 54; Hingorani, *Modern* (1984): 87; Jankovic, *Public International Law* (1984): 106.
77 Fenwick, *International Law* (3rd edn, 1948): 165–9; Azevedo, *Aspects généraux* (1953): 37; Oppenheim, *International Law* (5th edn., 1958), vol. 1: 133; Bindschedler, 'Die Anerkennung' (1962): 390; Dhokalia, *International Law* (1963): 213–18.
78 English translation of the Soviet government's statement in *International Legal Materials*, 7: 1323–5 (1968), repeating the *New York Times*'s error in dating publication to the 25 September 1969 issue of *Pravda*. It was first published the following day.
79 For a summary of much of the discussion in Soviet-bloc states and China see Bettati, ' "Souveraineté limitée" ou "internationalisme prolétarien" ?' (1972).
80 E.g. Tunkin, *Theory of International Law* (1974): 436 and 440.
81 E.g. Chi, 'Smash the New Tsars' Theory of Limited Sovereignty', in Cohen and Chiu, eds, *People's China and International Law*, vol. 1 (1974).
82 Dozer, 'Recognition' (1966): 325.
83 Inter-American Council of Jurists (1953): 16.
84 Reproduced in Whiteman, *Digest*, vol. 2: 89.
85 Officially this was based on Cuban efforts to subvert other governments rather than on the fact of its existence. The Castro government had been recognized – even by the USA – quickly in 1959 before the depth of its Leninism was clear to others.
86 English text in *AJIL*, 60: 398–9.
87 Arias, 'Disparación' (1969).
88 Cochran, 'The Recognition' (1969): 270; Rousseau, 'Chronique', *RGDIP*, 67: 182 (1963).
89 US statement in *Department of State Bulletin*, 47: 348–9 (1962).
90 Rousseau, 'Chronique', *RGDIP*, 90: 965 (1986).
91 Rousseau, 'Chronique', *RGDIP*, 71: 149 (1967) (Argentina) and 73: 876 (1969) (Peru).
92 *Congressional Quarterly Almanac*, 22: 714 (1966). Verhoeven, *La Reconnaissance* (1975): 606–7 relied on incomplete information when saying it passed.
93 Rousseau, 'Chronique', *RGDIP* 73: 506 (1969).
94 Cuban reaction noted in *British YBIL* 49:262 (1978); Mexican decision to break off diplomatic relations in *Mexican Newsletter*, No. 46 (31 Dec. 1974), p. 4.
95 Cochran, 'The Recognition' (1969): 189–91, 221–4, and 227–9.
96 Mehrish, *India's Recognition Policy* (1972): 59–60.
97 Warbrick, 'The New British Policy' (1981): 576, n. 36.
98 *Africa Diary*, 1963, pp. 1192, 1212 and 1218.

99 Peter Enahoro's advocacy and other journalists' reactions are noted in *Africa Contemporary Record*, 1980–81, p. A65.
100 This change has inspired a large political science literature on 'democratic transitions'. Early expositions include O'Donnell, Schmitter and Whitehead (eds), *Transitions from Authoritarian Rule* (1986); Boloyra, *Comparing New Democracies* (1987); and Pridham (ed.), *Encouraging Democracy* (1991).
101 According to Rousseau, 'Chronique', *RGDIP*, 85: 111 (1981) either the 181st or the 189th in Bolivia's 155 years of independence.
102 Brazilian action noted in 'Chronique', *Ann. française*, 1981, p. 951. Rousseau, 'Chronique', *RGDIP*, 85: 111 (1981) lists Argentina, Brazil, Paraguay, Uruguay, Egypt, Israel, South Africa, and the ROC as having formally recognized the junta.
103 Rousseau, 'Chronique', *RGDIP*, 85: 111 (1981), who gives the OAS vote as 18 to 3 (Bolivia, Chile, Paraguay) with 4 abstentions (Argentina, Brazil, Guatemala, Uruguay); Rousseau, 'Chronique', *RGDIP*, 87: 157 (1983).
104 *New Zealand Foreign Affairs Record* 1986/1, p. 11.
105 Debates noted and statement reproduced in *Canadian YBIL*, 25: 423–4 (1987).
106 *US Practice*, 1980–8, p. 323.
107 Rousseau, 'Chronique', *RGDIP*, 90: 689–90 (1986) notes that Soviet-bloc diplomats attended Marcos's ceremony.
108 Rousseau, 'Chronique', *RGDIP*, 92: 1001–2 (1988). This may have been encouraged by earlier history. Delvalle was chosen as vice-president in an election marked by widespread allegations of fraud, and succeeded to the presidency when Noriega forced the president to resign in 1986.
109 West and Murphy, 'The Impact' (1989): 458.
110 Rousseau, 'Chronique', *RGDIP*, 92: 494 (1990).
111 Security Council debates in *Official Records of the Security Council, 1989*, 2899th–2902nd meetings (20–23 Dec. 1989); General Assembly debates in *General Assembly Official Records, 44th Session*, Plenary Meetings, 88th meeting (29 Dec. 1989).
112 His career had earlier been advanced by elements of the US intelligence community. Dinges, *Our Man in Panama* (1990).
113 Statements relating to the situation in Panama, Nicaragua, Burma, and Haiti, *Ann. française*, 1990, p. 1059.
114 Mexico, which had severed relations in November 1974, Rousseau, 'Chronique', *RGDIP*, 92: 771 (1990).
115 UN General Assembly Resolution 45/150 (1990), *General Assembly Official Records, 49th Session*, Supplement 49, p. 254–5; CSCE Charter of Paris for a New Europe, 21 November 1990, *International Legal Materials*, 30: 190 (1991).
116 Statement by US President Bush, 20 August 1991, *Dispatch*, 30: 614–15 (1991); British Foreign Office statement, 20 August 1991, *British YBIL*, 62: 556 (1991); German government statement, 20 August 1991, *ZaoRV*, 53: 926 (1993).
117 *Keesing's Record of World Events*, 1991, p. 38370. Another $280 million of humanitarian aid was not suspended.

118 *Keesing's Record of World Events*, 1991, p. 38370.
119 Questions and responses in *Canadian YBIL*, 30: 366 (1992).
120 'Chronique', *Ann. française*, 1991, p. 1072.
121 Security Council Resolution 940 (1994), *Resolutions and Decisions of the Security Council, 1990*, pp. 51–2.
122 E.g. Franck, 'The Emerging Right of Democratic Governance' (1992).
123 E.g. Ruda, 'The Law' (1991): 458; Arbour, *Droit international* (1992): 174–5; Seidl-Hohenveldern, *Völkerrecht* (1992): 164.
124 General Assembly Resolutions 45/150 and 45/151, *General Assembly Official Records, 45th Session*, Supplement 49, pp. 254–6.
125 OAS General Assembly Resolution 1080 (1991).
126 Angola 1975–93, Chad 1979–88, Afghanistan 1978–88, Cambodia 1979–91.
127 Liberia 1990– ; Somalia 1991– ; Rwanda 1993– .
128 English translation as published in the *New York Times*, 27 September 1968. Also in *International Legal Materials*, 7: 1323–5.
129 Its character as a refusal of recognition became clear when Soviet delegates challenged the right of delegates sent by Pinochet to represent Chile at the International Maritime Organization's 1973 Conference on Marine Pollution (Fifth Plenary Meeting, 22 Oct. 1973, Doc. MP/Conf./SR.5).
130 *New York Times*, 26 September 1973, p. 3, col. 3.
131 Excerpts from their official statements are given in Bettati, '"Souveraineté limitée" ou "internationalisme prolétarien"?' (1972).
132 Soviet foreign ministry spokesman Gennady Gerasimov summed this up as the 'Sinatra Doctrine': 'Sinatra had a song "I did it my way..." So every country decides in its own way what road to take.' Quoted in *New York Times*, 26 October 1989, sec. 1, p.1.
133 Communiqué of the Warsaw Pact, 4 December 1989, *New York Times*, 5 December 1989, sec. 1, p. 1.
134 Lorimer, *Institutes* (1883), vol. 1: 109; Despagnet, *Cours* (1905): 93; Ullmann, *Völkerrecht* (1908): 125; Lawrence, *The Principles* (1913): 88.
135 Lorimer, *Institutes* (1883), vol. 1: 109–33 and 156–68; Lawrence, *The Principles* (1913): 88.
136 Verhoeven, *La Reconnaissance* (1975), and Lauterpacht, *Recognition* (1947) say that it was first applied by the US government to the Diaz government of Mexico in 1877. Chen, *Recognition* (1951): 125 credits the first application to British policy toward the Juarez government of Mexico in 1861.
137 Neumann, *Recognition of Governments in the Americas* (1947): 9.
138 E.g. Feldman, 'Recognition' (1969): 213.
139 Fauchille, *Traité* (1921), vol. 1: 321; Podesta-Costa, 'Règles' (1923): 55; Stinson, 'Recognition' (1924): 12; Pergler, 'Recognition of New Governments' (1925): 62; Anzilotti, *Cours* (1929), vol. 1: 180, Brown, 'La Reconnaissance' (1934): 347; Wolgast, 'Völkerrecht' (1935): 792; Accioly, *Traité* (1940), vol. 1: 170.
140 Baty, *Canons* (1930): 228; Grenard, 'Principes de la reconnaissance' (1931): 81; Arendt, *Anerkennung* (1938): 85.

141 Goebel, 'The Recognition Policy' (1915): 207; Gemma, 'Les Gouvernements' (1924): 342; Anderson, 'Recognition of Russia' (1925): 529; Spiropoulos, *De facto Regierung* (1926): 35–8; Hershey, 'Notes' (1927): 209; Kunz, *Anerkennung* (1928): 139–43; Huess, 'Zum probleme' (1935): 11.
142 English translation in *FRUS, 1932*, 5: 486 (1948).
143 Irizarry y Puente, 'Doctrine' (1953): 323.
144 *China Yearbook*, 1930: 824–5; Iriye, *After Imperialism* (1965).
145 Sibert, *Traité* (1951), vol. 1: 198, note 4; Inter-American Council of Jurists, 1949 draft and commentary (1953): 17–18 and 22; Berber, *Lehrbuch* (1960), vol. 1: 232; Chaudhari, *Public International Law* (1962): 96; Tandon, *Public International Law* (1965): 157; Takano, *Einführung* (1979): 146; Hingorani, *Modern* (1984): 87.
146 Fenwick, *International Law* (1948): 161; Starke, 'Recognition' (1950): 17–18; Azevedo, *Aspects généraux* (1953): 44–5; Patel, *Recognition* (1959): 71–3; American Law Institute, *Restatement, Second* (1965): 314.
147 Alexandrowicz, 'Quasi-Judicial' (1952): 635; Teuscher, *Die vorzeitige* (1958): 121; Oppenheim, *International Law* (8th edn, 1958), vol. 1: 132; Kozhevnikov, *International Law* (1961): 116; Dhokalia, *International Law* (1963): 312; Delbez, *Les Principes* (1964): 256; Menon, 'Some Aspects, III' (1990): 163–4. McChesney, 'International Law and Mexican Foreign Policy' (1969): 29 notes that most Mexican writers took this view.
148 Chen, *Recognition* (1951): 125–6; Irizarry y Puente, 'The Doctrine' (1953): 313–16; Bindschedler, 'Die Anerkennung' (1962): 390–1; Binavince, 'Canadian Practice' (1974): 172.
149 Briggs, *The Law of Nations* (new edn, 1952): 120–1; talks and resumption of diplomatic relations are noted in *Keesing's Contemporary Archives*, 1991, p. 38106.
150 Noted in Misra, *India's* (1966): 40.
151 Whiteman, *Digest*, vol. 2: 267.
152 Council on Foreign Relations, *Documents on American Foreign Relations*, 1964, pp. 340–1.
153 Noted by Cohen, 'Legal Problems of Normalization of Relations with China' (1974).
154 Memorandum of the Ministry of External Affairs Legal Advisor, 28 November 1973, reproduced in *Canadian YBIL*, 12: 300–1 (1974).
155 E.g. acceptance of the Argentine junta's assurances in 1976, *Canadian YBIL*, 15: 339 (1977).
156 E.g. statements by new Bangladesh and Chad governments quoted in *US Digest*, 1975: 23 and 34; by new leaders in Guinea and Sudan discussed in *Africa Contemporary Record*, 17: B74–5 and B447–78 (1984–5).
157 See pages 161–8.
158 Ruda, 'The Law' (1991): 456.
159 Arbour, *Droit international* (1992): 175; Oppenheim, *International Law* (9th edn, 1992), vol. 1: 152.
160 E.g. the rule that no participant change its form of government for 50 years in the proposed American General Confederation of 1825, noted in Irizarry y Puente, 'Doctrine' (1953): 319.

5. OTHER PROPOSED CRITERIA

1 Moore, *Digest*, vol. 1: 141.
2 Wharton, *Digest*, vol. 1: 326–7.
3 Bisschop, 'London International Law Conference' (1944): 204.
4 *Schweizerisches Jahrbuch*, 3: 115 (1946).
5 Marek, *Identity* (1954): 64–71; Brownlie, *International Law* (1966): 86; Feldman 'Recognition' (1969): 205; Blix, 'Contemporary Aspects' (1970): 591; Hingorani, *Modern* (1984): 87; Feldman, 'International Personality' (1985): 400; Tripathi, *India's* (1990): 40. Verhoeven, *La Reconnaissance* (1975): 93–5 was sympathetic but ultimately rejected it as too hard to apply.
6 Speech by President Truman, *Department of State Bulletin*, 13: 654 (1945).
7 Soviet delegate's statement to the General Assembly, *General Assembly Official Records, First Session*, part 2, pp. 1212–13 (1946).
8 The most elaborate statement came from the PRC in a lead article in *Peking Review* on 17 April 1970. Translation in Cohen and Chiu (eds), *People's China and International Law* (1974), vol. 1: 291.
9 Elias, *Africa and the Development of International Law* (1972): 113.
10 Umozurike, *Introduction* (1993): 67–8.
11 Rousseau, 'Chronique', *RGDIP*, 86: 549 (1982).
12 E.g. 1976 Canadian statement in *Canadian YBIL*, 15: 340 (1977); 1979 US statement in *US Practice*, 1979: 110.
13 Most pointedly in an Australian statement distinguishing the Ugandan and Cambodian situations, 22 November 1979, in *Australian YBIL*, 8: 277 (1983).
14 'Chronique', *Annuaire Française* 1990, p. 1100.
15 Rousseau, 'Chronique', *RGDIP*, 84: 832–4 (1980).
16 British statement in the UN General Assembly, 24 December 1981, noted in *British YBIL*, 52: 376 (1981).
17 Government statement to House of Commons, 19 July 1985, *British YBIL*, 56: 387 (1985).
18 India, Tripathi, *India's* (1990): 130.
19 General Assembly Resolution ES-6/2, 14 January 1980, *General Assembly Official Records, Sixth Emergency Special Session*, Supplement, p. 2.
20 'Chronique', *Ann. française*, 1980, p. 1009; Tripathi, *India's* (1990): 123.
21 British statements reported in *British YBIL*, 50: 297 (1979); French statements reported in *Ann. française*, 1980, pp. 888–9.
22 Which was quickly endorsed as the legitimate government of Cambodia by Bangladesh, China, Malaysia, Mauretania, North Korea and Pakistan, *Australian YBIL*, 10: 290 (1990).
23 US statements in *US Practice*, 1980–88, pp. 299–310; British statement of 4 May 1988 in *British YBIL*, 59. 436 (1988).
24 Australia established diplomatic relations on 2 July 1991, calling it 'the agreed embodiment of the sovereignty of Cambodia', *Australian YBIL*, 13: 367 (1993).
25 Oppenheim, *International Law* (9th edn., 1992), vol. 1: 152.

26 Phillimore, *Commentaries* (1879), vol. 2: 20; Fiore, *Nouveau droit* (1885), vol. 1: 275; Hall, *A Treatise* (1890): 46.
27 Stinson, 'Recognition' (1924): 20; Pergler, 'Recognition' (1925): 63; Anzilotti, *Cours* (1929), vol. 1: 180; McMahon, *Recent Changes* (1933), 115–16.
28 Hornbeck, 'Recognition' (1950), 187; Sibert, *Traité* (1951), 1: 198, note 4; Patel, *Recognition* (1959), 71.
29 Hence McMahon, *Recent Changes* (1933): 56–7 errs in crediting its invention to US opponents of recognizing the Soviet government.
30 The US, Swiss, and most Latin American governments were slower in coming to this view.
31 Molotov's report to the CPSU executive committee, December 1933, quoted in Degras (ed.), *Soviet Documents*, (1951), vol. 3: 56–7.
32 Newman, *Recognition of Communist China?* (1961) summarizes the debate.
33 Smith, *Great Britain and the Law of Nations* (1932), vol. 1: 232–3.
34 Albrecht-Carrié, *A Diplomatic History of Europe*, 240, note 40. Greater knowledge of the situation, and their own rivalry for influence, affected their views.
35 Hackworth, *Digest*, vol. 1: 288–9; later recalled in Rousseau, 'Chronique', *RGDIP*, 84: 390 (1980).
36 *FRUS, 1946*, 9: 367 (1972).
37 Červenka, *The Organization of African Unity* (1969): 39.
38 Mehrish, *India's* (1972): 27.
39 Rousseau, 'Chronique', *RGDIP*, 84: 390 (1980).
40 Comment on official French statements by Jean Charpentier, *Ann. française*, 1987, p. 975.
41 Doe made his point by televising the executions.
42 Umozurike, *Introduction* (1993): 69 did note that 'there may be methods of change that fall below civilized standards of which other states should show approprate disapproval' without saying that disapproval necessarily meant nonrecognition.
43 Feldman, 'Recognition' (1969): 205. His non-exhaustive list of basic norms included peaceful settlement of disputes with other states, respect for the political independence and territorial integrity of states, sovereign equality of states, international cooperation, the right of all states to participate in international cooperation, self-determination of peoples, and respect for human rights.
44 Contemporaneous opinion is explored from a position sceptical of the idea that there is such a category of basic norms in Sztucki, *Jus Cogens* (1974).
45 Mirkine-Guetzévitch, 'Droit international et droit constitutionnel' (1931): 338.
46 Fiore, *Nouveau droit* (1885), vol. 1: 281, note 2.
47 Arendt, *Anerkennung* (1938): 90.
48 Sibert, *Traité* (1951), vol. 1: 199; Azevedo, *Aspects généraux* (1953): 50; Patel, *Recognition* (1959): 77; Fenwick, 'Recognition De Facto' (1965): 965; Frowein, *Das de facto Regime* (1968): 231–2 for recognition beyond minimum 'de facto regime' status.
49 Lauterpacht, *Recognition* (1947): 170–4.
50 Quoted in Inter-American Council of Jurists (1953): 61–3.
51 English text in *AJIL*, 60: 398–9 (1966).

52 See discussion in Dugard, *International Law* (1994): 83.
53 Or taken on by a rival which is not in control of most of the state at the time of signature. See pages 113–14.
54 Foreign Minister's statement to the Senate, 28 February 1978, *Revue Belge*, 1980, p. 605.

6. THE FORMS OF RECOGNITION

1 Compare the 1926 Soviet response to the new King of the Hejaz in Degras, *Soviet Documents* (1951), vol. 2: 88, which used the word 'recognize', and the 1949 US response to the new government of Syria in Whiteman, *Digest*, vol. 1: 455, which did not.
2 E.g. Article 1 of the 1925 Soviet–Japanese Treaty concerning General Relations, specifying that 'The high contracting parties agree that with the coming into force of the present convention, diplomatic and consular relations shall be established between them.' Text in *AJIL*, 19: Supplement, p. 78 (1925).
3 While most nineteenth-century examples involved recognition of new states by Congresses of the Powers, the Supreme Allied Council used the form to recognize the Huszar government of Hungary in 1920. *British Documents on Foreign Policy, 1919–1939*, 1st ser., vol. 6, no. 307.
4 In a 2 October 1970 memorandum, the Canadian foreign ministry legal advisors said recognition expressed first in a statement to the press was unusual but legally valid, and warned that any such statement had to be worded carefully to avoid confusion. *Canadian YBIL*, 9: 304–5 (1971).
5 See pages 88–92.
6 E.g. Canadian Legal Bureau memorandum of 30 June 1988, *Canadian YBIL*, 26: 325 (1988).
7 McChesney, 'International Law and Mexican Foreign Policy', (1969): 57–61.
8 Quoted and discussed in Lauterpacht, *Recognition* (1947), p. 379. Canning was mainly concerned with new states, but the same considerations would apply to governments as well.
9 Foreign Ministry Legal Bureau memorandum, 30 June 1988, *Canadian YBIL*, 26: 325 (1988).
10 Press statement by Foreign Minister Estrada, 27 September 1930; English translation as published in *AJIL*, 25: Supplement, p. 203 (1931),
11 See pages 180–1.
12 Hsiung, 'China's Recognition Practice' (1972): 54–6.
13 E.g. US statement recognizing Corazon Aquino as President of the Philippines, to reinforce private warnings to Marcos that he should stand aside, *US Practice, 1980–88*, p. 323, and French recognition of Konan Bedie as President of the Ivory Coast, to forestall challenges by possible rivals in 1995, *Africa South of the Sahara*, 1995, p. 326.
14 E.g. Canadian telegram to the Provisional Revolutionary Government of South Vietnam, 14 May 1975, summarized in *Canadian YBIL*, 14: 347

(1976). The entire Canadian embassy had left the country before the final assault on Saigon.

15 Some variation of this phrase appears in almost every British press statement or ministerial response to parliamentary questions after 1980. See, e.g., *British YBIL*, 51: 368 (1980) on Afghanistan; 59: 436 (1988) on Cambodia; and 62: 556 (1991) on the Soviet coup attempt.

16 *FRUS, 1921*: 427–30 (1930).

17 Hackworth, *Digest*, vol. 1: 171–2.

18 Hackworth, *Digest*, vol. 1: 166.

19 Briggs, 'Relations Officieuses' (1940): 51–2.

20 Williams, 'Recognition' (1929): 75; Briggs, 'Relations Officieuses' (1940): 57.

21 Accioly, *Traité* (1940), vol. 1: 171; Baty, 'Abuse' (1936): 380.

22 Article 12 of its resolution on 'La reconnaissance des nouveaux États et de nouveaux gouvernements', read 'In the absence of a declaration or an act with similar effect, recognition must not be regarded as acquired.' *Annuaire de l'Institut de droit international*, 39: 303 (1936).

23 For a few examples see Whiteman, *Digest*, vol. 1: 55, and Erdmann, *Nichtanerkannte Staaten* (1962): 85.

24 *Department of State Bulletin*, 68: 346 (1973).

25 British statement in the Security Council, quoted in *British YBIL*, 51: 368 (1980).

26 Government statement to Senate, *Australian YBIL*, 8: 274 (1983).

27 Instructions noted in *Australian YBIL*, 11: 203 (1991).

28 Quoted in Inter-American Council of Jurists (1953): 69.

29 Whiteman, *Digest*, vol. 2: 60.

30 Dahm, *Völkerrecht* (1958), vol. 1: 141; Charpentier, *La Reconnaissance* (1956): 239; Patel, *Recognition* (1959): 98–9; Schwarzenberger, *A Manual* (1960), vol. 1: 62–5; Bindschedler, 'Die Anerkennung' (1962): 381; American Law Institute, *Restatement* (1965): 328; O'Connell, *International Law* (1965), vol. 1: 167.

31 Chen, *Recognition* (1951): 190; Wright, 'Some Thoughts' (1950): 558; Zivier, *Die Nichtanerkennung* (1969): 281–91; Gorus, *Manuel* (1980): 74.

32 Lauterpacht, *Recognition* (1947): 405–8.

33 Ross, *Textbook* (1947): 121; Fenwick, *International Law* (4th edn., 1965), vol. 2: 582; Shao, *Die Anerkennung* (1967): 147–52 and 159–60.

34 Akehurst, *Modern Introduction* (1970): 85. He drew an analogy to the English rule that anyone who signs a contract – even without reading it first – is assumed to have intended all the consequences.

35 Verhoeven, *La Reconnaissance* (1975), vol. 1: 352–4.

36 Verhoeven, 'La Reconnaissance' (1985): 22; Verhoeven, 'Relations internationales' (1993): 19.

37 Libyan Revolutionary Council announcement quoted in *Department of State Bulletin*, 61: 281 (1969).

38 Holtzendorff, *Handbuch* (1889), vol. 2: 88.

39 Lorimer, *Institutes* (1883), vol. 1: 101–3. Lorimer did not clearly distinguish between states and governments here and was a particularly strong exponent of the distinction between the 'civilized' (European or adopting European practices in international relations) and 'uncivilized' that some

diplomats and scholars used to deny that international law extended to relations with all political entities in the world. For a discussion of this doctrine, see Gong, *The Standard of 'Civilization' in International Law* (1984).

40 Klüber, *Droit des gens* (1874): 85.

41 Le Normand, *La Reconnaissance* (1889): 270.

42 This occurred after establishment of the Second French Republic (1848), the Second French Empire (1851), the Third French Republic (1871), the Brazilian Republic (1889), the Portuguese Republic (1911), and the Republic of China (1912).

43 Smith, *Great Britain and the Law of Nations* (1932), vol. 1: 125.

44 Lord Palmerston to Ambassador Abercrombie, 23 June 1848, in Smith, *Great Britain and the Law of Nations* (1932), vol. 1: 110–11.

45 Annual Message to Congress, 1 December 1890, Moore, *Digest*, vol. 1: 162.

46 Spiropoulos, *De facto Regierung* (1926): 17; Kunz, *Anerkennung* (1928): 134; Oppenheim, *International Law* (4th edn, 1928), vol. 1: 157; Politis, 'La Théorie' (1929): 181; Møller, *International Law* (1931), vol. 1: 159; Buza, 'Die juristische Natur' (1940): 81–2.

47 Gemma, 'Gouvernements de fait' (1924): 276–7; Hervey, *Legal Effects* (1926): 16; Strupp, *Éléments* (1930): 91; Brown, 'La reconnaissance' (1934): 346–7.

48 Hershey, 'Notes' (1927): 210; Wolgast, *Völkerrecht* (1935): 792; Arendt, *Die Anerkennung* (1938): 174.

49 To mean provisional and of limited competence: Liszt, *Völkerrecht* (12th edn, 1925): 92; Scelle, *Précis* (1932), vol. 1: 103; Institute of International Law (1936), Article 11; London International Law Conference (1943), Article 4. To mean provisional and with limited relations: Anzilotti, *Cours* (1929), vol. 1: 180; Accioly, *Traité* (1940), vol. 1: 172. To mean limited relations and of limited competence: Sastry, *International Law* (1937): 35–6. To mean provisional, of limited competence, and entailing limited relations: Schlüter, *De-facto Anerkennung* (1936): 4; and Raestad, 'La Reconnaissance' (1936): 312–13.

50 Kunz, *Anerkennung* (1928): 133; Møller, *International Law* (1931), vol. 1: 102; Schlüter, *De-facto Anerkennung* (1936): 26 (who believed this was the nineteenth-century meaning); Buza, 'Die juristische Natur' (1940): 81 (because provisional recognition was always extended tacitly).

51 Gemma, 'Gouvernements de fait' (1924): 372; Schlüter, *De-facto Anerkennung* (1936).

52 Baty, 'Abuse' (1936): 472–5.

53 Spiropoulos, *De facto Regierung* (1926), 18; Lécharny, *La validité* (1929): 17; Grenard, 'Principes de la reconnaissance' (1931): 82; Scelle, *Précis* (1933), vol. 1: 103; Bustamante y Sirven, *Droit international* (1934), vol. 1: 167–8; Arendt, *Anerkennung* (1938): 128.

54 Lauterpacht, 'Recognition of Insurgents' (1939–40): 2; Hyde, *International Law* (2nd edn, 1945), vol. 1: 194–5.

55 Baty, 'So-called' (1922): 487; Briggs, 'De Facto and De Jure Recognition' (1939): 699.

56 Hackworth, *Digest*, vol. 1: 203 and 204.

57 Foreign Office certificate in *The Gagara*, English Court of Appeal, 1919, *Annual Digest*, 1919–22, Case No. 25.
58 Hackworth, *Digest*, vol. 1: 216.
59 State Department instructions, 25 May 1920, in Hackworth, *Digest*, vol. 1: 261.
60 Instructions from the Acting Secretary of State, 9 December 1920, in Hackworth, *Digest*, vol. 1: 224.
61 Joint note to the Chinese foreign office, 9 December 1924, in Hackworth, *Digest*, vol. 1: 317.
62 Lauterpacht, *Recognition* (1947): 335.
63 *FRUS, 1925*, 2: 678–80 (1940). Secretary of State Kellogg instructed the US chargé to accord recognition as the *de facto* government, on grounds that the phrase was 'more exact and more in keeping with the general policy of the United States'.
64 Telegram to the Spanish foreign minister, 3 April 1939, in Hackworth, *Digest*, vol. 1: 297.
65 Zellwenger, *Die völkerrechtliche Anerkennung* (1954): 11.
66 Smith, *Great Britain and the Law of Nations* (1932), vol. 1: 78.
67 *British International Law Cases*, 2: 71, discussed in T. Chen, *Recognition* (1951): 279.
68 *British International Law Cases*, 2: 100, discussed in T. Chen, *Recognition* (1951): 279.
69 Foreign Office letter quoted in *British International Law Cases*, 2: 184.
70 Lauterpacht, *Recognition* (1947): 340; Brown, 'Effects' (1950): 639; Starke, 'Recognition' (1950): 15; Guggenheim, *Traité* (1955), vol. 1: 198; Oppenheim, *International Law* (8th edn, 1958), vol. 1: 136; Dahm, *Völkerrecht* (1958), vol. 1: 147; Patel, *Recognition* (1959): 49; Verdross, *Völkerrecht* (4th edn, 1959): 186; Schwarzenberger, *Manual* (1960), vol. 1: 68; Cavaré, *Le Droit* (1961), vol. 1: 323; Kozhevnikov, *International Law* (1961): 118; Bindschedler, *Anerkennung* (1962): 380–1; Brierly, *Law of Nations* (6th edn, 1963): 147; Dhokalia, *International Law* (1963): 218; Delbez, *Les Principes* (1964): 164; Tandon, *Public International Law* (1965): 152; Brownlie, *Principles* (1966): 87; Mugerwa, 'Subjects' (1968): 279.
71 Lauterpacht, Mugerwa, Guggenheim, Oppenheim, Dahm, Verdross, Cavaré, Dhokalia and Tandon regarded it as revocable.
72 Bierzanek, 'La Non-reconnaissance' (1962): 125; Zivier, *Nichtanerkennung* (1969): 57; Nedjati, 'Acts' (1981): 388–9.
73 Chatelain, 'La Reconnaissance' (1950): 719; Fenwick, 'Recognition De facto' (1964): 965–6; possibly Feldman, 'Recognition' (1969): 214; Balekjian, *Die Effektivität* (1970): 178.
74 Lazarev, *Mezhdunarodnoe pravo* (1951): 177, quoted in Frenzke, 'Stillschweigende Anerkennung' (1968): 142; Zivier, *Die Nichtanerkennung* (1969): 55.
75 Hsiung, 'China's Recognition Practice' (1972): 53.
76 Scelle, *Manuel* (1948): 128; Lador-Laderer, 'Recognition' (1957): 118; Dhokalia, *International Law* (1963): 218; American Law Institute, *Restatement* (1965): 325; Zivier, *Die Nichtanerkennung* (1969): 57; Oglesby, *Internal War* (1970): 80–1.

77 Provisional and involving limited relations: Azevedo, *Aspects généraux* (1953): 80; Chaudhari, *Public International Law* (1962): 95; Dhokalia, *International Law* (1963): 218; Tandon, *Public International Law* (1965): 154; Salonga and Yap, *Public International Law* (1966): 102. Provisional and of limited competence: Fenwick, *International Law* (3rd edn, 1948): 174–5; Berber, *Lehrbuch* (1960), vol. 1: 235. Involving limited relations and of limited competence: Bastid, *Droit international public* (1970): 171.

78 Wolf, 'Le Gouvernement de fait' (1956); Rousseau, *Droit international public* (10th edn, 1984).

79 Chen, *Recognition* (1951): 289; Kelsen, *Principles* (1952): 276–7; Charpentier, *La Reconnaissance* (1956): 302; Higgins, *Development* (1963): 145; Shao, *Anerkennung* (1967): 164; Frowein, *Das de facto Regime* (1968): 29; Bot, *Non-Recognition* (1968): 247; Blix, 'Contemporary Aspects' (1970): 601; Verhoeven, *La Reconnaissance* (1975).

80 Teuscher, *Die vorzeitige* (1958): 41; Brownlie, *Principles* (1966): 87; Visscher, *Theory* (1968): 239; Akehurst, *A Modern Introduction* (1970): 85.

81 Jessup, *A Modern Law of Nations* (1950): 57; Oppenheim, *International Law* (8th edn, 1958), vol. 1: 135; Brierly, *Law of Nations* (6th edn, 1963): 147; Schlüter, *De-facto Anerkennung* (1963): 12–13; O'Connell, *International Law* (1965), vol. 1: 174; Frowein, *Das de facto Regime* (1968): 29; Blix, 'Contemporary Aspects' (1970): 600.

82 Takano, *Einführung* (1979): 148; Loudwin, *Konkludente* (1983); Cruz, *International Law* (1984): 85; Starke, *Introduction* (1984): 137; Tunkin (ed.), *International Law* (1986) 115; Green, *International Law* (1988): 133; Dahm, *Völkerrecht* (2nd edn, 1988): 212–13; Ruda, 'The Law' (1991): 459.

83 Reuter, *Droit international public* (1983): 21; Visscher, *Cours* (1981); Frowein, 'Anerkennung' (1985): 9; Chen, *An Introduction* (1989): 43; Greig, 'Effects' (1991): 36.

84 Symmons, 'United Kingdom Abolition' (1981): 253–4; Frowein, 'Anerkennung' (1985): 9; Greig, 'Effects' (1991): 37.

85 Response to questions in the House of Commons, quoted in Whiteman, *Digest*, vol. 2: 446.

86 Response to questions in the House of Lords, quoted in Whiteman, *Digest*, vol. 2: 447.

87 Misra, *India's Policy* (1966): 137–9.

88 Mehrish, *India's Recognition Policy* (1972): 107.

89 Tripathi, *India's* (1990): 128.

90 Tripathi, *India's* (1990).

91 Hsiung, 'China's Recognition Practice' (1972): 39–40.

92 'Concerning the Establishment of Diplomatic Relations' (1956), in Cohen and Chiu (eds), *People's China* (1974), vol. 1: 208.

93 Wolf, 'Le gouvernement de fait' (1956): 125, who says the definition was established in March 1949.

94 Whiteman, *Digest*, vol. 2: 3; Binavince, 'Canadian Practice' (1974): 174–5.

95 Remarks to the Senate during a debate on recognition of the PRC, 5 March 1964, quoted in Verhoeven, *La Reconnaissance* (1975): 630–1.

96 Frowein, 'Anerkennung' (1985): 9 noted that they last used the term '*de facto* recognition' in initial recognition of Israeli statehood in 1948.

97 Brownlie, 'Recognition' (1986): 636.

98 Australian government statement on recognition, 8 January 1979, *Australian YBIL*, 8: 273 (1982); New Zealand statement regarding Pol Pot's faction in Cambodia, 31 October 1984, *New Zealand Foreign Affairs Review*, 1984/4, p. 25.
99 E.g. Symmons, 'United Kingdom Abolition' (1981): 253–4; Frowein, 'Anerkennung' (1985): 9; Kapoor, *International Law* (9th edn, 1992): 161; Detter, *International Law* (1992): 97; Dugard, *International Law* (1994): 85.
100 E.g. Oppenheim, *International Law* (9th edn, 1992), vol. I: 155–7; Umozurike (1993): 64.
101 Kozhevnikov, *International Law* (1961): 120–1; Feldman, 'Recognition' (1969): 206–7; Feldman, 'International Personality' (1985); Tunkin, *International Law* (1986).
102 Gorus, *Manuel* (1980): 54; Verdross and Simma, *Universelles Völkerrecht* (1984): 563; Feldman, 'International Personality' (1985): 401; Tripathi, *India's* (1990): 128; Umozurike, *Introduction* (1993): 69.
103 Compare discussions of procedure in the successive editions of Satow, *Guide to Diplomatic Practice*.

7. RECOGNITION IN BILATERAL RELATIONS

1 See Brownlie, 'Recognition' (1986): 628 and Warbrick, 'Recognition of States' (1996): 10–11. Oppenheim, *International Law* (9th edn, 1992), vol. 1: 183 also notes the three possibilities.
2 The absence of diplomatic relations between Saudi Arabia and the USSR, which started in 1938 and ended in 1990 (Rousseau, 'Chronique', *RGDIP*, 94: 132 [1990]), seems to be the world's longest suspension for reasons unrelated to the advent of a new regime.
3 See listings of resident missions in country sections of *Africa South of the Sahara*, and parliamentary discussions reported in *Revue belge*, 26: 219–20 (1991); *ICLQ*, 35: 978–9 (1986); and *Australian YBIL*, 12: 361 (1992).
4 See US State Department list of countries simultaneously recognizing PRC and having diplomatic relations with ROC in *International Legal Materials*, 11: 571–3 (1972).
5 Rousseau, 'Chronique', *RGDIP*, 88: 214–15 (1984).
6 *New York Times*, 25 May 1995, p. A6; *Wall Street Journal*, 8 January 1996, p. A9 (Eastern edition).
7 Moore, *Digest*, vol. 1: 235 (1906).
8 This is similar to a recognized government's right to break off or not initiate diplomatic relations with other states. The Pol Pot government of Cambodia expelled all foreign diplomats in April 1975 and as of November that year had authorized only the PRC and North Vietnam to maintain diplomatic missions in Phnom Penh. Rousseau, 'Chronique', *RGDIP*, 79: 1108 (1975).
9 *FRUS 1908*: 648–9 (1920).
10 Hackworth, *Digest*, vol. 2: 250–1.

11 *British Documents on the Origins of the World War, 1898–1914*, vol. 5: no. 115.
12 Most diplomats could indicate this by appearing in civilian clothes rather than diplomatic uniform.
13 Moore, *Digest*, vol. 1: 125. The Swiss minister was given similar instructions, but his were rescinded before the plebiscite.
14 Secretary of State Seward to Minister Dayton, 17 February 1864, in *FRUS 1864*, 3: 747 (1865).
15 Reaction reported to the US government by Minister Adams, 24 March 1864, in *FRUS 1864*, 3: 399 (1865).
16 Reports from US minister in Paris, *FRUS 1865*, 3: 747 (1866).
17 *British Documents on the Origins of the War, 1898–1914*, vol. 5: nos. 107 and 110.
18 *FRUS 1921*, 2: 419 (1936).
19 Hackworth, *Digest*, vol. 1: 346.
20 *Documents on British Foreign Policy, 1919–1939*, 1st series, vol. 6, nos. 81, 87 and 91 (1961).
21 *Grotius annuaire international pour l'année 1925*, p. 97.
22 Burckhardt, *Le droit fédéral suisse*, vol. 1: 188. The dispute involved whether a Soviet envoy to the Lausanne Conference had diplomatic status at the time he was murdered by a Russian émigré though the Soviets had not yet been formally invited to the conference.
23 Interwar discussion noted in Hackworth, *Digest*, vol. 1: 343–4, and post-1945 developments noted in Young, 'American Dealings with Peking' (1966–7): 77.
24 British efforts to start meetings between the Greek and Turkish governments in 1920–2, *Documents on British Foreign Policy, 1919–1939*, 1st series, vol. 17. French efforts to help the Swiss and Soviets start talks on the Vorovsky Affair; US arrangement of meetings between the Bolivian, Brazilian, Chilean, and Peruvian ambassadors and the Soviet ambassador in 1946, *FRUS 1946*, 9: 59 and 229–30 (1972).
25 Briggs, 'Relations officieuses' (1940), 47, and *Grotius annuaire international pour l'année 1939*, p. 107.
26 Brown, 'Legal Effects' (1950): 620.
27 *FRUS 1918*: 275 (1930).
28 Secretary of State Stimson to US chargé in Monrovia, 6 October 1931, in Hackworth, *Digest*, vol. 1: 279 (1940).
29 *Journal de droit international* (Clunet), 45: 1490–1 (1918).
30 *Journal de droit international* (Clunet), 45: 1478–9 (1918).
31 Burckhardt, *Le droit fédéral suisse* (1930), vol. 1: 186–7.
32 Hackworth, *Digest*, vol. 3: 1059.
33 Howard, *Strategic Deception* (1995): 124–5.
34 Gemma, 'Les Gouvernements de fait' (1924): 269–75; Schlüter, *De facto Anerkennung* (1936): 112–13.
35 Austrian Soviet and German–Soviet agreements, in Schapiro, *Soviet Treaty Series, 1917 1939*, 1: 136 and 168.
36 *Grotius annuaire international pour l'année 1925*, p. 97.
37 Report of the Foreign Affairs Committee to the Chamber of Deputies, 12 December 1924, in *Répertoire française*, 3: 81.

38 Telegram from the US ambassador in Brazil, 20 September 1932, *FRUS 1932*, 5: 608 (1948).
39 E.g. Indian communications to Presidents Ho and Diem of North and South Vietnam at a time when India did not even recognize their states, Misra, *India's Policy* (1966): 72–3; telegram from President Sekou Touré of Guinea to General Idi Amin immediately after the latter's coup in Uganda, *Africa Contemporary Record*, 4: C62–3 (1971–2).
40 Parliamentary statement, 22 February 1988, *British YBIL*, 59: 437 (1988).
41 Noted in *British YBIL*, 75: 508 (1986).
42 *British YBIL*, 60: 590 (1989).
43 Government explanation of policy noted in *Australian YBIL*, 10: 283–4 (1987).
44 *AJIL*, 62: 257–8 (1968).
45 Satow, *A Guide to Diplomatic Practice* (3rd edn, 1932), p. 113, quoted in *British Digest of International Law*, 7: 642–3.
46 Binavince, 'Canadian Practice' (1974): 166.
47 Public statements of Secretary of State for External Affairs to the House of Commons, 17 and 24 May 1966, quoted in *Canadian YBIL*, 5: 327 (1967).
48 *Canadian YBIL*, 4: 231 (1966).
49 Parliamentary discussion, *Canadian YBIL*, 15: 340–2 (1977).
50 *Foreign Service Manual*, 4: 113.63, quoted in Whiteman (ed.), *Digest*, vol. 2: 290.
51 Joint Under-secretary of State for Foreign Affairs to the House of Lords, 4 July 1958, quoted in *ICLQ*, 7: 94 (1958).
52 Rousseau, 'Chronique', *RGDIP*, 71: 149 (1967).
53 McChesney, 'International Law and Mexican Foreign Policy' (1969): 71–4.
54 The US–PRC ambassadorial talks in Warsaw, which began in 1955 with discussion of prisoner exchanges and then expanded to other topics, are discussed in Young, 'American Dealings' (1966): 77.
55 Public Law 93–22 of 30 April 1973, US Statutes at Large, 87: 24. This was the only way found to deal with the complications stemming from continuing US recognition of the Nationalist Chinese as the government of China and allowing its diplomats to use the Chinese embassy.
56 *United States Code*, 22: sec. 3301–16.
57 *Répertoire française*, 3: 82.
58 See page 118.
59 Hsiung, 'China's Recognition Practice' (1972): 26.
60 *Department of State Bulletin*, 66: 435–8 (1972).
61 Joint communiqué of 14 November 1973, in *New York Times*, 15 November 1973, p. 9, col. 1.
62 *British Practice in International Law*, 1964, p. 28.
63 Government statements reported in *Ann. française*, 1987: 969–70.
64 'Chronique', *Ann. française*, 1993: 1095.
65 Legal Consequences for States of the continued presence of South Africa in Namibia (South West Africa), notwithstanding Security Council Resolution 276 (1970), *ICJ Reports*, 1971, p. 16, para. 123. In his Separate Opinion, Judge De Castro indicated his view that consular and other

agents allowed in areas under de facto occupation could remain in Namibia.

66 Hingorani, *Modern International Law* (1984): 91.

67 Verhoeven, *La Reconnaissance*, 396–7 (1975) is among the few exceptions. He preferred focusing on ratification whenever it was required because legal obligations become effective at that time.

68 Westlake, *International Law* (2nd edn, 1913): 59.

69 Holtzendorff, *Handbuch* (1889), vol. 2: 28.

70 *Fontes Juris Gentium*, series B, sec. 1, vol. 1, pt. 1, no. 537.

71 *Répertoire française*, 3: 44.

72 Hudson, 'Recognition and Multipartite Treaties' (1929): 128; Møller, *International Law* (1931), vol. 1: 159; Jaffe, *Juridical Aspects* (1933): 112–19; Arendt, *Anerkennung* (1938): 141.

73 Gemma, 'Les Gouvernements de fait' (1924): 370; Lawrence, *The Principles* (7th edn, 1923): 87.

74 Spiropoulos, *De facto Regierung* (1926): 15; Kunz, *Anerkennung* (1928): 130.

75 Chen, *Recognition* (1951): 194.

76 Schapiro (ed.), *Soviet Treaty Series, 1917–1939* (1955): 41 and 47.

77 The Hungarians did likewise, but in their case the change involved the creation of a new state as well as new governing arrangements.

78 Schapiro (ed.), *Soviet Treaty Series, 1917–1939* (1955), vol. 1: 12, 17, 19 and 20 give the Treaty of Brest-Litovsk and related agreements, while vol. 1: 136 and 168 give the successor governments' agreements. Hungary and Turkey also made new agreements on diplomatic relations, Schapiro (ed.), *Soviet Treaty Series* vol. 1: 234 and vol. 2: 94.

79 Kelsen, *Principles* (1952): 282; Verdross, *Völkerrecht* (4th edn, 1959): 251; Chaudhari, *Public International Law* (1962): 92; Tandon, *Public International Law* (1965): 151; Ruda, 'The Law' (1991): 457.

80 Zivier, *Nichtanerkennung* (1969): 156–7; Gorus, *Manuel* (1980): 74. Zivier based his conclusion on the notion that recognition is a cumulative process of accepting particular competences of a foreign regime rather than an either–or proposition. Verhoeven, *La Reconnaissance* (1975): 412–16 leaves a similar impression because he tried to discuss several objects of recognition simultaneously and regarded state practice as subordinating consistency to maintaining discretion in recognition.

81 *Department of State Bulletin*, 33: 546 (1974).

82 *International Legal Materials*, 11: 443 (1972).

83 Coquia and Santiago, *Public International Law* (1984): 116.

84 Starke, *Introduction* (1984): 131.

85 Dahm, *Völkerrecht* (2nd edn, 1988): 204.

86 Greig, 'The Effects' (1991): 61; Kapoor, *International Law* (9th edn, 1992): 169; Menon, 'Some Aspects, Part V' (1991): 31–4; Oppenheim, *International Law* (9th edn, 1992), vol. 1: 174.

87 Gorus, *Manuel* (1980): 74; Umozurike, *Introduction* (1993): 61.

88 English translation in Cohen and Chiu, *People's China and International Law* (1974), vol. 1. 214.

89 Canadian statements, *Canadian YBIL*, 14: 398–9.

90 Japanese communiqué, *Japanese Annual*, 23: 78 (1980).

91 *US Practice*, 1979, p. 143.
92 Namibia Advisory Opinion, *ICJ Reports*, 1971, p. 16, para. 122. Judge De Castro included extradition and double taxation treaties among those that should not be applied in his Separate Opinion.
93 Memorandum of Secretary of State Fish, 7 January 1876, in Moore, *Digest*, vol. 5: 13.
94 Instructions of 19 October 1889 in Moore, *Digest*, vol. 1: 163.
95 Salis-Mayenfeld, *Le droit fédéral suisse* (2nd edn, 1904): 434.
96 *British Digest*, 8: 43–8. Fiji was annexed as a Crown Colony the following year.
97 E.g. US explanation to the unrecognized Ecuadorian junta in 1925, Hackworth, *Digest*, vol. 4: 694.
98 Degras, *Soviet Documents* (1951), vol. 1: 105.
99 *Journal de droit international* (Clunet), 48: 588 (France); *FRUS: The Soviet Union, 1933–1939* (1952): 38 (US). *FRUS, 1928* (1948): 828 notes the departure of the last US consul.
100 This had been US practice in the nineteenth century. See Hackworth, *Digest*, vol. 4: 687.
101 Hsiung, *Law and Policy in China's Foreign Relations* (1972): 180.
102 Kozhevnikov, *International Law* (1961): 313; Erdmann, *Nichtanerkannte* (1962): 191–2, both argue that consular relations depend on the simultaneous existence of diplomatic relations, so must end if diplomatic relations are broken off for any reason.
103 Article 2. *United Nations Treaty Series*, 596: 266.
104 Lee, *The Vienna Convention on Consular Relations* (1966): 41–2.
105 Rousseau, 'Chronique', *RGDIP*, 94: 487 (1990). Their informal status was indicated by the absence of a flag outside.
106 Bot, *Non-Recognition* (1968): 82–90; Zivier, *Nichtanerkennung* (1969): 109.
107 Communiqué released in Paris on 29 April 1975, quoted in Rousseau, 'Chronique', *RGDIP*, 79: 1107 (1975).
108 Cohen, 'Recognizing China' (1972): 31.
109 Germany, *ZaöRV*, 46: 309 (1986); Australia, *Australian YBIL*, 10: 284 (1987); France, *Ann. française*, 1990: 1075.
110 Rousseau, 'Chronique', *RGDIP*, 92: 711 (1988).
111 *ICJ Reports*, 1971, p. 16, para. 123.
112 Separate Opinion of Judge De Castro.
113 E.g. discussion of Norwegian acceptance of a trade mission in 1920 in Grzybowski, *Soviet Public International Law* (1970): 291.
114 Chen, *Recognition* (1951): 285–6.
115 Gemma, 'Les Gouvernements' (1924): 388–90.
116 *FRUS, 1928*: 828 (1942).
117 *Australian YBIL*, 11: 466–7 (1991).
118 *New York Times*, 3 June 1973, p. 4, col. 4.
119 Remarks of Foreign Minister to the Second Chamber of Parliament, 1 December 1971, *Netherlands YBIL*, 4: 308 (1973).
120 McChesney, 'International Law and Mexican Foreign Policy' (1969): 66.
121 Hackworth, *Digest*, vol. 1: 335, noting a lease transaction in 1929.
122 *British Practice in International Law, 1962–63*, pp. 153–4. See also Oppenheim, *International Law* (9th edn, 1992), vol. 1: 172.

123 Whiteman, *Digest*, vol. 2: 310 (Peru); *Ann. française*, 1967: 954 (Argentina); Cochran, 'Recognition' (1969): 279 (Guatemala).
124 *Africa Contemporary Record, 1968–69*: 28 and 472.
125 *Keesing's Contemporary Archives*, 1973, p. 26154.
126 Uchida, 'Legal Aspects' (1975).
127 Repatriation is regarded as humanitarian and has proceeded even in the face of nonrecognition of another state. See, e.g., the agreement between the North Korean and Japanese Red Cross societies regarding Koreans in Japan who wished to go to the North, in Nakamura, 'Korean Repatriation Question' (1960).
128 E.g. the extensive US private and government-supported relief effort in the USSR during the early 1920s. Brown, 'Some Unofficial Relations' (1923–4): 421.
129 *Japanese Annual*, 23: 78–80 (1980).
130 *British YBIL*, 60: 592 (1989).

8. RECOGNITION IN MULTILATERAL RELATIONS

1 Dispatch from the Russian foreign minister to the Russian ambassador in Paris, 20 October/1 November 1870, in *Fontes Juris Gentium*, B, sec. 1, vol. 1, pt. 1, no. 555.
2 The only clear exception is Rolin, 'Observations' (1934): 353.
3 E.g. sending a US delegation to Chile for the Fourth Interamerican Child Welfare Conference in 1924 during nonrecognition of the new Chilean junta. Hackworth, *Digest*, vol. 1: 346.
4 Hackworth, *Digest*, vol. 1: 301.
5 Hackworth, *Digest*, vol. 1: 347–52.
6 Hackworth, *Digest*, vol. 1: 349.
7 Hackworth, *Digest*, vol. 4: 327.
8 Hackworth, *Digest*, vol. 1: 347.
9 Whiteman, *Digest*, vol. 1: 410.
10 Azevedo, *Aspects généraux* (1953): 79; Dhokalia, *International Law* (1963): 229; Starke, *Introduction* (1984): 131 in some instances; Ruda, 'The Law of Friendly Relations' (1991): 457 if the conference produces decisions later ratified by governments.
11 E.g. Canadian Foreign Ministry Legal Bureau memorandum, 19 August 1988, in *Canadian YBIL*, 27: 388–9 (1989).
12 *General Assembly Official Records, 5th Session*, Supplement No. 20, p. 24.
13 See, e.g., debates about seating of a Hungarian delegation and non-invitation of Mongolia, East and West Germany, North Korea, and North and South Vietnam at the Vienna Conference on Diplomatic Intercourse and Immunities. UN Doc. A/CONF.20/14, (March 1962), pp. 2–4.
14 E.g. the 1959 Four Power Conference on Germany, the 1971–2 Paris negotiations on Vietnam, and the December 1973 attempt to convene the Geneva Conference on the Middle East, noted in Cohen, *Theatre of Power* (1987): 132–3.

15 Chen, *Recognition* (1951): 207, note 82.
16 E.g. the evolution of the Universal Postal Convention from its initial closed form in 1874 to a largely open convention where accession could be challenged later if a majority of the members agreed to challenge it, in 1878. Zivier, *Die Nichtanerkennung* (1969): 142–4.
17 Rolin, 'Observations' (1934): 353 argued it at least meant *de facto* recognition.
18 Hackworth, *Digest*, vol. 5: 337.
19 Hackworth, *Digest*, vol. 1: 349.
20 Hackworth, *Digest*, vol. 1: 349; and Chen, *Recognition* (1951): 207, note 85.
21 Hackworth, *Digest*, vol. 4: 327.
22 Distilled from instructions reported in Hackworth, *Digest* vol. 1: 350–2.
23 Hackworth, *Digest*, vol. 1: 353.
24 Chen, *Recognition* (1951); 202.
25 On the 1962 agreement see Czyzak and Salans, 'The International Conference', 306, and *British Practice in International Law*, 1962–4, pp. 154–5.
26 Convention on Diplomatic Asylum, *Pan American Union Treaty Series*, 18. Quoted in Whiteman, *Digest*, vol. 6: 438.
27 Most of the disclaimers were against recognition of states. See Canadian statement on the Test Ban, *Canadian YBIL*, 2: 283 (1964); US statement on the Nonproliferation Treaty, *Department of State Bulletin*, 53: 468–9; British statement on the Outer Space Treaty, *British Practice in International Law*, 1967, p. 52, and US statement on the Outer Space Treaty, in *Department of State Bulletin*, 56: 82 (1966).
28 Hyde, *International Law* (1945): 190–2; Oppenheim, *International Law* (1992), vol. 1: 171, n. 6.
29 Chen, *Recognition* (1951): 207.
30 Bot, *Non-Recognition* (1968): 30–1.
31 Starke, *International Law* (1984): 131; Ruda, 'Law of Friendly Relations' (1991): 457.
32 Chinese statements quoted in Cohen, 'Recognizing China' (1972).
33 E.g. Canadian Foreign Ministry Legal Bureau memorandum, *Canadian YBIL*, 14: 399.
34 *International Legal Materials*, 9: 567 (1972).
35 *ICJ Reports*, 1971, p. 16, para. 122.
36 League members included British dominions, which were not yet regarded as fully independent states in 1920.
37 Membership rule in League Covenant, Article 1, para. 2; seating in Burton, *Assembly* (1941): 175.
38 *USSR* v. *Luxembourg and Saar Company*, 1935, *Annual Digest and Reports of International Law Cases, 1935–37*, Case No. 33. Azevedo, *Aspects généraux* (1953): 76.
39 Oppenheim, *International Law* (4th edn, 1928), vol. 1: 145–6; Makarov, 'Sowjet Union und Völkerbund' (1935): 34; Resolution of the London International Law Conference, 1943, noted in Bisschop, 'London International Law Conference' (1943): 244.
40 Rougier, 'La première assemblée' (1921): 240; Hackworth, *Digest*, vol. 1: 196 (1940).

41 As conceded by a Swiss delegate to the Assembly in 1935, *League of Nations Official Journal*, vol. 15, special supplement 130, p. 18.
42 Admission involves favourable recommendation by the Security Council, giving the Permanent Five a veto, and acceptance by two-thirds of the General Assembly (UN Charter, Articles 4 and 18); and seating of delegations involves a two-thirds or a simple majority of the General Assembly depending on whether the matter is defined as an 'important question' in the particular case at hand (Peterson, *General Assembly* [1986]: 118–23).
43 Cuban proposal in *GAOR, 5th Session*, Annexes, Agenda item 61, p. 5, UN Doc. A/1308, noted in Fitzmaurice, 'Chinese Representation' (1952): 42.
44 E.g. Assembly subcommittee proposal in *GAOR, 5th Session*, Annexes, Agenda item 61, p. 9, UN Doc. A/AC.38/L.45 and discussion in Fitzmaurice, 'Chinese Representation' (1952): 43–4.
45 Paragraph 1, *General Assembly Official Records, 5th Session*, Supplement 20, p. 24.
46 Paragraph 4, *General Assembly Official Records, 5th Session*, Supplement 20, p. 24 (1950). This followed a Secretariat report on the matter, prepared at the Security Council's request, suggesting that linking membership or seating to recognition would be 'unfortunate from the practical standpoint and wrong from the standpoint of legal theory'. UN Doc. No. S/1466 (1950), p. 2.
47 Attitude of the Belgian government regarding the PRC and the Hoxha government of Albania noted in Verhoeven, *La Reconnaissance* (1975): 91 and 516, note 555. Prime Minister Nehru explained India's 1955 recognition of the Franco government of Spain as following from India's policy of recognizing any 'functioning country represented in the UN'. Quoted in Kapoor, *International Law* (3rd edn, 1992): 173.
48 Ethiopian and Tunisian delegates supported seating PRC delegations in the early 1960s at a time when their governments still recognized the ROC, Bot, *Non-Recognition* (1968): 174. Tunisian recognition came in January 1964 but Ethiopian not until November 1970. A larger number of governments voted in favour of seating in September 1971 but did not recognize the PRC government until later. Compare the report of the General Assembly vote, in *General Assembly Official Records, 26th Session*, 1976th plenary meeting, p. 41 (1971), with reports of later recognitions in Rousseau, 'Chronique', *RGDIP*, 75: 1117 (1971), and 76: 494 (1972). Japanese delegates did the same regarding delegates from the Yemeni Republic in 1963, *Japanese Annual*, 7: 103 (1963).
49 The Indian government maintained that recognition did so require in debates on whether to seat delegates from the PRC or the ROC as representatives of China in 1950–71. Mehrish, *India's Recognition Policy* (1972): 56. The British government maintained the contrary opinion in 1963, *British Practice in International Law*, 1962–4, p. 154.
50 Soviet-bloc challenges to seating of ROC delegates, e.g. Soviet delegate Malik's attempt to prevent ROC participation while he was presiding over the Security Council in 1950, noted in McDougal and Goodman, 'Chinese Participation' (1966): 678, and challenge to ROC participation on 31 January 1955, *Repertory of Practice of the Security Council*, Add. 1,

pp. 4–5. PRC challenge to participation by delegates sent by the Lon Nol government of Cambodia in the UN Economic Commission for Asia and the Far East, Cohen and Chiu, *People's China* (1974), vol. 1: 908–9, note 58. British statement that failure to challenge credentials does not imply recognition, *British YBIL*, 51: 377.

51 Verhoeven, *La Reconnaissance* (1975): 498–9.

52 Higgins, *Development of International Law* (1963): 162–4.

53 Higgins, *Development of International Law* (1963): 161–2.

54 Wright, 'Some Thoughts' (1950): 552–3; Berber, *Lehrbuch* (1960), vol. 1: 235; Tabata, 'Admission' (1961): 1; Chaudhari, *Public International Law* (1962): 100; Bot, *Non-Recognition* (1968): 173–4 (unless the vote was part of a package deal); Verhoeven, *La Reconnaissance* (1975): 516–17; Jhabvala, 'Credentials Approach' (1979): 626; Hingorani, *Modern International Law* (1984): 91; Ruda, 'Law of Friendly Relations' (1991): 457. Salonga and Yap, *Public International Law* (1966): 107 argued it would be if the rules of the organization so stated.

55 Lauterpacht, *Recognition* (1947): 166–9; Chatelain, 'La Reconnaissance' (1950): 719; Jessup, *A Modern Law of Nations* (1950): 45; Wright, 'Some Thoughts' (1950): 558–9; Chen, *Recognition* (1951): 222–3; Charpentier, *La Reconnaissance* (1956): 335–6; Patel, *Recognition* (1959): 79; Tabata, 'Admission' (1961): 1; Dhokalia, *International Law* (1963): 329; Mookerjea, *International Law* (1968): 129; Corbett, *Growth of World Law* (1971): 67. Dugard, *Recognition and the United Nations* (1986) makes the most elaborate case for this position.

56 Starke, 'Recognition' (1950): 19; Graham, 'Some Thoughts' (1950): 369; Kopelmanas, 'La Reconnaissance' (1957): 39–40; Kato, 'Recognition' (1970): 303–4; Coplin, *Functions of International Law* (1966): 59–60; Blix, 'Contemporary Aspects' (1970): 698–9; Yakemtchouk, *L'Afrique* (1971): 56.

57 *Repertory of Practice of the Security Council*, Add. 2, pp. 6–10.

58 *Keesing's Contemporary Archives*, 1974, pp. 26188 and 1975, p. 27149.

59 For example, the British Statement of 18 November 1981, *British YBIL* 52: 377–8 (1981).

60 Warbrick, 'Kampuchea' (1981): 238. The nonaligned adopted that solution for their own meetings.

61 Though criticized as contrary to the UN Charter because it has much of the effect of an expulsion without the qualified majority needed to decide the latter. E.g. Dutch government statement of 20 December 1973, in *Netherlands YBIL*, 6: 265–6 (1975).

62 Peterson, *General Assembly* (1986): 121. This involved having the credentials committee report at the end of the session with the Hungarian delegates participating in the meantime.

63 Jhabvala, 'Credentials Approach' (1979): 615–17; *UN Chronicle*, September 1994, p. 5 discusses seating of a delegation sent by the post-apartheid government on 23 June 1994.

64 Resolution 396(V), paragraph 3.

65 *International Legal Materials*, 9: 568 (1972).

66 *International Legal Materials*, 9: 568–9 (1972).

67 *International Legal Materials*, 9: 562 (1972).

68 *International Legal Materials*, 9: 565–6 (1972).
69 This was justified with an argument that the General Assembly's continued seating of ROC delegates had made it impossible for the PRC to express its views on whether China should be regarded as withdrawing. *International Legal Materials*, 9: 562–4 (1972). This did not keep other observers from treating China as a new member. E.g. comments in *Keesing's Contemporary Archives*, 1973, p. 28524.
70 *International Legal Materials*, 9: 566–7.
71 *International Legal Materials*, 9: 570 (1972).
72 Charter of the Organization of American States, 1948, Article 2. *United Nations Treaty Series*, 119: 48.
73 OAS Charter, 1967, Articles 6–7; *International Legal Materials*, 6: 312 (1967).
74 Aufricht, 'Principles and Practices' (1949): 677–8.
75 Article 54 of the 1967 Charter, *International Legal Materials*, 6: 326.
76 New Article 9 of the OAS Charter, *International Legal Materials*, 33: 1005 (1994).
77 *Latin America*, 7: 392 (7 Dec. 1973).
78 *Latin America*, 8: 65 (1 March 1974).
79 *Keesing's Contemporary Archives*, 1967, p. 22229.
80 *Afrique Contemporaine*, No. 24, p. 7 (March–April 1966). The protesters – the Algerian, Egyptian, Guinean, Kenyan, Malian, Somalian, and Tanzanian delegations were also perturbed by failure to take a strong stand on the Rhodesian question.
81 *Ann. française*, 1966, p. 394.
82 Mittelman, 'The Uganda Coup' (1972): 18–19.
83 *Keesing's Contemporary Archives*, 1978, p. 29258.
84 *Washington Post*, 16 January 1975, p. A31.
85 *Washington Post*, 6 May 1975, p. A11.
86 Robertson, 'Some Legal Problems' (1946): 149–50.
87 *Washington Post*, 12 May 1975, p. A1.
88 Noted in Cohen and Chiu, *People's China and International Law* (1974), vol. I: 278–90.
89 Zacklin, 'The Problem of Namibia' (1981): 308–27; Osieke, 'Admission' (1980).

9. RECOGNITION IN DOMESTIC ADMINISTRATION AND LAW

1 For an early discussion of this tension see Lachs, 'Recognition' (1959).
2 Hackworth, *Digest*, vol. 1: 355.
3 Hackworth, *Digest*, vol. 1: 340.
4 *Krimschansky* v. *Officier de l'état civil de Liège*, *Annual Digest*, 1929–30, Case No. 26.
5 Burckhardt, *Le droit fédéral suisse* (1930), vol. 1: 180.
6 In *re Samuel Leon Sack*, *Annual Digest*, 1935–7, Case No. 35.
7 See pages 148–50.

8 *Répertoire française*, 3: 34.
9 *United States* v. *John William Powell et al.*, US District Court for the Northern District of California, noted in Whiteman, *Digest*, vol. 2: 600–1.
10 Statement of Minister of State in the Home Office to the House of Commons, 25 October 1982, *British YBIL*, 53: 357 (1982). The immediate question involved North Koreans, but the response was cast in more general terms.
11 As with holders of passports issued by the 'Turkish Republic of Northern Cyprus'. See statement of facts in *Resat Caglar and Others* v. *Anthony Lawrence Billingham (H.M. Inspector of Taxes), Special Commissioners of Inland Revenue*, 1996, para. 51. *Simon's Tax Cases*, 150 (1996). Copy of judgment provided by Prof. Colin Warbrick.
12 *Foreign Service Manual*, 11: 113.6–9, quoted in Whiteman, *Digest*, vol. 2: 655.
13 Security Council Resolution 276 (1970), *Resolutions and Decisions of the Security Council, 1970*, p. 1.
14 Legal consequences for States of the continued presence of South Africa in Namibia (South West Africa), notwithstanding Security Council Resolution 276 (1970), *ICJ Reports*, 1971, 16, paragraphs 122 and 125.
15 Which was itself influenced by Security Council Resolutions 541 (1983) and 550 (1984) though the ECJ did not explicitly take this into account.
16 *R.* v. *Minister of Agriculture, Fisheries and Food, ex parte S. P. Anastasiou (Pissouri) Ltd and Others*, European Court of Justice, 1994, Case C-432/92, noted in *Common Market Law Review*, 33: 125–35 (1996). Though involving an unrecognized state, the opinion is phrased in terms of 'authorities'. The court reached this result without any reference to the Security Council resolutions calling on UN member states to avoid recognizing or having any relations with the Turkish Republic of Northern Cyprus.
17 Affirmed most recently in the USA by the Second Circuit Court of Appeals in *Goldwater et al.* v. *Carter et al.*, 617 F. 2d 697 (1979), noted in *International Legal Materials*, 19: 240–4 (1980). The Supreme Court later vacated the judgment as dealing with a political question beyond the courts' purview, 100 S.Ct. 533 (1980).
18 Verhoeven, 'Relations' (1985): 29–30.
19 Hardy, 'Certificats' (1977); Edeson, 'Conclusive executive certificates' (1981): 2–3; Verhoeven, *Relations* (1985): 30–3; Greig, 'The Effects' (1991): 44–5; Kindred et al., *International Law* (1993): 263.
20 Edeson, 'Conclusive executive certificates' (1981): 2–3, who dates conclusiveness to the House of Lords decision in *Duff Development Corporation* v. *The Sultan of Kelantan* (1924), D.C. 797. Mann, 'Judiciary and Executive' (1944) argued that British courts felt less bound at the turn of the century than in 1940 to follow the government's recognition policy when dealing with the acts of an effective government relating to its own territory.
21 All three noted in West and Murphy, 'Impact' (1989).
22 In the UK, *Luther* v. *Sagor* (English Court of Appeal, 1921), 3 K.B. 532; in Canada, *Re Chateau-Gai Wines Ltd and the Attorney General for*

Canada (1970), Ex. C.R. 366, discussed in Kindred *et al. International Law* (1993): 261–2.

23 Warbrick, 'New British Policy' (1981): 588, who felt this would make it easier for UK courts to adjust to the new situation created by abandonment of recognition of governments.

24 Nedjati, 'Acts' (1981); Warbrick, 'New British Policy' (1981): 579; West and Murphy, 'Impact' (1989); Davidson, 'Recognition' (1991); Greig, 'Effects' (1991): 47–8; Talmon, 'Recognition' (1992): 286; Kindred et al., *International Law* (1993): 270–8.

25 See particularly Judge Hobhouse's opinion in *Woodhouse, Drake* and the commentary by Kingsbury, 'Judicial Determination' (1993): 378–82.

26 Note, for example, the strong reaffirmations of the 'speak with one voice' doctrine in the Caglar case (cited above, note 11).

27 Aristodemou, 'Choice and Evasion' (1994) speculated on how judges may use this new discretion.

28 Edeson, 'Conclusive executive certificates' (1981): 2.

29 Verhoeven, *Relations* (1985): 60–7.

30 US decisions in *Ministry of Defense of the Islamic Republic* v. *Gould, Inc.* (1988) and *National Petrochemical Company of Iran* v. *M/T Stolt Sheaf* (US Court of Appeals, 2nd Circuit, (1988) 860 F.2d 551, noted in *AJIL*, 83: 368 (1989), are often cited in support. However, these involve making exceptions to the special restrictions on official or private contacts with the Iranian government rather than nonrecognition because the Carter administration said it would 'honor the will of the Iranian people' and deal with the new government. Press statement of 12 February 1979, *Department of State Bulletin*, March 1979, pp. 32–3.

31 Heuser, 'Zur Rechtsstellung' (1989): 342. Similar reasoning was part of the rationale for a US court decision enforcing a trade acceptance drawn on an East German government-owned corporation despite US nonrecognition of that government and state. *Upright* v. *Mercury Business Machines Co.*, Supreme Court of New York, Appellate Division, First Dept., 1961. 13 A.D.2d 36, 313; 213 N.Y.S. 2d 417. *ILR*, 32: 65–70.

32 E.g. *Amtorg Trading Corp.* v. *United States* (CCPa, 1934), 71 F2d 524, *Annual Digest*, 7: 75–6; *Transportes Aereos de Angola* v. *Ronair Inc.* (Federal District Court, 1982), 544 F. Supp. 858, *ILR*, 94: 202–9.

33 Noted in O'Connell, *International Law* (2nd edn, 1970): 181. See also the Swiss Federal Justice Office's determination that the new Iranian regime should be permitted to have information about property in Switzerland registered in the Shah's name in 1980, *Schweizerisches Jahrbuch*, 37: 225–6 (1981).

34 Taiwan Relations Act (1979), 22, *United States Code*, sec. 3301–16.

35 See examples of using these devices in *Republic of Somalia* v. *Woodhouse, Drake & Carey (Suisse) S.A. and Others*, English High Court, Queen's Bench Division, 1992, [1993] Q.B. 54, noted in *ILR*, 94: 608–23; *Caglar and Others* v. *Billingham* (cited above, note 11).

36 Warbrick, 'New British Policy' (1981): 581.

37 *Clerget* c. *Représentation commerciale de la République démocratique de Viet Nam*, Cour de Cassation, 15 March 1971, noted in Verhoeven, *Relations* (1985): 73.

38 *Wulfsohn* v. *Russian Soviet Federated Socialist Republic*, 234 N.Y. 372, 138 N.E. 24 (1923).
39 *The Arantzazu Mendi*, House of Lords [1939] A.C. 256, a result encouraged by the fact the Republicans were attempting to gain control of ships then in the UK that had been requisitioned by transfer of title in their home port of Bilbao, which the Nationalists controlled.
40 Warbrick, 'New British Policy' (1981): 581.
41 E.g. US Foreign Sovereign Immunities Act of 1976, *United States Code*, 28: 1330, 1332, 1391, 1401, 1602–11, *International Legal Materials*, 15: 1388–92; UK State Immunity Act, 1978, 26 and 27 Eliz. 2, ch. 33, *International Legal Materials*, 17: 1123 (1978); Canadian Act to Provide for State Immunity, 1982, 29, 30 and 31 Eliz. 2, ch. 93, *International Legal Materials*, 21: 798 (1982); Pakistani Act, Singapore Act, South African Act (all UN Doc. ST/LEG/SER.B/20 (1982).
42 Letter from Professor Colin Warbrick, 28 April 1996.
43 *Australian YBIL*, 11: 484 (1991).
44 *Somalia* v. *Woodhouse Drake & Carey* (cited above, note 25). Though nonrecognition was not involved because the premises were vacated in 1975, British government steps to ensure that squatters did not gain ownership of the vacant Cambodian embassy illustrate the general obligations regarding state property. *R.* v. *Secretaty of State for Foreign and Commonwealth Affairs, ex parte Samuel*, Court of Appeal, 28 July 1989, 83 ILR 231, noted in *ILR*, 96: 623–43.
45 *United States Code*, 28: sec. 1116(c)(1), *International Legal Materials*, 11: 1405 (1971) noted in Oppenheim, *International Law* (1992), vol. 1: 159.
46 E.g. French eviction of the ROC delegation to UNESCO from the offices and residential areas of the Chinese mission to UNESCO in March 1966, nine months after recognizing the PRC government but before the PRC began participating in the organization. *RGDIP*, 70: 740–3 (1966).
47 Act of 7 April 1941 (initially adopted to aid the governments-in-exile of Axis-occupied states), 55 Stat. 131 (1941) 12, *United States Code*, title 12, sec. 632.
48 For a recent example, see *Attorney General for Fiji* v. *Robt. Jones House*, New Zealand High Court, 1989, *ILR*, 80: 1–10. Also discussed in Davidson, 'Recognition' (1991).
49 A government indulging in prolonged nonrecognition of a new government will only allow appointees of the former regime to use the premises.
50 E.g. Australian statements regarding the empty Cambodian embassy, *Australian YBIL*, 11: 201 (1991).
51 [1939] A.C. 256, commentary in Henkin et al., *International Law* (1987): 263.
52 *The Spanish Government* v. *Felipe Campuzano*, Norwegian Supreme Court, 1938, *Annual Digest*, 1938–40, Case No. 27. The property was furniture and records of the Spanish legation in the custody of a Franco loyalist who refused to deliver them to the newly-appointed Minister.
53 *Republic of Panama* v. *Republic National Bank of New York and Others*, US District Court for the Southern District of New York (1988), 681 F. Supp. 1066 (1988), noted in *ILR*, 86: 1–9; *Republic of Panama* v. *Citizens and Southern International Bank and Others*, US District Court for the

Southern District of Florida, 682 F. Supp. 1544 (1988), noted in *ILR*, 86: 10–19.

54 *United States Practice of International Law*, 1980–8, pp. 318–20.

55 Diet debate on the Foreign Ministry's turning of the Chinese embassy over to PRC representatives in 1972, noted in *Japanese Annual*, 25: 81–4 (1982); Kokaryo case (*X.* v. *Taiwan [Republic of China]*), Osaka District Court, 1986, Kyoto High Court, 1988, noted in *Japanese Annual*, 31: 201–3 (1988).

56 PRC government and Chinese scholars' reactions discussed in Heuser, 'Zur Rechtsstellung' (1989): 339–40.

57 *United States Practice in International Law*, 1979, pp. 146–9.

58 *United States Practice in International Law*, 1979: 147.

59 22 *United States Code*, sec. 3301–16; *International Legal Materials*, 18: 873 (1974).

60 E.g. *Texas* v. *White* (US Supreme Court, 1868) 74 U.S. (7 Wall) 700; *United States* v. *Insurance Companies*, 22 Wall. 99, 89 US 99.

61 *Dreyfus Frères et Cie v. Chile*, Franco-Chilean Arbitral Panel, 1901, in Despagnet and Renault, *Receuil, Année 1901*, p. 180.

62 Nedjati, 'Acts' (1981): 408.

63 Nedjati, 'Acts' (1981): 409.

64 Dutch courts in *Herami Ltd* v. *Wladikawkao Eisenbanngesellschaft* (1940, *Annual Digest*, 11: 21–38; US courts in *Wulfsohn* v. *RSFSR* (appellate ruling, 1925), 235 N.Y. 375, 138 N.E. 25; *Annual Digest*, 2: 39–41, 42 and 125; *Russian Reinsurance Co.* v. *Stoddard*, 240 N.Y. 149, 147 N.E. 703, *Annual Digest*, 3: 54; *Salminoff* v. *Standard Oil Co.*, 1933, 262 N.Y. 220, 186 N.E. 679; *Annual Digest*, 7: 22–7.

65 E.g. *Petrogradsky Mejdunarodny Kommerchesky Bank* v. *National City Bank* (1930), 253 N.Y. 23, 170 N.E. 479; *Annual Digest*, 5: 38.

66 Tsutsui, 'Subjects' (1988): 325, n. 1.

67 Nedjati, 'Acts' (1981): 411; Verhoeven, *Relations* (1985): 112–15.

68 Verhoeven, *Relations* (1985): 115–23.

69 Verhoeven, *Relations* (1985): 123–34.

70 E.g. Allott, 'Courts' (1977): 273–4; Shaw, 'Legal Acts' (1978): 503–54.

71 Lord Wilberforce's opinion in *Carl Zeiss Stiftung* v. *V.E.B. Carl Zeiss, Jena* (House of Lords, 1966 [1967]) 1 A.C. 853, *ILR*, 61: 35; *Hesperides Hotels Ltd* v. *Aegean Turkish Holidays Ltd and Muftizade* (House of Lords, 1978) 3 WLR 378, noted in *ILR*, 73: 9–31.

72 Quoted in *British YBIL*, 49: 260. This statement was *obiter dictum* rather than a direct basis for the ruling.

73 E.g. Shaw, 'Legal Acts' (1978): 502.

74 Allott, 'Courts' (1977): 273, n. 46.

75 As anticipated and welcomed by Nedjati, 'Acts' (1981): 390–2, and Warbrick, 'New British Policy' (1981). See also Talmon, 'Recognition' (1992).

76 *British YBIL*, 62: 565–8 (1991).

77 Judgment of 7 July 1956, quoted in *Japanese Annual*, 1958, p. 149.

78 *Carl Zeiss Stiftung* v. *V.E.B. Carl Zeiss* (Federal District Court for the Southern District of New York, 1968), 293 F. Supp. 892.

79 *Bank Saderat* v. *Farshneshani* [1982], Commercial Law Reports 111, discussed in *British YBIL*, 53: 355 (1992).

80 *Gur Corporation* v. *Trust Bank of Africa*, English Court of Appeal, Queen's Bench Division, [1987] QB 599, noted in *ILR*, 75: 675–99.
81 *R.* v. *Minister of Agriculture, Fisheries and Food, ex parte S.P. Anastasiou (Pissouri) Ltd and Others*, European Court of Justice, Case No. C-432/92, 1994, noted in *Common Market Law Review*, 33: 125–35 (1966).
82 Legal consequences for States of the continued presence of South Africa in Namibia (South West Africa), notwithstanding Security Council Resolution 276 (1970), *ICJ Reports*, 1971: 16.
83 *ICJ Reports*, 1971: 16. See particularly the Separate Opinion of Judge Federico de Castro, who cautioned that concessions and other deals relating to public property should be regarded as invalid.
84 Kiss, *Répertoire française*, vol. 3: 44.
85 *Fenton Textiles Association* v. *Krassin*, *ILR*, 1: 295 (British); *Grotius annuaire internationale pour l'année 1933*, p. 33 (Dutch); Gemma, 'Les Gouvernements' (1924): 388–90 (Italy).
86 Wolf, 'Le Gouvernement de fait' (1956): 126.
87 Foreign Ministry *avis* of 16 December 1920, quoted in *Répertoire française*, 3: 80.
88 Dutch government statement that while the government was not interested in accepting even a trade mission from the Soviets it would not impede private efforts to increase Dutch–Soviet trade, quoted in *Grotius annuaire internationale pour l'année 1933*, pp. 33 and 133.
89 Discussed in Burckhardt, *Le Droit fédérale suisse* (1930), vol. 1: 180–90.
90 For the changing Soviet views see Boguslavskii, *Staatliche Immunität* (1965), and Osakwe, 'A Soviet Perspective' (1982).
91 Response to questions in the House of Representatives, 13 June 1968, quoted in Holder and Brennan, *The International Legal System* (1972): 188.
92 E.g. Australian and Canadian grain marketing board sales to PRC purchasing agencies. *Australian YBIL*, 1967, p. 237; *Canadian YBIL*, 2: 279–80 (1964).
93 Erdmann, *Nichtanerkannte* (1962): 157.
94 Erdmann, *Nichtanerkannte* (1962): 156.
95 Minister of External Affairs' response to questions in the House of Representatives, 13 June 1968, in Holder and Brennan, *The International Legal System* (1972): 188.
96 Johnson and Chiu (eds), *Agreements of the People's Republic of China, 1949–1967* (1968): 8–10 and 15. On the particularly complicated evolution of Japan–China trade see Hsiao, 'Nonrecognition and Trade' (1972); Uchida, 'Legal Aspects of Japan–China Trade' (1975).
97 Hsiao, 'Nonrecognition and Trade' (1972): 133–52.
98 Reghizzi, 'Legal Aspects' (1968): 91–2.
99 The Chileans later sued over the diverted cargos in British courts. See I Congreso del Partido, noted and discussed in *British YBIL*, 49: 262–3 (1978).
100 If not a new form, since the earlier mercantilists also favoured a strong role in foreign trade, then a new type of organization because the mercantilists operated through chartered companies rather than state agencies.

10. POLITICAL USES OF RECOGNITION

1 For a general discussion, see Wolfers, 'The Goals of Foreign Policy', in *Discord and Collaboration* (1962), ch. 5; for particular examples of international order-building motivated by such considerations see Burley, 'Regulating the World' (1993) and Kissinger, *A World Restored* (1957).
2 Australian Foreign Ministry announcement, 19 January 1988 in *Australian YBIL*, 11: 205; British government statement, 28 April 1980 in *British YBIL*, 51: 367 (1980); Dutch government statement of 4 July 1990 in *Netherlands YBIL*, 22: 237–8 (1991); US State Department memorandum, 'Diplomatic Recognition', *Department of State Bulletin*, 77: 462–3 (10 Oct. 1977).
3 Moore, *Digest*, vol. 1: 124 and 135–6.
4 Iriye, *After Imperialism* (1965).
5 *FRUS, 1936*, 2: 576.
6 Padelford, *International Law and Diplomacy in the Spanish Civil Strife* (1939): 17.
7 List from Misra, *India's Policy of Recognition* (1966): 107–8.
8 Recognitions noted in *Ann. française*, 1969: 947–51.
9 Tripathi, *India's Foreign Policy* (1990): 124.
10 'Chronique', *RGDIP*, 75: 158–9 (1971).
11 *Keesing's Contemporary Archives*, 1970: 24127.
12 *Washington Post*, 28 March 1975, p. A10.
13 'Chronique', *RGDIP*, 79: 1106–7 (1975); *Washington Post*, 18 April 1975, p. A15; 19 April 1975, p. A15; and 2 May 1975, p. A13.
14 *Ann. française*, 1965: 1084–5.
15 *Ann. française*, 1971: 1124.
16 *China Yearbook*, 1921: 623–6; Kiss (ed.), *Répertoire française*, 3: 85 (1965); comment in *Nonis* v. *Federation of Seamen* (Court of Appeal of Genoa, 1930), *Annual Digest and Reports of International Law Cases*, 1929–30: 45–6; Houghton, 'Policy of the United States' (1929): 96.
17 *New York Times*, 29 March 1977, p. 10.
18 See page 18.
19 Gemma, 'Les Gouvernements de fait' (1929): 341; Oppenheim, *International Law* (2nd edn, 1912), vol. 1: 426.
20 Smith, *Great Britain and the Law of Nations* (1932), vol. 2: 231–3.
21 Mirkine-Guetzévitch, 'Droit international et droit constitutionnel' (1931): 338.
22 Houghton, 'Policy of the United States and other Nations' (1929): 90–4 and 105, n. 99.
23 Hsiung, 'China's Recognition Practice' (1972): 54–5. The Saudis were among the last to relent, recognizing in July 1990. *Keesing's Record of World Events*, 1990: 37628.
24 *New York Times*, 15 April 1974, p. 13. Relations were ended on 18 March 1977 after the first post-Franco parliamentary elections, and relations established with the elected government on the 28th. *Keesing's Contemporary Archives*, 1977: 28329.
25 Chen, *Recognition* (1951): 285–8.

26 Burckhardt, *Le droit fédérale suisse* (1930), vol. 1: 189.
27 Particularly in the Australian case, where a newly-elected Labour Party government was making a break with the preceding National Party government's policy, these were also expressions of dissociation from US policy in the area.
28 *US Practice in International Law, 1977*: 23–5.
29 Compare, e.g., *US Practice in International Law, 1977*: 21–5 and 29–30.
30 All known examples accompanied recognition of new states. Chen, *Recognition* (1951): 265–9 discusses nineteenth-century and interwar examples in detail.
31 Scelle, 'Chronique des faits internationaux: Mexique' (1914): 129; Despagnet, *Cours* (1905): 96.
32 Dom Miguel refused the trade, Smith, *Great Britain and the Law of Nations* (1932), vol. 1: 179. The British then reverted to supporting Dona Maria and the constitutionalists.
33 See *Fontes Juris Gentium*, B, sec. 1, vol. 1, pt. 1, nos 517–58; *FRUS, 1883* (1884): 664; Barker, *The French Experience in Mexico* (1979) discusses the roots of the French venture.
34 Sharp, *Nonrecognition as a Legal Obligation* (1934): 43–5.
35 Sharp, *Nonrecognition as a Legal Obligation* (1934): 45–6.
36 Albrecht-Carrié, *Diplomatic History of Europe* (1958): 119–21.
37 These included adherence to the 1906 Act and all rules and decisions stemming from it, acceptance of responsibility for his predecessor's debts, continuation of Franco-Spanish supervision of the port police and sea-borne arms traffic, permitting the international claims commission set up after riots in Casablanca to complete its work, guarantee the safety and liberty of communications, guarantee orderly administration and treatment of foreigners by the standards of international law, and payment of a decent pension to the deposed sultan. *FRUS, 1908*: 648–9 (1912).
38 Dennis, 'Revolution, Recognition and Intervention' (1930–1): 207; Goebel, 'The Recognition Policy' (1915): 67; Baty, *Canons* (1930): 212; Scelle, *Manuel* (1943): 122; Anderson, 'Recognition of Russia' (1925): 519.
39 Article 6. Quoted in Irizarry y Puente, 'The Doctrine' (1954): 326.
40 Kunz, *Anerkennung* (1928): 162 said they could be used with *de facto* recognition only; Brown, 'La Reconnaissance' (1934): 349 said they could only be used with *de jure* recognition.
41 Scelle, *Précis* (1932), vol. 1: 101–2.
42 E.g. Spiropoulos, *Traité* (1933): 50; Bustamante y Sirven (1934), vol. 1: 169.
43 *Annuaire de l'Institut de droit international*, 30: 303 (1936).
44 *Documents on British Foreign Policy, 1919–1939*, 1st ser., vol. 6, no. 307.
45 *Documents on British Foreign Policy, 1919–1939*, 1st ser., vol. 12, nos 75 and 202.
46 Lauterpacht, *Recognition* (1947): 350, note 2. Chen, *Recognition* (1951): 102, and Kozhevnikov, *International Law* (1961): 121 said this was accomplished by withdrawing recognition from the provisional government until a republic was definitively established.

47 Yalta Conference Declarations on Liberated Europe, Poland and Yugoslavia, *FRUS, 1945: The Conferences at Malta and Yalta* (1955): 977–8, 980 and 980–1.
48 *Répertoire française*, 3: 59.
49 A few observers regarded this as a novel form of recognizing despite doubts that the new regime would abide by international law. See statements quoted in Brown, 'Legal Effects' (1950): 625.
50 Letter of 30 November 1933, quoted in Whiteman, *Digest*, vol. 2: 123–4. Texts of the agreements are given in *FRUS, The Soviet Union, 1933–1939* (1952): 28–29.
51 Report to the Third Party Congress, 13 May 1925, reported in Degras, *Soviet Documents* (1951), vol. 2: 30–1.
52 Chen, *Recognition* (1951): 285–8. Danish claims of compensation for expropriations added to the dispute.
53 Taracouzio, *The Soviet Union and International Law* (1935), Appendix XIV.
54 Burckhardt, *Le Droit* (1930), vol. 1: 189. The Vorovsky affair stemmed from the assassination of a Soviet delegate to the 1923 Lausanne Conference by a Russian émigré living in Switzerland.
55 Toynbee and Kirkwood, *Turkey* (1927), ch. 9.
56 Iriye, *After Imperialism* (1965): pp. 87–8.
57 Reynolds, 'Recognition Policy' (1928): 62.
58 Dinegar, 'Some Aspects' (1963): 234–5.
59 *FRUS, 1921* (1936), vol. 2: 399–419, *passim*.
60 *Répertoire française*, 3: 57.
61 *League of Nations Treaty Series*, 165: 19 (1936).
62 K'ung Meng 'A Criticism' (1958) in Cohen and Chiu, *People's China and International Law*, vol. 1: 246; Sibert, *Traité* (1951): 192; Oppenheim, *International Law* (8th edn, 1958), vol. 1: 148–9; Cavaré, *Le droit* (1961), vol. 1: 325; implied in Kozhevnikov, *International Law* (1961): 114–20; Coquia and Santiago, *Public International Law* (1984): 115.
63 Lauterpacht, *Recognition* (1947): 364; Azevedo, *Aspects généraux* (1953): 37; Kopelmanas, 'La Reconnaissance' (1957): 8–9; Hingorani, *Modern International Law* (1984), 88; Starke, *Introduction* (1984): 132.
64 Chen, *Recognition* (1951): 267–9; Mugerwa, 'Subjects' (1968): 282; Dahm, *Völkerrecht* (1958), vol. 1: 146–7.
65 Kelsen, *Principles* (1952): 275; Guggenheim, *Traité* (1953), vol. 1: 196–7; Verdross, *Völkerrecht* (4th edn, 1959): 252; Tandon, *Public International Law* (1965): 152; Brownlie, *Principles* (1966): 86.
66 Starke, 'Recognition' (1950): 19; Schwarzenberger, *A Manual* (1960), vol. 1: 62; Delbez, *Les Principes* (1964): 164; O'Connell, *International Law* (1964), vol. 1: 147; Fenwick, *International Law* (4th edn, 1965): 583; Salonga and Yap, *Public International Law* (1966): 96–7; Verhoeven, *La Reconnaissance* (1975), 651–6.
67 Starke, 'Recognition' (1950): 19.
68 Inter-American Council of Jurists (1953): 22.
69 Whiteman, *Digest*, vol. 2: 322–5. Unlike the Latin American cases, US citizens had little economic stake in this outcome.
70 Erasmus, 'General de Gaulle's Recognition' (1964): 196–7.

71 See pages 102–3.
72 *New York Times*, 10 June 1974, p. 1, col. 1.
73 Menon, 'Some Aspects, V' (1991): 29–31.
74 Oppenheim, *International Law* (9th edn, 1992), vol. 1: 154.
75 Kapoor, *International Law* (1992): 169; Oppenheim, *International Law* (9th edn, 1992), vol. 1: 175; Menon, 'Some Aspects, V' (1991): 29–31.
76 The Italians had encouraged President Zogu to establish a monarchy and proclaim himself king because they felt that would consolidate their influence in the country. See contemporaneous discussion in *FRUS, 1928*, 1: 849–51 (1942).
77 Schlüter, *De-facto Anerkennung* (1936): 44–5.
78 They did succeed in holding Helsinki for three months. Puntilla, *Political History of Finland* (1968): 102–9. Arto Mansala supplied this example.
79 Azevedo, *Aspects généraux* (1953): 39.
80 Degras, *Soviet Documents on Foreign Policy, 1917–1941* (1951): 405–47.
81 See discussions in *FRUS, 1940*, 4: 436–7 and 468.
82 Extra-legal changes of government calculated from Banks, *Cross-Polity Time Series Data* (1971), and notices of later instances in Rousseau, 'Chronique', *RGDIP*, *Latin American and Caribbean Review*, *Africa Contemporary Record*, and *Africa South of the Sahara*. The count may understate the number of extra-legal changes, but accurately indicates the trend over time.

11. ALTERING THE INSTITUTION OF RECOGNITION OF GOVERNMENTS

1 *Foreign Relations of the United States*, 1913: 433 (1914), also discussed on page 162.
2 *British Documents on the Origin of the War, 1898–1914*, nos. 65–74. Western Hemisphere governments had already extended recognition.
3 *FRUS, 1913*, pp. 114–15 and 132 (1920). These failed. The Brazilian, Cuban, Mexican, Peruvian and US governments extended recognition in May 1913 and the governments of Japan and the European powers in October 1913.
4 Lorimer, *The Institutes* (1883), vol. 1: 106–7; Pradier-Fodéré *Traité* (1885), vol. 1: 240–1.
5 *British Documents on Foreign Policy, 1919–1939*, 1st series, vol. 6, no. 307; Hackworth, *Digest*, vol. 1: 317.
6 Hackworth, *Digest*, vol. 1: 271–2. US opposition to a joint declaration forced this to be expressed in six separate notes to the new regime.
7 Oppenheim, *International Law* (4th edn, 1928), vol. 1: 145–6; Makarov, 'Sowjet-Union' (1935): 34.
8 Quoted in Bisschop, 'London International Law Conference' (1943): 294.
9 Lauterpacht, *Recognition* (1947): 166–9; Jessup, *Modern Law of Nations* (1950): 45; Chatelain, 'La Reconnaissance' (1950): 719; Wright, 'Some Thoughts' (1950): 558–9; Chen, *Recognition* (1951): 222–3; Charpentier, *La Reconnaissance* (1956): 317–18; Patel, *Recognition* (1959): 79; Tabata,

'Admission' (1961): 1; Dhokalia, *International Law* (1963): 205; Mooker - jea, *International Law* (1968), vol. 1: 129; Corbett, *Growth of World Law* (1971): 67.

10 Starke, 'Recognition' (1950) 19; Graham, 'Some Thoughts' (1950): 369; Coplin, *Functions* (1966): 59–60; Kopelmanas, 'La Reconnaissance' (1970): 39–40; Blix, 'Contemporary Aspects' (1970): 698–9; Kato, 'Recognition' (1970): 303–4; Yakemtchouk, *L'Afrique* (1971): 56.

11 Alexandrowicz, 'Quasi-Judicial' (1952): 631.

12 Dugard, *Recognition and the United Nations* (1987): 17–18.

13 UN Doc. S/1466, in *Security Council Official Records*, 5th Session, Supplement (Jan.–May 1950), pp. 18–22.

14 Warbrick, 'The New British Policy' (1981): 573.

15 E.g. the 'Monrovia Group' of moderates and the 1963 Togo coup, Ćervenka, *The Organisation* (1969): 5, n. 4; the francophone Conseil de l'Entente after the 1967 Togo coup, *Africa Diary*, 1967, p. 3261; examples noted in *Africa Contemporary Record*, 1: 506 (1968–9); the Franco-African Summit on the situation in the Central African Empire, *Ann. française*, 1980: 878.

16 Mittelman, 'The Uganda Coup' (1972): 18–19.

17 *Africa Contemporary Record*, 11: A27 (1978–9).

18 *Washington Post*, 2 May 1975, p. A13, col. 7.

19 McChesney, 'International Law' (1969): 38–40.

20 1949 consultation proposal in Inter-American Council of Jurists, p, 23; summary of debates, pp. 25–6 and 68.

21 Resolution of the Tenth Interamerican Conference (Caracas, 1962), quoted in Whiteman, *Digest*, vol. 2: 89.

22 Resolution 26 of the Second Special Interamerican Conference (Rio, November 1965), English version in *AJIL*, 398 (1966).

23 1990 amendment to Article 9 of the OAS Charter, text in *International Legal Materials* 33: 1005 (1994).

24 Williams, 'Recognition' (1929): 65 and 70.

25 Dinegar, 'Some Aspects' (1963): 107–28; Irizarry y Puente, 'The Doctrine' (1953–4). Relevant documents appear in *FRUS, 1943–7.*

26 *Keesing's Contemporary Archives*, 1990, p. 37373.

27 *Africa Contemporary Record*, 11: A31 (1978–9). Inclusion of Bob Denard, leader of the mercenaries, as a member of the delegation further irritated other members.

28 *Africa Contemporary Record*, 13: A65 (1980–1).

29 Rousseau, 'Chronique', *RGDIP*, 89: 1045–6 (1985).

30 On Namibia: SC Resolution 276 (1970); SC Resolution 566 (1985). On Rhodesia: SC Resolution 217 (1965); SC Resolution 277, 18 March 1970 (reacting to Smith's proclamation that Rhodesia was henceforth a Republic); SC Resolution 448 (1979) (calling on members to avoid recognizing Bishop Muzorewa as prime minister). All these were phrased as nonrecognition of government because of the UN's prior decision to treat Rhodesia as a British colony on the road to independence before the white minority regime derailed the process.

31 SC Resolution 841 (1993) aligned the UN with the existing OAS sanctions and SC Resolution 873 (1993) re-imposed them after the military regime

failed to go through with a promised transfer of power. SC Resolution 940 (31 July 1994) authorized military intervention.

32 Particularly operative was paragraph 2 of Resolution 940, which referred to 'the unique character of the present situation in Haiti and its deteriorating complex and extraordinary nature, requiring an exceptional response'.

33 Liszt, *Das Völkerrecht* (9th edn, 1913): 161. He repeated this in the 12th edition (1925): 243. The text refers to various situations, but the inclusion of recognition of governments among them does not depart from the spirit of his argument.

34 Rivier, *Principes* (1896), vol. 1: 283.

35 Louter, *Le droit international* (1920), vol. 1: 245; Huess, 'Zum Probleme' (1935): 4–5.

36 E.g. Bustamante y Sirven's argument in *Droit international* (1934), vol. 1: 237–8; endorsement of the Estrada Doctrine and the proposals for codification, in Brown, 'Recognition of New Governments' (1932): 339; Fenwick, 'The Recognition of New Governments' (1942): 452.

37 E.g. Stowell, 'Remarks' (1931): 179.

38 Raestad, 'La Reconnaissance' (1936): 257.

39 English translation of press statement issued by Foreign Minister Estrada, 27 September 1930, published in *AJIL*, 25: Supplement, 203 (1931).

40 Rodolfo Nervo, Mexican minister to France, suggested to a French audience that his government did not intend to abolish recognition, but only to give it the most democratic character possible, and would be shifting to tacit forms of conveying it. Nervo, 'La doctrine mexicaine' (1931).

41 Chen, *Recognition* (1951): 129; Patel, *Recognition* (1959): 40; Lachs, 'Recognition' (1959): 258–9; Aron, *Peace and War* (1968): 119.

42 Fenwick, *International Law* (3rd edn, 1948): 173; Brown, 'Legal Effects' (1950): 630–3; Jovanovic, 'Dualism' (1961): 135–6; Ulanova, 'Recognition of States and Governments' (1961); Dinegar, 'Some Aspects' (1963): 284–6, 321; Charvin, 'La République' (1971): 1022.

43 Viret, *La portée* (1953): 126–8; Blix, 'Contemporary' (1970): 699–700.

44 Ando, 'The Recognition' (1985): 40; Tsutsui, 'Subjects' (1988): 331; Detter, *International Law* (1992): 93–4; Arbour, *Droit international* (1992): 177.

45 Peterson, 'Recognition' (1981); Feldman, 'International Personality' (1985): 397 (who also argued that abolition was actually an effort to retain a free hand); Menon, 'Some Aspects, III' (1990): 184.

46 Reproduced in Inter-American Council of Jurists, 'Recognition' (1953): 14.

47 Inter-American Council of Jurists, 'Recognition' (1953): 33–4.

48 Reproduced in *OAS Annals*, 1: 136 (1949).

49 Verhoeven, *La Reconnaissance*, 1: 91 (1975).

50 French reaction to Boumédienne's coup in Algeria, *Ann. française*, 1966, p. 918; Belgian and Senegalese reaction to Mobutu's coup in Zaire, Yakemtchouk, *L'Afrique en droit international* (1971): 50–1.

51 Kenyan, Swiss, and Soviet reaction to Amin's 1971 coup in Uganda, *Africa Contemporary Record*, 4: C64–5 and C79; Spanish reaction to the 1975 coup in Portugal, Rousseau, 'Chronique', *RGDIP*, 79: 525 (1975); US

statement regarding the 1975 Bangladesh coup, *Digest of United States Practice in International Law*, 1975, p. 34.

52 Verdross and Simma, *Universelles Völkerrecht* (1984): 562, who also listed the Dutch among adopters.

53 Statement to Foreign Affairs Committee of the Chamber of Deputies, 1 March 1979, *Italian YBIL*, 4: 219 (1978–9).

54 Written answers to questions in the House of Commons and the House of Lords, 28 April 1980, *British YBIL*, 51: 367 (1980).

55 Federal Council's written answer to questions in the National Council, 17 February 1982, *Schweizerisches Jahrbuch*, 39: 208 (1982).

56 Foreign Minister's statement, 4 July 1990, *Netherlands YBIL*, 22: 237–8 (1991).

57 Dugard, *International Law* (1994): 83.

58 Foreign Minister's statement, 19 January 1988, *Australian YBIL*, 11 (1991): 205.

59 Memorandum of the Legal Bureau of the Ministry of External Affairs, 9 November 1988, *Canadian YBIL*, 27: 387.

60 Davidson, 'Recognition of Foreign Governments' (1991), and p. 162, n. 3 on the lack of any statement to Parliament or any other public forum before it was produced in court.

61 Statement of 20 August 1991, *Australian YBIL*, 13: 223 (1992).

62 Ando, 'The Recognition' (1985), 37 relying on Heinz Klarer (1981) 278–9.

63 Canadian Ministry of External Affairs Legal Bureau memorandum, 5 August 1975, *Canadian YBIL* 14: 341 (1976).

64 Ando, 'The Recognition' (1985): 35, based on an interview with the Chief of the First Section of the Treaty Bureau of the West German Foreign Ministry.

65 State Department Office of Legal Affairs memorandum, 25 September 1981, *Digest of United States Practice in International Law, 1980–88*, p. 296.

66 Statement of 25 April 1980 to the House of Commons, *British YBIL*; qualification emphasized in Symmons, 'United Kingdom Abolition' (1981): 252.

67 Greig, 'The Effects' (1991): 41.

68 Foreign Ministry announcement, 19 January 1988, *Australian YBIL*, 11: 205 (1991); repeated in 12: 357 (1992).

69 Opposition statement on the new recognition policy, 21 January 1988, *Australian YBIL*, 12: 357–8 (1992).

70 Last paragraph of Foreign Minister's statement of 19 January 1988, *Australian YBIL*, 11: 205 (1991).

71 Ministry of External Affairs Legal Bureau memorandum, 9 November 1988, *Canadian YBIL*, 27: 387 (1989).

72 Announcement of 4 July 1990, *Netherlands YBIL*, 22: 238 (1991).

73 Statement of 22 Feb. 1982, in *Ann. française*, 1982, p. 1083.

74 Foreign Minister's statement to the Senate, 14 July 1982, *Ann. française*, 1982, p. 1084.

75 Statement in the House of Commons, 13 December 1990, quoted in Warbrick, 'Recognition' (1993): 97, n. 31.

76 See page 66.

12. THE INTERNATIONAL SYSTEM AND RECOGNITION OF GOVERNMENTS

1 The full implications of the change are explored in Jackson, *Quasi States* (1990).
2 *FRUS, 1928*, 1: 849–51 (1942).
3 Slusser and Triska (eds), *Calendar of Soviet Treaties* (1959): 97.
4 Noted by Greig, 'Effects' (1991): 35; Warbrick, 'New British Policy' (1981): 570–1.
5 Such connections are central to various visions of better global order, for example, Kant *Perpetual Peace* (1795) and Marx, *Communist Manifesto* (1848). The connections have been noted by analysts of international relations as well, including Wolfers, 'The Goals of Foreign Policy' (1962): 74–7; Ruggie, 'International Regimes, Transactions, and Change' (1982); and Burley, 'Regulating the World' (1993).
6 On the difference between observable facts and meanings, see Kratochwil, *Rules, Norms, and Decisions* (1989): 21–5.
7 For a recent discussion see Krasner, 'Compromising Westphalia' (1996).

Bibliography

I LEGAL SCHOLARS' WORKS SURVEYED

Accioly, Hildebrando (Brazilian). *Traité de droit international public.* 3 vols. Translated by Paul Goule. Paris: Recueil Sirey, 1940–2.

Akehurst, Michael (British). *A Modern Introduction to International Law.* New York: Atherton Press, 1970. pp. 367.

Alexandrowicz, Charles H. (British scholar born in Austrian Poland). 'The Quasi-Judicial Function in Recognition of States and Governments'. *American Journal of International Law*, 46 (1952): 631–40.

——. 'The Theory of Recognition in Fieri'. *British YBIL*, 34 (1958): 176–98.

Allott, Philip (British). 'Courts and the Executive: Four House of Lords Decisions'. *Cambridge Law Journal*, 36 (November 1977): 255–83.

Alvarez, Alejandro (Chilean, member of the ICJ 1946–55). 'The Monroe Doctrine from the Latin American Point of View'. *St Louis Law Review*, 2 (1917): 135–46.

Ambros, Heino (United States). 'Nonrecognition: Its Development in International Law and Its Application by the United States, with Particular Reference to the Baltic States'. Ph.D. dissertation, New York University, 1965. pp. 362.

American Law Institute (private association of United States lawyers and scholars). *Restatement of the Law, Third: The Foreign Relations Law of the United States.* Washington, DC: American Law Institute, 1986.

——. *Restatement, Second: The Law of American Foreign Relations.* St Paul, Minn.: American Law Institute, 1965. pp. xxvi + 679.

Anand, Ram P. (Indian). *New States and International Law.* Delhi: Vikas Publishing House, 1972. pp. 119.

Anderson, Chandler P. (United States). 'Recognition of Russia'. *American Journal of International Law*, 28 (1934): 90–7.

Anderson, Louis (Costa Rican). 'De facto Government' (a translation of El gobierno de facto, San José, Costa Rica, 1925). *Inter-America*, 8 (1924–5): 503–34; and 9 (1925–6): 21–42.

Ando, Nisuke (Japanese). 'The Recognition of Governments Reconsidered'. *Japanese Annual of International Law*, 28 (1985): 29–46.

André-Vincent, H. (French). 'Le Problème de la reconnaissance'. *Revue de droit international*, 21 (1938): 399–411.

Anzilotti, Dionisio (Italian, member of the PCIJ 1922–45). *Cours de droit international.* 3rd edn. 3 vols. Translated by Gilbert Gidel (only vol. 1 appeared in translation). Paris: Recueil Sirey, 1929.

Arbour, J.-Maurice (Canadian). *Droit international public.* 2nd edn. Cowansville, Quebec: Les éditions Yvon Blais, 1992. pp. xxxiv + 514.

Arendt, Heinz-Carl (German). *Die Anerkennung in der Staatenpraxis.* Berlin: Buchdruckerei Franz Linke, 1938. pp. viii + 177.

Aristodemou, Maria. 'Choice and Evasion in Judicial Recognition of Governments: Lessons from Somalia'. *European Journal of International Law*, 5: 532–55 (1994).

Aron, Raymond (French social scientist). 'Evidence and Inference in History'. *Daedalus*, No. 87 (Fall 1958): 11–39.

——. *Peace and War*. Translated by Richard Howard and Annette B. Fox. New York: Praeger, 1968. pp. 820.

Asamoah, Obed Y. (Ghanaian). 'Recognition of States and Governments'. *University of Ghana Law Review*, 5 (1968): 122–32.

Aufricht, Hans (Austrian-born US citizen then serving as assistant counsellor of the IMF). 'Principles and Practices of Recognition by International Organizations'. *American Journal of International Law*, 43 (1949): 679–704.

Azevedo, J. L. Braganca de (Brazilian, member of the ICJ 1946–51). *Aspects généraux de la reconnaissance des gouvernements*. Paris: A. Pedone, 1953. pp. 104.

Balekjian, Wahe H. (Austrian). *Die Effektivität und die Stellung nichtanerkannter Staaten im Völkerrecht*. The Hague: Martinus Nijhoff, 1970. pp. 222.

Barnes, William S. (United States). 'US Recognition Policy and Cambodia'. In *The Vietnam War and International Law*, 3: 148–60. Edited by Richard A. Falk. Princeton: Princeton University Press, 1972.

Bastid, Suzanne (French). *Droit international public, principes fondamenteaux*. Paris: Les Cours de droit, 1970.

Baty, Thomas (British, long-time resident of Japan who often advised the Japanese government). 'Abuse of Terms: "Recognition", "War"'. *American Journal of International Law*, 30 (1936): 377–99.

——. 'So-called De Facto Recognition'. *Yale Law Journal*, 31 (1921–2): 469–88.

——. *The Canons of International Law*. London: John Murray, 1930. pp. xi + 518.

Berber, Friedrich J. (German). *Lehrbuch des Völkerrechts*. 3 vols. Munich: Beck, 1960–4.

Bettati, Mario (French). '"Souveraineté limitée" ou "internationalisme prolétarien"? Les liens fondamentaux de la communauté des États socialistes'. *Revue belge de droit international*, 8 (1972): 455–81.

Bierzanek, Remigiusz (Polish). 'La Non-reconnaissance et le droit international contemporain'. *Annuaire française de droit international*, 8 (1962): 117–38.

Binavince, Emilio S. (US-educated Filipino teaching in Canada). 'Canadian Practice in Matters of Recognition'. In *Canadian Perspectives on International Law and Organization*, 155–83. Edited by R. St J. MacDonald, Gerald L. Morris, and Douglas M. Johnson. Toronto: University of Toronto Press, 1974.

Bindschedler, Rudolf L. (Swiss). 'Die Anerkennung im Völkerrecht'. *Archiv des Völkerrechts*, 9 (1961–2): 376–97.

Bisschop, W. R. (British). 'London International Law Conference'. *American Journal of International Law*, 38 (1944): 290–6.

Black, Cyril E. and Falk, Richard A. (eds) (both United States). *The Future of the International Legal Order*. 5 vols. Princeton, N.J.: Princeton University Press, 1969– .

Blix, Hans M. (Swedish). 'Contemporary Aspects of Recognition'. *Hague Academy Recueil des cours*, 130 (1970): 591–703.

Bluntschli, Johann K. (German). *Das moderne Völkerrecht der civilisierten Staaten*. 3rd edn. Nordlingen: Verlag der C. H. Beck'schen Buchhandlung, 1878. pp. xii + 541.

Bonfils, Henry (French). *Manuel de droit international public*. 7th edn. Edited by Paul Fauchille. Paris: Rousseau, 1914. pp. viii + 1209.

Borchard, Edwin M. (United States). 'Remarks [on Hackworth's discussion of United States Recognition Policy]'. *Proceedings of the American Society of International Law*, 25 (1931): 171–3.

——. 'Recognition and Non-recognition'. *American Journal of International Law*, 36 (1942): 108–11.

Bot, Bernard R. (Dutch lawyer and diplomat). *Non-recognition and Treaty Relations*. Leyden: A. W. Sijthoff, and Dobbs Ferry, N.Y.: Oceana Publications, 1968. pp. xvi + 286.

Bozeman, Adda B. (United States). *The Future of Law in a Multicultural World*. Princeton, N.J.: Princeton University Press, 1971. pp. xviii + 229.

Brierly, James L. (British). *The Law of Nations*. 6th edn. Edited by Sir Humphrey Waldock. Oxford: Clarendon Press, 1963. pp. xii + 442.

Briggs, Herbert W. (United States). 'De Facto and De Jure Recognition: The Arantzazu Mendi'. *American Journal of International Law*, 33 (1939): 689–99.

——. 'Relations Officieuses and Intent to Recognize: British Recognition of Franco'. *American Journal of International Law*, 34 (1940): 47–57.

——. *The Law of Nations: Cases, Documents and Notes*. New York: F. S. Crofts, 1938. pp. xxix + 984.

——. *The Law of Nations: Cases, Notes and Documents*. 2nd edn. New York: Appleton-Century-Crofts, 1952. pp. xxvii + 1208.

British Institute of International and Comparative Law (a private association). *British International Law Cases*. 9 vols. London: Stevens & Son, and Dobbs Ferry, N.Y.: Oceana Publications, 1965–.

Brown, Everett S. (United States). 'Some Unofficial Relations with Soviet Russia'. *Michigan Law Review*, 22 (1923–4): 421–36.

Brown, Philip M. (United States). 'La Reconnaissance des nouveaux États et des nouveaux gouvernements: Rapport de l'Onzième commission'. *Annuaire de l'Institut de droit international*, 38 (1934): 302–50.

——. 'The Effects of Recognition'. *American Journal of International Law*, 36 (1942): 106–8.

——. 'The Legal Effects of Recognition'. *American Journal of International Law*, 44 (1950): 617–40.

——. 'The Recognition of New Governments'. *American Journal of International Law*, 26 (1932): 336–40.

——. 'The Recognition of New States and New Governments'. *American Journal of International Law*, 30 (1936): 689–94.

Brownlie, Ian (British). 'Recognition in Theory and Practice'. In *The Structure and Process of International Law*, R. St J. MacDonald and D. M. Johnston (eds), pp. 627–41. Dordrecht: Martinus Nijhoff, 1986.

——. *Principles of Public International Law*. Oxford: Clarendon Press, 1966. pp. xxxi + 646.

Bundu, A. C. (member of Commonwealth secretariat). 'Recognition of Revolutionary Authorities: Law and Practice of States'. *International and Comparative Law Quarterly*, 27 (1978): 18–45.

Bustamante y Sirven, Antonio S. de (Cuban, member of the PCIJ 1922–45). *Droit international public*. 5 vols. Translated by Paul Goule. Paris: Recueil Sirey, 1934–9.

Butler, William E. (United States expert on Soviet law now teaching in England). 'Book Review: Ramundo, *Peaceful Coexistence: International Law in the Building of Communism*'. *Harvard Law Review*, 83 (1969): 483–8.

——. '"Socialist International Law" or "Socialist Principles of International Relations"?' *American Journal of International Law*, 65 (1971): 796–800.

Buza, Ladislas (Hungarian). 'Die juristische Natur der Anerkennung im Völkerrecht'. *Zeitschrift für öffentliches Recht*, 20 (1940): 77–91.

Calvo, Carlos (Argentine diplomat). *Le droit international théorique et pratique*. 5th edn, rev'd. 6 vols. Paris: A. Rousseau, 1896.

Cansacci, Giorgio (Italian). 'Identité et continuité des sujets internationaux'. Hague Academy, *Recueil des cours*, 130 (1970): 1–94.

Carnazza-Amari, Giuseppe (Italian). *Traité de droit international public en temps de paix*. Translated by C. Montanari-Revest. 2 vols. Paris: L. Larose, 1880–2.

Castel, Jean G. (Canadian). *International Law, Chiefly as Interpreted and Applied in Canada*. Toronto: University of Toronto Press, 1965. pp. xii + 1402.

Cavaré, Louis (French). *Le droit international public positif*. 2 vols. Edited by Jean P. Quenendec. Paris: A. Pedone, 1961–2.

Červenka, Zdenek (Czech). *The Organisation of African Unity and Its Charter*. 2nd edn. New York: Frederick A. Praeger, 1969. pp. xii + 253.

Charpentier, Jean (French). *La Reconnaissance internationale et l'évolution du droit des gens*. Paris: A. Pedone, 1956. pp. 357.

Charvin, Robert (French). 'La République démocratique allemande et le droit international'. *Revue général de droit international public*, 75 (1971): 1014–59.

Chatelain, Jean (French). 'La Reconnaissance internationale'. In *La technique et les principes du droit public: Études en l'honneur de Georges Scelle*, vol. 2: 717–34. Paris: Librairie général de droit et de jurisprudence, 1950.

Chaudhari, Abdul R. (Pakistani). *Public International Law*. Lahore: Caravan Book House, 1962. pp. 510.

Chen, Chin-shan. 'American Recognition and Non-recognition Policies in China: A Legal, Historical and Political Analysis'. Ph.D. dissertation, Southern Illinois University, 1963. pp. 353.

Chen, Lung-chu (Chinese-born? US scholar). *An Introduction to Contemporary International Law: A Policy-Oriented Perspective*. New Haven: Yale University Press, 1989. pp. xii + 500.

Chen, Ti-chiang (English-educated Chinese who taught at National Peking University, 1950–8). *The International Law of Recognition*. Edited and brought up to date by L. C. Green. New York: Frederick A. Praeger for the Royal Institute of International Affairs, 1951. pp. xxvii + 461.

Chi, Hsiang-yang, 'Smash the New Tsars' Theory of Limited Sovereignty'. *Peking Review*, 23 May 1969, pp. 20–2. English translation in Jerome A. Cohen and Hungdah Chiu (eds), *People's China and International Law: A Documentary Study*. Princeton, NJ: Princeton University Press, 1974, vol. 1, pp. 153–5.

Cochran, Charles L. (United States). 'The Recognition of States and Governments by President John F. Kennedy: An Analysis'. Ph.D. dissertation, Tufts University, 1969. pp. 366.

——. 'De Facto and De Jure Recognition: Is There a Difference?' *American Journal of International Law*, 62, (1968): 457–60.

——. 'The Development of an Inter-American Policy for the Recognition of De Facto Governments'. *American Journal of International Law*, 62 (1968): 460–4.

Cohen, Jerome A. (United States expert on PRC law). 'Recognizing China'. *Foreign Affairs* (New York), 50 (1970–1): 20–43.

——. 'Legal Problems of Normalization of Relations with China'. Lecture given at the Columbia University School of Law, New York, 4 February 1974.

——. 'Remarks [on Soviet influence on People's Republic of China international legal doctrine]'. *Proceedings of the American Society of International Law*, 62 (1968): 210–12.

——. and Chiu, Hungdah (Chinese-born, teaching in the United States) (eds). *People's China and International Law: A Documentary Study*. 2 vols. Princeton, N.J.: Princeton University Press, 1974.

Cohen, Raymond. *Theatre of Power: The Art of Diplomatic Signalling*. London: Longman, 1987.

Coplin, William D. (United States). *The Functions of International Law*. Chicago: Rand McNally, 1966. pp. xi + 294.

Coquia, Jorge R. and Miriam Defensor Santiago (both Filipinos). *Public International Law*. Quezón City: Philippine Jurisprudence Project, 1984. pp. xlix + 901.

Corbett, Percy E. (Canadian-born United States scholar). *The Growth of World Law*. Princeton, N.J.: Princeton University Press, 1971. pp. xii + 216.

——. *Law and Society in the Relations of States*. New York: Harcourt, Brace, 1951. pp. 337.

Crawford, James (British). 'Democracy and International Law'. Inaugural lecture delivered 5 March 1993. Cambridge: Cambridge University Press, 1993. pp. 43.

Cruz, Isagani A. (Filipino). *International Law*. Quezón City: Central Lawbook Publishing Company, 1984. pp. xvii + 347.

Dahm, Georg (German). *Völkerrecht*. 2., Völlig neu bearbeitete Auflage, Jost Delbruck and Rudiger Wolfrum (eds). Vol. 1, part 1. Berlin: Walter de Gruyter, 1988.

——. *Völkerrecht*. 3 vols. Stuttgart: W. Kohlhammer, 1958.

Dai, Poeliu (teaches in Canada). 'Recognition of States and Governments under International Law'. *Canadian Yearbook of International Law*, 3 (1965): 289–305.

Davidson, Scott (New Zealander). 'Recognition of Foreign Governments in New Zealand'. *International and Comparative Law Quarterly*, 40 (1991): 162–70.

Davis, George B. (United States). *The Elements of International Law*. 3rd edn. New York: Harper & Bros, 1908. pp. xxx + 673.

Decaux, Emmanuel. 'Le statut de chef d'État déchu'. *Annuaire française de droit international* 1980, pp. 101–39.

Delbez, Louis (French). *Les Principes généraux de droit international public*. 3rd edn. Paris: Librairie général de droit et de jurisprudence, 1964. pp. 666.

'Democracy and Legitimacy: Is there an Emerging Duty to Ensure a Democratic Government in General and Regional Customary International Law?' (Symposium). *Contemporary International Law Issues: Sharing Pan-European and American Perspectives*, pp. 126–41. Washington: American Society of International Law, and Nederlandse Vereniging voor International Recht.

Dennis, Lawrence (United States). 'Revolution, Recognition and Intervention'. *Foreign Affairs* (New York), 9 (1930–1): 204–21.

Despagnet, Frantz (French). *Cours de droit international public*. 3rd edn. Paris: Librairie de la Société de recueil général des lois et des arrêts, 1905. pp. 907.

Detter, Ingrid (British-trained Swedish scholar). *International Law*. Stockholm: Stockholm Institute for Research in International Law, 1992. pp. xxviii + 628.

Deutsch, Karl W. (Czech-born United States political scientist). 'The Probability of International Law'. In *The Relevance of International Law: Essays in Honor of Leo Gross*, pp. 80–114. Edited by Karl Deutsch and Stanley Hoffmann. Garden City, N.Y.: Doubleday, Anchor Books, 1971.

Dhokalia, R. P. (Indian). *International Law*. Allahabad: Central Book Depot, 1963. pp. 652.

Dickinson, Edwin D. (United States). 'Remarks [on Hackworth's discussion of United States recognition policy]'. *Proceedings of the American Society of International Law*, 25 (1931): 131–5.

——. 'The Unrecognized Government or State in English and American Law'. *Michigan Law Review*, 22 (1923–4): 118–34.

Dinegar, Caroline A. (United States). 'Some Aspects of the Use of the Recognition of New Governments as an Instrument of United States Foreign Policy'. Ph.D. dissertation, Columbia University, 1963. pp. 322.

Dozer, Donald M. (United States). 'Recognition in Contemporary Inter-American Relations'. *Journal of Inter-American Studies*, 8 (1966): 318–35.

Dugard, John (South African). *International Law: A South African Perspective*. Kenwyn, South Africa: Juta, 1994. pp. xxxviii + 372.

——. *Recognition and the United Nations*. Cambridge: Grotius Publications, 1987. pp. xiii + 192.

Edeson, W. R. (Australian). 'Conclusive Executive Certificates in Australian Law'. *Australian Yearbook of International Law*, 7 (1981): 1–26.

Elias, Taslim O. (Nigerian, member of the ICJ 1975–xx). *Africa and the Development of International Law*. Leiden: A. W. Sijthof, and Dobbs Ferry, N.Y.: Oceana Publications, 1972. pp. xiii + 261.

Erasmus, Stephen (British). 'General de Gaulle's Recognition of Peking'. *China Quarterly*, 18 (April–June 1964): 195–200.

Erdmann, Ulrich (German). *Nichtanerkannte Staaten und Regierungen*. Göttingen: Institut für Völkerrecht an der Universität Göttingen, 1962. pp. 217.

Erich, Rafael Waldemar (Finnish). 'La naissance et la reconnaissance des Etats'. Hague Academy, *Recueil des cours* 13 (1926): 431–507.

Fatouros, Arghyrios A. (Greek, then teaching in the United States). 'Participation of the "New" States in the International Legal Order of the Future'. In *The Future of International Law*. 4 vols. *Volume I: Trends and Prospects*, pp. 317–71. Edited by Cyril E. Black and Richard A. Falk. Princeton, N.J.: Princeton University Press, 1969.

Fauchille, Paul (French). *Traité de droit international public*. 8th edn. 2 vols. Edited by Henry Bonfils. Paris: Rousseau, 1921–6.

Feldman, D. I. (Soviet). 'Recognition of States and Governments in Present-Day International Law'. In *Contemporary International Law*, pp. 204–15. Edited by Grigory I. Tunkin and translated by G. Ivanov-Mumjiev. Moscow: Progress Publishers, 1969.

——. 'International Personality'. Hague Academy, *Recueil des cours*, 191 (1985–II): 343–414.

Fenwick, Charles G. (United States). 'Recognition De Facto – in Reverse Gear'. *American Journal of International Law*, 58 (1964): 863–6.

——. 'The Recognition of New Governments Instituted by Force'. *American Journal of International Law*, 38 (1942): 448–52.

——. *International Law*. 3rd edn. New York: Appleton-Century-Crofts, 1965. pp. l + 744.

——. *International Law*. 4th edn. New York: Appleton-Century-Crofts, 1965. pp. liii + 849.

Ferguson, Jan H. (Dutch diplomat). *Manual of International Law*. 2 vols. The Hague: Martinus Nijhoff, 1884.

Field, David D. (United States). *Outlines of an International Code*. 2nd edn. New York: Baker, Voorhis, and London: Trubner, 1876. pp. 712.

Fiore, Pasquale (Italian). *Nouveau droit international public*. 3 vols. Translated by Charles Antoine. Paris: A. Durand et Pedone-Lauriel, 1885–6.

Fitzmaurice, Gerald C. (British, member of the ICJ 1960–73). 'Chinese Representation in the United Nations'. *Yearbook of World Affairs* (London), 6 (1952): 36–55.

Fountain, Edwin L. (United States). 'Out from the Precarious Orbit of Politics: Reconsidering Recognition and the Standing of Foreign Governments to Sue in US Courts'. *Virginia Journal of International Law*, 29 (1989): 473–515.

Frenzke, Dietrich (German). 'Stillschweigende Anerkennung durch Vertragsschlüss in der östlichen Völkerrechtslehre'. *Österuoparecht*, 14 (1968): 133–58.

——. 'Völkerrechtliche Anerkennung und das Recht auf Tielnahme an internationalen Konferenzen'. *Recht in Ost und West*, 11 (1967): 185–94.

Friedmann, Wolfgang G. (German refugee of 1933 who later settled in the United States). *The Changing Structure of International Law*. New York: Columbia University Press, 1964. pp. xvi + 410.

——. 'The Reality of International Law – A Reappraisal'. *Columbia Journal of Transnational Law*, 10 (1971): 46–60.

Frowein, Jochen Abr. (German). *Das de facto Regime im Völkerrecht*. Cologne: Carl Heymanns Verlag, 1968. pp. xii + 243.

——. 'Anerkennung'. In *Lexikon des Rechts: Völkerrecht*. Edited by Ignaz Seidl-Hohenveldern, pp. 8–10. Neuweid: Luchterhand, 1985.

Fuhrmann, Peter (German). 'Die Anerkennung von Staaten und Regierungen nach Völkerrecht'. *Politische Studien* (Munich), 16 (1965): 432–40.

Funck-Brentano, Théophile (French) and Sorel, Albert (French diplomatic historian). *Précis du droit des gens*. 3rd edn. Paris: E. Plon, Nourrit 1900. pp. 528.

Gardner, Daniel (United States). *A Treatise on International Law*. Troy, N.Y.: Press of N. Tuttle, 1844, pp. 315.

Gareis, Karl (German). *Institutionen des Völkerrechts*. 2nd edn. Giessen: Verlag von Emil Roth, 1901. pp. xi + 319.

Gemma, Scipione (Italian). 'Les Gouvernements de fait'. Hague Academy, *Recueil des cours*, 4 (1924): 297–413.

Gibbs, Frederick W. (British). *Recognition: A Chapter from the History of the North American and South American States*. London: W. M'Dowall, 1863. pp. 46.

Goebel, Julius, Jr (United States). 'The Recognition Policy of the United States'. Ph.D. dissertation, Columbia University. New York: n.p., 1915. pp. 229.

Gorus, Jan (Belgian-trained, teaches at University of Rwanda). *Manuel de droit international public avec référence aux nouveaux États africains*. Butare: Faculté de droit, Université nationale de Rwanda, 1980. pp. 159.

Gott, Virginia L. (United States). 'The National Socialist Theory of International Law'. *American Journal of International Law*, 32 (1938): 704–18.

Gould, Wesley L. and Barkun, Michael (both United States). *International Law and the Social Sciences*. Princeton, N.J.: Princeton University Press, 1970. pp. xx + 383.

Graham, Malbone W. (United States). 'Some Thoughts on the Recognition of New Governments and Regimes'. *American Journal of International Law*, 44 (1950): 356–60.

Green, L. C. (Canadian). *International Law: A Canadian Perspective*. 2nd edn. Toronto: Carswell, 1988. pp. vii + 409.

Greig, A. M. (Australian). 'The Effects in Municipal Law of Australia's New Recognition Policy'. *Australian YBIL, 11 (1991): 33–65.*

Grenard, Joseph F. (French diplomat). 'Principes de la reconnaissance des nouveaux gouvernements'. *Séances et travaux de l'Académie diplomatique internationale*, 5 (1931): 79–83.

Gross, Leo (Austrian scholar who became a US citizen). 'Die Haftung des Staates für Akte einer Zwischenherrschaft'. *Zeitschrift für öffentliches Recht*, 13 (1933): 375–407.

Grzybowski, Kazimierz (expert on Soviet law who left Poland during World War II and later settled in the US). *Soviet Public International Law: Doctrines and Diplomatic Practice*. Leiden: A. W. Sijthoff, and Durham, N.C.: Rule of Law Press, 1970. pp. xx + 544.

Guest, Stephen (South African). 'Three Juridical Doctrines of Total Recognition of Revolutionary Governments'. *Acta Juridica*, 1980, pp. 1–48.

Guggenheim, Paul (Swiss). *Traité de droit international public*. 2 vols. With the collaboration of Denise Bindschedler-Robert. Geneva: Georg, 1953.

Hackworth, Green H. (United States, then Solicitor of the State Department). 'Policy of the United States in Recognizing New Governments in the Past Twenty-five years'. *Proceedings of the American Society of International Law*, 25 (1931): 120–31.

Hall, William E. (British). *A Treatise on International Law*. 3rd edn. Oxford: Clarendon Press, 1890. pp. xxvii + 788.

Halleck, Henry W. (United States). *International Law*. New York: D. van Nostrand, 1861. pp. 907.

Hardy, Vincent, 'Certificats présentés en cour par le Ministère des Affaires Extérieures: La pratique canadienne'. *Canadian Yearbook of International Law* 15 (1977): 236–52.

Harvard Law School. Research in International Law. 'Draft Convention on Diplomatic Privileges and Immunities'. *American Journal of International Law*, 26 (1932): Supplement, 15–187.

——. 'Draft Convention on the Law of Treaties'. *American Journal of International Law*, 29 (1935): Supplement, 653–1228.

——. 'Draft Convention on the Legal Position and Function of Consuls'. *American Journal of International Law*, 26 (1932): Supplement, 189–449.

Hatschek, Julius (German). *Völkerrecht*. Leipzig: A. Deichertsche Verlagsbuchhandlung, 1923. pp. iv + 429.

Hazard, John N. (United States expert on Soviet law). 'Renewed Emphasis on Socialist International Law'. *American Journal of International Law*, 65 (1971): 142–8.

Heffter, August W. (German). *Le droit international de l'Europe*. 4th French edn, rev'd. Edited by F. H. Geffke and translated by Jules Bergson. Berlin: H. W. Muller, and Paris: A. Cotillon, 1883. pp. xv + 578.

Henkin, Louis (United States). 'International Law: Politics, Values and Functions'. Hague Academy, *Recueil des cours*, 216: 9–416 (1989).

Hershey, Amos S. (United States). 'Notes on the Recognition of De Facto Governments by European States'. *American Journal of International Law*, 14 (1920): 499–518.

——. *The Essentials of International Public Law and Organization*. Rev'd edn. New York: Macmillan, 1927.

Hervey, John G. (United States). *The Legal Effects of Recognition in International Law as Interpreted by the Courts of the United States*. Philadelphia: University of Pennsylvania Press, and London: Oxford University Press, 1928. pp. xiv + 170.

Heuser, Robert (German). 'Zur Rechtsstellung des de facto-Regimes in Völkerrecht', *Zeitschrift für ausländisches öffentliches Recht und Völkerrecht*, 89 (1989): 335–41, and English language summary, pp. 341–2.

Higgins, Rosalyn (British, member of the ICJ 1995–). *The Development of International Law through the Political Organs of the United Nations*. London: Oxford University Press, 1963. pp. 402.

Hingorani, R. C. (Indian). *Modern International Law*, 2nd edn. New York: Oceana Publications, 1984. pp. xii + 472.

Holder, William E. and Brennan G. A. (both Australian). *The International Legal System*. Sydney: Butterworth's, 1972. pp. xi + 1048.

Holtzendorff, Franz von (ed.) (German). *Handbuch des Völkerrechts*. 4 vols. Berlin: C. Habel, 1885–9.

Hornbeck, Stanley K. (United States expert on China, long in the State Department). 'Recognition of Governments'. *Proceedings of the American Society of International Law*, 44 (1950): 181–92.

Houghton, Nealie D. (United States). 'Policy of the United States and Other Nations, with Respect to the Recognition of the Russian Soviet Government, 1917–1929'. *International Conciliation*, 247 (February 1929): 83–108.

Hsiao, Gene T. (United States). 'Nonrecognition and Trade: The Fourth Sino-Japanese Trade Agreement'. In *China's Practice of International Law*, pp. 129–53. Edited by Jerome A. Cohen. Cambridge: Harvard University Press, 1972.

Hsiung, James C. (China-born scholar in the United States). 'China's Recognition Practice and its Implications in International Law'. In *China's Practice of International Law*, pp. 14–56. Edited by Jerome A. Cohen. Cambridge: Harvard University Press, 1972.

——. *Law and Policy in China's Foreign Relations*. New York: Columbia University Press, 1972. pp. 435.

Hudson, Manley, O. (United States, member of the PCIJ 1936–45). 'Recognition and Multipartite Treaties'. *American Journal of International Law*, 23 (1929): 126–32.

Huess, Alfred (German). 'Zum Probleme juristischer Unterscheidung völkerrechtlicher Anerkennungsarten'. *Zeitschrift für Völkerrecht*, 19 (1935): 1–38.

Hyde, Charles C. (United States scholar, once Solicitor of the State Department). *International Law, Chiefly as Applied and Interpreted by the United States*. 2nd rev'd edn. 3 vols. Boston: Little, Brown, 1945.

Institut de droit international (private association of lawyers and scholars, very selective in membership). 'La Reconnaissance des nouveaux États et des nouveaux gouvernements'. (Resolutions.) *Annuaire de l'Institut de droit international*, 39 (1936): 300–5.

Inter-American Council of Jurists (a group of lawyers and scholars, advising the OAS). 'Recognition of De Facto Governments'. Washington, DC: Pan American Union Department of International Law, 1953. pp. 75.

Irizarry y Puente, Julius (United States citizen who once served as Honduran consul in Chicago). 'The Doctrine of Recognition and Intervention in Latin America'. *Tulane Law Review*, 28 (1953–4): 313–42.

Jaffe, Louis L. (United States). *Juridical Aspects of Foreign Relations, in particular the Recognition of Foreign Powers*. Cambridge: Harvard University Press, 1933.

Jankovic, Branimir M. (Yugoslav). *Public International Law*. New York: Transnational Publishers, 1984. pp. xxi + 423.

Jessup, Philip C. (United States, member of the ICJ 1961–70). 'The Estrada Doctrine'. *American Journal of International Law*, 25 (1931): 719–23.

——. *A Modern Law of Nations*. New York: Macmillan, 1950. pp. vii + 236.

Jhabvala, Farrokh. 'The Credentials Approach to Representation Questions in the United Nations'. *California Western International Law Journal*, 7 (1979): 615–38.

Jones, J. Mervyn (British). 'The Retroactive Effects of Recognition of States and Governments'. *British Yearbook of International Law*, 16 (1935): 42–55.

Jovanovič, Bozidar (Yugoslav). 'Dualism of the Institution of Recognition of States in International Law'. In *New Trends in International Law*, pp. 121–37. Edited by Dejan Janca. Belgrade: Institute of Politics and Economy, 1961. (Also a French translation: 'Dualité de l'institution de la reconnaissance de l'État en droit international', in *Le Nouveau droit yougoslave*, 12 [1961]: 125–41.)

Kaplan, Morton A. and Katzenbach, Nicholas de B. (both United States). *The Political Foundations of International Law*. New York: John Wiley & Sons, 1961. pp. xii + 372.

Kapoor, S. K. (Indian). *International Law*. 9th edn. Allahabad: Central Law Agency, 1992. pp. liii + 862.

Kato, L. L. (Tanzanian). 'Recognition in International Law: Some Thoughts on Traditional Theory, Attitudes of and Practice by African Governments'. *Indian Journal of International Law*, 10, (1970): 299–323.

Kelsen, Hans (Austrian, exiled in US during World War II). 'Théorie générale de droit international public: problémes choisis'. Hague Academy, *Receuil des cours*, 42: 117–351 (1932).

——. 'Recognition in International Law: Theoretical Observations'. *American Journal of International Law*, 35 (1941): 605–17.

——. *Principles of International Law*. New York: Rinehart, 1952. pp. xviii + 461.

Kindred, Hugh M. et al. (eds) (all Canadians). *International Law, Chiefly as Interpreted and Applied in Canada*. 5th edn. Toronto: Edmund Montgomery Publications, 1993. pp. lxiii + 957.

Kingsbury, Benedict, 'Judicial Determination of Foreign "Government" Status'. *Quarterly Law Review*, 109 (1993): 377–82.

Klüber, Jean-Louis (Badenese active in the service of many German states). *Droit des gens moderne de l'Europe*. 2nd edn. Edited by M. A. Ott. Paris: Librairie de Guillaumin, 1874. pp. xxxii + 573.

Kopelmanas, Lazare (Lithuanian-born Frenchman then Legal Advisor to the UN Economic Commission for Europe). 'La Reconnaissance en droit international'. *Communicazioni e studi*, 9 (1957): 1–45.

Korovin, Evgenii A. (Soviet). 'Le République des soviets et le droit international'. *Revue général de droit international public*, 32 (1925): 292–312.

——. 'Soviet Treaties and International Law'. *American Journal of International Law*, 22 (1928): 753–63.

Kozhevnikov, Fedor I. (ed.) (Soviet, member of the ICJ 1953–61). *International Law: A Textbook for Use in Law Schools*. Translated by Dennis Ogden. Moscow: Foreign Languages Publishing House, 1961.

K'ung Meng. 'A Criticism of the Theories of Bourgeois International Law on the Subjects of International Law and the Recognition of States'. *Kuo-chi wen-t'i yen-chu (Studies in International Problems)*, No. 2, April 1958. English translation in Jerome Cohen and Hungdah Chiu (eds), *People's*

China and International Law: A Documentary Survey (Princeton: Princeton University Press, 1974), vol. 1, pp. 246–50.

Kunz, Josef L. (Austrian exiled in US during World War II). *Die Anerkennung der Staaten und Regierungen im Völkerrecht*. Stuttgart: W. Kohlhammer, 1928. pp. 218.

——. 'Critical Remarks on Lauterpacht's *Recognition in International Law*'. *American Journal of International Law*, 44 (1950): 713–20.

——. 'On the Theoretical Basis of International Law'. *Transactions of the Grotius Society*, 10 (1925): 115–42.

Lachs, Manfred (Polish, member of the ICJ 1967–93). 'Recognition and Modern Methods of International Cooperation'. *British Yearbook of International Law*, 35 (1959): 252–9.

Lador-Laderer, J. J. (Norwegian). 'Recognition – a Historical Stocktaking'. *Nordisk tidsskrift for international ret*, 27 (1957): 64–92 (part 1) and 117–42 (part 2).

Larnaude, F. (French). 'Les Gouvernements de fait', *Revue générale de droit international public*, 28 (1921): 457–503.

Lauterpacht, Sir Hersh (British, member of ICJ 1954–60). *Recognition in International Law*. Cambridge: Cambridge University Press, 1947. pp. 442.

——. 'Recognition of Governments'. *The Times* (London), 6 January 1950, page 5, column 6.

——. 'Recognition of Insurgents as a de facto Government'. *Modern Law Review*, 3 (1939–40): 1–20.

Lawrence, Thomas J. (British). *The Principles of International Law*. 4th edn. London: Macmillan, 1913. pp. xii + 745.

——. *The Principles of International Law*. 7th edn. Edited by Percy H. Winfield. Boston: D. C. Heath, 1923. pp. xix + 766.

Lécharny, Louis (French). *La validité des actes internes des gouvernements de fait à l'égard des étrangers*. Paris: Librairie Arthur Rousseau, 1929. pp. 181.

Lee, Luke T. (China-born scholar working in the United States). 'Consular Status under Unrecognized Regimes'. *British YBIL*, 32 (1956): 295–300.

—. *Consular Law and Practice*. New York: Frederick A. Praeger, 1961. pp. xii + 431.

——. *The Vienna Convention on Consular Relations*. Leiden: A. W. Sijthoff, and Durham, N.C.: Rule of Law Press, 1966. pp. 315.

Leng, Shao-chuan and Chiu, Hungdah, (eds) (both China-born scholars in the US). *Law in Chinese Foreign Policy: Communist China and Selected Problems of International Law*. Dobbs Ferry, N.Y.: Oceana Publications, 1972. pp. 435.

Le Normand, René (French). *La Reconnaissance internationale et ses diverses applications*. Paris: Imprimerie Camis, 1899. pp. viii + 285.

Li, Victor H. (United States expert on Chinese law). 'Legal Aspects of Trade with Communist China'. *Columbia Journal of Transnational Law*, 3 (1964): 57–71.

Liszt, Franz von (Austrian). *Das Völkerrecht systematisch dargestellt*. 9th edn. Berlin: Verlag von O. Haring, 1913. pp. xii + 565.

——. *Das Völkerrecht systematisch dargestellt*. 12th edn. Edited by Max Fleischmann. Berlin: Verlag von Julius Springer, 1925. pp. xviii + 764.

Livonius, Ernst M. von (German). *Die völkerrechtliche Anerkennung, unter besonderer Berücksichtigung Sowjet-Russlands.* Charlottenburg: Druck Studentenwerk, 1934. pp. xi + 118.

Lorimer, Sir James (British). *The Institutes of the Law of Nations.* 2 vols. Edinburgh: William Blackwood and Sons, 1883. (The section on recognition appeared in French as 'La doctrine de la reconnaissance' in *Revue de droit international et de législation comparée,* 16 [1st ser.] [1884]: 333–59.)

Loudwin, Bernd. *Konkludente Anerkennung im Voikerrecht.* Berlin: Dencker and Humblot, 1983.

Louter, Jan de (Dutch). *Le Droit international public positif.* 2 vols. Oxford: Oxford University Press, 1920.

McChesney, Robert M. (United States). 'International Law and Mexican Foreign Policy'. Ph.D. dissertation, University of Virginia, 1969. pp. 346.

MacCorkle, Stuart A. (United States). *American Policy of Recognition Towards Mexico.* Baltimore: Johns Hopkins Press, 1933. pp. 119.

McDougal, Myres S. (United States) and Feliciano, Florentino P. (Filipino). *Law and Minimum World Public Order.* New Haven, Conn.: Yale University Press, 1961. xxvi + 872.

——. and Goodman, Richard M. (United States). 'Chinese Participation in the United Nations: The Legal Imperatives of a Negotiated Solution'. *American Journal of International Law* 60, (1966): 671–727.

Mackintosh, Sir James (British). 'Speech ... in the House of Commons on the 15th of June 1824'. *Miscellaneous Works.* 3 vols. London: Longman, Brown, Green and Longmans, 1854. Vol. 2: 433–78.

McKittrick, Seward (United States). 'Recognition of Changes in Government'. *St Louis Law Review,* 2 (1917): 37–48.

McMahon, John L. (United States). *Recent Changes in the Recognition Policy of the United States.* Washington, DC: The Catholic University of America, 1933. pp. vi + 138.

McNair, Sir Arnold D. (British, member of the ICJ 1946–55). *The Law of Treaties: British Practice and Opinion.* New York: Columbia University Press, and Oxford: Clarendon Press, 1938. pp. xxx + 578.

——. *The Law of Treaties.* Oxford: Clarendon Press, 1961. pp. xxi + 789.

McWhinney, Edward (Canadian). *Conflit idéologique et ordre public mondial.* Paris: A. Pedone, 1970. pp. 157.

Makarov, A. (Russian, settled in Germany after losing his Petrograd University post in 1923). 'Sowjet-Union und Völkerbund'. *Zeitschrift für ausländisches öffentliches Recht und Völkerrecht,* 5 (1934): 360–83.

Mamaini della Rovere, Terenzo, Conte de Saint' Angelo (Sardinian, at the time a member of the Cabinet). *The Rights of Nations.* Translated by Roger Acton. London: W. Jeffs, 1860. pp. xl + 377.

Mann, F. A. (British). 'Judiciary and Executive in Foreign Affairs', *Transactions of the Grotius Society,* 29: 143–70 (1944).

Marek, Krystyna (Polish émigré who left in 1939 and later settled in Switzerland). *Identity and Continuity of States in Public International Law.* Geneva: Librairie E. Droz, 1954. pp. 613.

Marre, Franz-B. (German). 'Rechtsnatur der Gesetzgebungsakte von De facto-Regimes: Ein Urteil des Obersten Gerichtshofes Uruguays', *Verfassung und Recht in Übersee,* 22 (1989): 23–30.

Martens, Fedor F. (Russian). *Traité de droit international public*. 3 vols. Translated by Alfred Leo. Paris: Chevalier-Marescq, 1883–7.

Martens, George F. von (Hanoverian). *Précis de droit des gens moderne de l'Europe*. 3rd edn. Göttingen: Librairie de Dieterich, 1821. pp. xii + 502.

Matthews, Rebecca (United States). 'Conditional Recognition'. *Cumulative Digest of International Law and Relations*, 2 (1932): 53–4.

Meeker, Leonard C. (United States, then Legal Advisor to the State Department). 'Recognition and the Restatement'. *New York University Law Review*, 41 (1966): 83–95.

Mehrish, Brijesh N. (Indian). *India's Recognition Policy towards the New Nations*. Delhi: Oriental Publishers, 1972. pp. 228.

Menon, P. K. (teaches at the University of the West Indies, Barbados). 'Some Aspects of the Law of Recognition, Part I: Theories of Recognition', *Revue de droit international de sciences diplomatiques et politiques*, 67 (1989): 161–82.

——. 'Some Aspects of the Law of Recognition, Part III: Recognition of Governments'. *Revue de droit international de sciences diplomatiques et politiques*, 68 (1990): 157–96.

——. 'Some Aspects of the Law of Recognition, Part V: Modes of Recognition'. *Revue de droit international de sciences diplomatiques et politiques*, 69 (1991): 19–50.

——. 'Some Aspects of the Law of Recognition, Part VI: The Effects of Recognition'. *Revue de droit international de sciences diplomatiques et politiques*, 69 (1991): 83–113.

——. 'Some Aspects of the Law of Recognition, Part VII: The Doctrine of Non-Recognition'. *Revue de droit international de sciences diplomatiques et politiques*, 69 (1991): 237–58.

——. *The Law of Recognition in International Law*. Lewiston, NY: Edwin Mellen Press, 1994. pp. 278 (assembles all 7 of the earlier articles).

Merignhac, Alexandre (French). *Traité de droit public international*. 3 vols. Paris: Librairie de droit et de jurisprudence. 1905–12.

Mirkine-Guetzévitch, Boris (Russian émigré who became a French citizen). 'Droit international et droit constitutionnel'. Hague Academy, *Recueil des cours*, 38 (1931): 307–465.

Misra, Kashi P. (Indian). *India's Policy of Recognition of States and Governments*. Bombay: Allied Publishers, 1966. pp. 214.

Mittelman, James H. (United States expert on Africa). 'The Uganda Coup and the Internationalization of Political Violence'. *Munger Africana Library Notes*, number 14 (September 1972). pp. 36.

Møller, Axel (Danish). *International Law in Peace and War*. 2 vols. Translated by H. M. Pratt. London: Stevens, 1931–5.

Mookerjea, Sobhanlal (Indian). *International Law*. 2nd edn. 2 vols. Calcutta: A. Mukherjee & Co., 1968–70.

Morrison, Fred L. (United States). 'Recognition in International Law: A Functional Reappraisal'. *University of Chicago Law Review*, 34 (1966–7): 857–83.

Mugerwa, Nkambo (Ugandan). 'Subjects of International Law'. In *Manual of Public International Law*, pp. 247–310. Edited by Max Sørensen. London: Macmillan, and New York: St Martin's Press, 1968.

Munch, Fritz (German). 'Quelques problèmes de la reconnaissance en droit international'. In *Miscellanea W. J. Ganshof van der Meersch*, 1: 157–72. Brussels: Université libre, 1972.

Musgrave, R. Kenton (United States). 'Nonrecognition of a Foreign Government: Its Effects and Ramifications'. *Journal of Public Law*, 1 (1952): 239–43.

Nedjati, Zaim M. (British-trained). 'Acts of Unrecognized Governments'. *International and Comparative Law Quarterly*, 30 (1981): 385–415.

Nervo, Rodolfo (Mexican). 'La Doctrine mexicaine "d'Estrada" sur la reconnaissance'. *Revue de droit international*, 7 (1931): 436–45.

Neumann, Leopold Freiherr von (Austrian). *Éléments du droit des gens moderne*. 3rd edn. Translated by M. A. de Riedmatten. Paris: A. Rousseau, 1886. pp. 332.

Neumann, William L. (United States). *Recognition of Governments in the Americas*. Washington, DC: Foundation for Foreign Affairs, 1947. pp. 52.

Noël-Henry (member of the French consular service). 'La Doctrine américaine en matière de reconnaissance de gouvernements étrangers'. *Revue général de droit international public*, 35 (1928): 201–67.

Nomura, Issei (Japanese, then Director of the Legal Division of the Foreign Ministry Treaties Bureau). 'Recognition of Foreign Governments'. *Japanese Annual of International Law*, 25 (1982): 67–72.

Nys, Ernest (Belgian). *Le droit international*. New [3rd] edn. 3 vols. Brussels: M. Weissenbruch, 1912.

O'Connell, Daniel P. (New Zealander who later taught in Australia and the UK). *International Law*. 2 vols. London: Stevens, 1965.

Oppenheim, Lassa F. (British). *International Law*. 2nd edn. 2 vols. London: Longmans, Green, 1912.

——. *International Law*. 4th edn. 2 vols. Edited by Sir Arnold D. McNair. London: Longmans, Green, 1928.

——. *International Law*. 8th edn. Vol. 1 only published. Edited by Sir Hersh Lauterpacht. London: Longmans, Green, 1958.

——. *International Law*. 9th edn. 2 vols. Edited by Sir Robert Jennings and Sir Arthur Watts. London: Longman, 1992.

Padelford, Norman J. (United States). *International Law and Diplomacy in the Spanish Civil Strife*. New York: Macmillan, 1939. pp. xxvii + 710.

Patel, Satyavrata R. (Indian). *Recognition in the Law of Nations*. Bombay: N. M. Tripathi, 1959, pp. 122.

Pergler, Charles (United States). 'Recognition of New Governments'. *Central Law Journal*, 98 (1925): 61–3.

Pessoa, Epitacio (Brazilian, member of the PCIJ 1922–30). 'Draft of a Code of Public International Law for the Americas'. Typescript of a proposal to the Fourth International American Conference, 1911, in the Columbia University School of Law Library, pp. 246.

Peterson, M. J. (United States). 'Recognition of Governments should not be Abolished'. *American Journal of International Law*, 77 (1983): 31–50.

Phillimore, Sir Robert (British). *Commentaries upon International Law*. 3rd edn. 4 vols. London: Butterworths, 1879–89.

Podesta-Costa, Luis A. (Argentine). 'Règles à suivre pour la reconnaissance d'un gouvernement de facto étranger'. *Revue générale de droit international public*, 29 (1922): 47–59.

Politis, Nicolas (Greek). 'La Théorie de la reconnaissance'. In *Mélanges Antoine Pillet*, 1: 179–93. Paris: Recueil Sirey, 1929.

Pollock, Sir Frederick (British). '"De jure" Recognition'. Letter to *The Times* (London), 5 February 1924, page 11, column 5.

Potter, Pitman B. (United States). 'Membership and Representation in the UN'. *American Journal of International Law*, 49 (1955): 234–5.

Pradier-Fodéré, Paul L. E. (French, taught for some years at the University of Lima). *Traité de droit international public européen et americain.* 8 vols. Paris: A. Durand et Pedone-Lauriel, 1885–1906.

Preuss, Lawrence (United States). 'National Socialist Conceptions of International Law'. *American Political Science Review*, 29 (1935): 594–609.

Price, Pamela P. (United States). 'The Impact of Constitutive Recognition on the Right to Self-Determination'. *Valparaiso University Law Review*, 14 (1979): 123–56.

Raestad, Arnold C. (Norwegian). 'La Reconnaissance internationale des nouveaux États et des nouveaux gouvernements'. *Revue de droit international et de législation comparée*, 63 (1936): 257–313.

Ramundo, Bernard A. (United States). *Peaceful Coexistence: International Law in the Building of Communism.* Baltimore: Johns Hopkins Press, 1967. pp. x + 262.

Reghizzi, Gabriele C. (Italian). 'Legal Aspects of Trade with China: The Italian Experience'. *Harvard International Law Journal*, 9 (1968): 85–139.

Reuter, Paul. *Droit international public.* 6th edn. Paris: Presses universitaires de France, 1983. pp. 595.

Reynolds, George M. (United States). 'The Recognition Policy of the United States as Applied in the Caribbean'. M.A. essay, Columbia University, 1928. pp. ii + 85.

Rivier, Alphonse P. (Swiss). *Principes de droit des gens.* 2 vols. Paris: A. Rousseau, 1896.

Robertson, Arthur H. (British, then assistant general counsel of UNRRA). 'Some Legal Problems of the UNRRA'. *British Yearbook of International Law*, 23 (1946): 142–50.

Robinet de Cléry (French). 'Des emprunts contractés par un gouvernement éphémère'. *Journal de droit international*, 8 (1881): 42–6.

Rolin, Henri (Belgian). 'Observations'. *Annuaire de l'Institut de droit international*, 38 (1934): 350–7.

Rosenau, James N. (ed.) (United States). *International Aspects of Civil Strife.* Princeton, N.J.: Princeton University Press, 1964. pp. vii + 322.

Ross, Alf (Danish). *A Textbook of International Law, General Part.* Translated by Annie L. Fansbøll. London: Longmans, Green, 1947. pp. 313.

Rougier, Antoine (French). *Les Guerres civiles et le droit des gens.* Paris: L. Larose, 1903. pp. xvi + 569.

Rousseau, Charles. *Droit international public.* 10th edn. Paris: Dalloz, 1984. pp. xxii + 433.

Ruda, José María (Argentine, member of ICJ, 1973–91). 'The Law of Friendly Relations between States: Recognition of States and Governments'. In M. Bedjaoui (ed.), *International Law: Achievements and Prospects*, pp. 449–65. Paris and Dordrecht: Martinus Nijhoff, 1991.

Salonga, Jovito R. and Yap, Pedro L. (both US-educated Filipinos). *Public International Law.* 3rd edn. Manila: Regina Publishing Corp., 1966. pp. xxi + 581.

Sastry, Kadayan R. R. (Indian). *International Law.* Allahabad: Kitabistan [1937]. pp. xxxi + 472.

Scelle, Georges (French). 'Chronique des faits internationaux: Mexique'. *Revue général de droit international public*, 21 (1914): 117–32.

——. *Manuel de droit international public.* Paris: Éditions Domat-Montchrestien, 1948. pp. 1008.

——. *Précis de droit des gens.* 2 vols. Paris: Recueil Sirey, 1932–4.

Schapiro, Leonard B. (British expert on the USSR). 'The Soviet Concept of International Law'. *Yearbook of World Affairs* (London), 2 (1948): 272–310.

Schlüter, Ferdinand (German). *De-facto Anerkennung im Völkerrecht.* Wurzburg: Triltsch, 1936. pp. 133.

Schwartz, Benjamin I. (United States expert on China). 'The Maoist Image of World Order'. *Journal of International Affairs* (New York), 21 (1967): 92–102.

Schwarzenberger, Georg (German who settled in England in the mid-1930s). 'The Recognition of Governments'. Letter to *The Times* (London), 9 January 1949, page 5, column 5.

——. *A Manual of International Law.* 4th edn. 2 vols. London: Stevens & Son and New York: Frederick A. Praeger, 1960.

——. *The Inductive Approach to International Law.* London: Stevens & Son, and New York: Oceana Publications, 1965. pp. xv + 209.

Seidl-Hohenveldern, Ignaz (Austrian). *Völkerrecht.* 7th edn. Cologne: Carl Heymanns Verlag, 1992. pp. xxviii + 475.

Sereni, Angelo P. (Italian exiled in the US 1939–45). *The Italian Conception of International Law.* New York: Columbia University Press, 1943. pp. xi + 402.

Shao Tzu-ping (ROC citizen educated in Germany). *Die Anerkennung im Völkerrecht durch die Aufnahme konsularischer Beziehungen.* Heidelberg: A. Grosch, 1967. pp. v + 178.

Sharp, Roland H. (United States). *Nonrecognition as a Legal Obligation.* Liège: Imprimerie Georges Thone, 1934. pp. x + 232.

Shaw, Malcolm (British). 'Legal Acts of an Unrecognized Entity'. *Law Quarterly Review*, 94 (1978): 500–5.

Sibert, Marcel (French). *Traité de droit international public.* 2 vols. Paris: Librairie Dalloz, 1951.

Spiropoulos, Ioannes (Greek, member of the ICJ 1958–67). *Die de facto Regierung im Völkerrecht.* Verlag des Instituts für Internationales Recht an der Universität Kiel, 1926. pp. xvi + 188.

——, 'Nichtanerkannte Staaten und Regierungen vor dem Standigen Internationalen Gerichtshofe'. *Revue de droit international*, 5 (1927): 35–45

——. *Traité théorique et pratique de droit international public.* Paris: Librairie général de droit et de jurisprudence. 1933. pp. 465.

Starke, Joseph G. (Australian, later lived in England). 'Recognition at International Law'. *Australian Quarterly*, March 1950, 13–20.

——. *Introduction to International Law*. 9th edn. London: Butterworth's, 1984. pp. xxviii + 664.
Stierlin, Peter (Swiss). *Die Rechtsstellung der nichtanerkannten Regierung im Völkerrecht*. Zurich: Polygraphischer Verlag, 1940. pp. 200.
Stinson, J. Whitla (United States). 'Recognition of De Facto Governments and the Responsibility of States.' *Minnesota Law Review*, 9 (1924–5): 1–20.
Stowell, Ellery C. (United States). 'The Doctrine of Constitutional Legitimacy'. *American Journal of International Law*, 25 (1931): 302–6.
——. 'Remarks [on Hackworth's discussion of United States recognition policy]'. *Proceedings of the American Society of International Law*, 25 (1931): 178–9.
Strupp, Karl (German). *Éléments du droit international public*. 3 vols. 2nd edn. Paris: Les éditions internationales, 1930.
Symmons, C. R. (British). 'United Kingdom Abolition of Recognition of Governments: A Rose by Another Name?' *Public Law* (1981): 249–62.
Tabata, Shigjiro (Japanese). 'Admission to the UN and Recognition of States'. *Japanese Annual of International Law*, 5 (1961): 1–14.
Takano, Yuichi (Japanese). *Einführung in das Völkerrecht*. 14th edn. Translated by Ingo Richter. Cologne: Carl Heymanns Verlag, 1979.
Talmon, S. 'Recognition of Governments: An Analysis of the New British Policy and Practice'. *British Yearbook of International Law*, 63: 231–97 (1992).
Tandon, Mahesh P. (Indian). *Public International Law*. 10th edn. Allahabad: Allahabad Law Agency, 1965. pp. xi + 893.
Taracouzio, T. A. (Russian émigré). *The Soviet Union and International Law*. New York: Macmillan, 1935. pp. xvi + 530.
Teuscher, Hans-Herbert (German). *Die vorzeitige Anerkennung im Völkerrecht*. Munster: Max Kramer, 1958. pp. xxi + 127.
Tripathi, Manjul Rani. *India's Foreign Policy on Diplomatic Recognition of States and Governments*. Delhi: B.R. Publishing Corp., 1990. pp. viii + 216.
Tsutsui, Wakamizu (Japanese). 'Subjects of International Law in the Japanese Courts'. *International and Comparative Law Quarterly*, 37 (1988): 325–36.
Tucker, Robert W. (United States). 'The Principle of Effectiveness in International Law'. In *Law and Politics in the World Community: Essays on Hans Kelsen's Pure Theory and Related Problems of International Law*, pp. 31–48. Edited by George Lipsky. Berkeley: University of California Press, 1953.
Tunkin, Grigory I. (Soviet). *Droit international public*. Translated by the Centre de recherches sur l'U.R.S.S. et les pays de l'est of the University of Strasbourg. Paris: A. Pedone, 1965. pp. 250.
——. *Theory of International Law*. Translated by William E. Butler. Cambridge: Harvard University Press, 1974. pp. xxv + 497.
——. 'Conflit idéologique et le droit international contemporain. In *Recueil d'études de droit international en hommage à Paul Guggenheim*', pp. 888–98. Geneva: Faculté de droit de l'Université de Genève and Institut universitaire des hautes études internationales, 1968.
——. 'Peaceful Coexistence and International Law'. In *Contemporary International Law*, pp. 5–35. Edited by Grigory I. Tunkin and translated by A. Ivanov-Mumjiev. Moscow: Progress Publishers, 1969.

——, ed. *International Law: A Textbook*. Moscow: Progress Publishers, 1986.

Twiss, Sir Travers (British). *The Law of Nations*. 2 vols. Oxford: Oxford University Press, and London: Longman, Green, Longman & Roberts, 1861.

Ulanova, N. N. (Soviet). 'Recognition of States and Governments and Participation in Multilateral Treaties'. (English summary of article) *Soviet Yearbook of International Law*, 1961, 320–2.

Ullmann, Emanuel Ritter von (German). *Völkerrecht*. 2nd edn. Tübingen: Verlag von J. C. B. Mohr, 1908. pp. viii + 555.

Umozurike, U. O. (Nigerian). *Introduction to International Law*. Ibaden: Spectrum Law Publishing, 1993. pp. viii + 261.

United Nations. International Law Commission. *Fourth Report on the Law of Treaties (the Effects of Treaties)*. G. G. Fitzmaurice, special rapporteur. U.N. Doc. A/CN.4/120, 17 March 1960.

——. *Second Report on the Law of Treaties*. G. G. Fitzmaurice, special rapporteur. U.N. Doc. A/CN.4/107, 15 March 1957.

——. Secretary-General (Lie). Letter dated 8 March 1950 from the Secretary-General to the President of the Security Council transmitting a Memorandum on the Legal Aspects of the Problems of Representation in the United Nations. UN Doc. 5/1466.

Verdross, Alfred von (Austrian). 'Die völkerrechtliche Anerkennung, kritische Bemerkungen zu Lauterpachts "Recognition in International Law"'. *Juristische Blätter* (Vienna), 70 (1948): 521–3.

——. *Völkerrecht*. Berlin: Verlag von Julius Springer, 1937. pp. xv + 362.

——. *Völkerrecht*. 4th edn. With the collaboration of Karl Zemanek. Vienna: Springer Verlag, 1959. pp. xx + 584.

——. and Bruno Simma. *Universelles Völkerrecht: Theorie und Praxis*. 3rd edn. Berlin: Duncker & Humblot, 1984. pp. xxx + 956.

Verhoeven, Joe (Belgian). *La reconnaissance internationale dans la pratique contemporaine: les relations internationales*. Paris: Pedone, 1975. pp. xi + 861.

——. 'La Reconnaissance internationale: déclin ou renouveau?' *Annuaire française de droit international*, 39 (1993): 7–40.

——. 'Relations internationales de droit privé en l'absence de reconnaissance d'un État, d'un gouvernement ou d'une situation'. Hague Academy, *Recueil des cours*, 192 (1985–III): 9, 232.

Verzijl, Jan H. W. (Dutch). *International Law in Historical Perspective*. Volume 2: *International Persons*. Leiden: A. W. Sijthoff, 1969. pp. xi + 606.

Villari, Luigi (Italian). *Italian Foreign Policy under Mussolini*. New York: Devin-Adair, 1956. pp. xii + 396.

Viret, Jacques (Swiss). *La portée extra-territoriale des actes de souveraineté interne d'un gouvernement non reconnu*. Montreux: Imprimerie Corbaz, 1951. pp. 139.

Visscher, Charles de (Belgian, member of the PCIJ 1937–45 and of the ICJ 1946–52). *Les Effectivités en droit international public*. Paris: A. Pedone, 1967. pp. 175.

——. *Theory and Reality in Public International Law*. 3rd edn. Translated by Percy E. Corbett. Princeton, N.J.: Princeton University Press, 1968. pp. xii + 527.

Visscher, Paul de (Belgian). *Cours de droit des gens (partie générale)*. Louvain-la-Neuve: Cabay, 1981. pp. 257.

Warbrick, Colin (British). 'Kampuchea: Representation and Recognition'. *International and Comparative Law Quarterly*, 30 (1981): 234–46.

——. 'The New British Policy on Recognition of Governments'. *International and Comparative Law Quarterly*, 30 (1981): 568–92.

——. 'Recognition of Governments'. *Modern Law Review*, 56 (1993): 92–7.

Wegner, Arthur (German). 'Über Anerkennung im Völkerrecht'. In *Festgabe für Paul Heilborn*, pp. 181–202. Breslau: M. and H. Marcus, 1931.

Weisse, Carlos (Peruvian). *Le droit international appliqué aux guerres civiles*. French edn, revised and brought up-to-date. Lausanne: B. Benda, 1898. pp. viii + 364.

West, Mary Beth and Sean D. Murphy (both United States). 'The Impact on US Litigation of Non-recognition of Foreign Governments'. *Stanford Journal of International Law*, 26 (1989–90): 435–78.

Westlake, John (British). *International Law*, 2nd edn. 2 vols. Cambridge: Cambridge University Press, 1910–13.

Wheaton, Henry (United States, diplomat). *Elements of International Law*. 2 vols. London: B. Fellowes, 1836.

——. *Elements of International Law*. 2 vols. 6th English edn. Edited by F. Barriedale Keith (British). London: Stevens & Son, 1929.

Whelan, Joseph G. (United States). 'The US and Diplomatic Recognition: The Contrasting Cases of Russia and Communist China'. *China Quarterly*, No. 5 (January–March 1961): 62–89.

Williams, Sir John F. (British). 'La Doctrine de la reconnaissance en droit international et ses développements récents'. Hague Academy, *Recueil des cours*, 44 (1933): 203–314.

——. 'The New Doctrine of "Recognition"'. *Transactions of the Grotius Society*, 18 (1933): 109–29.

——. 'Recognition'. *Transactions of the Grotius Society*, 15 (1929): 53–76.

Wilson, George G. (United States). 'British Recognition De Facto and De Jure of the USSR'. *American Journal of International Law*, 28 (1934): 99–101.

Wolf, Ernest (Swiss). 'Le gouvernement de fait en droit suisse'. *Schweizerisches Jahrbuch für internationales Recht*, 13 (1956): 115–32.

Wolgast, Ernst (German). 'Völkerrecht'. In *Das gesamte deutsche Recht*, 2: 691–980. Rudolf Stammler (ed.). Berlin: G. Stilke, 1935.

Woolsey, Lester H. (United States). 'The Non-recognition of the Chamorro Government in Nicaragua'. *American Journal of International Law*, 20 (1926): 543–9.

——. 'The Recognition of the Government of El Salvador'. *American Journal of International Law*, 28 (1934): 325–30.

Woolsey, Theodore D. (United States). *Introduction to the Study of International Law*. 5th edn. New York: Charles Scribner's Sons, 1883. pp. xvii + 526.

Wright, Quincy (United States). 'Recognition, Intervention, and Ideologies'. *Indian Yearbook of International Affairs*, 7 (1958): 89–118.

——. 'Some Thoughts about Recognition'. *American Journal of International Law*, 44 (1950): 548–59.

Yakemtchouk, Romain. *L'Afrique en droit international.* Paris: Librairie général de droit et de jurisprudence, 1971. pp. ix + 319.
Young, Kenneth T. (United States, former diplomat). 'American Dealings with Peking'. *Foreign Affairs* (New York), 45 (1966–7): 77–87.
Zachari, H. A. (German). 'Über die Verpflichtung restaurierter Regierungen aus den Handlungen einer Zwischenherrschaft'. *Zeitschrift für die gesamte Staatswissenschaft*, 9 (1853): 79–114.
Zellwenger, Éduard (Swiss). 'Die völkerrechtliche Anerkennung nach schweizerischer Staatenpraxis'. *Schweizerisches Jahrbuch für internationales Recht*, 11 (1954): 11–42.
Zivier, Ernst R. (German). *Die Nichtanerkennung im modernen Völkerrecht.* Berlin: Berlin Verlag, 1969. pp. 311.

II OFFICIAL AND UNOFFICIAL REPORTS OF STATE PRACTICE

Africa Contemporary Record. Vol. 1 (1968/69). London: Africa Research Ltd, 1969.
Africa Diary (annual, 1961, vol I. –). New Delhi.
Africa South of the Sahara (annual, 1971–). London: Europa Publications Limited.
American Journal of International Law. Vol. 1 (1906)–.
'Annual Review of Japanese Practice in International Law'. *Japanese Annual of International Law.* Vol. I (1957)–.
Annuaire française de droit international. Vol. 1 (1955)–.
Australia. Department of Foreign Affairs. *Australian Foreign Affairs Record.* Vol. 1 (1973). (Superseded *Current Notes on International Affairs.*)
——. *Current Notes on International Affairs.* Vol. 1 (1935) – Vol. 43 (1972).
'Australian Practice in International Law'. *Australian Year Book of International Law.* Vol. I (19)–.
Bruns, Viktor (ed.). *Fontes Juris Gentium. Series B. Digest of the Diplomatic Correspondence of the European States, 1871–1878.* Berlin: Carl Heymanns Verlag, 1933.
Burckhardt, Walter (Swiss). *Le droit fédéral suisse: Jurisprudence du Conseil fédéral et de l'Assemblée fédérale en matière de droit public et de droit administratif depuis 1903.* 5 vols. Translated by George Bouet. Neuchâtel: Delachaux & Niestle, 1930.
Canadian Yearbook of International Law. Vol. I (1963).
China Handbook Editorial Board (semi-official ROC organization). *China Handbook*, 1950–1956/57. Subsequently titled *China Yearbook, 1957/58.* New York: Rockport Press, 1950; and Taipei: China Publishing Co., 1951–.
'Chronique juridique international'. *Annuaire francaise de droit international.*
Council on Foreign Relations (US private association of scholars and US policy-makers). *Documents on American Foreign Policy, 1964–.* New York: Harper & Row, 1965–6 and Simon & Schuster, 1967–.

Degras, Jane (ed.) (British). *Soviet Documents on Foreign Policy, 1917–1941*. 3 vols. London: Oxford University Press, 1951.
Despagnet, Franz and Louis Renault, comp. *Recueil international des traités du XXe siècle*. 7 vols. Paris: Arthur Rousseau, 1900–7.
France. Ministère des Affaires Etrangères. *Documents diplomatiques*. Paris: Imprimerie impériale, 1861–70, and Imprimerie nationale, 1896–1939.
——. *Documents diplomatiques français, 1871–1914*. 41 vols. Paris: Imprimerie nationale, 1929–59.
Germany. Auswärtigen Amtes. *Die grosse Politik der europäischen Kabinette, 1871–1914*. 40 vols. Berlin: Deutsche Verlagsgesellschaft für Politik und Geschichte, 1924–7.
——. *Documents on German Foreign Policy, 1918–1945. Series C: The Third Reich, First Phase*. 5 vols. *Series D: The War Years*. 13 vols. Washington, DC: United States Government Printing Office, and London: Her Majesty's Stationery Office, 1949–66.
Great Britain. Foreign Office. *British Documents on the Origins of the War, 1898–1914*, 10 vols. London: His Majesty's Stationery Office, 1932–8.
——. *Documents on British Foreign Policy, 1919–1939*. 46 vols. London: Her Majesty's Stationery Office, 1949–69.
Grotius annuaire international pour l'année—, 1913–41. The Hague: Martinus Nijhoff, 1914–43.
Hackworth, Green C. (ed.). *Digest of International Law*. 8 vols. Washington, DC: United States Government Printing Office, 1940–4.
'Italian Practice relating to International Law: Diplomatic and Parliamentary Practice'. *Italian Yearbook of International Law*.
Japanese Annual of International Law. Vol. 1 (1957).
Johnson, Douglas H. (Canadian) and Chiu, Hungdah (eds). *Agreements of the People's Republic of China, 1949–1967*. Cambridge: Harvard University Press, 1968.
Journal de droit international privé (Clunet). Vol. I (1873).
Keesing's Contemporary Archives, 1963–95.
Kiss, Alexandre C. (ed.). *Répertoire de la pratique française en matière de droit international public*. 7 vols. Paris: Éditions du Centre national de la recherche scientifique, 1962–72.
'La pratique du pouvoir executif et la controle des chambres législatives en matière de droit international'. J. A. Salmon and others, comp. *Revue belge de droit international*. Vol. I (1965)–.
'La pratique suisse en matière de droit international public'. Lucius Caflisch and others, comp. *Schweizerisches Jahrbuch für internationales Recht*. Vol. I (1944)–.
Latin American and Caribbean Contemporary Record. Vol. 1 (1981–82)–. New York and London: Holmes and Meier.
Lauterpacht, Elihu (ed.). *British Practice in International Law, 1962–1967*. London: British Institute of International and Comparative Law, 1964–71.
——. 'The Contemporary Practice of the United Kingdom in the Field of International Law'. *International and Comparative Law Quarterly*, 5–10 (1955–61).

Lauterpacht, Sir Hersch (ed.). *Annual Digest and Reports of Public International Law Cases*. London: Butterworth's, 1919–49.

——and Lauterpacht, Elihu (eds). *International Law Reports*. London: Butterworth's, 1950–.

McNair, Arnold Duncan (ed.). *International Law Opinions*. 3 vols. Cambridge: Cambridge University Press, 1956.

Moore, John B. (ed.). *A Digest of International Law*. 8 vols. Washington, DC: Government Printing Office, 1906.

'Netherlands State Practice for the Parliamentary Year'. *Netherlands Yearbook of International Law*. Vol. 1 (1970).

New Zealand. Ministry of Foreign Affairs. *New Zealand Foreign Affairs Review*. Quarterly, cited by year and number. 1950–88.

Parry, Sir Clive (ed.). *A British Digest of International Law*. 8 vols. London: Stevens, 1965.

'Pratique française du droit international'. *Annuaire française de droit international*. Vol. I (1955)–.

Rousseau, Charles (French). 'Chronique des faits internationaux'. *Revue générale de droit international*. Vols 62 (1958) to 97 (1993). Continued by Maurice Torrelli and others with Vol. 98 (1994).

Salis-Mayenfeld, Ludwig R. von (Swiss). *Le droit fédéral suisse: Jurisprudence du Conseil fédéral et de l'Assemblée fédérale en matière de droit public et de droit administratif depuis le 29 mai 1874*. 5 vols. 2nd edn. Translated by Eugène Borel. Berne: K. J. Wyss, 1904.

Schapiro, Leonard (ed.). *Soviet Treaty Series, 1917–1939*. 2 vols. Washington, DC: Georgetown University Press, 1955.

Schweizerisches Jahrbuch für internationales Recht. Volume 1 (1944).

Slusser, Robert M. and Triska, Jan F. (eds). *A Calendar of Soviet Treaties, 1917–1957*. Stanford, Calif.: Stanford University Press, 1959. pp. xii + 530.

Smith, Herbert A. (ed.). *Great Britain and the Law of Nations*. 2 vols. London: P. S. King & Son, 1932.

Temperley, Harold and Penson, Lillian (eds) (both British). *Foundations of British Foreign Policy from Pitt (1792) to Salisbury (1902)*. Cambridge: Cambridge University Press, 1938. pp. xxx + 375.

United States of America. Congress. Senate. Committee on Foreign Relations. *United States Recognition of Foreign Governments*. Hearings before the Committee on S. Res. 205. 91st Cong., 1st Sess., 1969.

——. Department of State. *Department of State Bulletin*. Volume 48 (January–June 1963) –89 (July–December 1989).

——. *Dispatch*. Vol. 1 (1990).

——. *Foreign Relations of the United States*. 1862–. Washington, DC: United States Government Printing Office, 1863–.

——. *Digest of United States Practice in International Law* (annual, 1975–80). Marian Nash Leich, comp. Washington: Department of State.

——. *Cumulative Digest of United States Practice in International Law, 1980–1988*, Book 1. Marian Nash Leich, comp. Washington: Department of State, 1993.

'Völkerrechtliche Praxis der Bundesrepublik Deutschland in Jahre—'. *Zeitschrift für ausländisches öffentliches Recht und Völkerrecht*, vol. 13 (1950)–.

Wharton, Francis (ed.). *A Digest of the International Law of the United States*. 2nd edn. 3 vols. Washington, DC: Government Printing Office, 1887.
Whiteman, Marjorie M. (ed.). *Digest of International Law*. 15 vols. Washington, DC: United States Government Printing Office, 1963–71.
Woodhead, H. G. W. (ed.) (British, lived in China). *China Yearbook*, 1919–30. Tientsin: Tientsin Press, 1920–31.
Zeitschrift für ausländisches öffentliches Recht und Völkerrecht. Volume 13 (1950).

III OTHER WORKS CITED

Albrecht-Carrié, René. *A Diplomatic History of Europe since the Congress of Vienna*, New York: Harper & Row, 1958.
Arias, L.G. 'La disparación de la doctrina Betamcourt sobre no reconocimiento de gobiernos *de facto*'. *Revista español de deritto internacional*, 1969, pp. 104–6.
Banks, Arthur S. *Cross-Policy Time Series Data*, Cambridge: MIT Press, 1971.
Barker, Mary Nichols, *The French Experience in Mexico, 1821–1861*. Chapel Hill: University of North Carolina Press, 1979.
Boguslavskii, (Rathfelder, trans.) *Staatliche Immunität*. West Berlin: Berlin Verlag, 1965.
Boloyra, Enrique A. *Comparing New Democracies: Transition and Consolidation in Mediterranean Europe and the Southern Cone*. Boulder, Col.: Westview Press, 1987.
Burley, Anne-Marie. 'Regulating the World: Multilateralism, International Law, and the Projection of the New Deal Regulatory State'. *In Multilateralism Matters*. John G. Ruggie ed., pp. 125–56. New York: Columbia University Press, 1993.
Burton, Margaret E. *The Assembly of the League of Nations*. Chicago: University of Chicago Press, 1941.
Buzan, Barry, Charles Jones, and Richard Little. *The Logic of Anarchy: Neorealism to Structural Realism*. New York: Columbia University Press, 1993.
Carr, E. H. *The Twenty Years' Crisis*. 2nd edn. London: Macmillan, 1946.
Chase-Dunn, Christopher. *Global Formation: Structures of the World Economy*. Oxford: Basil Blackwell, 1989.
Cohen, Raymond, *Theatre of Power: The Art of Diplomatic Signalling*. London: Longman, 1987.
Corten, Olivier. 'La Résolution 940 du Conseil de sécurité autorisant une intervention militaire en Haiti: L'émergence d'un principe de légitimité démocratique en droit international?' *European Journal of International Law*, 6: 116–33 (1996).
Cox, Robert W. *Production, Power, and World Order: Social Forces in the Making of History*. New York: Columbia University Press, 1987.
Czyzak, John J. and Carl F. Salans. 'The International Conference on the Settlement of the Laotian Question and the Geneva Agreements of 1962'. *American Journal of International Law* 57: 300–17 (1963).

Diamond, Larry and Marc F. Plattner (eds). *The Global Resurgence of Democracy*. Baltimore: Johns Hopkins University Press, 1993.

Dinges, John. *Our Man in Panama: How General Noriega used the United States and made Millions in Drugs and Arms*, New York: Random House, 1990.

Falk, Richard A. (ed.). *The Vietnam War and International Law*. 3 vols. Princeton, N.J.: Princeton University Press, 1968–72.

——(ed.). *The International Law of Civil War*. Baltimore, Md: The Johns Hopkins Press, 1971.

Franck, Thomas. 'The Emerging Right to Democratic Governance'. *American Journal of International Law* 86: 46–91 (1992).

——. *The Power of Legitimacy among Nations*. New York and Oxford: Oxford University Press, 1990.

George, Alexander. *Presidential Decisionmaking in Foreign Policy: The Effective Use of Information and Advice*. Boulder, CO: Westview Press, 1980.

Gilderhus, Mark T. *Diplomacy and Revolution: US–Mexican Relations under Wilson and Carranza*. Tucson: University of Arizona Press, 1977.

Gill, Stephen. *American Hegemony and the Trilateral Commission*. Cambridge: Cambridge University Press, 1990.

Goldstein, Judith and Robert O. Keohane (eds). *Ideas and Foreign Policy: Beliefs, Institutions, and Political Change*. Ithaca, N.Y.: Cornell University Press, 1993.

Gong, Gerrit W. *The Standard of 'Civilization' in International Society*. Oxford: Clarendon Press, 1984.

Haas, Peter M. (ed.). *Epistemic Communities and International Policy Coordination*. Special Issue of *International Organization*, 46: 1– (1992).

Henkin, Louis, Richard C. Pugh, Oscar Schachter, and Hans Smit. *International Law: Cases and Materials*. 2nd edn. Minneapolis, MN: West Publishing Company, 1987.

Hoffmann, Stanley. 'International Systems and International Law'. In *The State of War*, pp. 88–122. New York: Frederick A. Praeger, 1965.

——. 'The Study of International Law and the Theory of International Relations'. In *The State of War*, pp. 123–33. New York: Frederick A. Praeger, 1965.

Holbraad, Carsten. *The Concert of Europe*. London: Longman, 1970.

Howard, Michael. *Strategic Deception in the Second World War*. New York: W. W. Norton, 1995.

Iriye, Akira. *After Imperialism: The Search for a New Order in the Far East, 1921–1931*, Cambridge: Harvard University Press, 1965.

Jackson, Robert H. *Quasi-States: Sovereignty, International Relations and the Third World*. Cambridge: Cambridge University Press, 1990.

Jowitt, Ken. *The New World Disorder: The Leninist Extinction*. Berkeley: University of California Press, 1992.

Kant, Immanuel. 'Perpetual Peace' [1795] in *Kant's Political Writings*. H.B. Nisset, trans. Cambridge: Cambridge University Press.

Khong, Yuen Foong. *Analogies at War: Korea, Munich, Dien Bien Phu and the Vietnam Decisions of 1965*. Princeton, N.J.: Princeton University Press, 1992.

Kissinger, Henry A. *A World Restored: Metternich, Castlereagh and the Problems of Peace, 1812–1822*. Boston: Houghton Mifflin, 1957.

Koskenniemi, Martii. *From Apology to Utopia* (1989). Helsinki: Finnish Lawyers' Publishing Co., 1989.

Krasner, Stephen D. 'Compromising Westphalia', *International Security*, 20: 115–51 (1995–6).

Kratochwil, Friedrich. *Rules, Norms and Decisions: On the Conditions of Practice and Legal Reasoning in International Relations*. Cambridge: Cambridge University Press, 1991.

Marx, Karl. *The Communist Manifesto* [1848]. Frederick L. Bander (ed.), New York: W.W. Norton, 1988.

Mill, John Stuart, 'A few Words on Nonintervention'. *Fraser's Magazine*, December 1859.

Morgenthau, Hans. *Politics among Nations*. New York: Alfred A. Knopf, 1948.

Nakamura, 'Korean Repatriation Question and Positive International Law', *Japanese Annual of International Law*, 4: 68–78 (1960).

Newman, Robert P. *Recognition of Communist China?* New York: Macmillan, 1961.

O'Donnell, Guillermo, Philippe C. Schmitter, and Laurence Whitehead. *Transitions from Authoritarian Rule: Prospects for Democracy*. Baltimore: Johns Hopkins Press, 1986.

Oglesby, Roscoe R. *Internal War and the Search for Normative Order*. The Hague: Martinus Nijhoff, 1971. pp. xii + 142.

Ohira Zengo and Kuwahara Terumichi. 'Fishery Problems between Japan and the People's Republic of China'. *Japanese Annual of International Law*, 2 (1958): 109–25.

Onuf, Nicholas. *World of Our Making: Rule and Rules in Social Theory and International Relations*. Columbia: University of South Carolina Press, 1989.

Osakwe, Christopher. 'A Soviet Perspective on Foreign Sovereign Immunity: Law and Practice', *Virginia Journal of International Law*, 23: 13 (1982).

Osieke, Ebere. 'Admission to Membership in International Organizations: The Case of Namibia'. *British Yearbook of International Law* 189 (1980).

Peterson, M. J. *The General Assembly in World Politics*, London: George Allen & Unwin, 1986.

Pridham, Geoffrey (ed.). *Encouraging Democracy: The International Context of Regime Transition in Southern Europe*. New York: St Martin's Press, 1991.

Reisman, Michael and F. Willard. *International Incidents: The Law that Counts in World Politics*. Princeton, N.J.: Princeton University Press, 1988.

Ruggie, John G. 'International Regimes, Transactions and Change: Embedded Liberalism in the Postwar Economic Order'. In *International Regimes* ed. by Stephen D. Krasner, pp. 195–232. Ithaca, NY: Cornell University Press, 1983.

Satow, Sir Ernest. *A Guide to Diplomatic Practice*. London: Longmans, Green, 1917; 2nd edn 1922; 3rd edn 1932; 4th edn 1957 corrected 1964; 5th edn 1979.

Schroeder, Paul. *The Transformation of European Politics, 1763–1848*. Oxford: Clarendon Press, 1994.

Sztucki, Jan. *Jus Cogens and the Vienna Convention on the Law of Treaties: A Critical Appraisal.* Vienna: Springer Verlag, 1974.

Toynbee, Arnold J. and Kenneth P. Kirkwood. *Turkey*. New York: Scribner, 1927.

Uchida, Hisashi (Japanese). 'Legal Aspects of Japan–China Trade between 1949 and 1975', *Japanese Annual of International Law*, 19: 39–79 (1975).

Vattel, Emmerich de. *The Law of Nations* [1758]. Charles G. Fenwick trans. Washington: Carnegie Institution, 1916.

Wallerstein, Emmanuel. *The Capitalist World-Economy*. Cambridge: Cambridge University Press, 1979.

Waltz, Kenneth M. *Theory of International Politics*. Lexington, Mass.: Addison-Wesley, 1979.

Warbrick, Colin. 'Recognition of States: Recent European Practice'. In EC International Law Forum II: *Prospects of Statehood and Institutionalism in Contemporary Europe*, ed. Malcolm D. Evans. Aldershot: Dartmouth (forthcoming).

Wendt, Alexander. *Social Theory of International Relations* Cambridge: Cambridge University Press, forthcoming.

Wolfers, Arnold. *Discord and Collaboration: Essays on International Politics.* Baltimore: Johns Hopkins University Press, 1962.

Zacklin, Ralph. 'The Problem of Namibia in International Law', Hague Academy, *Recueil des cours*, 171: 225–339 (1981).

Index